THE MARCH AND THE MUSTER

A Day-book, Commonplace Book, Muchness,
Omnium Gatherum, Nightcap & Cornucopia

by *Frank McManus*

Best wishes; Frank McManus

  Born in Southport in 1927, Frank McManus was educated at St Philip's CE primary and King George V boys' secondary schools there, and at Gonville and Caius College Cambridge. Married to Benita in 1953, and now with family grown up, he served as a Chemistry lecturer at Lancaster and Morecambe College of Further Education for 14 years, and then as Head of Science in two London girls' comprehensive schools for 12; and also as an Open University tutor.

  A local-league football referee for 20 years, he has been a local councillor for 28, now at Todmorden, and a parliamentary candidate three times. A Reader and diocesan synod member in the Church of England, his hobbies include fell-walking and classical music, with Tennyson Society membership. He is also a Friend of Dove Cottage Grasmere where Wordsworth lived. "The March and the Muster" is his first and maybe his only book.

MARDALE BOOKS
TODMORDEN

Published by MARDALE BOOKS at 97 Longfield Rd., Todmorden OL14 6ND in AD 2007.

© Frank McManus, 2007; see also the acknowledgements, at the back of this book.

All rights are reserved. No part of this book may be stored on a retrieval system, or transmitted in any form, without the prior written permission of the publisher, who will consider with sympathy requests to reproduce the author's work herein.

Frank McManus hereby asserts and gives notice of his right under s.77 of the Copyright, Design & Patents Act 1988 to be identified as the author of the items in this book not attributed to others.

Printed and bound by KIRKFIELD PRESS, Dewsbury.

ISBN 978.0.9555167.0.2

<u>By way of dedication</u>: I stayed at the Haweswater Hotel on 16th July 2005 to celebrate the completion of this Daybook over a period of 10 years. At the valley-head I turned my back on Manchester's reservoir (see entry for 27th February), and on the 60 parked cars, to face the sunlit splendour before me:

> "Oh the Mardale hills are glorious,
> The Mardale hills are grand;
> If ye climb the hills of Mardale, boys/girls,
> Ye'll view the promised land." — Old song.

Of course "East or West, home's best"; and in West Cumbria they say:

> "The best hills are the Wasdale hills
> When spring comes up the vale."

So I quote from Sarah Hall's best novel to date (see entry for 11th October) and apply to the entire world her toast to a fictional old worthy of the soon-to-be-drowned Mardale Green:

"To Nathaniel Holme, God rest him well, and to all the noble men and women ever of this dale." *Frank.*

"For, behold, I create new heavens and a new earth: and the former shall not be remembered, nor come into mind. But be ye glad and rejoice forever in that which I create: for behold, I create Jerusalem a rejoicing, and her people a joy." — Isaiah 65:17-18.

FOREWORD by VALERIE PURTON.

More than a Day-book, indeed a very Un-common Commonplace Book, Frank McManus's <u>The March and the Muster</u> is that very rare publication, a cornucopia of Wit and Wisdom which spans poetry and politics, religion and radicalism in a way which refuses neat classification but (perhaps because of this) is a delight to read.

Whether unearthing a little-known Tennyson illustration, explaining the origins of St. Thomas' Day or preaching against the war method, the author is always engagingly himself, beholden to a variety of political and literary traditions and to none, increasing our enjoyment of literature and the arts while encouraging us to participate fully in a world which, despite its dangers, remains in his eyes rich and rewarding.

There is an unsentimental good-heartedness about all the entries. They can be read day by day or in a more sustained way. The book would make an excellent Christmas present, especially perhaps as a tonic for the cynical or depressed: I challenge anyone not to respond to the sheer appetite for life evident in these pages — a sense of the glory and delight of 'things being various'.

Dr Valerie Purton,
Senior Lecturer,
Anglia Ruskin University.

"BY SAINT AGNES FOUNTAIN"

Julia's Pool, Upper Swindale.   N. Mercer.

A Book of Days for the Bleak Midwinter
(8th January to 29th February)

"The March and the Muster"
Part I

Frank McManus

"THE MARCH AND THE MUSTER." — Welcome and Introduction.

by Frank R. McManus.

Dear Readers,

Locksley House,
97 Longfield Road,
Todmorden OL14 6ND.
1st January 2007.

This six-part Book of Days, commonplace-book or "omnium gatherum" dipping-book has circulated privately among some of my friends over six recent Christmastides. I now make bold to present it to a wider public, hoping as before that if the serious items pall, the frivolities may yet please — and vice versa, of course! My year is divided into six sections as follows, and begins on 8th January so as not to bisect the Twelve Days of Christmas:

8 Jan. – 29 Feb.:	"By Saint Agnes' Fountain"	(J.M. Neale).
1 March – 3 May :	"Voice and Vision"	(William Morris).
4 May – 5 July :	"Below the Darksome Bough"	(Wm. Barnes).
6 July – 5 Sept.:	"Summer Suns are Glowing"	(W.W. How).
6 Sept. – 6 Nov.:	"England Arise"	(Edward Carpenter).
7 Nov. – 7 Jan.:	"The Morn on our Mountains"	(W. Scott).

Each of these sectional titles is taken from a poem by the named author:— see 10.1 for Neale's carol; 3.5 Morris; 26.5 Barnes; 31.7 How; sectional cover for Carpenter; and Drumossie-day 16.4 for Sir Walter Scott and my main title also. My valedictory "Splendour of the Morning" comes from a love-poem by Violet Morgan to her near-fiancé Bertram Pollock (28.5).

I began my collection in 1996, and some items from that year are dated accordingly. I thank all who have encouraged, helped and criticised me, and shall welcome corrections of such errors as may remain as my sole responsibility. Summaries of Contents conclude every section, and an Index of Main Themes follows at the end. Joy & Peace to you all! *Frank.*

Plough Monday 8th January 1996/2007.

With the street-illuminations ended and the joys and stresses of the Festive Season too often followed by one of financial stringency, the workaday world looms large, and the morning darkness is only just beginning to lift. In pre-industrial days the plough was blessed on the Sunday after Twelfth Night, and until the Reformation the "Plough Light" was maintained before a saint's image by a guild. In some places there were Sword Dances, Mumming Plays, or Morris Dances. To this day an old horse-plough is blessed in some churches to the words "God speed the plough; the plough and the ploughman, the farm and the farmer, machine and beast and man."

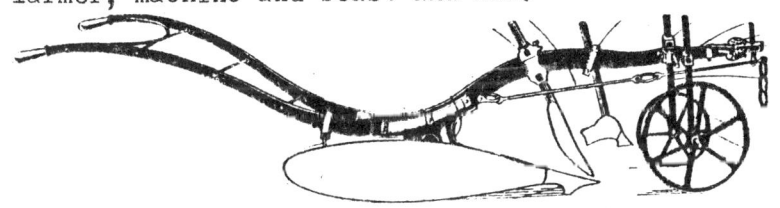

Fieldwork was resumed on Plough Monday (or on 7 January if a weekday): but I feel it could hardly be deferred till a Plough Monday as late as the 13th. It is unclear what happened in any interval between Twelfth Night and the start of work. The first day in the fields was often one of licensed frivolity and flirtation to ease the resumption of hard labour, and it could end early to prepare for men and women to join in evening partying. Robert Herrick wrote in "Hesperides" (1648):

```
         "Partly work and partly play,
(*)      You must on St Distaff's day;
         From the plough soon free your team;
(ɸ)      Then come home and fother them;          (ɸ) fodder
         If the Maides a-spinning go,
         Burn the flax and fire the tow,
(+)      Scorch the plackets but beware            (+) pockets
         That ye singe no maiden hair.
         Bring in pails of water then,
         Let the maids bewash the men.
         Give St Distaff all the right;
         Then bid Christmas sport good-night
         And next morrow, everyone
         To his own vocation."
```
— — — — — — — — — —

(*) There is of course no such saint, but the day marked the women's return to the spindle, as the "distaff side".

9th January.   HOW MUCH WOOD?

Riddles have always been a source of amusement:
1. What's the difference between a sick lion and a dead bee?
2. And between a cat and a comma?
3. When is a voice not a voice?   4. And a door not a door?
5. Why does a hen lay an egg?   6. Why did the chicken run?
7. Why is a raven like a writing-desk? (Lewis Carroll).
8. What goes into Beds, and Hunts, and ends up in the Wash?
9. How much wood would a woodchuck chuck if a woodchuck could chuck wood?   (Answers below.)

- - - - - - -

Some folksongs contain riddles, e.g. "I will give my love an apple" which Ralph Vaughan Williams collected and published for school use in 1912. (Ask at you local library for the related rhyme "My love sent me a chicken without e'er a bone".)

- - - - - - -

"I will give my love an apple without e'er a core,
I will give my love a house without e'er a door,
I will give my love a palace wherein she may be,
And she may unlock it without any key.

"My head is the apple without e'er a core,
My mind is the house without e'er a door,
My heart is the palace wherein she may be,
And she may unlock it without any key."

- - - - - - -

Answers. (1) One's a seedy beast and the other's a bee deceased.
(2) On has its claws at the end of its paws; the other has its pause at the end of its clause. (3) When it's a little ho(a)rse.
(4) When it's ajar. (5) Because it can't lay a brick.
(6) Because it saw the pillar box (political version: ballot box).
(7) The first has flapping fits and is a pest for wrens; the second has fitting flaps and is a rest for pens. (from entries to *Spectator* 1991.)
(8) The River Ouse (but Hunts. ceased to be a county in 1974).
(9) It depends which woodchuck it is.

4

<u>10th January.</u>   "And in the Frosty Season" (Wordsworth).

Christmastide has now ended except for those who follow the Eastern Orthodox tradition which, not having changed in 1752 from the Julian to the Gregorian calendar, keep Christmas Day on 7 January (which is sensible since it puts the holiday further into the "bleak midwinter" when it is most needed). Mention of that phrase prompts me to wonder whether John Mason Neale (1818-1866), who set in snow his song "Good King Wenceslas", paused to ask himself whether a poor man who lived "right against the forest fence, by St Agnes' fountain" really needed to go "a good league" to get firewood. Neale, who translated from the Latin some of our most popular hymns, certainly disapproved of the toning-down of his carol by a teetotal vegetarian whose version ran:

> "Bring me milk and bring me bread,
> Bring me pine-logs hither;
> Thou and I shall see him fed..."

But that was before the days of cruel intensive animal-husbandry, which the compassionate writer would have abhorred. It might be thought that bread and milk failed to fortify against "the rude wind's wild lament", just as I smile at the failure of some illustrators of Keats' "St. Agnes' Eve" who show Madeleine eloping in a party-dress on just such a night.

With the end of the festive season, Berlioz' "Childhood of Christ" deserves mention. It is in three parts, beginning with "Herod's wrath" and ending with the Holy Family finding hospitality among Ishmaelite "infidels" in Sais (Port Said), Egypt. (Is this Berlioz' fantasy, or is there an old tradition?) The central "Fuite (flight) en Egypt" section is very beautiful, with a consistency seldom found in Berlioz. Brahms rated it the French composer's best work. It comprises an overture of archaic gravity, for woodwind and strings; then the well-known "Shepherds' Farewell"; and then a conclusion portraying the angelic adoration and blessing of the refugees as they rest by the wayside.

Berlioz based his Shepherds' Chorus on a theme he had improvised for the album of an architect called Duc. Peeved by the generally-destructive attitude of the music-critics of his era, he mischievously presented the overture and the chorus as a "discovery" of a work by the non-existent "Pierre Ducré, master of music in 17th-century Paris". Only one critic was suspicious enough to doubt the genuineness of the "discovery" and to avoid being hoaxed by Berlioz.

11th January.   ASK FOR THE OLD PATHS.

A former student of mine wrote to me on Christmas Day from a boys' home in Goa where she spent six weeks with 36 orphans aged from 4 to 20 years. She took full 24-hour care whilst the two brothers-in-charge made their retreat. "I am more than ever convinced", she writes, "that the Indian culture has everything right, and the Western world has everything wrong." Everything? – one may demur, yet from the practical standpoint she's correct!

> "The world is too much with us; late and soon, (Wm. Words-
> Getting and spending, we lay waste our powers: worth.)
> Little we see in Nature that is ours;
> We have given our hearts away, a sordid boon!"

Thus splendidly wrote Wordsworth by 1807 when the First Industrial Revolution was scarcely under way. For years I regarded industrialism as the cause of proletarian oppression. As Goldsmith wrote in "The Deserted Village":

> "A time there was, ere England's griefs began,
> When every rood of ground maintained its man."

– and I accepted from R.H. Tawney's famous book "Religion and the Rise of Capitalism" that "Puritanism, not the Tudor secession from Rome, was the true English Reformation, and it is from its struggle against the old order that an England which is undoubtedly modern emerges." By 1750, says Tawney, most educated Englishfolk concurred with Pope's lines:

> "Thus God and Nature formed the general frame,
> And bade self-love and social be the same."

Alas today the Global Market is all too often treated as sacrosanct by its Western "beneficiaries", so that philanthropy and respect for values are confined to those parts of life which fall outside mainstream commerce and industry. But Hilaire Belloc, in his book "The Servile State", rightly goes further back: "Capitalism was here in England before the Industrial System...England...was <u>already</u> captured by a wealthy oligarchy <u>before</u> the series of great discoveries began." "No such material cause determined the degradation from which we suffer. It was the deliberate action of men, evil will in a few and apathy of will among the many."

(Continued.

The root of our present evils was in fact the hijacking of the Reformation for selfish purposes, and the seizure of the monastic lands. This created a landed oligarchy and destroyed the civilisation of the late Middle Ages, in which the distributive system of property and the organisation of the guilds had been slowly creating a society in which all men should be "economically free through the possession of capital and land." Collectivist measures, wrote Belloc of radicalism a century ago, will merely make capitalism endurable within its essential terms. What is being brought about is not a collectivist but a servile state, in which "the mass of men shall be constrained by law to labour for the profit of a minority, but...shall enjoy a security which the old capitalism did not give them."

(The "bond system" imposed on Durham miners in the 19th century afforded an extreme confirmation of Belloc's views. We now know, however, that the high industrial age has in its turn yielded to a "global market" era of high instability.)

Best of all perhaps is Wilfrid Mellers' diagnosis in his "Vaughan Williams and the Vision of Albion" (Pimlico 1991 p45): "...the Catholic and Universal Church was undermined as man substituted individualised human power for what had been thought of as the will of God...when once the immense wealth of the Church had been plundered by desperate men, power went to their heads. As reform brought material profit to the reformers, the spiritual impulses that justified reform were obscured."

Accordingly I find myself something of a medievalist, even though I'm well aware of the harshness of life for the many in those days. So far as life on earth is concerned, humanity will do well to insist that alongside the benign application of the marvels of modern technology, it is even more important that in the field of ethics and morality we shall "ask for the old paths, for they are good, and walk in them." Jeremiah: (chapter 6, verse 16).

"Ill fares the land, to hastening ills a prey,
Where wealth accumulates and men decay." (Oliver Goldsmith.)

12th January 1996. A HUMAN-SIZED CAPITAL CITY.

A visit to York, where even the new Archbishop, David Hope, found as a schoolboy that the railway station rivalled the Minster as chief attraction. If Isaiah had seen the station in the heyday of steam he might have exclaimed in a different context that "His Train filled the Temple"! Spring and Autumn are the best times to visit this walled city which the Danes held for two centuries before the Norman Conquest. Today the Minster was dark by mid-afternoon, though there was light enough to review the statues of post-1066 kings on the screen:

"Willie, Willie, Harry, Stee; Harry, Dick, John, Harry 3; 1,2,3 Neds, Richard 2; Henries 4,5,6 - then who?"

(Well, nobody so far as the Minster is concerned, so I'll leave completing this mnemonic-rhyme until tomorrow.)

More brightly lit was the National Railway Museum, where I always thrill at the presence of Mallard, the preserved L.N.E.R. streamliner whose steam record 126m.p.h. has stood for some 60 years, and on seeing the giant Chinese locomotive. I delight too on seeing Coppernob from the Furness Railway, displaced by a World War 2 bomb from its glass conservatory outside Barrow station; the sole surviving Aspinall 2-4-2 tank engine from the L. & Y. ("Lanky"); the huge 2-10-0 Evening Star, which was British Rail's last steam locomotive; and other such fine machines, the most elegant ever to have moved on earth. (The figures are wheel-arrangements - in the middle we have the number of large driving-wheels, which is preceded by the number of wheels on the leading bogie and followed by the number on the trailing bogie, as provided for optimal running.) The names given to steam locomotives were generally more attractive than those of their successors. Interestingly the G.W.R. "Star Class" included three locomotives, Lode Star, North Star, and Pole Star, which were all named after the same heavenly body.

Among the more poignant artefacts in the York Museum is a poster published by the railway companies in the wake of the 1926 General Strike in which, doubtless to secure an indemnity for their members, the rail unions stated that they had been wrong to strike. Duress? The museum's "Thomas the Tank Engine" section, celebrating Wilbert Awdry's work, quotes from a book: "Early in the morning, Down at the station, All the little engines, Standing in a row. Along comes the driver, Pulls the little lever, Puff, puff, chuff, chuff! Off we go." This was parodied by the strikers who doubted that the middle-class volunteers of 1926 could run railways safely. They varied the second half as follows: "Darcy on the footplate Pulls a little lever, Puff, puff, chuff, chuff! UP we go!'"

8

13th January 1996.   A TRIP TO BRONTËLAND.

Another, albeit minor, railway-day; I took the bus from my home town of Todmorden to the "Brontë Village" of Haworth, then took the 4.51pm steam train on the Worth Valley Railway to Keighley to return home by British Rail. This was an exercise in nostalgia which renewed my long-forgotten experience of steam travel from and through gas-lit stations, adding yet further confirmation to my belief, shared by many, that in the wake of steam traction "there hath past away a glory from the earth" (Wordsworth, in a different connection, in his "Ode - Intimations of Immortality...")

I recall some of the salvaged signs in the Worth Valley museum at Oxenhope:

"Only the Company's Horses are allowed to drink from this trough." (Probably not meanness, but for avoiding congestion.)

"These closets are intended for the convenience of passengers only. Workmen, Cabmen, Fish Porters and Idlers are not permitted to use them - BY ORDER." (Well, well!!)

Most chauvinistically the L.N.W.R. in 1901 produced a sign stating that "It is forbidden for Vagrants, Beggars, Itinerant Musicians and Females of Doubtful Reputation to enter these premises - BY ORDER." (For "Doubtful" read "Rotten"! - then ask whether the old "North Western" employed Males of Similar Reputation for the work that could be had from them.)

Finally there's the following from the toilet compartments of L.M.S. corridor-trains: "NOTICE - The public are requested to assist in keeping the W.C. in a clean condition, and to see that proper use is made of the toilet paper - BY ORDER."

Sad to say, the "golden ages of steam railways", including the 1900s and 1920s, have all but passed from living memory. The Preserved Railways tend to maintain the later ambiences of the Post-Grouping Big Four and of B.R. which though fine were slightly "below peak".

- - - - - - - -

To complete the "Monarchs jingle" from yesterday:
"Edwards two and Dick the bad; Harries two then Ned the lad; Mary, Bess, and James the vain; Charlie, Charlie, James again; William 'n Mary, Anna Gloria; 4 Georges, William and Victoria; Edward, George and Edward 8; George - now Betty's Head of State, Gentle George's Lillibet - Here comes Charlie! no, not yet, Lizzie 2 is still alive; then Charlie 3 and Willie 5." (But "Nay, let each voter have a voice, and Tony Benn will be my choice." The conclusion may be varied according to taste!)

14th January. FROM A KINDLIER DAY AND AGE

(in many places, that is, though life was hard for
many, and total war was soon to shatter Europe's peace.)

By MARGARET CRAMS (28) in 1913. Found during Eppleton Church
      Others.   1983 centenary, Co. Durham.

Think before you take a step to injure or offend.
Thoughtless words may break a link that time may never
mend. Pause before you make a move, examine heart and
mind. Make quite sure your motive, based on something
true and kind.
Other people are affected by the things we do. No one
lives unto himself; so keep that truth in view — when
you talk about your rights remember, if you can, the
rights, the problems and the feelings of the other man.
Learn to put yourself aside, your worries, wants and
woes. See things from the angle of the person you op-
pose. What a different place the world would be if all
agreed to *practise in their daily lives this plain and simple creed*

Charles Dalmon's Hymn for Justice and Peace, sung to Wir
Pflügen, is useable for any good radical cause. In the 1930s
John Groser chose it for street-processions in support of an
East London rent-strike; and in the 80s it was sung at Moles-
worth for "beating the bounds" of the H-bomb missile base. I
can send copy (s.a.e. please); here are three verses:

2. In many a golden story,
On many a golden page,
The poets in their poems
Have sung the golden age;
The age of love and beauty,
The age of joy and peace,
When everyone lived gladly
And shared the earth's increase.

4. God is the only Landlord
To whom our rents are due.
He made the world for all folk
And not for just a few.
The four parts of Creation —
Earth, water, air and fire —
He made & blessed & stationed
For everyone's desire.

5. God made the earth for all folk
And He alone is Lord,
And we shall win our birthright
With truth's prevailing sword;
And all the powers of darkness
And all the hosts of pride
Shall pass and be forgotten
For God is on our side.

(Chorus):
Raise the people's banner
And let the ancient cry
For justice, peace & freedom
Re-echo to the sky!

Heartsearch, New Statesman, 1977: "Extremely well-travelled
female, 50, slim, attractive & crazy for life. Looking for
a tall & attractive male who knows how to treat a girl."

15th January. "Stitch that would awaken the dead."

On 15 January 1996 the *Independent* printed the following letter from Mr. Tim Craig of Hindford in Shropshire:

"Sir: The recent revival of Daphne Banks from a mortuary reminded me of the following:

"On one of the ships I sailed as a cadet in the Merchant Navy in the early 1960s, there was a death on board off the West African coast. As there were two doctors on the ship to sign the death certificate and no refrigerated space, it was decided to "commit the body to the deep".

"The mate sent me down to assist the bo'sun to prepare and stitch up the corpse, as he said I would be unlikely to witness such an occurrence again. The bo'sun, a North Sea Chinaman (i.e. he hailed from the Orkney Isles), was in his sixties and had performed the task several times before. He was a deft hand with the palm (leather glove) and needle used to sew the heavy canvas into a shroud around the body, and when he came to the final stitches around the face he pushed the large triangular-shaped needle right through the nose. I winced, and he looked up at me and said, 'That's the law of the sea, the last stitch through the nose, if that don't wake him up I know he's dead.'

"Apparently, it was not uncommon for sailors or passengers to be mistakenly pronounced dead. This was the final test. Yours sincerely, TIM CRAIG."

DERIVATIONS of common English words are not always well known. "Crossing the Threshold" to enter a house is an expression from the days of slate or stone floors which were slippery unless spread with straw or thresh which also gave warmth in winter. The board at the door that kept this in place was called the thresh-hold.

MAURICE'S JOTTINGS, first set, from my late friend M. Darwin.

If humble pie has to be eaten, BOLT IT WHOLE.
An ounce of love is worth a pound of knowledge.
Lie down with dogs, get up with fleas.
Delicacy is to love what grace is to beauty.
A delay is better than a disaster. Who can enjoy, alone?
A poor man knows his friends. The eagle does not hurt flies.
Do a little at a time, that you may do more. (J.Wesley).dead.
I reverence the young, because they may be useful when I am /
I do not believe in the big way of doing things. (MotherTeresa
In mediation get both sides' confidence and see the loser is not humiliated.

16th January.   "MALE AND FEMALE".   (Some Epigrams).

Feminism: No thank you, I'd much prefer an orange. (Eve, allowed a re-run.)

No-one should have to dance backward all their lives.
(Jill Ruckelshaus.)

Beware of the man who praises women's liberation; he is about to quit his job. (Erica Jong.)

I wish Adam had died with all his ribs in his body. (Boucicault.)

In the world we live in, feminism is a trivial cause. (Doris Lessing.)

A celibate young lady duck Made a shelter of wattle and muck; And there she did stay For many a day - That sensible young lady duck. (Anonymous.)

Alimony: Buying oats for a dead horse (Author not known by compiler.)

The high cost of leaving. (Anonymous.)

Bounty after the mutiny. (Max Kaufmann.)

Fission after fusion. (Rita Mae Brown.)

Billing minus cooing. (Mary Dorsey.)

Love (see also 14th February):

is - an island of emotions surrounded by an ocean of expenses. (after T.R.Dwyer.)
    - the irresistable desire to be irresistably desired. (Robert Frost.)

Sex is a part of love, but not a very good part. (School essay.)

Love never gives up. (Saint Paul, 1 Corinthians 13 verse 8.)

"Yet each man kills the thing he loves, By each let this be heard,
Some do it with a bitter look, Some with a flattering word,
The coward does it with a kiss, The brave man with a sword!

"Some kill their love when they are young, And some when they are old;
Some strangle with the hands of Lust, Some with the hands of Gold:
The kindest use a knife, because
            The dead so soon grow cold.

"Some love too little, some too long, Some sell, and others buy;
Some do the deed with many tears, And some without a sigh:
For each man kills the thing he loves, Yet each man does not die."
.....
(Oscar Wilde, "The Ballad of Reading Gaol".)

Wednesday 17th January 1996 - Centenary of the Motor Car!

This event was marked by a service in Coventry Cathedral during which a vintage Daimler and an electric battery-car were driven up the central aisle. Several anti-road organisations had protested at these plans, saying the car is no unmixed blessing:

* The motorist is more terrible than the terrorist in respect of lives cut short.
* The private-vehicle-based transport system isn't safe enough
* The car promotes a privatised lifestyle, with out-of-town hyper-markets capturing shoppers from town centres. This may even make spouses strainfully over-dependent on each other!
* The car removes responsible adults from urban streets and makes town centres less safe; this may even inhibit the development of local friendships through people meeting.
* The car erodes public transport, thus being self-proliferating.
* The road-transport lobby secures the maiming of beautiful places by road-construction (e.g. Keswick bypass under Skiddaw mountain) and by bridge-building (e.g. Skye bridge).
* Exhaust-fumes pollute the air and damage the environment.
* Motorists are tempted to laziness and lack of exercise.

Of course the car has obvious advantages, giving mobility to the disabled and flexibility of door-to-door journeys to families. The vehicle itself is not malign but it serves as a focus for the good and bad traits of human nature. Provost John Petty at first declined to involve protesters in the centenary event, saying this would be discourteous to guests from the industry; but he rightly softened this stance on the day, taking some protesters into the old cathedral, and publicising the forthcoming "Victims of Road Accidents" service.

All this, however, was "upstaged" by Lucy Pearce (35), who lost her mother in a road accident when she was 2. This lady was brave or exhibitionist enough, or most probably both, to assume the role of Lady Godiva Mark 2, by stripping in front of the congregation of 1000 to display anti-car slogans on her body as she spoke for 4 minutes, claiming to mourn 17 million people killed directly by the motor car. Though she was hustled out, charged, and later released, she secured the reporting of the event in the tabloid press as well as in the broadsheets, making people blend thankfulness for the car with thoughtful penitence.

18th January,   Andy Capp Dies Hard.

In spite of Doris Lessing's comment set out two days ago, the feminists do have right on their side in claiming that women in general have been "put on" by men in general. This was inevitable during the era of heavy industry when men were exploited by the baleful commercial system, and worked to exhaustion. Too often, however, the Andy Capp type of husband perpetuated this when it was no longer fair. Of course this may not be wholly a result of social conditioning, for a special nurturing role falls to women as with breastfeeding of infants. The male blackbird gathers the twigs, and the female builds the nest with them. I once mentioned this to a good female friend who had an outside job, and she remarked "What if the female blackbird has to gather the sticks and build the nest as well?" I could only think of the callous reply "More fool she!" - and women know now that they have been liberated from the tyranny of the husband into the tyranny of the boss and the economic system. All too often they have added paid employment to their existing housework, whilst too many men have become drones without real purpose in life.

Anne Fazackerley's poem "What About Me?" is about a mother whose husband is in jail:

"Unspoken rules which I must obey,
These are the things I am told every day -
'Think of the children, think of the home,
Think of your husband locked up all alone.

- - - -

"Consider the neighbours, consider the cat,
Go on a diet - you're no good to us fat!
Think of the future, don't live for today;
If you're not careful it'll all slip away.

- - - -

"Do all the housework, pay all the bills,
Got the self-pity? - There, have some pills.
Keep it inside you, don't let it out,
Control it at all costs, forbidden to shout.

- - - -

"But it winds up inside me, and I've lost the key.
When my head's in the oven, who'll think of me?"

(The last line 'dates' this poem to the era when coal-gas, with its content of carbon monoxide in small amount, provided a kindly mode of suicide for the despairing. Car-exhaust fumes now serve this role.)

19th January.

THE SCHOOLGIRL'S GUIDE TO THE SONNET.

Sonnets are compact poems much loved by poets and by their readers. The great William Wordsworth wrote two such poems in praise of their structure — "Nuns fret not" and "Scorn not the Sonnet". He did not, however, explain sonnet-form for the benefit of the uninitiated; nor to my knowledge did any other poet of note. Here then is my exposition, using the specimen rhymes "Pig, bat, etc." from the Oxford English Dictionary's definition of "sonnet":

A Sonnet is a poem of fourteen lines,

Each one "iambic" — five "ti-tums" (you know)

Unless the poet makes the last one go

On longer, as when Wordsworth thus inclines,

Portentously, to make his feelings plain.

The first eight rhyme "Pig bat cat wig jig hat

Rat fig" in Petrarch's scheme, though Shakespeare sat

More lightly to such rules as would constrain

His tenderness of love. Till Milton's time

The last six lines observed a break of sense

From the first "octet". The "sextet" might rhyme

In diverse ways; Petrarch would fain devise

A two- or three-fold plan, in some such wise

As seldom had a final pair in evidence.

— — — — — — —

The "rhyming scheme" for the above verse may be set out thus: ABBA CDDC EFEGGF, as may be checked. The reader may like to locate and read the following favourite sonnets in an anthology or elsewhere, and to note their rhyming schemes (check on 29 February):
"I am the great sun, but you do not see me" (Causley).
"When I consider how my life is spent" (Milton).
"What passing-bells for these who die as cattle?" (Owen).
"The world is charged with the grandeur of God" (Hopkins).
"Much have I travell'd in the realms of gold" (Keats).
and the two named above by Wordsworth.

20th January – "St. Agnes' Eve – ah, bitter chill it was!"; a date made famous by Keats' ode about the Lady Madeline:-

> Whose heart had brooded, all that wintry day,
> On love, and winged St. Agnes' saintly care,
> As she had heard old dames full many times declare.
>
> They told her how, upon St. Agnes' Eve,
> Young virgins might have visions of delight,
> And soft adorings from their loves receive
> Upon the honeyed middle of the night,
> If ceremonies due they did aright;
> As, supperless to bed they must retire,
> And couch supine their beauties, lily white;
> Nor look behind, nor sideways, but require
> Of Heaven with upward eyes for all that they desire.

The mellifluous verses tell of Porphyro's dangerous access to "her hushed and silken room", as portrayed by artists including Arthur Hughes of the famous triptych. Others have depicted their chaste elopement "away into the storm"; Holman Hunt's Madeline has her arms bare below the elbows although "the iced gusts still rave and beat" (an oversight, surely – but please see tomorrow; the artist was, in his own words, just concerned to contrast "the sacredness of honest responsible love" with "the weakness of proud intemperance".) Some artists have painted the bedroom scene; Maclise's version is brashly over-rich, and Millais', once held by the Queen Mother, was considered by the viewing public to have too ugly, thin, and stiff a woman.

Tennyson's short "St. Agnes' Eve" poem spiritualises the theme into that of a nun yearning for Christ her Heavenly Bridegroom:

> "Make Thou my spirit pure and clear
> As are the frosty skies,
> Or this first snowdrop of the year
> That in my bosom lies."

It has been pointed out somewhat churlishly that Keats' poem, which I hope all who read this page will study, errs in portraying the coloured tincturing of objects lit by the moon through stained glass:

> "Full on this casement shone the wintry moon,
> And threw warm gules on Madeline's fair breast,
> As down she knelt for Heaven's grace and boon;
> Rose-bloom fell on her hands, together prest,
> And on her silver cross soft amethyst..."

Millais found when working at midnight that even a full moon is too weak to achieve this! But Keats can claim poetic licence.

21st January.

Hunt (detail).

A Literary Discovery!

Two further stanzas of the Keats ode have recently come to light. Written on a separate sheet of paper, they are marked "Insert before the three final verses". It is to be feared, alas, that their authenticity is doubtful to say the least - even if Keats had foreseen rail transport, as Tennyson had predicted the aeroplane in his first <u>Locksley Hall</u> poem.

Millais (detail).

"You silly girl, you <u>can't</u> elope like that! -
Romance has turned your mind and swamped your brain!
<u>Get something on!</u> - here! catch this coat and hat,
These boots to march you to the night-mail train,
With thornproof cloak against the snowy rain.
Throw me your gown and bodice sweet and slim;
To part with silken hose do not disdain;
Then don these woollen combinations trim,
And take this lamp for paths and places dark and dim.

"Now here's a skirt of warmest Harris tweed,
And stockings red from wool of Herdwick sheep;
Two leathern gloves; a bag with meats and mead,
And Fair Isle shawl for snugness when you sleep.
- My darling Maddy, don't you fret or weep,
Our foes' response is neither here nor there! -
Just leave those fruits for Angela to keep -
Quick! - down the steps and through the gate we fare
To pledge our nuptial vows by Book of Common Prayer."

- - - - - - - -

Now please obtain and read Keats' "Isabella & the Pot of Basil"

17

Victorian advertising was not manipulative in informing.

JOSEPH GILLOTT'S STEEL PENS
GOLD MEDALS   PARIS. 1878:1889.
V.R.
Numbers for Ladies' use, Medium & Broad Points
166 M, 166 B, 225 M, 287 M, 352, 616 M, 616 B, 909 M, 983 (oblique). Fine Points - 163, 166, 287, 808, 909.

22nd January. "O for the Wings, for the Wings of a GOOSE!"

— for they are far more useful than a dove's for escaping our bleak midwinter. The light is now returning but the late winter snows may yet freeze us, and we should expect some "false springs" before the yearly rebirth of the northern world. At least we're spared the extremes of Scandinavia, whose main cities had but two hours of daylight at last month's solstice.

Geese are usually and with truth considered to be stupid, aggressive, and given to sticking their necks out. Even so, they can teach humans at least these five lessons:

1. Geese when flying in V-formation, as when migrating, help one another's "lift" which is 70 % greater than when flying solo. (This accords with my experience on mountains, which I believe is fairly general. Climbers in a party boost one another's energies.)

2. Geese at the rear encourage their leaders by "honking" their support, in contrast with humans who all too often speak to belittle.

3. If the leading goose feels tired after a while, it drops back a little, and another takes over. Humans by contrast display pride of place.

4. If a wilful goose departs from the V-formation, it finds the going tough and it soon returns to its place.

5. If, however, a bird falls to earth as a result of some mishap such as being shot, it never flies alone. Two or three other geese go to earth with it and remain until it either recovers or dies. The geese then catch up with their "V" if they can, or join another gaggle if they can't.

MORAL — "Government and co-operation are in all things eternally the laws of life. Anarchy & competition, eternally and in all things, the laws of death." (John Ruskin).

The Iona Community's Publications Division is called Wild Goose Publications (4th fl., Savoy House, 140 Sauchiehall St., Glasgow G2 3DH; tel. 0141.3326292) The Wild Goose is a Celtic symbol of the Holy Spirit.

<u>23rd January.</u> "<u>Savage Ruskin....sticks his tusk in.</u>"
(Punch, 1855).

John Ruskin, one of the most famous of all Victorians, was born in London in 1819 and died in Coniston in 1900 A.D. That at least can be said with easy certainty about this otherwise most complex visionary man. His intense low-church mother taught him a narrow version of Christianity from which he defected in adulthood, to regain a freer and more loving understanding of the Faith in later life. His sherry-merchant father, partner to Signor Domecq whose name still graces some sherries, gave him a protected upbringing, and bought him into Oxford University after a school-free childhood under tutors. He excelled as artist and as critic of art and architecture, and his espousal of Turner and the Pre-Raphaelites is well known. More literally he married Euphemia Gray; but (in Kenneth Clark's vivid phrase) "after almost six years of increasing neglect, he pushed her into the arms of his brilliant young protégé, John Everett Millais, and his marriage was annulled." Incapable of ordinary relationships with women, he "had a passion for little girls", whom he like Lewis Carroll did not harm (except, psychologically, for Rose La Touche whose death in 1875 "probably hastened his mental collapse"). Alas for our sexually-obsessed era there tends to be **over-emphasis** on this aspect of Ruskin studies, to the detriment of his unique social criticism and attack on burgeoning capitalism. He bore bravely the obloquy but it did his state of mind no good. Kenneth Clark's anthology "Ruskin Today" (Penguin 1964) - well worth reading even though it devoted more space to the seer's art than to his sociology - says that Ruskin's 1859 putting-aside of art to devote himself to critical economics, brought out the best in him.

Sheltered by his parents from Victorian squalor, he in his twenties became aware that their visitors from the Spanish landowning society spoke of their peasants as encumbrances save for producing wealth for them by their labour. He asked himself why the Andalusians got none of the wine which "came to crown our Vandalic feasts", nor the money it was sold for; and he thus was led "necessarily" into earnest political work. His Manchester lectures "A Joy for Ever" were followed in the <u>Cornhill Magazine</u> by four papers "Unto This Last" (1860) that were reviled by all their readers save the older radical Thomas Carlyle, who now is seldom read but whose dictum (that a society with cash payment as the sole nexus between men will be spiritually empty) is masterly in its overview.[1] Published in book form in 1862, "Unto This Last" served as a laserbeam piercing the "smokescreen of classical economics" (Clark) to reveal the underlying "true human realities." (1 - 2.1)
(continued.

Ruskin regarded the work as his best book, to stand "surest and longest", and time has vindicated this (though alas it is no longer certain to be on town libraries' open shelves, or even those of Ruskinian honeypots which emphasise his art). It was followed in 1864 by two lectures printed as "Sesame and Lilies" in the following year, and from 1871 to 1884 by the strident "Letters to the Workmen and Labourers of Great Britain" preciously entitled "Fors Clavigera" - the Angel of Destiny. When not concerned with promoting his fanciful "Guild of St. George", which induced Oscar Wilde to do road-work at Hinksey, or with his views on miscellaneous matters, "Fors" railed in Swiftian fury at "a social system which condemned four-fifths of the population to poverty and squalid ugliness" (Clark); "He thought that all investment was a form of usury, and so contrary to Christian and the best pagan teaching". Amazingly, or typically, the final letter bore a drawing of a girl and two children, entitled "Rosy Vale", by his friend Kate Greenaway. Alongside this activity, and despite being plagued by bad dreams and the like, he served seriously as Oxford's Slade Professor of Fine Art from 1869 till he resigned it a decade later on health grounds and in protest at the University's tolerance of vivisection. His last years were spent quietly at Brantwood overlooking the lake at Coniston, where the churchyard has a fine obelisk at his graveside. Oxford remembers him too through his endowing Ruskin College for working folk such as Hardy's fictional Jude who otherwise were excluded from higher education.

24th January.   WHO KEEPS THE BANK?   ("Unto This Last", 226.)

"Men of business do indeed know how they themselves made their money, or how, on occasion, they lost it....But they neither know who keeps the bank of the gambling-house, nor what other games may be played with the same cards, nor what other losses and gains, far away among the dark streets, are essentially, though invisibly, dependent on theirs in the lighted rooms. They have learned a few, and only a few, of the laws of mercantile economy; but not one of those of political economy."
- - - -

(also Ruskin on Usury: "The idea that money could beget money, though more absurd than alchemy, had yet an apparently practical and irresistibly tempting confirmation in the wealth of villains and the success of fools...But all wholesome indignation against usurers was prevented, in the Christian mind, by wicked and cruel religious hatred of the race of Christ....to this day, the worship of the Immaculate Virginity of Money, 20 mother of the Omnipotence of Money, is the Protestant form of Madonna worship." ("Val d'Arno, x.277). -see also 28 January.

<u>Thursday 25th January 1996.</u> St. Paul's Day and Burns' Nicht — they make an uneasy pairing, but it's the bard's bicentenary of death in 1796 so he'll have this entry to himself.

> Wee, sleekit, cow'rin', tim'rous beastie,
> Oh, what a panic's in thy breastie!
> Thou need na start awa sae hasty,
>   Wi' bickering brattle!   *hurrying scamper*
> I wad be laith to rin an' chase thee,
>   Wi' murd'ring pattle!   *plough-staff*

Born at Alloway this day in 1759 he laboured on poor, under-capitalised farms (Mount Oliphant, Lochlea, Mossgiel, Ellisland), and later as an exciseman, which role he mocked:

> "There's threesome reels, there's foursome reels,
> There's hornpipes and strathspeys, man,
> But the ae best dance ere cam to the land
> Was The Deil's Awa wi' th' Exciseman!"

Feted in Edinburgh where he met the teenaged boy Walter Scott, he nevertheless died at 37 in dire poverty, weakened by over-hard fieldwork and impaired by rheumatic fever. He was boisterous, vivacious, perceptive and charitable, and his Muse was irrepressible: "The poet who laughed the Devil out of Hell (and - more difficult - banished him from Scots Presbyterian theology)...the first poet of common humanity...if Shakespeare (for example) be regarded as the poet who scaled the highest

(continued.

peaks....Burns may be likened to the broad rolling plains of mankind's triumph and travail". (James Barke, Collins, 1955)

Who else would even think of dedicating a song "To a Mouse, on turning her up in her nest with the plough, November 1785"? —

6
That wee bit heap o' leaves an' stibble,
Has cost thee monie a weary nibble!
Now thou's turned out, for a' thy trouble,
But house or hald,
To thole the winter's sleety dribble,
An' cranreuch cauld!

7
But Mousie, thou art no thy lane,
In proving foresight may be vain:
The best-laid schemes o' mice an' men
Gang aft agley,
An' lea'e us nought but grief an' pain,
For promis'd joy!

And who could put paid to a hypocrite and to Calvinist excess?

HOLY WILLIE'S PRAYER

1
O Thou that in the Heavens does dwell,
Wha, as it pleases best Thysel,
Sends ane to Heaven an' ten to Hell
A' for Thy glory,
And no for onie guid or ill
They've done before Thee!

6
But yet, O Lord! confess I must:
At times I'm fash'd wi' fleshly lust; irked
An' sometimes, too, in warldly trust,
Vile self gets in;
But Thou remembers we are dust,
Defiled wi' sin.

5
Yet I am here, a chosen sample,
To show Thy grace is great and ample:

7
O Lord! yestreen, Thou kens, wi' Meg—
Thy pardon I sincerely beg—

Yet the same poet who rejoices, in formal Spenserian stanzas, over the cotters' Saturday evening devotions (see tomorrow) did also perpetrate some very bawdy rhymes that fit hardly, if at all, with "The Burns We Love", though I don't balk at the mischief of "Love and Liberty" in which the roisterers cock a snook at the sober (tune: Jolly Mortals, Fill Your Glasses".)

CHORUS
fig for those by law protected!
Liberty's a glorious feast,
ourts for cowards were erected,
Churches built to please the priest!

2
What is title, what is treasure,
What is reputation's care?
If we lead a life of pleasure,
'Tis no matter how or where!

5
Life is all a variorum,
We regard not how it goes;
Let them prate about decorum,
Who have character to lose.

1
ee the smoking bowl before us!
Mark our jovial, ragged ring!
Round and round take up the cho-
And in raptures let us sing: rus

4
Does the train-attended carriage
Thro' the country lighter rove?
Does the sober bed of marriage
Witness brighter scenes of love?

6
Here's to budgets, bags and wallets!
Here's to all the wandering train!
Here's our ragged brats and callets!
One and all, cry out, Amen!

Everyone knows the perhaps overworked "Auld Lang Syne", but near to the heart are the love-lyrics including "Flow gently sweet Afton", "Ca' the yowes", "John Anderson, my jo", "Ye banks and braes", and "My love is like a red red rose". All are worth looking up, as are many more including the comic tale of "Tam O' Shanter", the heroic "Scots wha hae", the lighthearted "Duncan Gray", "Charlie is my darling", "My Heart's in the Highlands", "A Man's a Man for a' that", & "The Twa Dogs". As Wordsworth epitomised Lakeland, so Burns was Scotland's voice at the same era of history.

(*) wayfarers' bundles.
(∅) sluts.

22

26th January. THE COTTER'S SATURDAY NIGHT, in its portrayal of poor farmworkers' devotions, reveals the Bard's universal sympathies by its seriousness at polar remove from the giddy "Love and Liberty". He rejoices in the formal "Spenserian stanzas" (with rhyme-scheme ABABBCBCC as with Keats, 20 January, and extended final line) into which he sneaks the occasional Scots word.

13

They chant their artless notes in simple guise,
  They tune their hearts, by far the noblest aim;
Perhaps *Dundee's* wild-warbling measures rise,
  Or plaintive *Martyrs*, worthy of the name;
  Or noble *Elgin* beets the heaven-ward flame,
The sweetest far of Scotia's holy lays:
  Compar'd with these, Italian trills are tame;
The tickl'd ears no heart-felt raptures raise;
Nae unison hae they, with our Creator's praise.

14

The priest-like father reads the sacred page,
  How Abram was the friend of God on high;
Or, Moses bade eternal warfare wage
  With Amalek's ungracious progeny;
  Or, how the royal Bard did groaning lie
Beneath the stroke of Heaven's avenging ire;
  Or Job's pathetic plaint, and wailing cry;
Or rapt Isaiah's wild, seraphic fire;
Or other holy Seers that tune the sacred lyre.

15

Perhaps the Christian volume is the theme,
  How guiltless blood for guilty man was shed;
How He, who bore in Heaven the second name,
  Had not on earth whereon to lay His head;
  How His first followers and servants sped;
The precepts sage they wrote to many a land:
  How he, who lone in Patmos banished,
Saw in the sun a mighty angel stand,
And heard great Bab'lon's doom pronounc'd by
  Heaven's command.

16

Then kneeling down to Heaven's Eternal King,
  The saint, the father, and the husband prays:
Hope 'springs exulting on triumphant wing,'
  That thus they all shall meet in future days,
  There, ever bask in uncreated rays,
No more to sigh or shed the bitter tear,
  Together hymning their Creator's praise,
In such society, yet still more dear;
While circling Time moves round in an eternal sphere.

17

Compar'd with this, how poor Religion's pride,
  In all the pomp of method, and of art;
When men display to congregations wide
  Devotion's ev'ry grace, except the heart!
  The Power, incens'd, the pageant will desert,
The pompous strain, the sacerdotal stole;
  But haply, in some cottage far apart,
May hear, well-pleas'd, the language of the soul,
And in His Book of Life the inmates poor enroll.

18

Then homeward all take off their sev'ral way;
  The youngling cottagers retire to rest:
The parent-pair their secret homage pay,
  And proffer up to Heaven the warm request,
  That He who stills the raven's clam'rous nest,
And decks the lily fair in flow'ry pride,
  Would, in the way His wisdom sees the best,
For them and for their little ones provide;
But, chiefly, in their hearts with Grace Divine preside.

23

The worship is of course led by "the sire", with "His lyart haffins (grey sidelocks) wearing thin and bare". Overblown in one or two places, the poem's a joy to read overall.

27th January. USURY — a nasty thing, we all agree, as we think of rapacious moneylenders who prey on the deprived. Yet we like to condemn them for demanding excessive interest, whilst we ourselves as a rich Western nation accept a coerced inflow of wealth from the Third World. The churches to their credit play a leading role in debt-cancellation campaigns; yet although Jesus said "Lend expecting nothing in return" (Luke 6^{35}) it tends to be left to our Muslim friends to uphold the biblical tradition on the topic (e.g. Exodus 22^{25}, Nehemiah 5$^{7-12}$, Psalm 15^{6}, Ezekiel 18^{8}). A clear reassertion of the traditional Christian ban on "The attempt to draw profit and increment without labour, cost or risk out of a thing (i.e. money) that does not fructify" would be most welcome. That is the teaching of the Church, worked out in medieval times and asserted in 1515 by the 5th Lateran Council of the undivided Western Church including England; and again in 1745 by Pope Benedict XIV whose encyclical "Vix Pervenit" has been put on the Internet. For that is the traditional meaning of the term "usury" — unjustified interest, not excessive interest! The Oxford English Dictionary shows the fatal drift in the popular understanding of the term, for its definition is "The fact or practive of lending money at interest; especially in later use excessive or illegal rates of interest".

The drift from the traditional understanding of "usury" isn't easy to trace; but R.H. Tawney's "Religion and the Rise of Capitalism" (Murray 1926; Penguin etc.) portrays it, and shows that the success of diligent able Puritans in exploiting new scientific discoveries led to some good men getting rich, from which influential people concluded, illogically but conveniently, that riches are a sign of God's favour. The way was made clear for 19th-century capitalists to exploit low-wage industrial communities; and now the impersonal and anarchic "global market" has spread this activity to the Far East, devastating Britain's **heavy industry and preying on poor nations** (See Part 5 foreword).

In The Sunset ("Im Abendrot") by J. Von Eichendorff, set by Richard Strauss, Four Last Songs, No.4.

"We have gone hand in hand through pain and joy. The air is already growing dark in the valley. Only two larks rise upwards. Come close andd let them flutter. Soon it is time to sleep, so that we do not lose each other in the solitude. How tired we are of wandering. Can that perhaps be death?"

Preceded by three Hesse poems this 1948 masterwork has lark-trills and a final cadence from Death & Transfiguration (1889).

<u>28th January.</u> <u>The Greater Money-Trick.</u>

Robert Tressall's novel "The Ragged Trousered Philanthropists" brilliantly evokes the author's life and work as a Brighton housepainter a century ago, and his socialistic opinions. It contains a famous chapter on "The Great Money Trick", in which his hero gives a talk to his fellow-workers showing how the boss, by virtue of his possessing wealth and the means of production, could force his employees to work for far less a return than their productive efforts secure for him. Some Liverpool apprentices in the late 1940s were given copies of this chapter on their first day at work, because the older workers were anxious to see that the youngsters knew how the system worked to the disproportionate benefit of the rich.

The clarity of this understanding has alas been lost in recent years as local firms have been superseded by large impersonal conglomerates including multinationals. Work lacks its old permanency, as witness the calls for "labour flexibility" which means the readiness of people to move from one job and one place to another whenever the vagaries of the market so require. Add to this the lower political awareness of the comfortably-placed, and the fatalism of many in the deprived minority, and we can see that there is little understanding of the Greater Money Trick of the "global market", Capitalist International, or Capintern. Interest-payments by the poor cosset the rich!

Ruskin (24 January) asked "Who Keeps the Bank?" - and in Letter 80 of "Fors Clavigera" he attacked usury:

"The dullest of all excuses for usury is that some kind of good is done by the usurer. Nobody denies the good done; but the principle of Righteous dealing is, that if the good costs you nothing, you must not be paid for doing it. Your friend passes your door on an unexpectedly wet day, unprovided for the occasion. You have the choice of three benevolences to him – lending him your umbrella, lending him eighteenpence to pay for a cab, or letting him stay in your parlour till the rain is over. If you charge him interest on the umbrella, it is profit on capital - if you charge him interest on the eighteenpence, it is ordinary usury - if you charge him interest on the parlour, it is rent. All three are equally forbidden by Christian law, being actually worse, because more plausible and hypocritical sins, than if you at once plainly refused your friend shelter, umbrella, or pence. You feel yourself to be a brute, in the one case, and may some day repent into grace; in the other you imagine yourself an honest and amiable person, rewarded by Heaven for your charity; and the whole frame of society is rotten to the core..."

29th January.

THE LIM'RICK packs laughs anatomical
Into space that is quite economical,
   But the good ones I've seen
   So seldom are clean,
And the clean ones so seldom are comical.

Thus complained Vyvian Holland in his book "An Explosion of Limericks" (Cassell 1967). Style comes into it, and choice of rhyme and of sound. I agree with Holland that many by Lear who restored the form fall flat. Many limericks give improbable information:

The Bishop of Glasgow and Galloway
Preferred Artie Shaw to Cab Calloway.
   When he sang Artie's mass
   They could hear the loud brass
In the Highlands and over to Scalloway.

Another example tells of a poet's grandson who captained England:

The cricketing Lord L.H. Tennyson
Preferred fish and chips to roast venison.
   He dined at the wicket,
   Ignoring the cricket,
But looking exceedingly mennyson.

Some are topical; this one won a New Statesman prize in 1999:

The currency known as the Euro
Is welcomed from Oder to Douro,
   But it gets on the tits
   Of the d-mn-d little Brits
Who reject it from Thurso to Truro.

Some abbreviate long stories such as Gotterdammerung's ecological disaster:

Brunnhilde's distress was so dire
Till Siegfried came riding through fire;
   Then ('tis a long story)
   His fate was too gory
And she leapt with her horse on a pyre.

Others portray a moment's misunderstanding:

There was a young girl named Bianca
Who retired while the ship lay at anchor;
   But she rose in dismay
   When she heard the mate say
"We must hoist up the topsheet and spanker".

Also sexily:

There was a young lady of Kent
Who said that she knew what it meant /and wine;
   When men asked her to dine, Gave her cocktails
She knew what it meant —(but she went.)

30th January.   Charlie Gets The Chop.

This gruesome Tabloid Headline won a "New Statesman" prize for how today's Press would present important events in history, the episode in question being the execution of King Charles I on 30 January 1649. Whether even our worst papers would sink to quite such coarseness we can but guess. It portrays the trivialising of values, the disrespect for fellow-humans, and the cheapening of life which now plagues our country. There is much talk these days of Education; why then do so many Britons, when they read at all, buy and tolerate our destructive daily papers? Studdert Kennedy wrote in 1919 that you can't build an A1 nation out of people who are morally C3.

(Why was Charles killed, and his henchman Archbishop William Laud to boot? Because they stood in the way of the free marketeers who resented their dictatorial methods which stemmed from their sincere belief in theocracy and the Divine Right of Kings. Alongside its less reputable reasons of finance, King Charles' Privy Council protected tenants, and ensured the grain-harvest by harrying the depopulating landlord, removing enclosures, ordering grass-land to be re-ploughed, and maintaining poor relief and minimum wages. Its "Ship Money" taxes were resented, as was the coercive "Court of Star Chamber" with its cruel punishments. Laud strove to enforce the old laws against usury, but made himself unpopular because his methods fell short of his doctrinal ideals. Tawney held that unlike many present-day campaigners for social unity or classless society, Laud was as ready to condemn the rich and powerful people who stand in its way as he was to plead to the lowly poor for their patience.)

- - - - - - -

One shudders at the headline "Golgotcha" proposed for the Crucifixion in the same competition. More happily I would suggest two alternatives for the Creation:

"It was the Lord wot did it"; or

"Your Page Three on our Day Three".

27
_____

U.K. postage stamp for commemoration of
        Robert Burns (see 25 January).

31st January.   C A T S.

When I was asked to contribute to a collection of cat stories, I was able to share one which had appeared in the magazine of Gonville and Caius (pron. "Keys") College, Cambridge. Maisie Anderson lived in the Master's Lodge there in the 1930s and played a trick on her father's cat by inducing a friendly Chemistry student to provide her with a substance, probably acetamide, which smells like concentrated mouse. She put it in a small hole in a flower bed and hid at a window to watch. The Wumpus "crouched for a spring, tense with a most unusual excitement. He pounced but found nothing. Again he crouched and sprang - on nothing." Then, having lost face, he "stalked off in offended dignity and would not speak to her for a week.

(Advert. pre-dated awareness of health-hazard.)

Another critical cat was Joey of Blackrod near Wigan, who had a discerning ear for music. Whenever there was chamber-music by Haydn or Mozart on the radio he would lie in front to absorb the pleasant euphony. But if a rumbustious Beethoven quartet followed, he would stalk off in some dudgeon. Fortunately my friends there never played Wagner, Shoenberg, jazz, rock, or pop.

I myself was given a tomcat when Tomas O'Fiaich (pron. O'Fee) was Cardinal Archbishop of Armagh in the 1980s. I was told that the animal was named Tomas O'Fiaichline in his honour. A delightful cat, he offered me an unforgettable apology one morning. On going to bed the night before, I had left a folder of papers on the balustrade at the top of the stairs. On going out at dawn I saw the papers strewn down the stairway, with Tomas sitting where the folder had been before he dislodged it. He looked into my eyes and miaowed loudly four times, which I interpreted as "May I still be your cat, please?" He was very happy to be immediately reassured that he was.

1st February. St. Brigid's Day, coinciding with the old Irish feasts of Brig (valour), Imbolc (returning light), and Brigit or Brigantia (the high goddess of the poetic arts and crafts). Legends of the saint abound as set out in the Encyclopaedia Britannica, tradition holding that she, like St. David, was born after royal seduction of her mother. Certainly the virgin abbess Brigid of Kildare (d.ca.525) is honoured as Ireland's second saint. Her sacred fire at her "double abbey" with its houses for nuns and monks was tended by women for nearly 1000 years; and a disputed tradition says Ibor consecrated her as bishop. (2-12)

February 1

Brigid

2nd February.

"THE DARK IS BEHIND US AND SPRING'S ON ITS WAY
WHEN CHRISTMAS MEETS EASTER ON CANDLEMAS DAY."

February for northern people is an improvement on January, for it is lighter even when it is colder. (Yesterday, St. Brigid's day, coincides with the Celtic "Imbolc" which celebrates the return of the light.) The Candlemas rhyme refers of course to physical light and lengthening days. Traditionally this festival marks the presentation of the child Jesus in the Jerusalem temple, and it ends the 40-day season of Christmas and Epiphany, which was joyful though shadowed by King Herod's cruelty. It looks forward to Lent and Passiontide with their message that light comes only from darkness.

So I offer my selection of favourite verses by Masefield,

"A CONSECRATION."

Not of the princes and prelates with periwigged charioteers
Riding triumphantly laurelled to lap the fat of the years,
Rather the scorned - the rejected - the men hemmed in with
             the spears.
Not the ruler for me but the ranker, the tramp of the road,
The slave with the sack on his shoulders, pricked on with
             the goad,
The man with too weighty a burden, too weary a load.

Others may sing of the wine and the wealth and the mirth,
The portly presence of potentates goodly in girth; -
Mine be the dirt and the dross, the dust and scum of the earth.

Of the maimed and the halt and the blind in the rain and
             the cold -
Of these shall my songs be fashioned, my tale be told. Amen.

Next some lines from T.S. Eliot, "ROCK" part X, rearranged:
Therefore we thank Thee for our little light, that is dappled
             with shadow.
We thank Thee for the lights that we have kindled,
The light of altar and of sanctuary;
And when we have built an altar to the Invisible Light, we may
    set thereon the little lights for which our bodily vision is
             made.
And we thank Thee that darkness reminds us of light.
O Light Invisible, we give Thee thanks for Thy great glory!

3rd February.

We look on cats more benignly than do mice, and we envy their threefold adaptation to life on earth; they obtain fur coats without cruelty, they move in three dimensions, and they cannot be conscripted into armies. Here is Munro's poem,

"MILK FOR THE CAT."

When the tea is brought at five o'clock
And all the neat curtains are drawn with care
The little black cat with bright green eyes
   Is suddenly purring there.

At first she pretends, having nothing to do,
She has come in merely to blink by the grate
But, though tea may be late or the milk may be sour,
   She is never late.

And presently her agate eyes
Take a soft large milky haze,
And her independent, casual glance
   Becomes a stiff hard gaze.

Then she stamps her claws, or lifts her ears,
Or twists her tail or begins to stir,
Till suddenly all her lithe body becomes
   One breathing, trembling purr.

The children eat and wriggle and laugh,
The two old ladies stroke their silk;
But the cat is grown small and thin with desire,
   Transformed to a creeping lust for milk.

The white saucer like some full moon descends
At last from the clouds of the table above;
She sighs and dreams and thrills and glows,
   Transfigured with love.

She nestles over the shining rim,
Buries her chin in the creamy sea,
Her tail hangs loose; each drowsy paw
   Is doubled under each bending knee.

A long, low ecstasy holds her life,
Her world is an infinite shapeless white,
Till her tongue has curled the last holy drop,
   Then she sinks back into the night;

Draws and drips her body to heap
Her sleepy nerves in the great armchair,
Lies defeated and buried deep
Three or four hours unconscious there.

4th February.

> "In the spring a young man's fancy
> Lightly turns to thoughts of love."

So wrote Tennyson in his first "Locksley Hall" poem. I am perhaps past my prime, and my thoughts thus turn at any time given the necessary provocation. In early February, however, they turn to poetry because it is the time of the Wordsworth Winter School in Grasmere, which I like to attend if only for three days or so. It is ironic that my train journey to Windermere, where I pick up the Grasmere bus, falls foul of the poet's philippics, for in 1844 he wrote this sonnet:

"ON THE PROJECTED KENDAL AND WINDERMERE RAILWAY."

Is there no nook of English ground secure
From rash assault? Schemes of retirement sown
In youth, and 'mid the busy world kept pure
As when their earliest flowers of hope were blown,
Must perish;- how can they this blight endure?
And must he too the ruthless change bemoan
Who scorn a false utilitarian lure
'Mid his paternal fields at random thrown?

Baffle the threat, bright Scene, from Orrest-head
Given to the pausing traveller's rapturous glance:
Plead for thy peace, thou beautiful romance
Of nature; and, if human hearts be dead,
Speak, passing winds; ye torrents, with your strong
And constant voice, protest against the wrong.

The elderly Poet Laureate, long past his best, was neatly answered thus by Monckton Miles M.P.:

The hour may come, nay must in these our days,
When the swift steam-car with the cat'ract's shout
Shall mingle its harsh roll, and motley rout
Of multitudes these mountain echoes raise.
But Thou, the Patriarch of these beauteous ways,
Canst never grudge that gloomy streets send out
The crowded sons of labour, care, and doubt,
To read these scenes by light of thine own lays.

Disordered laughter and encounters rude
The Poet's finer sense perchance may pain,
But many a glade and nook of solitude
For quiet walk and thought will still remain,
Where He those poor intruders can elude,
Nor lose one dream for all their homely gain.

Monday 5th February 1996.

Snow at Grasmere where I arrived yesterday for a Wordsworth Winter School week. The beautifully-gentle though heavy fall began at 11am and was well over a foot deep when it stopped at supper-time. It removed nearly all traffic from the roads, to re-create the peace and quiet that the village has steadily lost to the "infernal combustion engine". The low pass over Dunmail Raise to Keswick, now used by the busy A591 main road, used to provide the Lake Poets and others with a fine 12-mile walk between Grasmere and Keswick via the shore of Thirlmere which used to exist as two lakes, Leathes Water and Thurston Water, prior to flooding a century ago to make a reservoir for thirsty Manchester. The "Four-In-Hand Hotel" at Keswick has a display of pictures showing top-hatted civic worthies travelling by charsabancs to the opening ceremony for this undertaking. Wythburn village (pronounced Wyburn) was inundated save for the hillside church, which hosts but five regular services each year now, on the third or fourth Sunday afternoons from May to September. Of the dwellings in the parish there remain but the odd farm or house and the Dale Head guesthouse to the north of the deepened lake.

Wordsworth enjoyed providential good fortune in being able to settle into Dove Cottage at Grasmere, formerly the "Dove and Olive Branch" inn, when there was little demand for local dwellings there. Having withdrawn from politics in revulsion from the aftermath of the French Revolution on which the high youthful hopes of many had been set, he wrote magnificent sonnets and other poems there before regentrifying and moving to the larger Rydal Mount for his final decades. The railway-sonnet "Is there no nook..?" typifies his narrowing sympathies Was it of him, or of Bonnie Prince Charlie, that the rhyme was written:

> "Sir, I have heard another story -
> He was a most confounded Tory,
> And grew (or he is much belied)
> Extremely dull before he died"?[1]

It may even be wondered whether an extension of the offending railway from Windermere to Keswick, by tunnel under Dunmail Raise, might have safeguarded the pass from the later "rash assault" of the road transport lobby!

---

1. No - it was Swift, "Death of Dr Swift"!

Dove Cottage is now owned and maintained by the Wordsworth Trust, which has also established the nearby Grasmere and Wordsworth Museum. For details of visiting: 015394.35544.

5th February.

Are poets any use? - or are the arts merely there to entertain well-heeled middleclass Westerners? There is a saying of Solomon that "Where there is no vision the people perish" (Proverbs 29.18) - and the best poets and prophets are "seers" whose gift is to penetrate further than the rest of us into the realities of existence, and to help us along life's path by sharing their insights. All peoples have looked to their bards for encouragement, but today's commercialised media tend not to enlighten their readers and viewers. "Muzak" and "pop" bring millions of pounds to some entertainers and promoters, whereas Mozart, Schubert and Burns died in poverty. Schubert's String Quintet, now hailed as a supreme masterpiece of chamber music, lay unpublished on a shelf for twenty years before Diabelli found it there and galvanised the firm into printing it.

Britain's poets range from the early Caedmon and Chaucer, through the "classical" Shakespeare, Spenser, Milton, Goldsmith and Pope, to the great Romantic flowering two centuries ago, and on to Browning, Hopkins, Kipling, Masefield, Eliot, Idris Davies, Betjeman, and contemporaries, avant-garde and otherwise. Among the great Romantics, alongside people like Southey and Scott, are:

William Blake	1757 - 1827
Robert Burns	1759 - 1796
William Wordsworth	1770 - 1850
Samuel Coleridge	1772 - 1834
George Gordon, Lord Byron	1788 - 1824
Percy Shelley	1792 - 1822
John Keats	1795 - 1821
Alfred, Lord Tennyson	1809 - 1892;

and we may take equal pride in the concurrent renewal of Christian hymnody, led by the mighty Charles Wesley and by John Mason Neale, translator of many ancient songs and author of "Good King Wenceslas"; also by Fanny Alexander whose fine translation of St. Patrick's hymn far excels her "All things bright and beautiful"; Bishop Christopher Wordsworth (not closely related to the poet); Alford, Dix, How and many others. I lament that all but one of the listed names are male - I demur at including Felicia Hemans for her much-parodied Battle of the Nile poem with its remarkable first line "The boy stood on the burning deck", and I regard Emily Brontë as a special case since she wrote little but this included some gems. I shall, however, try to offer a few pointers towards the most interesting works of the Romantics.

7th February.

"Bliss was it in that dawn to be alive,
But to be young was paradise indeed."

Thus did Wordsworth, the greatest of the Lake Poets and a contestant for the accolade of our greatest poet of all, hail the radical success of the French Revolution of 1789, before the sickening Terror which followed turned him to study the nature of the human mind and soul as the way to improve the world. After a spell in Somerset, at Racedown and then Alfoxden (near Coleridge at Nether Stowey), he and his sister Dorothy moved in late 1799 to Dove Cottage, where he was enabled by a friend's legacy to live as a full-time writer. In "Home at Grasmere" (1800) he rhapsodised the wonderful scene as:

"This small abiding place of many men,
A termination, and a last retreat,
A centre, come from wheresoe'er you will,
A whole without dependence or defect,
Made for itself, and happy in itself,
Perfect contentment, unity entire."

His best-known poem describes the host of dancing golden daffodils near Ullswater:

"A poet could not but be gay   (* or "laughing" Words-)
In such a jocund* company!"   (worth kept varying his)
                                     (verse.   )
-and its attractiveness leads many who didn't encounter his poems at school, and some even who were alas repelled by their treatment there, to look at more of them. In "Lines Written a Few Miles Above Tintern Abbey" (on 13th July, 1798) he testified to the human spiritual experience in words of famous clarity, miraculously expressing the inexpressible "some-thing":

".... And I have felt
A presence which disturbs me with the joy
Of elevated thoughts, a sense sublime
Of something far more deeply interfused,
Whose dwelling is the light of setting suns,
And the round ocean, and the living air,
And the blue sky, and in the mind of man —
A motion and a spirit that impels
All living things, all objects of all thoughts,
And rolls through all things."

This accords with the Judaeo-Christian tradition (e.g. Isaiah 57[15]) that God is both immanent, dwelling in material things, and transcendent, "upholding all things by the word of His power" (Heb. 1[3] - this although the poet only moved to full orthodoxy in later life.

8th February.

Wordsworth's "keeping open house" in the smallish cottage must have been burdensome for Dorothy, and for his bride Mary Hutchinson when she joined them. In spite of rats and mice he wouldn't let them keep a cat, lest it scared the birds away.[1] Their plain living led Sir Walter Scott, visiting them, to go through his window, very possibly with the tacit concurrence of his host, for breakfast at "the famous Swan" of Wordsworth's lighthearted "Waggoners" poem.(1. Eventually the ladies prevailed!)

The masterpieces of Wordsworth's best years, too numerous for listing here, include "Michael", "Resolution and Independence", "Elegaic Stanzas suggested by a picture of Peele Castle in a Storm", and the famous "Ode, Intimations of Immortality from Recollections of Early Childhood" which has as its pregnant motto the last three lines of this separate little poem:

> "My heart leaps up when I behold
>   A rainbow in the sky;
> So was it when my life began;
> So is it now I am a man;
> So be it when I shall grow old,
>   Or let me die!
> The child is father of the man;
> And I could wish my days to be
> Bound each to each by natural piety."

We owe some of the greatest English sonnets to Wordsworth's decade at Dove Cottage:

> "The world is too much with us. Late and soon,
> Getting and spending, we lay waste our powers..."
> "Milton, thou shouldst be living at this hour..."
> "It is a beauteous evening, calm and free..."
> "Nuns fret not at their convent's narrow room..."(But they do!)

and the supreme Toussaint sonnet about the leading African slave, set free by the 1794 French Convention, who in 1802 was jailed in Paris for opposing Napoleon's revival of slavery in San Domingo (Haiti). Written while Toussaint languished for ten months before his death, it concludes impressively:

> "Though fallen thyself, never to rise again,
> Live, and take comfort. Thou hast left behind
> Powers that will work for thee; air, earth, and skies;
> There's not a breathing of the common wind
> That will forget thee; thou hast great allies;
> Thy friends are exultations, agonies,
> And love, and man's unconquerable mind."

9 February. "AS IT HAPPENED" is the quiet title of the biography of the young M.P. whom Ramsay Macdonald chose as one of his Parliamentary Private Secretaries. He was Clement Attlee, who was destined to be Prime Minister himself from 1945 to 1951, and to establish Britain's finest social framework, at least since the Reformation. The taciturn Attlee used his maiden speech, on the 1922 Address on the King's Speech, to set out his approach to the economic problem of the day.

Asking "Why was it that in the war we were able to find employment for everyone?", he remarked that it was simply because the Government controlled the purchasing power of the nation... "We must have rifles...shells...uniforms...saddles." "They took, by means of taxation and by methods of loan, control...and directed that purchasing power into making those things that are necessary... Today the distribution of purchasing power in the nation is enormously unequal. I recall a speech by the present Prime Minister, in which he said that one of the greatest reforms in our national life would be a better distribution of wealth among the individuals composing this nation. I entirely agree with him. While the purchasing power of this nation is concentrated in the hands of a few, there will be production of luxuries and not of necessaries. It was found necessary during the war for the Government to take hold of the purchasing power—which,

(Attlee added) is what we are demanding shall be done in time of peace. It is possible for the Government, by methods of taxation and by other methods, to take hold of that purchasing power, and to say that, exactly as they told manufacturers and workers that they must turn out shells and munitions of all sorts to support the fighting men, so they must turn out houses and necessities for those who are making the country a country of peace."

Tax-and-spend indeed! But better than do this only for bombs and guns. In this 21st century there are many younger folk with no conception of the pre-war unemployment and poverty which the private sector alone could not and did not cure. British socialism hasn't concurred with state absolutism on the Soviet model; but neither have we condoned uncontrolled capitalism; as Carlyle held (2.1): A community with cash-payment as the sole nexus between people will be spiritually empty. So in 1945 the people trusted the team led by Clem Attlee who reiterated that

"... The Labour Party believes that if you want certain results you must plan to secure them; that in peace as in war the public interest must come first, and that if in war...despite the conditions, we were able to provide food, clothing and employment for all our people, it is not impossible to do the same in peace, provided the Government has the will and the power to act..."

10th February.

Wordsworth intended the "Prelude" to be one of three parts of a great philosophical trilogy "The Recluse"; but he found the task beyond him, although another part, the "Excursion" which he completed in later life contains much of value. He was of course the recipient of poetic ripostes and the target of parodies. Such is the lot of the famous. Such squibs can provide enjoyment and light relief, or they can wound cruelly. The "vernal wood" verse quoted on 18 July comes from one of two early Wordsworth poems depicting an exchange between friends. His "Skylark" poem in its original 3-stanza version (1825/7), with its middle verse "To the last point of vision and beyond" which he later transferred into "A Morning Exercise", prompted G.K. Chesterton to offer the bird's reply "as it might have appeared to Byron":

> "Ephemeral minstrel, staring at the sky,
> Dost thou despise the earth where wrongs abound,
> Or, eyeing me, hast thou the other eye
> Still on the Court, with pay-day coming round,
> That pension that could bring thee down at will,
> Those rebel wings composed, that protest still?
>
> \- - - -
>
> "Past the last trace of meaning and beyond
> Mount, daring babbler, that pay-prompted strain.
> 'Twixt thee and Kings a never-failing bond
> Swells not the less their carnage o'er the plain.
> Type of the wise who drill but never fight,
> True to the kindred points of Might and Right."

More cruel was J.K. Stephen's "Lapsus Calami", which begins strongly with Wordsworth's own first line, but alas contains too much merely offensive calumny for quoting in full:

> "Two voices are there: one is of the deep......
> And one is of an old half-witted sheep
> Which bleats articulate monotony,
> And Wordsworth, both are thine..."

The Bard's best work is, of course, so great that such snipings may safely be ignored, as can a few of his own works that are best forgotten. Other poets' pride, or purported pride, was similarly brought to earth, as with:

"You must wake and call me early, call me early, Vicky dear"

when the Queen made Tennyson a Lord.

(More Wordsworth lore on 18.7)

11th February.

Having mentioned Byron I must in fairness cite some works of this brilliant wordsmith and poetic corsair, who did not demur to portray the licence of his scandalous private life in his comic masterpiece "Don Juan". He nevertheless showed tremendous bravery in public life. At 24 his maiden speech in the Lords was a passionate attack on the Bill to impose the death penalty on starving Luddite workers who smashed the automatic looms that had robbed them of their livelihood. In later life he devoted all his wealth and energy to liberate Greece from Turkish oppression in their revolution of 1821. He died there in 1824 after a convulsive fit, and was mourned throughout Greece, where to this day he is honoured as liberator, with a Byron Street in nearly every town:

"THE DESTRUCTION OF SENNACHERIB" - based on Isaiah 37^{36}!

> The Assyrian came down like the wolf on the fold,
> And his cohorts were gleaming in purple and gold;
> And the sheen of their spears was like stars on the sea,
> When the blue wave rolls nightly on deep Galilee.
>
> Like the leaves of the forest when summer is green,
> That host with their banners at sunset were seen:
> Like the leaves of the forest when autumn hath blown,
> That host on the morrow lay withered and strown.
>
> For the Angel of Death spread his wings on the blast,
> And breathed in the face of the foe as he passed;
> And the eyes of the sleepers waxed deadly and chill,
> And their hearts but once heaved, and for ever grew still.
>
> And there lay the steed with his nostril all wide,
> But through it there rolled not the breath of his pride:
> And the foam of his gasping lay white on the turf,
> And cold as the spray of the rock-beating surf.
>
> And there lay the rider distorted and pale,
> With the dew on his brow, and the rust on his mail,
> And the tents were all silent, the banners alone,
> The lances uplifted, the trumpet unblown.
>
> And the widows of Ashur are loud in their wail,
> And the idols are broke in the temple of Baal;
> And the might of the Gentile, unsmote by the sword,
> Hath melted like snow in the glance of the Lord!

Marvellous the word-play - as also in "Don Juan", with Canto I devoted to a "bedroom farce" par excellence involving poor Donna Julia, "married, charming, chaste, and twenty-three" and her 16-year old protégé. Alas the real-life girl on whose scandalous lapse the tale is based was sent to a convent. One hopes that her behaviour when found out was less blatantly hypocritical than in the poem!

(continued.

CIX.

Julia had honour, virtue, truth, and love
  For Don Alfonso; and she inly swore,
By all the vows below to powers above,
  She never would disgrace the ring she
    wore,
Nor leave a wish which wisdom might re-
    prove;
  And while she ponder'd this, besides much
    more,
One hand on Juan's carelessly was thrown,
Quite by mistake—she thought it was her
own....

CXI.

The hand which still held Juan's, by de-
    grees
  Gently, but palpably confirm'd its grasp,
As if it said, "Detain me, if you please;"
  Yet there's no doubt she only meant to
    clasp
His fingers with a pure Platonic squeeze;
  She would have shrunk as from a toad,
    or asp,
Had she imagined such a thing could rouse
A feeling dangerous to a prudent spouse.....

CXIII.

The sun set, and up rose the yellow moon:...

CXIV.

There is a dangerous silence in that hour, ...
  The silver light which, hallowing tree and
    tower,
Sheds beauty and deep softness o'er the
    whole,
Breathes also to the heart, and o'er it throws
A loving languor, which is not repose.

CXV.

And Julia sate with Juan, half embraced
  And half retiring from the glowing arm,
Which trembled like the bosom where 't was
    placed;
Yet still she must have thought there was
    no harm,
Or else 't were easy to withdraw her waist;
  But then the situation had its charm,
And then——God knows what next—I can't
    go on;
I'm almost sorry that I e'er begun......

CXVII.

And Julia's voice was lost, except in sighs,
  Until too late for useful conversation;
The tears were gushing from her gentle eyes,
  I wish, indeed, they had not had occasion;
But who, alas! can love, and then be wise?..etc!

<u>12th February.</u>

    Byron's verse has however been criticised for its limited spirituality. Matthew Arnold wrote, in his preface to a selection of Byron's poetry, that "Wordsworth has an insight into permanent sources of joy and consolation for mankind which Byron has not; his poetry gives us more which we may rest upon than Byron's...and which men may rest upon always." Even so we have the marvellous poignancy of "Waterloo";

From "Childe Harold's Pilgrimage" Canto III

There was a sound of revelry by night,
And Belgium's capital had gathered then
Her beauty and her chivalry, and bright
The lamps shone o'er fair women and brave men;
A thousand hearts beat happily; and when
Music arose with its voluptuous swell,
Soft eyes looked love to eyes which spake again,
And all went merry as a marriage bell;
But hush! hark! a deep sound strikes like a rising knell!

Did ye not hear it?—No; 'twas but the wind,
Or the car rattling o'er the stony street;
On with the dance! let joy be unconfined;
No sleep till morn, when Youth and Pleasure meet
To chase the glowing hours with flying feet.—
But hark! that heavy sound breaks in once more,
As if the clouds its echo would repeat;
And nearer, clearer, deadlier than before!
Arm! arm! it is—it is—the cannon's opening roar!.....

(continued.

> Ah! then and there was hurrying to and fro,
> And gathering tears, and tremblings of distress,
> And cheeks all pale, which but an hour ago
> Blushed at the praise of their own loveliness;
> And there were sudden partings, such as press
> The life from out young hearts, and choking sighs
> Which ne'er might be repeated: who could guess
> If ever more should meet those mutual eyes,
> Since upon night so sweet such awful morn could rise!
>
> And Ardennes waves above them her green leaves,
> Dewy with Nature's tear-drops, as they pass,
> Grieving, if aught inanimate e'er grieves,
> Over the unreturning brave—alas!
> Ere evening to be trodden like the grass
> Which now beneath them, but above shall grow
> In its next verdure, when this fiery mass
> Of living valour, rolling on the foe,
> And burning with high hope, shall moulder cold and low....

Although Byron in self-derogation called "Don Juan" "A nondescript and ever-varying rhyme", adding that he hoped

> "it is no crime
> To laugh at all things - for I wish to know
> What, after all, are all things but a show?",

Leslie Marchand, in "Byron, A Portrait" (John Murray, 1971) rightly comments that although this poet had the strength of mind to see through the heresies and insincerities of insincere religious posturing, he was himself too sincere to tolerate the label of infidel, which he categorised as a cold, chilling word. Byron's sense of the mysteries of life and the universe was too great, too deep for him to settle for mechanical viewpoints and negative stances.

Byron wrote small gems too:

SO, WE'LL GO NO MORE A ROVING.

So, we'll go no more a roving
  So late into the night,
Though the heart be still as loving,
  And the moon be still as bright.

For the sword outwears its sheath,
  And the soul wears out the breast,
And the heart must pause to breathe,
  And love itself have rest.

Though the night was made for loving,
  And the day returns too soon,
Yet we'll go no more a roving
  By the light of the moon.

SHE WALKS IN BEAUTY.

She walks in beauty, like the night
  Of cloudless climes and starry skies;
And all that's best of dark and bright
  Meet in her aspect and her eyes:
Thus mellow'd to that tender light
  Which heaven to gaudy day denies.

One shade the more, one ray the less,
  Had half impair'd the nameless grace
Which waves in every raven tress,
  Or softly lightens o'er her face;
Where thoughts serenely sweet express
  How pure, how dear their dwelling-place.

And on that cheek, and o'er that brow,
  So soft, so calm, yet eloquent,
The smiles that win, the tints that glow,
  But tell of days in goodness spent,
A mind at peace with all below,
  A heart whose love is innocent!

and celebrated his Land of Heart's Desire:

> "The isles of Greece, the isles of Greece!
> Where burning Sappho loved and sung..." - and where
> "the heart must pause to breathe, and love itself find rest.

13th February.

All days no doubt are sad anniversaries, but this day has special poignancy in Britain and Western Europe. Shamefully King William III, a.k.a. the Dutch Usurper, was privy to what happened this night in 1692 in Glencoe. The massacre of the Macdonald clan was mitigated by some Campbells who, disgusted by their orders, warned their hosts to escape into the night.

Then in 1945 there occurred the infamous air-raid on Dresden in the closing stages of World War 2. With many refugees from the Eastern Front in the city, Bomber Command took 25000 lives according to the historian A.J.P. Taylor. The Germans alleged 250,000 and other sources 135,000, compared with 83793 in Tokyo 9-10 March 1945 and 71379 at Hiroshima 6 August 1945. Bishop George Bell of Chichester had protested in the Lords against this "strategic bombing" by firestorm of civilian populations for motives of terror. It had been approved by Churchill, Air Minister Sinclair, and the War Cabinet, but they allowed the bellicose Sir Arthur Harris, C-in-C Bomber Command, to be held responsible by the public.

Bell was largely a lone figure, though Vera Brittain's "Bombing Restriction Committee" tried to help; and on 31st March 1943 Richard R. Stokes, Labour M.P. for Ipswich, challenged Sinclair in the Commons, refusing to be deflected by several scornful remarks. He elicited the reply that "the targets of Bomber Command are always military"; but this wasn't true, for Sinclair's minute to Sir Charles Portal, 28 October 1943, stated that only thus "could he satisfy the inquiries of the Archbishop of Canterbury, the Moderator of the Church of Scotland, and other significant religious leaders whose moral condemnation of the bombing offensive might disturb the morale of the Bomber Command crews." (So it would if they knew the Bible - Luke 9.51+).

The extent of the tragedy did not become common knowledge until the last quarter of the 20th century. In 1995 its 50th Anniversary was marked in Dresden by a concert by an English orchestra at which Lord Menuhin conducted Mozart's Requiem, and by a service at which Simon Barrington-Ward, the Bishop of Coventry, said he had lived through London's Blitz and seen the sky glow over Coventry, but nothing had prepared him for the devastated cities of Germany. Our press spoke of the barbarism of Hitler's Germany, and the voice of Coventry's Provost was not heard in England. "He had said no to revenge and had spoken of forgiveness." The Litany of Reconciliation, which is also prayed in Dresden's Kreuzkirche, begins with the biblical words "All have sinned..." "It is true; we all have the death of countless people on our conscience."   (continued.

Bishop Simon had however seen more than ruins; he had met the Christian resistance to Hitler, who had "experienced the presence of a suffering, compassionate God" and had pointed him to faith, hope and love. New cities arose, yet often built on weak spiritual foundations, whilst the ruins in human souls often remained unrepaired, though much that is good was done.

"To guide our feet into the way of peace (Luke 1^{79}) is no easy task: to create justice between East and West, North and South, rich and poor, between cultures and races...Not only has communism failed, capitalism too is in the process of failing." Repentance and forgiveness is needed in our public life. "The short walk from Coventry's poignant Cathedral-ruin into our new Cathedral has become a symbol of our hope, the journey from darkness to light for all who still walk in the shadow of death. May the much-debated reconstruction of your Frauenkirche also become a symbol of a humanity, still torn apart, that is healed of its divisions. As a Coventry poet has written:

> "God needs no second site on which to build,
> But on the old foundation, stone by stone,
> Cementing sad experience with grace,
> Fashions a stronger temple of his own."

<u>14th February.</u> (Saints Valentine, for there were two, or more!)

If these men were "into" romantic love they left no record. The sending of greetings, much fomented by the greetings-card industry to bridge the gap between Christmas and Mothering (Mid-Lent) Sunday with its Mother's Day offshoot, has proliferated in recent years. It grew from tentative Victorian beginnings as in Hardy's novel "Far From the Madding Crowd", and from root in the distasteful Lupercalia fertility-festival of old Rome.

The happy anthology "The Wit of Love" (Frewin, 1972) is a fruitful source of epigrams and quotations, including some of:

<u>KISSING A GIRL</u> is like opening a bottle of olives; the first may come hard but it is a cinch to get the rest. (Jack Paar). Kisses are things a woman gets in bushels before marriage but in pecks thereafter. (Anon.) (E. Paul

<u>LOVE IS</u> - something that should sneak up on a woman, gradual-li
- the triumph of imagination over intelligence (H. Menck
- the most subtle form of self-interest. (H. Jackson)
- "It is a prick, it is a sting;   (Geo. Peele, in)
  It is a pretty, pretty thing;   ("The Hunting of)
  It is a fire, it is a coal   Cupid.")
  Whose flame creeps in at every hole." (continued.

43

(But, very seriously, "Love is the firm intention of will to promote the highest good of the one beloved." (Maurice Darwin.))

<u>MEN</u> - the only thing original about some is original sin. (Helen Rowland.)
- When a man brings his wife flowers for no reason, there usually is a reason. (Anon.)

<u>SEX</u> - (a) is Latin for six (b) means that each tree has two grandmothers (Self, fending off tiresome school-pupils.)
- I never give it a second thought. (Marilyn Monroe.)
- Glamour is when a man knows a woman is a woman (Gina Lollobrigida.)

---

from "<u>The Old Bachelor</u>" by William Congreve: "I am melancholy when thou art absent; look like an ass when thou art present; wake for thee when I should sleep; and even dream of thee when I am awake; sigh much, drink little, eat less, court solitude, am grown very entertaining to myself, and (as I am informed) very troublesome to everybody else. If this be not love, it is madness, and then it is pardonable."

Among the great love-stories that of the theologian Peter Abelard and his young pupil Heloise is perhaps the most remarkable. The sad story is well outlined in Helen Waddell's novel "Peter Abelard" which is well worth reading also for his "Moral Theory of the Atonement", which holds, rightly I think, that humans are made whole through being moved to love and repentance by the contemplation of Christ's life, passion, and resurrection. After they married in secret, Heloise gave him up to pursue his academic career and entered a convent. After this renunciation for the sake of his vocation, she wrote of "pleasure that surpassed all ointments in sweetness." "There are times, even when I pray, that the images and pleasureable scenes of our love-making stir my miserable heart until the voluptuous memories of these moments even distract me from my prayers - and people praise my chastity...when in reality I am aflame with desire to re-live again those passions we have together experienced...it was for you alone, and not for any divine vocation, that I donned my monastic habit", wrote she.

Heloise could only feel divine cruelty in their tragedy, and seek a kind word: "These torments of the flesh are greatly inflamed: my lust, by the ardour of my youth and my experience of these most intoxicating pleasures. Men...have not discerned the hypocrite in me." Thus from a respected Abbess! Abelard replied kindly, urging oh so correctly that she turn her love from him to God. He died at 63 in 1142; she, a score of years younger, in 1163. I don't think she had fair treatment.

15th February.

THE SEEKERS   by John Masefield.

Friends and loves we have none, nor wealth nor blessed abode,
But the hope of the City of God at the other end of the road.
Not for us are content, and quiet, and peace of mind,
For we go seeking a city that we shall never find.

There is no solace on earth for us - for such as we -
Who search for a hidden city that we shall never see.
Only the road and the dawn, the sun, the wind, and the rain,
And the watch fire under stars, and sleep, and the road again.
We seek the City of God, and the haunt where beauty dwells,
And we find the noisy mart and the sound of burial bells.
Never the golden city, where radiant people meet,
But the dolorous town where mourners are going about the street.
We travel the dusty road till the light of the day is dim,
And sunset shows us spires away on the world's rim.
We travel from dawn to dusk, till the day is past and by,
Seeking the Holy City beyond the rim of the sky.
Friends and loves we have none, nor wealth nor blest abode,
But the hope of the City of God at the other end of the road.

"Real love begins where nothing is expected in return". Antoine de Saint-Exupery.

"...for here we have no continuing city, but we seek one to come.'
New Testament Epistle to the Hebrews, chapter 13, verse 14, q.v.

45

16th February, returning to the Dresden topic.

"One of the most grim and graphic descriptions of massacre bombing", wrote the journalist Vera Brittain in the US magazine <u>Christian Century</u>, 1 August 1945, "was published by the United States forces' newspaper <u>Stars and Stripes</u>, 5 May 1945, in relation to the Allied raid on Dresden on 13-14 February:

> Nine British POWs were working in Dresden during the raid and said the horror and devastation caused by the Anglo-American 14-hour raid was beyond human comprehension unless one could see for himself. One British sergeant said, 'Reports from Dresden police that 300,000 died as a result of the bombing didn't include deaths among 1,000,000 evacuees from the Breslau area trying to escape from the Russians. There were no records of them. After seeing the results of the bombings, I believe their figures are correct. They had to pitch-fork shrivelled bodies onto trucks and wagons and cart them to shallow graves on the outskirts of the city. But after two weeks of work the job became too much to cope with and they found other means to gather up the dead. They burned bodies in a great heap in the centre of the city, but the most effective way, for sanitary reasons, was to take flame-throwers and burn the dead as they lay in the ruins.

"In the *Observer* for 8 April, its war correspondent, George Orwell (who last year adversely reviewed my booklet, *Seed of Chaos*), commented from Germany as follows:

> The people of Britain have never felt easy about the bombing of civilians ... but what they still have not grasped – thanks to their own comparative immunity – is the frightful destructiveness of modern war and the long period of impoverishment that now lies ahead of the world as a whole. To walk through the ruined cities of Germany is to feel an actual doubt about the continuity of civilization."

I myself agree that we Britons have not all realised how total is war's destruction – or that World War 2 was at its vastest on the Russian front. Perhaps the television coverage of conflicts not involving the UK and therefore not "sanitised" to allay viewers' concern is opening everyone's eyes? Brittain continued by saying that in spring 1945 Western opinion was distracted by the death of President Roosevelt, the reports from the Nazi death-camps, VE day, the British general election, and the Far Eastern war. But "There can be no question that the ruthless bombing of congested cities is as great a threat to the integrity of the human spirit as anything which has yet occurred on this planet...By denying the divine spark in Man, it denies the God in whose image he is made...even from the standpoint of the 'national interest', the efficacy of massacre bombing is by no means established..."

46

17th February.

Vera Brittain's life-story is well known through the televising of her early experiences which she recorded in "Testament of Youth". She was a rebellious Buxton schoolgirl and Oxford student who was caught up in the horrors of World War I trench-warfare, which took her fiancé and her brother and led her via front-line nursing to peace-campaigning and journalism. I was privileged to meet her in 1952. She was incredibly brave and was not to be silenced by "patriotic" critics and papers during World War 2. Her Open Letter of 17 June 1943 proclaimed:

> I am obviously one of the voices selected for condemnation by the *Sunday Express*. Mine is only a small voice. But if I were the only voice left in England to say it, and were to be shot tomorrow for saying it, I should still maintain that by every civilized standard, Christian or otherwise, it is brutal and wicked to attempt to win a war by burning and starving to death the young and helpless, and by letting loose overwhelming floods upon unsuspecting mothers and their innocent children in the small crowded homesteads of an industrial area. And judging by the conversations that I hear in trains and shops, I believe that the great majority of England's population agree with me, though most of them dare not say so.

She mentioned that in 1918 she was nursing in a military hospital at Étaples when the Germans dropped leaflets prior to attacking the nearby railway; and she asked <u>re</u> the famous Dambuster raids:

> Could not our rulers who pride themselves on their superiority to German brutality have done at least as much for the women and their children in the Ruhr valleys, before they were swept away with no chance of escape when the dams were broken?

Counter-attacking the <u>Sunday Express</u> for saying that "sentimentalists" such as herself were "probably encouraged by the sound of voices made in Germany", she declared that not she but the newspaper carried a sound like that of those German and Italian teachers whose work laid the foundations of Nazism, e.g.

> Heinrich von Treitschke, the German historian, who wrote: 'We live in a warlike age; the over-sentimental philanthropic fashion of judging things has passed into the background ... The greatness of war is just what at first sight seems to be its horror – that for the sake of their country men will overcome the natural feelings of humanity.'
>
> I am proud to be one of those voices derided by the *Sunday Express* – and by Treitschke. I take courage from the echoes of other and greater voices which have spoken throughout history in the accents of pity, mercy, toleration, and love:

– Confucius, Buddha, Jesus, St. Paul (see Matt.5.7, Eph.4.32.)

18th February.

Eppleton near Hetton was a mining village on the Durham coalfield prior to the closure in 1986 of the colliery which was its raison d'etre. It had

ALL SAINTS EPPLETON
Be watchful, stand firm in your faith, be courageous, be strong.
(1 Cor 16 13)

brief unwanted fame because of the pit explosion which took eight lives in 1951 some two months after the big disaster at nearby Easington. The Thatcher Government's sacrifice of our coal industry struck further at the heart of the local community, yet the traditions are maintained at the Big Meeting or Miners' Gala in Durham every 2nd Saturday in July (but check with Tourist Information Office) and a commemoration of the brave Tommy Hepburn, founder of the Miners' Federation in the area.

Here is a sonnet by my friend who was vicar of Eppleton from 1979 till he retired in 1995. It expresses his deep concern...

for Peace

Come, God, and cleanse the sins of man from earth
With soft sweet water falling from the skies,
Your raindrops have baptised us since our birth,
Mixed with the tears that flow from tired eyes...
Come, purge this earth of man's horrific deeds,
Expel the hate and falsehood deep within
Which threatens peace, denies the poor their needs,
False peace which nuclear weapons underpin...
This planet earth, polluted, poisoned, raped.
Bears witness to the boor and beast in men,
The murder that men do in God's good name
A younger generation does again...
So come, good God, our sanity restore,
Root out the sin that makes a god of war.
                    John Stephenson

Peace is the fruit of anxious daily care to ensure that each person lives in justice as God intends (Pope Paul VI)

Give yourselves to the service of life, not to the work of death.... true courage lies in working for peace.
(Pope John Paul at Drogheda)

<u>19th
February.</u>

---- "THE GOOD OLD DAYS" ----

"We were taught to work jolly hard. We were taught to prove ourselves; we were taught self-reliance; we were taught to live within our income. We were taught that cleanliness is next to godliness. We were taught self-respect. We were taught to give a hand to our neighbour; we were taught tremendous pride in our country. All these things are Victorian values, they are also perennial values".

Mrs. Margaret Thatcher, April 1983.

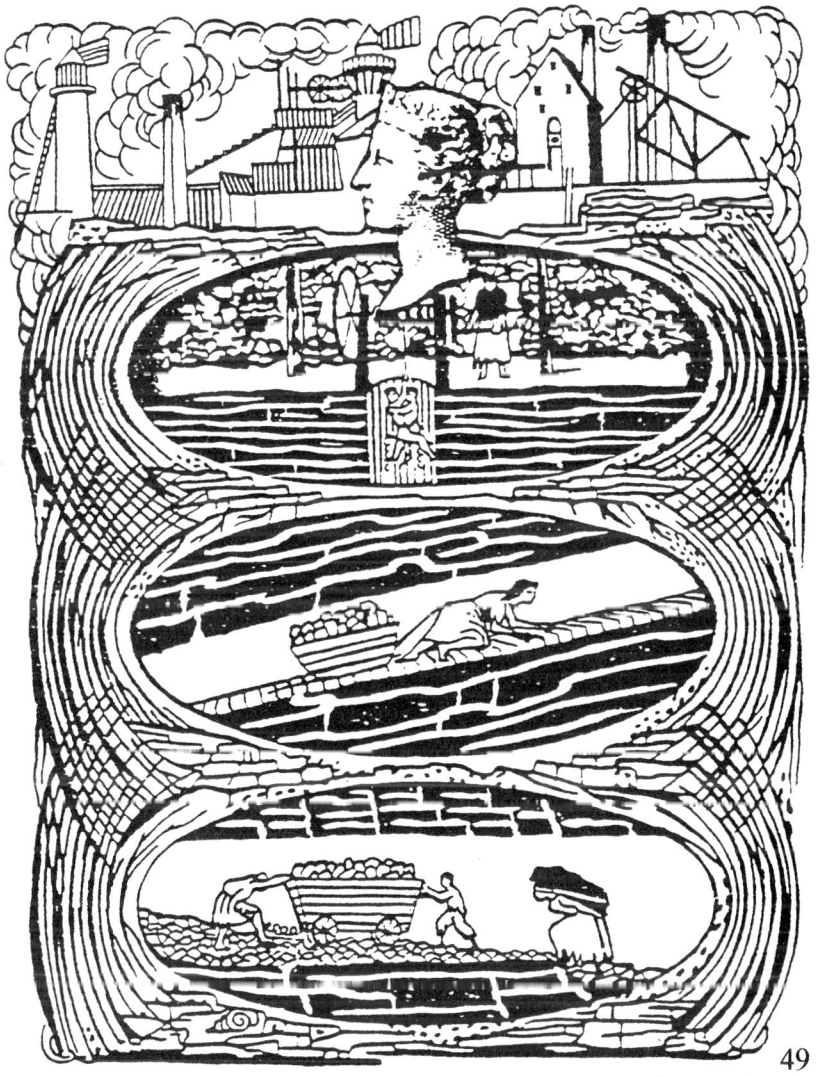

"Who robbed the miner?" cry the grim bells of Blaina...
"Put the vandals in court" cry the bells of Newport.
Idris Davies.

Shrove Tuesday 20th February 1996.

Shriving (confession of sins followed by absolution) was universal in Western Europe on the day before Lent – in the Church of England it remains available on request – and a "Pancake Bell" was rung from each church at noon to end the day's work for that purpose. It gained its name because it prompted the housewives to make pancakes from their remaining eggs and fats which they would forgo, along with meat, from the morrow, Ash Wednesday, till Easter. Shrove Tuesday was and is something of a Carnival Day (Latin "carnem levare", meat-removal!), with street football and "thread-the-needle" dances in several towns, the latter to the song:

"Shrove Tuesday, Shrove Tuesday, when Jack went to plough,
His mother made pancakes she didn't know how;
She tipped them, she tossed them, she made them so black,
She put so much pepper she poisoned poor Jack."

In Scarborough the Mayor still rings the bell to inaugurate skipping in Foreshore Road, and throughout England the holiday afternoon persisted long after the Reformation. Schools enjoyed the half-holiday until recently – we had it in Southport in the 1930s – and extended sometimes by tolerated pupil-rebellion linked with "mischief" and with outdoor games renewed to mark the "expulsion of winter". (At Bainbridge in the Yorkshire Dales the Hornblower, who gives three blasts daily at 9pm from 28 September as a direction-guide to anyone lost in the surrounding woods, desists after Shrove Tuesday.)

In France the day is called "Mardi Gras" (fat Tuesday), and this extended to French Louisiana, where the famous New Orleans Carnival attracts a million people thronging the streets. Parades were started there by masked students in 1827 and by the "Comus group" in 1857. They now occupy two weeks, day and night, and culminate with the Rex Parade on Shrove Tuesday itself.

It is not clear why eggs were banned for Lent; indeed it was customary in some places to boil them hard on Shrove Tuesday and to claim that only their cooking was forbidden during the fast. Perhaps the ban was to ensure that enough eggs were put under the hens to maintain the supply of chickens. Did Lent add virtue to necessity when food was in short supply?

Ash Wednesday 21st February 1996 marks the start of the 40-weekday season of spiritual discipline (Lent, the lengthening of days) kept by Christians to mark Jesus' 40 days of temptation in the wilderness (Matthew 4.1-11) and to prepare for the solemnities of Passiontide and Easter. The day passes largely unnoticed by the "secular world"; maybe the papers carry a small paragraph next day about CND demonstrators' arrests for writing "Repent" in charcoal on the wall of the Ministry of Defence building. (The police were too quick one year, and the cases were dropped after the magistrate asked how five people could be involved since only three letters REP had been written.) But a "personal spring-clean and MOT" is no bad thing, even if fasting merely to lose weight is to trivialise the season somewhat. It is good to ringfence one's hedonism, minimise one's enslaving addictions, and sacrifice a little First-World comfort so as to help where there is need "The world is too much with us", and entertainment has marginalised serious thought, so a bit of say Bible study is no bad thing - politics too, for a century ago the doings of Bill (Gladstone) and Ben (Disraeli) won the excited attention in pubs and clubs which is now reserved for sporting "heroes"

The temptations resisted by Jesus "on retreat" were (1) to win an ephemeral following just by providing material plenty. Ye "shall not live by bread alone!", he insisted. (2) to say that ends justify any means, and to compromise oneself without limit so as to gain power to do good is possible without being corrupted. "Ye shall worship and serve God alone!" (3) to take short cuts by trick methods which turn no hearts - spin-doctoring such as throwing oneself from pinnacles won't do. Dostoevsky's verdict, put in the mouth of the Grand Inquisitor in "The Brothers Karamazov", is that the formulation of these is pivotal to life on earth and was the greatest of miracles!

So now the Church proclaims that life is real and earnest. There are lugubrious hymns that challenge our courage, yet Percy Dearmer's "White Lent", sung to "O leave your sheep", makes the season of discipline one of good cheer (cf Isaiah 58

To bow the head
  In sackcloth and in ashes,
    Or rend the soul,
      Such grief is not Lent's goal;
But to be led
  To where God's glory flashes,
    His beauty to come nigh,
      To fly, to fly,
      To fly where truth and light do lie.

For is not this
  The fast that I have chosen?
    (The prophet spoke)
      To shatter every yoke,
Of wickedness
  The grievous bands to loosen,
    Oppression put to flight,
      To fight, to fight,
      To fight till every wrong's set right.

(Continued.

An alternative commercially-rooted Calendar of Festivals which doesn't include Shrove Tuesday or recognise the place of Mother's Day in mid-Lent has evolved. (As 'Mothering Sunday', this day relates to Mother Church and the Heavenly Jerusalem also.) Now we have cards for Father's Day too, and Cup Final Day is a folk festival, as are the Blackpool Lights switch-on and the Last Night of the Proms. The diminished religious awareness marks the closing stages of a process that has been going on for half a millennium. In his book "The Stripping of the Altars" (Yale, 1992) Eamon Duffy surveys the state of popular religion in England 1400-1580, showing that the old and admittedly-flawed spiritual customs flourished right up to Henry VIII's reformation, or rather deformation, and were not abandoned to his commissioners without a struggle. "We have given our hearts away, a sordid boon." Now we need to win them back.

22nd February.

German resistance to Nazism - The White Rose Martyrs.

On this date in 1943 three Munich University students in their early twenties were executed for distributing anti-Nazi leaflets - Hans and Sophie Scholl and Christoph Probst. Two others followed later, as did their philosophy-professor Kurt Huber. The Scholls' sister Inge, in her book "Six Against Tyranny" (Murray, 1955) tells how Hans and Sophie had become aware of politics when Hitler gained power ten years previously and everyone expected Germany to become happy and prosperous again. They enjoyed walks, cycle-runs and "Home Evenings" with their new friends of the Hitler Youth. Soon alas a dark side began casting its shadow - rearmament, book-bans, concentration-camps, hounding of Jews, and the enforcement of conformity. Hans and his younger brother moved to the earlier and still-innocent "Jungenschaften", till this was suppressed and its members jailed for some weeks.

World War Two began, and Hans was conscripted as a medical orderly in Munich. The grip of the Gestapo tightened on all the people, with secret ears listening everywhere for the most casual questioning of the State, Yet several leaflets were distributed in 1942 quoting Bishop Galen's astonishing attack on Nazi killings of the insane and suppressions of church establishments: "The Secret State Police...wish to reshape the German people by force, especially our young men and women..." Yet the bishop, brave to the point of reck-
(Continued.

lessness, survived, doubtless through Nazi fear of alienating worldwide church opinion.

After the young men had been sent to the Russian front for a spell, and had seen Jews performing forced labour in Poland, the students were all back in Munich. Further leaflets of better quality appeared, and wall-slogans "Down with Hitler" seventy times over - all whilst the newspapers carried big slogans underlined in red: "Hatred is our prayer, Victory our wages". Inevitably they were caught and betrayed by the university head-porter, "tried", and killed. Obvious traitors in the eyes of "patriots", they testified to Inge's verdict that "the tiniest step towards peace means more both to the individual and the nation than great victories on the battlefield". Their names, including those of Willi Graf and Alexander Schmorell, alongside those of the more famous Dietrich Bonhoeffer, Maximilian Kolbe, and Franz Jagerstatter, deserve mention at Remembrancetide and All-Saintstide as representing all loyal citizens who nevertheless serve higher loyalties too.

23rd February.

How did a major European nation come to embrace Nazism with its "evil logic of territorial aggression and racial hatred...which was to prove the most catastrophic and pitiless regime Europe or indeed the world had seen"? And how can we guard against a recurrence? These questions are posed by my friend Peter Walker, who was Bishop of Ely 1977-89, in his Church Times review, 11 April 1997, of William Brustein's book "The Logic of Evil" (Yale, 1997). This Minnesota professor had analysed 42,000 Nazi Party membership cards, and had concluded that the Nazis had cloaked their hidden agenda to gain power democratically over a nation desperate to gain a better life after the near-despair of defeat and depression. "When 'rational self-interest' becomes the very air we breathe", writes Bishop Peter, "does there not come with it a blunting of sensitivity to, and perception of, evil when evil is at the door?" He goes on to find an answer in the sermon-notes of an unknown pastor returned from holiday in Vienna. Speaking on the text John 8.32,36 about the violence he had seen done to Jews, the pastor concluded: "Don't let us suppose that freedom is simply the result of our own virtue. It is God's gift...come to us in the power and influence of the Holy Spirit and centuries of faithful discipleship. Not least the pastoral work of the Church has leavened our homes and institions with the Spirit of JesusChrist. Give thanks for our liberty. Remember the persecuted. Don't wait until liberty is threatened. Keep alive true religion!"

53

24th February.

" WHO ROBBED THE MINER? "

Margaret Thatcher's words as quoted on 19 February are true, bus alas she was myopic in delivering them on the basis of her Grantham childhood, in ignorance of, if not in indifference to, the very different circumstances of traditional industrial communities. Archie Kinnock, grandfather of her parliamentary opponent, was a coalface miner near Tredegar in South Wales. Nine people lived in his tiny "two up, two down" terrace house around the start of World War 1. Robert Harris notes in his book "The Making of Neil Kinnock" (Faber, 1984) that the family lacked a proper diet and went hungry, surviving mainly on bread, jam and chips. The floor was flagged and uncarpeted; the table was covered by newspaper in lieu of cloth; a toilet visit entailed carrying a bucket of water with you to the end of the yard. These details were "typical of place and period", an expression which appears to have covered all our coalfields and some overseas. Ned Cowen who was born in 1891 wrote as follows in "Bands and Banners" magazine about his early life in Bewicke Main village five miles from Gateshead in County Durham:

"Each house had only one door... Water was carried in pails from a tank in the square...the houses were lit by oil lamps and candles, but there was no outside lighting at all." At 12 or 13 Ned collected his little lamp at 6am and "entered the cage carrying a bait poke on my arm and a bottle of tea in my pocket. There were no gates on this cage, and the men made me stand in the middle...I was terrified...At this time the only daylight I saw was at the weekend, for it was dark when I set out to work and dark when I returned home." I shall tell more northern stories another day; for the moment returning to South Wales, I have an NUM postcard of Risca celebrating the 1947 nationalisation as "the dawn of a new era", but the sun set during Thatcher's ascendancy. It was said in some fashionable circles that some miners drew 5-figure wages; but I have met a man in Abertillery who in the mid-1980s worked 6 days for £100 p.w. to support his wife & 2 Children; and a double shift on the 7th to pay his electricity.

54

ó double shift was quarterly.

25th February.   THE CLERIHEW.

Though not so famous as a verse-form as Edward Lear's re-invention of the Limerick, yet more so than the earlier Triolet and Villanelle, the Clerihew, named after its inventor Edward Clerihew Bentley, is well-suited for extravagant comments (and lies) about the famous. He is said to have devised it, with 4 lines of any length and rhyme-scheme AABB, as a schoolboy during a chemistry lesson:

> "Sir Humphrey Davy
> Abominated gravy.
> He lived in the odium
> Of having discovered sodium."

I recall visiting the Royal Institution, Albemarle St., London and handling Davy's working notebook which contained a jumble of calculations, drawings, and verses by this versatile man who edited the first edition of "Lyrical Ballads" by Coleridge and Wordsworth. Then a later Clerihew came my way in the mid-1990s, celebrating in nonsense the very great 20th-century polymath famed for his encyclopaedic project on "Science and Civilisation in China". He died at 94 on 24.3.95:

> "Doctor Joseph Needham
> Dances with philosophic freedom.
> You must mind your toes if
> You chance to dance with Joseph."

No less scurrilous is:

> "Edvard Grieg
> Was no stranger to intrigue.
> He wrote _Finlandia_ under the alias
> Of Jan Sibelius."

More plausibly, _re_ a celebrated mid-century musician:

> "The Royal Philharmonic
> Can hardly be described as chronic;
> But, if they were, Beecham
> Would teach 'em." -

and it was said of the founding Head of our pioneer N. London Collegiate girls' high school & her friend the Head of Cheltenham Ladies' College 1858-1906:

> "Miss Buss and Miss Beale
> Cupid's darts do not feel-
> Oh, how different from us,
> Miss Beale and Miss Buss."

And certainly: "When Charles the Second / Beckoned,/Nell /Fell!

26th February. FENLAND CAMP-FOLLOWERS.

The amazingly-flat and often-bleak fen country of East Anglia has a distinctive life and feel from the rest of England. Vulnerable to wind and water, from the latter of which it was only won by Vermuyden's drainage-schemes of the 18th century. James Wentworth Day's book "Rum Owd Boys" (East Anglia Magazine Ltd., Ipswich, 1974, £3.50) tells of the pre-industrial "poachers, wildfowlers, longshire pirates, cut-throat islanders, smugglers and 'fen-tigers' who abounded in its earlier years. Day writes of a Fenland village:

"Between the lot of them, the Wesleyans, the Ranters, and the 'Camp-followers' - not what you think for a minute - Sunday is pretty lively. The church, poor old grey thing among the trees, sits in almost unattended majesty... A Camp Meeting must be seen to be believed... Take first a four-wheeled wagon, built like a ship, cocked up fore and aft with a curved girlish waist, painted red, blue and yellow, and at least 100 years old. Place firmly in the midst of the village green and garnish with worshippers... One local preacher: he is the main dish...Brother Tobias the pork butcher... small, round and fat, with little porcine eyes and a rare memory for minute debts... He leered at them confidentially:-

"'All on ye work for a master. If ye don't muck them fields of his'n, your master don't harvest no crops. An' ye don't draw no harvest money. Thass a true piece, ain't it?

"'Well, then, brothers and sisters, the Good Lord above is your Master, ain't he? Your souls are his fields, ain't they? Do ye mind you muck them owd souls o' yourn with plenty of good deeds. Do ye don't, brothers and sisters, ye 'on't git no harvest money from the Lord above - that means no harps in Heaven... You'll git Hell-fire and brimstone everlastin' an' perish in that there Pit of Abomination, what's a-garpin', for ye right now, flames an' all. So muck yar souls with good deeds, else yew perish. Now lift up yar 'earts and sing.' They sang. The rooks flew off in a body. The ducks flew off the pond. Dogs bolted for their kennels..."

- - - - - - -

(The more conventional Brother Zebedee, on seeing the squire) - "There my friends go the Quality. They give 14 pence a pound for lamb. Yew come here, and git the Lamb of God for Nawthin'."

- - - - - - -

27th February.   WONDERS OF THE NORTH.

As a Southport-born "Sandgrounder" I admit to a superiority complex in respect of the Southern English, which they no doubt reciprocate. But we welcome them to enjoy our Seven Wonders, even though we fight among ourselves to identify them. Setting aside football and entertainment as being dependent on local loyalties and tastes, there are four wonders that few would query

1. Durham Cathedral (see it from the railway viaduct!)
2. The Lake District (a compact miracle, 20 miles square with fresh delights of changeability each visit.)
3. York Railway Museum (well-kept and marvellous); and
4. Settle-Carlisle Railway, epitomised by the great (*) viaduct just south of the long tunnel at Ribblehead

The "Dales" town of Settle is a treat, with thousands of snowdrops in the churchyard, thousands of books in the second-hand shop (almost facing Tourist Office by the square), and a quiet and simple meeting-house of the "Religious Society of Friends. A magazine there cited schoolchildren's opinions; one wrote that the society was founded by a Mr George Quaker, and another claimed that Quakers eat oats at their meetings and talk among themselves.

The famous railway north was built by hundreds of navvies for the then Midland Railway in mid-Victorian days. Too many paid with their lives as commemorated where they rest by the church at Chapel-le-Dale near Ingleton. The line gave the "Midland" a direct and independent route to Scotland, crossing bleak moorland to reach Carlisle via the lusher Eden Valley.

Dent station is the highest main-line one in England, and it is hardly possible to run for a train there, since its access-road has gradient 1 in 3. A local farmer, asked why the station is $4\frac{1}{2}$ miles from Dent town (whose most famous son was Professor Adam Sedgwick the Cambridge geologist) replied famously "'Appen they wanted it near t'lines."

To complete the tally of seven wonders, possibilities include: Hadrian's Wall; Calder Hall/Windscale/Sellafield nuclear site (like it or hate it!); Liverpool Maritime Museum; the vast Kielder Reservoir which saved Yorkshire and the North-East during the 1995 drought. I thought of Thirlmere (with its stone dam and crenellated water-tower) but the loss of two natural lakes was too high a price. - the later drowning of Haweswater is the subject of Sarah Hall's evocative novel of that name (ff, 2002). Further alternatives include Rievaulx Abbey; Southport's restored extended pier; model villages Port Sunlight and Saltaire; & the "pre-Raphaelite" St Martin's Church, Scarborough with Liz Siddal modelling Our Lady

28th February. "In the Spring a Young Man's Fancy...."

The line quoted on 4 February may be Tennyson's best-known in the first of his two Locksley Hall poems, where he portrays the zest of the jilted young hero as he sets out into the world to drown his sorrows in adventure: The poem contains a remarkable prophesy of air-warfare and the United Nations:

> For I dipt into the future, far as human eye could see,
> Saw the Vision of the world, and all the wonder that would be ;..
>
> Heard the heavens fill with shouting, and there rain'd a ghastly dew
> From the nations' airy navies grappling in the central blue ;..
>
> Till the war-drum throbb'd no longer, and the battle-flags were furl'd
> In the Parliament of man, the Federation of the world.
>
> There the common sense of most shall hold a fretful realm in awe,
> And the kindly earth shall slumber, lapt in universal law.

Its sequel, "Locksley Hall Sixty Years After", written at 77 years of age, shocked the educated Victorian public with its stunning social comment far exceeding any from Tennyson before:

> Is it well that while we range with Science, glorying in the Time,
> City children soak and blacken soul and sense in city slime?
>
> There among the glooming alleys Progress halts on palsied feet,
> Crime and hunger cast our maidens by the thousand on the street.
>
> There the Master scrimps his haggard sempstress of her daily bread,
> There a single sordid attic holds the living and the dead.
>
> There the smouldering fire of fever creeps across the rotted floor,
> And the crowded couch of incest in the warrens of the poor.

There is much more to this fine poem which deserves reading in full, for it integrates the poet's feelings on personal, scientific, religious and historical matters too, whilst holding to the "the larger hope" behind the world's sadnesses.

29th February.   Leap-Year Day.

(Answers for 19 January: Hopkins & Keats are both ABBA ABBA CDCDCD; Milton is ABBA ABBA CDECDE; Owen is ABAB CDCD EFFEGG; Nuns - ABBA ABBA CDDCCD; and Scorn - ABBA ACCA DEDEFF; Causley is ABAB CBCB DBDB EE).

I traversed a dominion
Whose spokesmen spake out strong
Their purpose and opinion
Through pulpit, press, and song.
I scarce had means to note there
A large-eyed few, and dumb,
Who thought not as those thought there
That stirred the heat and hum.

When, grown a Shade, beholding
That land in lifetime trode,
To learn if its unfolding
Fulfilled its clamoured code,
I saw, in web unbroken,
In history outwrought
Not as the loud had spoken,
But as the mute had thought.

('Mute Opinion', T. Hardy's squib against "Expert-domination"!)

58

Shall I to the Byre go down?

Shall I to the Byre go down
   Where the stalled oxen are?
Or shall I climb the mountain's crown
   To see the rising star?
Or shall I walk the golden floor
   Where the King's feast is spread?
Or shall I seek the poor man's door
   And ask to break his bread?

It matters not. Go where you will,
   Kneel down in cattle stall,
Climb up the cold and starlit hill,
   Enter in hut or hall,
To the warm fireside give your cheek,
   Or turn it to the snow,
It matters not; the One you seek
   You'll find where'er you go.

His sandal-sole is on the earth,
   His head is in the sky,
His voice is in the baby's mirth
   And in the old man's sigh,
His shadow falls across the sea,
   His breath is in the wind,
His tears with all who grieve left He,
   His heart with all who sinned.

Whether you share the poor man's mite,
   Or taste the king's own fare,
He whom you go to seek tonight
   Will meet you everywhere:
For He is where the cattle wend,
   And where the planets shine –
Lo, He is in your eyes! Oh friend,
   Stand still, and look in mine.

   (*Tomfool* of the DAILY HERALD, 1926
     probably George Lansbury.)

   Suitable for Christmas & other times!

Summary of contents.

January:

8 - Plough Monday.
9 - Riddles.
10 - Christmas Music.
11 - The Old Ways.
12 - York / Mnemonic.
13 - Railway Notices.
14 - "Others".
15 - Stitch / Epigrams.
16 - Male & Female.
17 - Car Centenary.
18 - Andy Capp.
19 - The Sonnet.
20 - St Agnes' Eve.
21 - do. ("Discovery").
22 - Geese.
23 - Ruskin (biographical).
24 - Ruskin on Banking.
25 - Burns' Nicht.
26 - Cotter's Saturday Night.
27 - Usury.
28 - Ruskin on Usury.
29 - The Limerick.
30 - Charles I, K. M.
31 - Cats.

February:

1 - St Brigid
2 - Masefield "Consecration".
3 - Milk for the Cat.
4 - Windermere Railway.
5 - Dove Cottage.
6 - Romantic Poets.
7 - Wm. Wordsworth (I).
8 - do. (II).
9 - Attlee Biography.
10 - Poetic Parodies.
11 - Byron (I).
12 - do. (II).
13 - Dresden 1945.
14 - Valentines.
15 - Masefield "Seekers".
16 - Dresden (II).
17 - Brittain.
18 - Eppleton / Sonnet.
19 - Good Old Days?
20 - Shrove Tuesday.
21 - Ash Wednesday.
22 - German Martyrs.
23 - Nazism.
24 - Miners.
25 - The Clerihew.
26 - Camp-Followers.
27 - Wonders of the North.
28 - Tennyson "Locksley Hall".
29 - Hardy "Mute Opinion", and Tomfool's poem.

"VOICE and VISION"

(contact the Tennyson Society at Central Library, Lincoln.)   *Roberts Fecit: Tennyson in his library*

A Springtime Book of Days
[1st March to 3rd May]

"The March and the Muster" Part 2

Frank McManus

"1966 And All That." (foreword to "Voice and Vision".)

"Pirating" my title from Sir Geoff Hurst's footballing autobiography which inevitably centres on the World Cup Final hat-trick which gave England our sole victory in the competition to date, via linesman Bakharov's hairsbreadth goal-award – (Was the ball wholly over the line? Repeated video-viewings at Preston's national football museum fail to confirm or refute it) – I look back on the vast cultural changes, for better and/or for worse, of those heady times that Philip Larkin famously epitomised in his lines:

"Sexual intercourse began
In nineteen sixty-three...
Between the end of the
  Chatterley trial
And the Beatles' first LP."

"Dear dead days" – for some! Picture:– Queen Victoria at Kate Kearney's Cottage, near Killarney (now an expanded tourist-amenity). PHOTOGRAPHER UNKNOWN, 1861

I turn to Callum Brown's melodramatically-titled book, (Routledge, 2001)

"The Death of Christian Britain." (!)

on page 2 of which he notes that "a formerly religious people have entirely forsaken organised Christianity on a sudden plunge into a secular condition".

That of course is not true; churchgoing is only a small part of Christian living, yet the numbers attending on Sundays exceed the numbers paying to watch Saturday afternoon football. Even so there has been too much marginalisation into a distinct part of life. The language of God is far less heard in public than it was before World War Two. The present interest in books on "Body, mind & spirit" seems overcentred on the individual self; so I present for Passiontide (2-7.4) a look at the more traditional thinking on the Sacred Mystery (See also Isa. 57.15). Is it poor ministry, public inattention and hedonism, and doubt born of SHAM (science, horror and money!) that have weakened the hold of GOSPEL (God's offer:– salvation, peace, eternal life!)? Or is it the perception of insincerity over modern war (13.8) & commerce (11.1 &c. as per topic-index 29.2)?

62 The 1960s, dubbed "the Devil's decade" by a Susan Howatch character, also saw a grave weakening of the UK postwar social consensus. "V. & V." therefore ends with May-day-related topics.

1st March. St. David for Wales, and for me a particularly happy day since the light has returned and all Spring and Summer are yet to come. I recall from my days at St. Philip's C.E. primary school, Southport (my native town) this rhyme which taught us the names of THE MONTHS:

January brings the snow,
Makes our feet and fingers glow.

February brings the rain,
Thaws the frozen lake again.

March brings breezes loud and shrill
To stir the dancing daffodil.

April brings the primrose sweet,
Scatters daisies at our feet.

May brings flocks of pretty lambs,
Skipping by their fleecy dams.

June brings tulips, lilies, roses,
Fills the children's hands with posies.

Hot July brings cooling showers,
Apricots and gillyflowers.

August brings the sheaves of corn,
Then the harvest home is borne.

Warm September brings the fruit,
"Sportsmen" then begin to shoot.

Fresh October brings the pheasant,
Then to gather nuts is pleasant.

Dull November brings the blast,
Then the leaves are whirling fast.

Chill December brings the sleet,
Blazing fire and Christmas treat.

Schooldays in the early 20th century were not always the happiest, for the belief remained prevalent (in some places even till the 1980s) that to spare the rod was to spoil the child. Yet the universal appeal of nursery-rhymes in the playground and infants' class made those days seem good for many.

CAT HAS ATE THE PUDDING-STRING

Sing, sing, what shall I sing?
The cat has ate the pudding-string!
Do, do, what shall I do?
The cat has bit it quite in two.

LITTLE POLLY FLINDERS

Little Polly Flinders
Sat among the cinders
Warming her pretty little toes!
Her mother came and caught her,
And whipped her little daughter
For spoiling her nice new clothes.

CLAP HANDS, CLAP HANDS

Clap hands, clap hands!
 Till father comes home;
For father's got money,
 But mother's got none.
  Clap hands till father comes home!

I recall from the time of the "Munich crisis" of 1938 the variant on a current pop-song which spread like wildfire among Britain's older schoolchildren: "Underneath the spreading chestnut tree/ Mr Chamberlain said to me/ "If you want to get your gas-mask free,/ Join the blinking A.R.P." (Air-raid precautions, but war brought and brings sorrow to the world.)

2nd March.   T A R A N T E L L A.

    I was 72 before I discovered this poem in "The Collins Book of Best-Loved Verse" (1986). One can <u>hear</u> the music and <u>see</u> the flamenco-dancer! –

> Do you remember an Inn,
> Miranda?
> Do you remember an Inn?
> And the tedding and the spreading
> Of the straw for a bedding,
> And the fleas that tease in the High Pyrenees,
> And the wine that tasted of the tar?
> And the cheers and the jeers of the young muleteers
> (Under the vine of the dark verandah)?
> Do you remember an Inn, Miranda,
> Do you remember an Inn?
> And the cheers and the jeers of the young muleteers
> Who hadn't got a penny,
> And who weren't paying any,
> And the hammer at the doors and the Din?
> And the Hip! Hop! Hap!
> Of the clap
> Of the hands to the twirl and the swirl
> Of the girl gone chancing,
> Glancing,
> Dancing,
> Backing and advancing,
> Snapping of a clapper to the spin
> Out and in –
> And the Ting, Tong, Tang of the Guitar!
> Do you remember an Inn,
> Miranda?
> Do you remember an Inn?
>
> Never more;
> Miranda,
> Never more.
> Only the high peaks hoar:
> And Aragon a torrent at the door.
> No sound
> In the walls of the Halls where falls
> The tread
> Of the feet of the dead to the ground
> No sound:
> But the boom
> Of the far Waterfall like Doom.

                                                                      HILAIRE BELLOC

3rd March. On this date in 1931 the Senate of the United States of America adopted Francis Scott Key's "The Star-Spangled Banner" as the Union's National Anthem, arguably the world's most impressive both verbally and musically.[a] In 1812/4 the British were in minor hostilities against their erstwhile colonies, and on 13 September 1814 Key went to them from Baltimore, with a flag of truce, to seek the release of his friend Dr Beanes. Detained temporarily because of their secret plans to attack Baltimore, he had to watch their bombardment of Fort McHenry. The "desolating foe" was mild enough to release him speedily then, and the Baltimore Patriot published his verses on the 20th. Previous British help for the defiant anthem had been given by John Stafford Smith, sometime organist at the Chapel Royal, London, who composed its exalted tune under the title "Anacreon in Heaven". The Oxford Dictionary of Music faults such national songs which arise from wartime events (e.g. the French Marseillaise) on the ground that they foster narrow patriotism in schoolchildren; does this take them too serious-ly. (see foot overleaf.)

1. Oh say can you see by the dawn's early light
   What so proudly we hailed at the twilight's last gleaming?
   Whose broad stripes and bright stars through the perilous fight
   O'er the ramparts we watch'd were so gallantly streaming?
   And the rocket's red glare, the bombs bursting in air,
   Gave proof thro' the night that our flag was still there.
   Oh say does that star-spangled banner still wave
   O'er the land of the free and the home of the brave?

2. On that shore dimly seen through the mists of the deep,
   Where the foe's haughty host in dread silence reposes,
   What is that which the breeze, o'er the towering steep,
   As it fitfully blows, now conceals, now disposes?
   Now it catches the gleam of the morning's first beam,
   In full glory reflected now shines on the stream;
   'Tis the star-spangled banner; oh long may it wave
   O'er the land of the free and the home of the brave.

3. And where is that band who so vauntingly swore
   That the havoc of war and the battle's confusion
   A home and a country should leave us no more?
   Their blood has washed out their foul footsteps' pollution.
   No refuge could save the hireling and slave
   From the terror of flight, or the gloom of the grave;
   And the star-spangled banner in triumph doth wave
   O'er the land of the free and the home of the brave.

(a - compare 9 April.)   (continued.

4. Oh thus be it ever when freemen shall stand
   Between their loved home and the foe's desolation.
   Blest with vict'ry and peace may the heav'n-rescued land
   Praise the power that hath made and preserv'd us a nation!
   Then conquer we must, when our cause is just,
   And this be our motto, "In God is our Trust",
   And the star-spangled banner in triumph shall wave
   O'er the land of the free and the home of the brave.

(Verses 2 & 3 are generally omitted out of courtesy to Britain!)

<u>4th March.</u> That of course wouldn't do for the <u>20th century</u>; still less will it serve for the 21st. Even so, I can still enjoy such simplistic writings which trust God to treat our "enemies" as always His own!

"O Lord forgive the pride of human sin;
Man's fall into himself to love himself,
to seek experience that he should know
himself to be the centre of all he seeks,
in disobedience to the call of God
to wait on Him to do His will.

Love is the end, for when the flow of circumstance
has come to be simplicity
of loving mutuality
wherein the timeful experience of individuality
is become the individual experience of unity,
when all is rest, dependent on the love
that is the Being of all love."

So wrote Gilbert Shaw, a Church of England parson in the first half of the 20th century and a master of contemplative prayer who steered clear of the war-method altogether. In the words applied by G.K. Chesterton to Blake in his book "William Blake" (Duckworth, 1910), Shaw "was on the side of historic Christianity on the fundamental question on which it confronts the East; the idea that personality is the glory of the universe and not its shame; that pardon is higher than Nemesis, because it is more personal". He held that humanity's goal was the communion of forgiven saints and not a Nirvana of oblivion! It is a tragedy that the 21st century and 3rd Christian millennium have started with a catastrophic lapse by the USA from the idealism of its founders — and even from that of President Eisenhower who said in 1953 that the way of the US people was "faithful to the spirit that inspired the UN: to prohibit strife...to banish fears...We pay for a single fighter with half a million bushels of wheat....Hearts must turn!

5th March. Tennyson's "Crossing The Bar", which he wrote at age 80, was jotted down on the opened-up inside of a used envelope during the 20-minute voyage from Lymington to Yarmouth en route to his Isle of Wight home at Farringford. His son Hallam, on being shown the lines after dinner that night, said "That is the crown of your life's work"; to which the poet replied "It came in a moment". The bar in question is of course the sandbank deposited from a river where its estuary enters deep water, a particularly fine example existing at Salcombe in Devon. Sailors would take an experienced local pilot on board to guide them through the shallows, after which the pilot might be "dropped" - though not always, so that Tennyson's hopeful conclusion forms a reasonable analogy.

SUNSET and evening star,
 And one clear call for me!
And may there be no moaning of the bar,
 When I put out to sea,

But such a tide as moving seems asleep,
 Too full for sound and foam,
When that which drew from out the
    boundless deep
 Turns again home.

Twilight and evening bell,
 And after that the dark!
And may there be no sadness of farewell,
 When I embark;

For tho' from out our bourne of Time
    and Place
The flood may bear me far,
I hope to see my Pilot face to face
 When I have crost the bar.

Tennyson knew Charles Kingsley's doleful "The Three Fishers", which I believe prompted the "may there be no moaning at the bar" riposte. Joan Baez loved to sing Kingsley's dirge in three verses of which the first is:

Three fishers went sailing away to the West,
 Away to the West as the sun went down;
Each thought on the woman who loved him the best,
 And the children stood watching them out of the town;
 For men must work, and women must weep,
 And there's little to earn, and many to keep,
    Though the harbour bar be moaning.

Another instance of effortless composition by a poet who normally had to work hard on rhyme and diction is "The Battle Hymn of the American Republic" by Julia Ward Howe - "Mine eyes have seen the glory". She scribbled it down and went back to sleep (10.11). It spread to "singing millions" (Sandburg) and brought tears to President Lincoln's eyes when sung at a rally.

My own experience of the Yarmouth ro-ro ferry in 1996 was practical rather than idyllic. With about 80 enthusiastic young motorcyclists aboard for a rally, all I could think of was:

Mirror and Morning Star, and no big bill for me;
You'll never catch me propping up the bar When I put out to sea!

(The Micklegate Bar tollgate museum on York city wall once had a notice "No Beer - we are not that sort of bar!")

6th March.   "THE BIG SHIP SAILS."

[musical notation]

The playground verse noted on 1 March appears in the very fine book by Iona and Peter Opie, "The Lore and Language of Schoolchildren", which adds a World War 2 song that spread by a similar nationwide bush-telegraph:

"Whistle while you work, Mussolini had a shirt;
Hitler wore it, Chamberlain tore it, Whistle while you work."

Strangely this celebrates Chamberlain rather than Churchill who superseded him as Prime Minister when war flared up in 1940.

The Opies' later anthology "The Singing Game" (Oxford, 1985) records many playground-ditties not all of which may survive in the era of commercial TV jingles. "The Big Ship Sails" may have been the only "needle-threading" game to last till around 1980. Its tune (above) has a fascination matching that of the archway-dance itself, in which a tall girl (more girls than boys would link hands for the game) puts one palm high against a wall, and the child at the other end leads the chain through the arch thus formed, until the tall girl is pulled round 180° so as to finish with her arms crossed. The chain then goes under the arch between that girl and her neighbour; then under that between the naighbour and the next child; and so on till all arms are crossed. All this is done to the words: "The big ship sails on the alley alley oh, the alley alley oh, the alley alley oh; The big ship sails on the alley alley oh, on the last day of September." This was featured in the 1961 film of Shelagh Delaney's play "A Taste of Honey". What the words mean, if anything, is conjectural.

Some sea-shanties use the nautical order "a lee, a lee-oh" and other dances use "Sally-go". Maybe the Manchester Ship Canal (1894) led Lancashire children to think of a ship on an alley-like waterway. Be that as it may, when all arms are crossed, the end children join hands, and all sing (with action) "We all dip our hands in the deep blue sea". Then they loose hands for "The captain said 'This will never never do'", with wagging fingers. This is sometimes followed by "The big ship sank to the bottom of the sea" (all fall down); or by linking hands and whirling round quickly. The date in the song could be changed, e.g. to "December" or "the 14th of November."

7th March. "I ONCE SAW A MIRACLE."

In the last issue of the "Church Times" for the year 1999, John Pridmore, the rector of Hackney, East London tells of an experience nearly a quarter of a century previously, when he was "in a remote village in southern Chile (on) the last night of a week-long evangelistic mission. Lots were 'gloriously converted', as we used to say; and they all stayed on to be healed. The evangelist told them, 'Put your hand where you need healing.' Then I saw how the poor suffer, for most there touched their teeth .. The evangelist prayed for them - rather loudly I recall - then invited some of them on to the platform, telling them to look into each other's mouths. Seeing doubting Thomas in the midst, the evangelist hauled me up with them, handed me a torch, and invited me to make my own inspection.

"Then I saw what was the cause of the ecstasy around me. Those teeth had been filled, each filling in the form of a silver cross - except for one small boy (God keeps his best gifts for children) who showed me a tooth in which was distinctly set a golden cross. Incidentally there were no dentists in that part of Chile. Moreover these people were malnourished - they needed food not fillings. Also a nasty little dictator called Pinochet had just taken over. And I'd seen the gold torn from teeth at Auschwitz - no signs and wonders there. Miracles are appallingly equivocal things. No wonder Jesus told those he healed to keep quiet about it. Perhaps I should have shut up, too."

PRAYER OF ST. COLUMBA OF IONA
Be thou a bright flame before me,
Be thou a guiding star above me,
Be thou a smooth path below me,
Be thou a kindly shepherd behind me,
Today - tonight - and forever

Paranormal happenings occur - I have experienced a few - and the universe cannot be enmeshed completely within the conceptual cage of physical science!

8th March. — _Our Lady of Threadneedle Street?_

No, that's not the dedication of this feast-day which falls between those of the Celtic saints David (1st March) and Patrick (17th March). Christians today honour St Felix of East Anglia; the beloved Edward King, Bishop of Lincoln 1885-1910; and the great Geoffrey Studdert Kennedy (Padre 'Woodbine Willie' of the 1st world war who became Missioner of the Industrial Christian Fellowship and a pacifist before his early death this day in 1929). He made clear his belief that the "capitalist money-system", which he hated, isn't really a system at all but is a _growth_ arising from a myriad of actions by individuals after the Reformation and Commonwealth philosophies had detached public opinion from the ideas of "collective endeavour" and "pursuing God's will". Further drastic deterioration has stemmed from the worldwide electronic communication underlying the "global market" which has transformed commerce and economics beyond recognition over the last third (or more) of the twentieth century.

What is money and where does it originate? Prior to and for some time beyond the "Middle Ages" it was just a token of value, useful in exchange; but now it is a mere abstraction, with no mechanisms at either national or international level to link the amount in circulation to the goods and productive capacities which it ought to represent. How did this change come about, bringing with it the scandal of third-world debt, with a malign flow of capital in the 1980s and 1990s from S to N?

(Pennies from Heaven!)

Not everyone realises that the big Western banks lend ten or more times the amount of money which has been deposited with them. The term "bank" literally denoted the shelf on which the banker used to put for safe keeping the deposits of coin entrusted to him. Soon the bankers found it highly unlikely that all depositors would wish to withdraw their holdings at the same time. They began to risk "lending" paper money (promissory notes) of their own making, over and above the deposits which they held. Occasionally a rumour that the bank was at risk might panic the depositors, causing a crisis if they demanded more money back than the bank held. — some 18th-century paintings of "Saving the Bank" show the arrival of a stagecoach bringing enough bullion from London HQ to pay the clients. But for most of the time the banks enjoyed a private monopoly of the creation of credit from nothing!

9th March.   **Pennies from Heaven?**

So where **does** money come from? Long ago, when barter was found difficult and cowry-shells inconvenient, the local king would order his Royal Mint to produce coins (now known among economists as "M0 money") and circulate them by spending them on goods (e.g. food, works of art) and on wages (e.g builders') If he were devoutly Christian he would see that the supply of money was such as maintained it as a stable measure of value, as taught by St Thomas Aquinas. Islam and other faiths had similar practices. **But** most money today isn't minted! Rather than being embodied in coins or notes, it is an **abstraction**, appearing on the screens and print-outs of the so-called financial services industry.

For over 300 years, since the Tunnage and Poundage Act of William III gave the Bank of England a private monopoly of credit-creation in recognition of "services to the State" in establishing him as king rather than Dutch Usurper, it (plus a few other finance-houses who later received a similar privilege) provided Britain with most of its money by <u>creating it out of nothing</u> by taking the risk outlined yesterday - see the "Encyclopaedia Britannica". Banks however don't put clients in credit by spending the created money or donating it; they issue it with strings attached in the form of interest-charges on loan-debt, so that their role is far too parasitic. Indeed if they have the sole power to create money, and they want back more than they have made, they ask the impossible, and peoples' debts grow, placing a crushing burden of interest on National and Local Government as well as on very many individuals.

The nature of money has changed dramatically during our lifetimes! Banks' activities have grown so greatly since 1963, when "M0 money" represented 21% of the total UK supply; compare 3.6% in 1997! Through the inattention, deliberate I suspect, of schools and media to the public as distinct from private aspects of monetary practice, not many citizens are aware that the property-owning democracy of which some politicians boast is more truly a debt-bound nation through mortgages and other loan The effect of "globalisation" which instant communication has made possible is yet more baleful, with Third World Debt irredeemable by Third World activity. To end the genocide whereby a child dies every 2½ seconds of hunger or preventable illness, money **must** be created, free of debt, by public authorities, and spent or given into circulation rather than lent at interest. As the prophet said, "LEAVE OFF THIS USURY" (Nehemiah 5.10)!

See also "The Invalidity of Third World Debt", by Michael Robotham. For my précis please send s.a.e

10th March. It is much to be hoped that the Friendly Greetings being distributed by this benign Victorian vicar on his rounds are a cut above such works as William Carus Wilson's Friendly Visitor and its companion penny-periodical Children's Friend (1824), also Psalms and Hymns by Isaac Watts, author of the fine "Our God, our help in ages past" (1714) but alas also of such offerings as "My thoughts on awful subjects roll, Damnation and the dead...", and of his Divine and Moral Songs for children:

> "If this rebellious heart of mine
> Despise the gracious calls of heaven,
> I may be hardened by my sin
> And never have repentance given."

Carus Wilson is notorious as the original of the Revd Mr Brocklehurst, whose "Lowood" in Jane Eyre is based on Wilson's "Clergy Daughters School founded at Cowan Bridge in 1824, which has evolved into the reputable Casterton School, where I have seen its records of the Brontë sisters exhibited as part of an Open Day exhibition.

In Chapter II of her outstanding biography of Charlotte Brontë (Methuen, 1988) Rebecca Fraser asks whether the sadistic Brocklehurst is a portrait or caricature of headmaster Wilson. Little can be added to her assessment of the extraordinary scenes. The seemingly cruel hypocrisy of the independently wealthy Wilson may well have stemmed from his stupid-ity. He wrote that "The pupils are necessarily put into a very simple and uniform attire. Many of them no doubt feel it. They have been unfortunately accustomed...to excess in this...love of dress..."

(continued)

72

It is no defence of the Cowan Bridge punishments to say they were typical of all schools of their date. For a time at least there was a disastrous combination of damp site, unpleasant staff and silly regime. The matter was ventilated in public after the appearance in 1857 of Elizabeth Gaskell's biography of Charlotte, the Halifax Guardian serving as battlefield. Charlotte's widower Arthur Nicholls championed Mrs Gaskell's attacks with the aid of ex-pupils whilst the Wilson faction saw their parson as sacrosanct -losing credibility when their written evidence from "superintend-ent A.H." turned out to be written by the original of Miss Scatcherd the chief villainess of Jane Eyre! "Well she would, wouldn't she?!"

THRESHER & GLENNY,
CLERICAL TAILORS & HATTERS,
152 & 153, STRAND, LONDON, W.C.
Church Times ——— 5.i.1900
Having acquired the business recently carried on by Mr. THOMAS COLE, late of 155, STRAND, which is being conducted under the same management, Messrs. THRESHER and GLENNY retain full particulars of all goods supplied, and respectfully assure the very large number of CLERGY whose confidence in the Firm has for so many years been placed, that orders will be carried out to their entire satisfaction.

CLERICAL SILK & FELT HATS
OF EVERY DESCRIPTION.
Goods sent on approval in Town or Country.

ONLY ADDRESS—
152 & 153, STRAND, LONDON,
(Next door to Somerset House)

11th March. English Hymnody Saved!

One child who at 8 **cried bitter tears** over the harsh Calvinistic doctrines of the Georgian Evangelicals grew to be the very great champion of Western orthodoxy against their excess. He was John Mason Neale (1818-1866), author of "Good King Wenceslas" (but why did the poor man have to go gathering wood three miles from his home against a forest fence? There must have been a malign landowner on the scene) and founder and warden of the Society of St Margaret, East Grinstead.

Attacking children's hymns such as the one quoted yesterday, he protested that instead of being taught that the work of salvation (from human sins, negligences and ignorances) is already accomplished for them, and all they have to do is to continue therein till their dying day, they are furiously told to begin that work themselves, reading and praying lest they be sent to eternal death. That is heresy, saying they should trust in themselves for salvation, rather than in God who gives it! (Source of information: "The Influence of John Mason Neale" by A.G. Lough; SPCK, 1962).

Neale's other priceless gift to the Church is his finding and translating many old hymns of the West and the East. Some are recondite; others are much-loved - All glory laud and honour, Christ is made the sure foundation, O come Emmanuel, and Sing my tongue the glorious battle. Look these hymns up!

12th March.   "SALLY GO ROUND THE SUN."

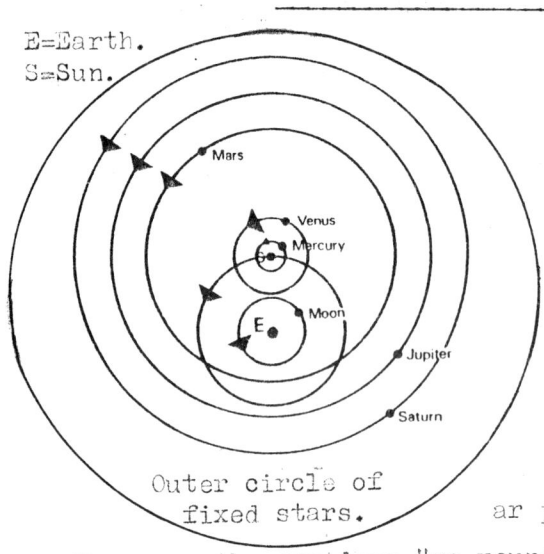

E = Earth.
S = Sun.

Outer circle of fixed stars.

Prompted by a professor's "aside" in the press that but for science we would still believe that the sun goes round the earth, I recall the system of Tycho Brahe (1546 – 1601), which is intermediate between the entirely earth-centred model of Aristotle & Ptolemy and the now-familiar one of Copernicus, published in 1543, with the sun at the centre of planetary orbits including the Earth's. Later astronomers added near-circular paths for Uranus Neptune & Pluto.

Even so, the sun _does_ "go round the earth"! – I can see this happen from my window as I write (and have done so o'er Galway Bay!) This is not to deny that the earth goes round the sun, as Galileo tried to prove from the tides after his telescopic discovery of the phases of Venus had established the orbiting of _that_ planet round the sun not the earth. The "God's eye view" of the estimated "hundred billion trillion (10^{23}) stars out there" (Sarah Woodward, _Cam_ magazine, Easter 2000AD), and such satellites as exist, is obviously complex beyond human grasp, and all or most are moving _relative to one another_!

The 1633 trial of Galileo by the Roman Inquisition is a well-known part of popular culture, and all including the R.C. church now accept that the Inquisitors were wrong – but what was their mistake? I think it was twofold in claiming (a) that observational science is unacceptable as a way to truth about Nature if it clashes with existing ideas; and (b) that the Roman Curia had final jurisdiction over all culture. Nevertheless unless the universe embodies an absolute standard of rest, the Inquisitors were just as entitled to deem the earth to be at rest in accordance with our everyday experience, as Galileo the sun.

Those interested in relativity-theories are advised to refer to the popular book "The Evolution of Physics" by A. Einstein & L. Infeld. Physicists and philosophers are still arguing about whether they entail a fixed standard of rest. Pending the establishment of one, we can but be pragmatic and use what serves our purposes best – the sun for planetary astronomy, the star-map of the distant heavens for stellar astronomy, and "dear mother earth" for everyday life.

13th March. "The good Old Times of England".
(from "A Mirror of Faith – Lays and Legends
of the Church of England" by J.M. Neale, 1845)

— — — — — —

John Neale (see 11 March) looked back, albeit
idealistically, to pre-Reformation days (see
11 January, 'By St Agnes' Fountain') with
longing for our nation to be permeated once
more by the catholic Christian Faith, in his
sense of the universal Western Faith not necessarily tied to Rome.
We may still learn from his verses which I can supply in full-(sa
This selection refers to the separation of man & wife in workhouse

Oh, the good old times of England! ere, in her evil day,
From their Holy Faith and their ancient rites her people fell away;
When her gentlemen had hands to give, and her yeomen hearts to feel;
And they raised full many a bede-house, but never a bastile:
And the poor they honoured, for they knew that He, Who for us bled,
Had seldom, when He came on earth, whereon to lay His Head; ...

But times and things are altered now; and Englishmen begin
To class the beggar with the knave, and poverty with sin:
We shut them up from tree and flower, and from the blessed sun;
We tear in twain the hearts that **God** in wedlock had made one,
The hearts that beat so faithfully, reposing side by side
For fifty years of smiles and tears from eve till morning tide; ...

Yet...still our solemn festivals from age to age endure,
And wedded troth remains as firm, and wedded love as pure;
And many an earnest prayer ascends from many a hidden spot;
And England's Church is Catholic, though England's self be not!

England of Saints! The hour is nigh---far nigher may it be
Than yet I deem, albeit that day I may not live to see,---
When all thy commerce, all thy arts, and wealth, and power, and fame,
Shall melt away---at thy most need---like wax before the flame;
Then shalt thou find thy truest strength thy martyrs' prayers above,
Then shalt thou find thy truest wealth their holy deeds of love;
And thy Church, awaking from Her sleep, come glorious forth at length,
And in sight of angels and of men display Her hidden strength:
Again shall long processions sweep through Lincoln's minster pile:
Again shall banner, cross and cope gleam thro' the incensed aisles;
And the faithful dead shall claim their part in the Church's thankful prayer,
And the daily sacrifice to **God** be duly offered there;
England of Saints! the peace will dawn,---but not without the fight;
So, come the contest when it may,---and **God** defend the right!

75

(side margin:) Neale when young wrote occupational ballads too, e.g. Engine-Drivers on the new railways - "While the sleepers quake below, and the wheels like lightning go, Through the tunnel and the bridge we dare" but he strengthened the Church mightily and his stress on spiritual renewal is vital to this day!

14th March. "The Joy of Music".

Susan Sharpe, prominent in BBC Radio 3's excellent team of "DJs", whist introducing a 1996 broadcast of Beethoven's much-loved Fourth Piano Concerto, told the story of its first performance as part of a four-hour-long concert in a chilly hall one evening. Beethoven himself was the soloist — but, lacking all selfconsciousness, he rose when the piano part required silence and started to conduct with his usual extravagant gestures, with the result that he knocked the two lamps off the ends of the piano and on to the floor. He demanded a re-start, and the precaution was taken to find two boys to hold the lamps. Unfortunately they leaned too close in order to read the music, so that when the same point was reached and the maestro repeated his gesture, one boy was quick enough to duck, but the other was struck on the cheek. He dropped his lamp, the audience was convulsed with laughter, and Beethoven never conducted or performed as soloist in public again.

— — — — —

In his book "The Joy of Music" (Panther Arts, 1969) the American conductor-composer Leonard Bernstein wrote of "The inexplicable ability to know what the next note has to be". Beethoven, he claimed, "had this gift in a degree that leaves them all panting in the rearguard. When he really *did* it, as in the Funeral March of the *Eroica* symphony, he produced an entity that always seems to me to have been previously written in Heaven, and then merely dictated to him. Not that the dictation was easily achieved....There is a special space carved out in the cosmos into which this movement just fits, predetermined and perfect."

Bernstein has a further comment, in conversation with a "Lyric Poet", which includes this exchange:

L.B. — "Our boy has the real goods, the stuff from Heaven, the power to make you feel at the finish — 'Something is right in the world. There is somethingg that checks throughout, that follows its own law consistently — something we can trust, that will never let us down.'"

L.P. (quietly) "But that is almost a definition of God."

L.B. — "I meant it to be."

— — — — —

I believe that Sibelius shared Beethoven's gift. Mozart could write divinely without visible effort, as "a musical instrument played by God". As for the rivalry between Bach's champions and Beethoven's, it has been said that Bach's music is God speaking to man, and Beethoven's is man addressing God. But there is more to each of them than that.

<u>15th March.</u>   <u>Beware the Ides of March!</u>

Pope Benedict XVI, a year after his appointment, is claimed by some pope-watchers to have metamorphosed from John Paul II's "grand inquisitor" and doctrinal Rottweiler into a benign German Shepherd. Be that as it may, he has won smiles by human touches such as sharing his homes including the Vatican papal apartments with his cats, and criticising the overwork which mars Western life. His views reflect mine and those of the writer Ivor Mills among many others. Mills' arguments in an article that I cannot trace are on the following lines:

Following the run-down of the high industrial era, the developed West risks a breakdown of civilisation. Competition leads too many people to strain for too much affluence, and we need to allow normal human inefficiency at work and in all places of education

— — — — — — —

Overstated, yes! – <u>every</u> job? – and doubtfully focussed, for a more equitable distribution of land would support our present population less stressfully; but there is much truth in Mills' overview. In recent decades British voters have given more weight to their selfcentred (yes, and familycentred I accept) prospects of material benefit than in my youth. This is a direct cause of the loss of public peace which we all bewail; and of the desolation of marginalised people and communities which entails total disengagement, and unemployment of a sizeable minority whilst too many others are overworked and dehumanized.

As recently as the early 1960s it was possible in Britain to send children of 8 or so on train-journeys of 100 miles, with the guard keeping a watchful eye on them till he saw them met at their destination. Bottles of concentrated acids and of poisonous solutions including cyanides could be seen on the open shelves of college and school chemistry laboratories, without fear of misuse or dangerous horseplay. Nowadays in protecting people from the consequences of irresponsibility, we give them the message that they are fundamentally untrustworthy, and so teach folly into some of them.

77   "Equality of opportunity" is so rightly lauded these days that it needs shouting from the housetops that it isn't enough unless the social ethos or climate of public opinion insists that individual go-getting needs tempering by a framework that ensures that the interests of the community and especially its weaker members are sufficiently upheld, the race will be to the strong, and Studdert Kennedy's epigram of the 1920s will apply: "Everyone for themselves and God be with us all, as the elephant said, as it danced among the chickens." (cf. 24.3.)

16th March. A Mousetail and a Backward Glance:

WE LIVED BENEATH THE MAT,
WARM AND SNUG AND FAT,
BUT ONE WOE, AND THAT
WAS THE **CAT**!

Robert Burns' poem "To a Mouse" has done well to remind us of the precariousness of the lives of mice and other little creatures. We ourselves are, of course, more vulnerable to disaster (except God help) than we care to think.

To our joys a clog; In our eyes a jog; On our hearts a log was the **DOG**!

More innocently and lightheartedly we may recall the mousetail in the "Caucus Race" chapter of "Alice in Wonderland". It isn't widely known that Lewis Carroll composed this other and arguably superior mousetail!

When the Cat's away,
Then
The mice
 will
  play,
 But alas!
  One day, (so they say)
   Came the Dog and
    Cat, hunting
     for a
      Rat,
     Crushed
      the mice
       all flat,
      Each
       one
        as
         he
          sat,
          u_n_d_e_r_n_e_a_t_h the mat, warm and snug and fat, Think of that!

MOTHER MOUSE IS COOKING.

MOTHER mouse is cooking
 In a green pan;
Come along, children,
As quickly as you can.

Come and eat your supper,
Run, run, run;
Here is lovely porridge
Enough for everyone.

Can today's toddlers enjoy the quiet rhymes of 100 years ago? Programmes on television which flicker from one thing to another can hardly fail to latch them to a media-defined subculture. A headteacher-friend tells me that primary-school poetry books now contain only amusing verse, to the pupils' detriment.

17th March.   Saint Patrick for Ireland - and beyond!

Patrick, writes David Adam in his book "The Cry of the Deer" (Triangle, 1987), "was born about A.D.414 near the western coastline of the Roman province of Britannia, most likely.... opposite Ulster" - perhaps near Dumbarton. The most celebrated saint of Europe's western isles, his day is kept by Irish and other folk throughout the world, no less in parades and Guinness as in High Mass. Famously, continues Adam, "When Patrick was only sixteen, he was captured by a raiding party from Ireland and sold as a slave to a petty king in Armagh." His home lost to him in a trice, he found he could still meet up with fellow-Christians, and pray when tending sheep and in wild places and weather - in his "Confessions" he wrote "The Spirit seethed in me". Escaping after six years, he had "Come Back to Erin" dreams of his friends and the Irish people calling him back. Returning around 455 to preach, he went on to Gaul for training (and ordination if not already secured), then back to Tara to challenge the old ways of witchcraft and idolatry based there.

"When Easter approached", says Adam, "Patrick was determined to keep the festival in Tara...it coincided with a great pagan festival...all lights were to be extinguished and all fires put out, only the king would provide people with fire and light. Patrick and his companions pitched their tent, collected wood and kindled the Paschal fire, which lit up the whole of Mag Bre so that the king's wise men warned him that unless the fire was extinguished immediately it would flood Ireland with its light and burn until Doomsday....The king was in no doubt that Patrick had to be stopped...Soldiers were sent to capture Patrick and prevent him from coming to Tara; they surrounded him and his men. When Patrick saw them, he quoted the Psalms: 'Some put their trust in chariots and some in horses; but we in the Lord our God'. He was able to escape...and entered Tara itself...

"Legend grew that Patrick was more powerful than the Druids...that when the army attacked him, he turned himself into a deer and so escaped them. Whatever we make of that, tradition says that this is when he composed the hymn known as 'The Deer's Cry[1]' or 'The Breastplate of St Patrick[2]."

- "I bind unto myself today The strong Name of the Trinity."
 −(2.6).

(Psalm quoted is No. 20, verse 7.)   Translators: 1. Kuno Meyer. 2. Fanny Alexander.

18th March.   ST PATRICK'S BREASTPLATE.

This hymn as we know it, adds David Adam, "may belong to three canturies after Patrick, but that does not matter. It expresses so well much of the early Celtic Christian Faith. It vibrates still with the God who surrounds us, the Christ who is with us, and the Spirit within us...The Divine Glory is woven into all of life like a fine thread; there is a Presence and a Power that pervades everything...The glory is not something we create, it is God's gift of Himself to us. It is a mystery to be enjoyed, not a problem to be solved..."

Patrick went on from Tara to evangelise, all over Ireland, 'preaching, baptising, and building churches...a lion in boldness'; when asked by the King of Connaught's daughters who and where his God was, he, "filled with the Holy Spirit, replied:

> Our God is the God of all, God of Heaven and earth, sea and river. He has His dwelling in heaven and earth and sea and all that are therein. He inspires all things; He quickens all things. He kindles the light of the sun and of the moon. He has a Son, co-eternal with Himself and like unto Him. And the Holy Spirit breathes in them. Father, Son and Holy Spirit are not divided. I desire to unite you to the Son of the Heavenly King, for you are daughters of a king of earth."

In another book, "The Eye of the Eagle" (Triangle, 1990), in which his main concern is to interpret another Celtic hymn "Be Thou My Vision", David Adam claims that "The early Celtic Church had many breastplate-prayers or <u>lorica</u> which declared the surrounding and encompassing of God...not to make God come — He is already there — but to open our eyes to the reality, as with the "Chariots of Fire" vision of Elisha's servant (2 Kings 6.17). <u>Divine Defence</u> is mentioned in Psalms 20, 23 ('The Lord is my shepherd' which promises God's help even in death's dark vale), 91 (R.C.90) pledging deliverance from hunter's snare and noisesome pestilence, and several others; yet the preface to "I bind..." in the <u>Liber Hymnorum</u>, folio 196, at Trinity College Dublin is amazingly strong:-

> Patrick made this hymn... And this is the corslet of faith for the protection of body and soul against the devils and human beings and vices. Whoever shall sing it every day, with pious meditation on God, devils will not stay before him. It will be a safeguard to him against all poison and envy. It will be a defence to him against sudden death. It will be a corslet to him after dying."

(Note also the medieval English mystic Lady Julian of Norwich: God says not "You shan't be tempested" but "You shan't be overcome".

19th March.   Jail for 33 Seconds!

The use of nuclear weapons against Japan in 1945 gave a new dimension to warfare, creating superpowers that appeared at times to threaten all life on earth. Canon Charles Raven declared in a mid-century lecture that if Christians were prepared in any circumstances to wipe out the entire population of a city, it would be difficult to see how our worship and prayer and talk of love, service and sacrifice could be anything but cant and hypocrisy. I go along with that, for Jesus wouldn't countenance the destruction of a village by fire from heaven (Luke 9.51-6). When H-bomb bases were established in Britain they attracted "peace-camps" of protesters, who made minor attacks and forays on occasion, albeit less dramatic than that in George Target's fine novel "The Americans". (Duckworth, 1964)! The CND (Campaign for Nuclear Disarmament) magazine "Sanity" used to report on some ensuing cases.

In June 1988 a defendant charged with marking an MOD wall during an Ash Wednesday Christian CND action in London was stated to have been acquitted because he had only drawn a line and the charge read that he had "written". The next issue said that Christine Steers had been found not guilty of affixing a copy of "Sanity" to a police-cell window after it was found by Alconbury magistrates that affixing is only an offence when objects are attached to a perimeter fence. (Dr Linda Patterson was fined at Pateley Bridge for affixing a daffodil to the Menwith Hill fence, a crime which prompted me to write a parody of Wordsworth's "Daffodils" poem for our local press. -3.6)

On 26 November 1988 a Welsh court sentenced the Revd.A.Gwynedd to be "detained until the court rises" for non-payment of a fine imposed after the Brawdy action of 1987. It then rose, and a BBC reporter timed Aled's imprisonment at 33 seconds. A record?!

81

Then on 22 February 1989 a man was arrested on Salisbury Plain for "displaying a symbol representing a dove within the sight of a person liable to be caused harassment, alarm or distress thereby"! The prosecution service had a better sense of proportion, and maybe of humour, than the local police, for it offered no evidence in court, counsel stating that it is recognised that "a dove is a symbol of peace and wouldn't cause offence to anyone". And Lytham magistrates on 10 March that year **lifted a £200 fine** imposed on the Revd.S.Tedesco for action at Springfield; they said they were remitting the fine because it was Red Nose Day and the defendant was a Xaverian who believed in giving all one's goods to the poor. To this day many courts refuse to toe the MOD line automatically and insist on considering international law; but somehow the Ministry of Defence has yet to appear in court under the 1969 Genocide Act, and the RAF joins far too readily with the United States' Air Force in raids on Iraq & elsewhere.

20th March.   ## CO-DELINQUENTS.

The "Campaign" section of "Sanity" magazine for August 1989 reported, under the heading "Peace in Court", that "Hexham magistrates find Karen Glover, Sheila McBrien and Annette Moran guilty of criminal damage during Snowball action at (Albermarle) base in January. Each fined £50...." The same issue published a letter from Karen Glover and Sheila McBrien, of "Newcastle Opposes a Nuclear Environment". It read:

"We thought we'd mistaken Sanity for The Sun when we read in "Peace in Court" that six women had entered the base at Greenham dressed as schoolgirls - why on earth dress as schoolgirls? This only perpetuates the male stereotype view of women, i.e. they exist to dress as men want, as little girls and schoolchildren. It's perverted and very dangerous and extremely offensive. You shouldn't have printed it."

This assault brought Campaign Editor Diana Shelley to her knees. "Yes, you're right. 'Peace in Court' tries to be an accurate record of peace activists' brushes with the law (whether or not we personally agree with all the activities recorded) but I agree this report should either not have been printed or should at least have been commented on. Apologies to anyone who may have been offended. We have also been asked to make it clear that the actions reported were by women from Woad Gate."

Not all readers were of that mind, however; in November the following riposte appeared, headed "Spotty", on the letters page: "I am 18 and am made to dress as a schoolgirl even in my A-level year. I've just seen the August issue of your magazine, in which Karen Glover and Sheila McBrien criticise six women from Woad Gate for having entered the base at Greenham dressed as schoolgirls....The implication is that the six should dress as Glover and McBrien want. I think these two complainants should develop a sense of humour and proportion about what was clearly in part a tease, devised without reference to men - as was the schooldress, which was evolved by Victorian headmistresses and maintained by woman teachers who have done more than any other group of people to secure women's equality in many walks of life. As for the action, far be it from me to compare its worthwhileness with that...at Albemarle by your correspondents....Our hearts are just as spotty as (peaceable men's re) pride, anger etc.
"Francesca Foxwell, Manchester."

<u>21st March.</u>   A YOUNG MAN'S FANCY.

    Spring has come – "officially"! – and I lightly turn to thoughts of Tennyson – Queen Victoria's laureate 1850-1892:

> Step by step we gain'd a freedom known to Europe, known to all;
> Step by step we rose to greatness, — thro' the tonguesters we may fall.

So he warned the nation in his second Locksley Hall poem which he wrote at 77, and alas we weren't vigilant enough against manipulative advertisers, spin-doctoring media-moguls and politicians, and corrupters of the arts in the late 20th century. Tennyson's social comment, concentrated almost exclusively in the above-mentioned poem, tends like Ruskin's to be denied due attention. There are depths in Tennyson which are not sounded by his "popular" output of The Brook, The Lady of Shalott, Blow Bugle Blow, Mariana, and his worst and most famous poem The Charge of the Light Brigade. J.B. Steane's "Tennyson" (Evans, 1966) is a fine introduction to the poet's work as a whole. Of this last-named poem he writes: "....a great success with every-one except the other branch of the Tennyson family, where it was pronounced 'horrid rubbish'. The lines are so familiar by this time that it is hard to judge the merits of that critical comment: on the whole I think there might be something in it." I agree; its insistent rhythm is certainly evocative, but it lacks pity for the stupidly-doomed men – and horses.

    Much more important are Tennyson's philosophical works, in which we may discover and drink from the life-giving fountain from which they flow. Poets and visionaries have always and everywhere testified to the existence of a spiritual realm, of which our familiar material world is a shadow. Tennyson held this belief from childhood, and at 14 he wrote of a spiritual experience parallel with Wordsworth's by Tintern Abbey (7 Feb.):

> "All sense of Time
> And Being and Place was swallowed up and lost
> Within a victory of boundless thought,
> I was a part of the Unchangeable,
> A scintillation of Eternal Mind,
> Bemix'd and burning with its parent fire."   (Armageddon.)

At the same youthful age he also wrote a play, The Devil and The Lady, in which the Devil is made to ask:

> "O suns and spheres and stars and belts and systems,
> Are ye or are ye not?
> Are ye realities, or <u>semblances</u>
> Of <u>that</u> which men call real?"

A similar insight by the Apache poet Black Elk declares, of a fellow-American, that "Crazy Horse dreamed and went into the world where there is nothing but the spirit of all things. (see also Hebrews 11[3]) That is the real world that is behind this one, And everything we see here is something like a shadow from that world."

22nd March. Alfred Tennyson lived from 1809 to 1892, and this drawing was made by his young friend James Spedding, of Mirehouse nr Keswick, around 1831, before the tragic death in 1833 of his even closer friend Arthur Hallam exposed him to the temptations of the nihilism born of grief: "A life of nothings, nothing worth,/ From that first nothing ere his birth,/ To that last nothing under earth." (The Two Voices). His earlier viewpoints which remained with him all his life came under eclipse whilst the passage of time, slowly, slowly brought healing balm. After a decade of silence his reticent masterpiece "In Memoriam" was published anonymously in 131 parts or cantos plus prologue and epilogue. It is best read in full, or where this is impossible in representative selection including "anthology-favourites". (Incidentally when buying a second-hand "Tennyson" it is wise to check that it ends with "Crossing The Bar", for the collections printed during the poet's lifetime are necessarily incomplete.)

A short selection from "In Memoriam" might include Prologue;
- 11 — "Calm is the morn without a sound";
- 20 — "The lesser griefs that may be said" (also 21 & 22);
- 28 — "The time draws near the birth of Christ" (also 29 & 30);
- 54 — "O yet we trust that somehow good" (also 55, 56, & 57);
- 73 — "So many worlds, so much to do";
- 87 — "I past beside the reverend walls" (also 93, 95, & 96);
- 106 — "Ring out, wild bells" (and the preceding 104 & 105);
- 117 — "O days and hours, your work is this" (also 120 & 124);
- 126 — "Love is and was my Lord and King" (also 125 & 131).

Thus the long poem advances, like Beethoven's 3rd Symphony, from heartrending grief to strong hopes which enter from an altogether higher realm of the Spirit of Life. In Canto 93 the poet pleads for the mercy of spiritual communion with his lost friend:
"That in this blindness of the frame,
My Ghost may feel that thine is near."
and in Canto 95 he tells us that this prayer is granted:
"And all at once it seemed at last,
The living soul was flash'd on mine."
but that doubt supervened about the validity of the experience of "the powers of the world to come" (Hebrews 6.5), as happens with many who have enjoyed such intimations. (continued on 26 March.

23rd March.   The Fiddler of Dooney.

Ireland has her own musical tradition, or rather traditions; for the old-time harpists with their range of instruments including steel,- the traditional fiddlers with their zest who are still to be found in the pubs,- and the Parlour Musicians of the great houses of the "protestant-ascendancy years" all made, or make, valuable contributions.

The central hotel of Sligo city in the north-west, by the river where I saw 46 swans peacefully afloat, recently used this poem by Yeats (pronounced Yates) in a publicity-brochure: 'Every year traditional Irish musicians and fans flood into the Hotel Silver Swan for the coveted "Fiddler of Dooney" competition. "The Fiddler Dooney" is the inspiration and heritage for this battle between some of Ireland's most talented musicians. A must for any traditional Irish music lover....' (as is the hotel for visitors to Yeats' Land of Heart's Desire).

Now locate and read:
* Under Ben Bulben (see also 30 March).
* Lake Isle of Innisfree.
* Down by the Salley Gardens.
* The Pity of Love.
* The Lover Pleads.
* Easter 1916.
* The Second Coming.
* The Fiddler of Dooney:

> And the merry love to dance:
> And when the folk there spy me,
> They will all come up to me,
> With "Here is the fiddler of Dooney!"
> And dance like a wave of the sea.

The poem reminds me of the final movement of Beethoven's String Quartet Opus 131, of which Wagner wrote: "It is the world's own dance - wild pleasure painful weeping, the ecstasy of love, supreme joy, fury, voluptuousness, and suffering; lightning cuts through the air, thunder growls - and above all, the Great Fiddler, urging and leading all the villagers, proud and sure through the whirlwind, guides us towards the abyss; he smiles to himself, because for him this enchantment was but a game. Then night calls him; his day is done."

(But the romantic Wagner, I believe, was wrong to use the term "abyss", for Beethoven's intense music maintains its foothold; and his last quartet of all, Op. 135, which is easier listening, ends humorously as the composer himself looks cheerfully into the Unknown!)

85

- - - - - - -

Yeats' celebrated "Lake Isle of Innisfree" is on Lough Gill, a fairly short walk, ride or drive from Sligo. I fail, however, to share his enthusiasm for "Nine bean-rows"; for one sufficed to satisfy my zeal for gardening.

24th March. Death of an Archbishop, and other stories.

At times my pen takes up perpetual motion, with results to be seen in local and occasionally national papers. I "made" the Church Times with this little tribute which corrected a common misapprehension about British politics over the decade from 1982. Labour's 1983 election-manifesto was famously called the longest suicide-note ever; but the attempted suicide was Britain's, and the Labour Party's fate was "grievous bodily harm during attempted murder". When the Thatcher government was re-elected in 1983 a lady said to me "If I make a mistake in my housekeeping I can't put it right overnight; the family has to suffer. This nation has just made such a mistake, and it'll take 50 years to correct it". Seventeen years afterwards, a third of way through the half-century, I reminded her about that view. She said she sitll stands by it. So did I, and so I still do. The Maastricht Treaty is a trick rather than a treat!

In the same month a lighter squib appeared as follows. Football is now big business, with far too many penalty kicks being awarded as a consequence of rule-changes & the introduction of shootouts.

OBSERVER
Sports
Magazine
2.7.2000

Runcie's stand against Tories

From Councillor Frank McManus
Sir, — I demur at one point only in David Edwards's warm and worthy obituary of Archbishop Runcie, namely the statement that, "What kept the Tories in power was the looniness of the Left." I write as a Labour activist and a Reader.

Granted that some local and national Labour politicians, including a former Prime Minister, displayed a degree of indiscipline which their successors avoided in 1997, our 1983 defeat and wilderness years were due to two main causes.

First, the "Falklands Factor", which provided a focus for a national bellicosity and imperial hankering which Britain is normally loath to acknowledge. Michael Foot was well ahead of Margaret Thatcher in all the opinion polls before the clash with Galtieri, which was grist to the tabloid-media mill.

Second, the deep division of radical voters in southern England between Labour and Liberal, whereby our flawed electoral system yielded over a hundred Tory MPs on minority votes.

The erosion of the fabric of society under the ethos of individual go-getting, epitomised by Studdert-Kennedy's aphorism, "Everyone for himself and God be with us all, as the elephant said while it danced among the chickens", bit deep as it shattered many communities and produced deprived and disaffected young adults by the tens of thousands.

But the faithful few fought bravely to guard the nation's life, and Bob Runcie held an honourable place in this spiritual conflict, for which he will be lovingly remembered.
FRANK McMANUS
Locksley House
97 Longfield Road
Todmorden

Penalty drama in 1938

Your feature on the 10 worst penalty misses (Issue 2) put me in mind of Mutch's penalty goal for Preston in the last minute of extra-time in the 1938 Cup final. He said the goal looked small and distant and filled by the Huddersfield goalie, but Shankly the captain told him to shut his eyes and blast it in – which he did via the underside of the crossbar.

It may not have been a recent memory, but it is vivid nevertheless; as a boy of 10 in Southport I couldn't bear the suspense and left the room with the wireless at full-time. I went back in when I had timed it as over, only to hear the commentator say 'It's a penalty...'
Frank McManus

86

25th March.   **Does Football Matter?**

Wembley Stadium 30.4.1938.

It adds colour to life's routines, is like chess a game of infinite variety, and is accessible to nearly everyone, with young men and woman playing at local and national level and beyond. I was born in Southport in 1927 and my father used to take me by train (steam, stopping, and slow) to watch Preston North End. He had turned down a trial with that club because it offered no security for later life – the wage-limit held the greatest players, Stanley Matthews, Tom Finney and Co., to upper working class wages, and kept the clubs related to their towns – and this may have lost the game a famous bulldog-type defender.

People then still remembered the PNE "Old Invincibles" who in 1889 won the F.A. Cup without conceding a goal and the League Championship without losing a match. Their 26-0 victory over Hyde on 15.10.1887 remains the record score in first-class English football. That season they were so confident of winning the Cup that they borrowed it for a photograph before the Final. They lost, showing the unwisdom of counting chickens before they are hatched. Many a slip twixt Cup and lip! Fifty years later they regained the limelight, losing the 1937 Cup Final to Sunderland but winning dramatically in 1938. It is a pity that the game has recently been trivialised and made cruel by penalty shootouts, when nearly all drawn games could be determined by treating the first goal scored as a "silver goal" to decide the outcome, except for goalless draws which could go on corner kicks secured. But surely the American poet Grantland Rice should have the last word with his atrocious "Alumnus Football":
"For when the One Great Scorer comes to write against your name, He marks not that you won or lost, but how you played the game.

26th March. "Matter-moulded forms of speech".

Are paranormal experiences of sight or hearing, such as appearances of ghosts or inexplicable movements of objects (Uri Geller's bent spoons, Elijah's fire on Mount Carmel) to be accepted at face-value? (I don't refer to cases of fraud, which have trivialised the topic in the public mind.) Tennyson, facing this question after feeling that his departed friend's "living soul was flash'd on mine...all at once" (In Memoriam, Canto 95), realised that "matter-moulded forms of speech" are all but unable to specify, and that "intellect" is scarcely able to conceive, what happens at the meeting of two living spirits. This being the case with our earthly loves and friendships, how much more true is it then of the relationships in the last three cantos, 129 to 131, of the poem? Tennyson, who had in cantos 54 to 56 and 120 agonised over the implications of evolutionary theory, appears to have concluded that our "matter-moulded" senses, developed slowly to combat the material difficulties of life, are inadequate for the proper apprehension of the underlying spiritual world. Later, in 1874, he expressed this conclusion very neatly in his lyric "The Voice and The Peak":

"A deep below the deep,/ And a height beyond the height!
Our hearing is not hearing,/ And our seeing is not sight."

I understand that the poet's grandson and biographer Sir Charles Tennyson concurs with this assessment, for in his book "Alfred Tennyson" (Macmillan, 1968, pp373/4) he writes that in "The Higher Pantheism" (1869) the poet "explored the idea ...that the material universe, which often seems so menacing and purposeless, may be the vision of God, if not actually a part of God Himself, though man, with his limited powers, can only get a distorted and partial view of the reality. Yet, if man will only make the effort, he will find that the barrier can be surmounted and direct communion with God achieved"!! I quote from "Higher Pantheism":

> THE sun, the moon, the stars, the seas, the hills and the plains—
> Are not these, O Soul, the Vision of Him who reigns?
>
> Earth, these solid stars, this weight of body and limb,
> Are they not sign and symbol of thy division from Him?
> Glory about thee, without thee; and thou fulfillest thy doom
> Making Him broken gleams, and a stifled splendour and gloom.
>
> Speak to Him thou for He hears, and Spirit with Spirit can meet—
> Closer is He than breathing, and nearer than hands and feet.

88

All this is redoubtably restated in the "All The Boundless Heavens" quatrain of '2nd Locksley Hall'. This claim may stagger the people of our secular culture, but it tallies with the New Testament (see 1 Cor 13.12 & Heb 12.22!)

27th March.   Time For More Limericks.

The "Book of Judges" (Old Testament) is gruesome, e.g. ch.4 v.2

> The treacherous woman called Jael
> When angered was wont to impale.
>   While Sisera slept,
>   To his bedside she crept,
> And did him with hammer and nail.

If that were all the Bible had to offer by way of heroic idealism I'd feel bound to concur with the Frenchman in this verse:

> Il y avait un jeune homme de Dijon
> Qui n'avait que peu de religion.
>   Il dit: "Quant à moi
>   Je déteste tous les trois,
> Le Père et le Fils et le Pigeon".

From the "Meccano Magazine" from the 1930s, with no 24-hr. clock:

> There was an old lady called Carr
> Who caught the 3.3 to Forfar.
>   She said "I believe
>   That the 3.3 will leave
> Before the 4.4 to Forfar".

Distinguished folk indulge in merry pranks:

> The Sultan of Oman and Muscat
> Preferred his racoon to his puss-cat.
>   He sang in the street
>   To keep it in meat
> Till he found a good corner to busk at.

Wagner's "Ring" (29 January) was followed by Puccini's Yukon:

> The Girl of the wild Golden West
> Ruled her tavern with scriptural zest
>   Till she fell for the robber
>   Whom the miners would clobber,
> And her vehement tongue did the rest.

Classically: There was a young curate of Kew
> Who kept a tom cat in a pew.
>   He taught it to speak
>   Alphabetical Greek –
> But it never got further than μ.   mu.
>
> He said to it, "Pussy, you know,
> Is that really as far as you go?
>   I'm sure if you'd try
>   You would soon manage π pi.
> Or even o, or ρ ".   omikron, rho.

28th March.   **THE GOLIATH REHABILITATION SOCIETY.**

From the Hon. Secretary.   (date as postmark)
Dear John,

We were — or, rather, I was — delighted to receive your recent enquiry enclosing the excellent leaflet saying "Out of the Bible goes David slaying Goliath — it's far too 'Roy of the Rovers'".

Abraham had lived peacefully in the Philistines' land (Gen. 21.34), and Joshua 13.1-2 deals with "the borders of the Philistines" not yet conquered. Thus the Israelites were the aggressors in the long war, although they thought that they were still obeying the Lord after their great Exodus from Egypt. Their prophetess Deborah even sang that Jael (Judges 5.24; see 27.3) was "Blessed above women"!

Thus though the Philistines shared the general barbarism of their days their campaign was defensive so that it conformed with "just-war doctrine"; and Goliath, if no saint, at least spared the people "collateral damage" by proposing single combat between champions.

Of course David grew in wisdom, writing the penitential "Miserere" psalm following his murderous abduction of Bathsheba. Yet nice little boys don't throw stones; and readings of the Goliath episode need following by the hymn which honours Jesus as "Great David's Greater Son", showing that the human quest for God was only beginning.

Please join us and double our membership.

                    Yours sincerely,

(King David and King Solomon lived very merry lives,
With very many lady-friends and very many wives;
But when they both grew older and began to have some qualms,
King Solomon wrote <u>Proverbs</u> & King David wrote the <u>Psalms</u>.)
See 1 Kings 11.3; not 300 porcupines as a pupil once wrote.

<u>29</u>th March.   "THE BABY'S OPERA."

We sang this song from "The Baby's Opera" in junior school (or was it infants?) in the early 1930s. I rediscovered it "sixty years after" in a book, illustrated by Kate Greenaway, which was displayed in the City Art Gallery, Manchester.

1. There was a lady loved a swine.   "Honey!" said she;
   "Pig-hog, wilt thou be mine?"   "Hunc!" said he
2. "I'll build thee a silver sty, Honey!" said she;
   "And in it thou shalt lie!"   "Hunc!" said he.
3. "Pinned with a silver pin, Honey!" said she;
   "That thou mayest go out and in."   "Hunc!" said he
4. "Wilt thou have me now, Honey?" said she;
   "Speak, or my heart will break!"   "Hunc!" said he.

91

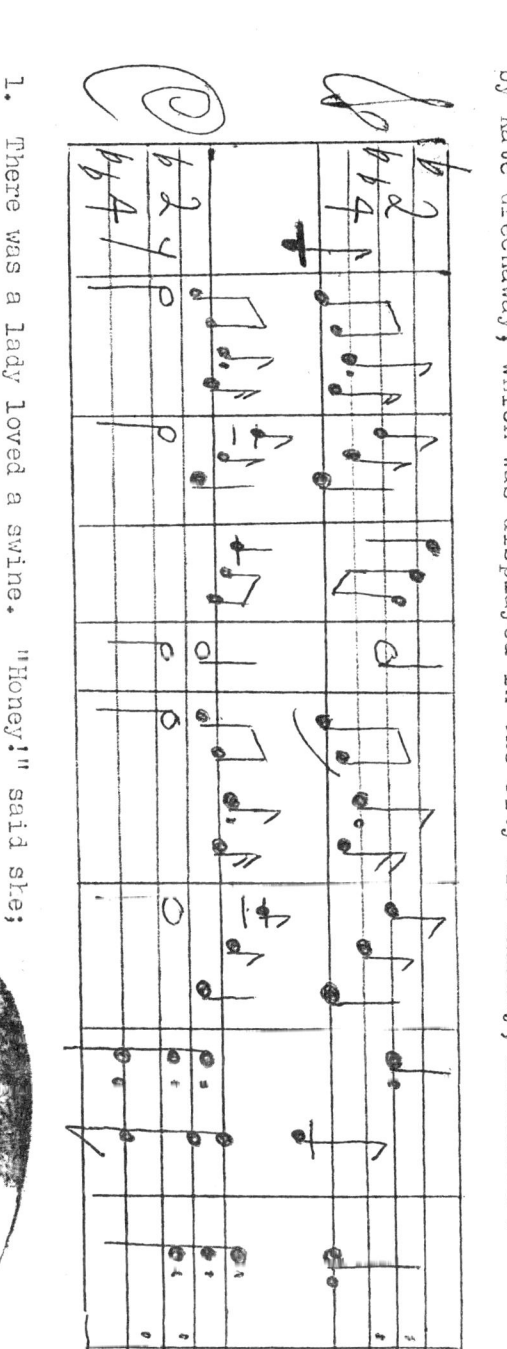

30th March. "Irish poets, learn your trade,
Sing whatever is well made.....

Yeats

Under bare Ben Bulben's head
In Drumcliff churchyard Yeats is laid.
An ancestor was rector there
Long years ago, a church stands near."

Well known by virtue of the lovely Innisfree lyric of his late twenties, with its evocative alliterations of lakeside sounds on an islet in dear County Sligo, William Butler Yeats (1865 - 1939) is Ireland's finest poet. Descended from in-comers from Cornwall and Yorkshire, and dividing his time between Sligo and London, he was drawn into the politics of Irish liberation via his friendship with Maud Gonne, who spurned his love, but who triggered his interest in seances which he shared with his wife Georgie Hyde-Lees whom at last he married when he was 52 and she was 25. (He had mistresses both before and after so doing.) Friendly too with other republicans, especially women - Lady Augusta Gregory, Eva Gore-Booth, Constance Markiewicz - he was from 1922 a quiet member of the Irish Senate, and in 1923 he won the Nobel Prize for literature. It has been truly said that poetry for Yeats came near to religion (as for Hardy who hinted that they modulated into each other). Poetry was knowledge beyond natural philosophy, as per Tennyson, "The Voice and the Peak".

A brief critical review of Yeats' late poem Under Ben Bulben:- The strangely-calm ending cited on this page embodies the poet's awareness of being in the deep republican tradition of Irish freedom, yet neither dominated by nor scorning the powerful Church. It shows Yeats as a Bard par excellence of Passion and of Mirth, his trade well-learnt and productive; for he wasn't physically earth-bound in his multi-faceted life.

This curiously attractive poem nevertheless links life to Place and to Nature, with its integrated feeling of life in community which enhances individuality rather than dulling it. Yeats is Ireland like Sibelius is Finland. He does alas slip up in ascribing "rest for the people of God" to Palmer, since it originates in Hebrews chapter 4 v. 9.

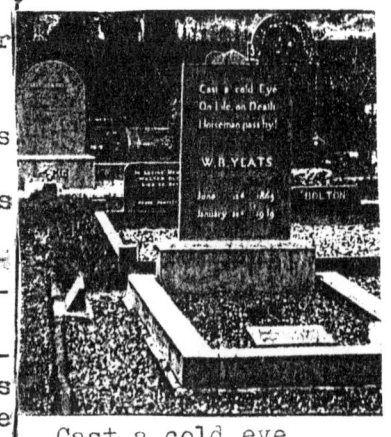

"...By his command
these words are cut:

Cast a cold eye
On life, on death.
Horseman, pass by!"

92

31st March.   Pioneers of Methodism.

The first "circuit-meeting" of the 18th-century Methodist movement within the Church of England took place at Todmorden Edge Farm in the town where I now live. Our Calder Valley was visited by John Wesley during his evangelistic tours of England. The octagonal chapel at the hill-village of Heptonstall is among the earliest places of worship used by the movement which seceded from the C. of E. after the Wesley brothers died. I recently sent this query to the "Church Times":

Blaenwern, one of the world's most marvellous tunes, to which the hymn "Love Divine" is sung, is by William Rowlands, who was Welsh, and lived from 1860-1937. Has anyone any further information about him?

Answers (28.7.2000) were:

William Penfro Rowlands was born at Llys Brân, Maenclochog, Pembrokeshire, on 19 April 1860. His second forename (meaning Pembroke) was, in fact, his bardic name. A schoolteacher by profession, he settled in Morriston, Swansea, in 1881, where he became precentor at Bethania Chapel, and then at Morriston Tabernacle, the largest chapel in Wales, from 1892-1927. For many years, he also conducted the Morriston United Choral Society. He died at his home in Morriston on 22 October 1937.

Blaenwern, the only tune by which he is now known, dates from the Welsh Revival of 1904-5. In England, its popularity began in the late 1940s, through various evangelistic campaigns, and broadcasting.
Bernard S. Massey
Redhill
Surrey

William Rowlands was born in the parish of Llys-y-Frân in 1860, in a cottage named Dan-y-Coed (under the trees). This was inhabited within living memory, but is now in ruins. The farm Blaenwern, which gives its name to the tune, is about three miles from here. When Rowlands was living in Morriston, his son, who had been seriously ill, was sent back to recover at Blaenwern, which lies at the foot of the Preseli hills. It is said that Rowlands wrote *Blaenwern* in thanksgiving for his son's recovery.

A memorial to Rowlands was unveiled in 1993, and stands next to the ruins of his birthplace, at the foot of what is now the impressive Llys-y-Frân dam. Some bars of the tune are cut into the slate of the upper section of the memorial.
(The Revd) John Livingstone
Llys-y-Frân
Pembrokeshire

Blaenwern first appeared in 1915 in *Cân a Moliant (Song and Praise)*. It seems to have become known in England and elsewhere after being issued on a single-sheet leaflet in the 1920s.
Gwilym Beechey (Dr)
Hull

John Wesley's brother Charles was the 18th child in the family — some died young — and was also a travelling preacher; but his "great change" or spiritual experience (21.5.1738) made writing his chief work. He wrote, according to the excellent "Penguin Book of Hymns" (1990) at least 8989 religious poems. "Love divine, all loves excelling", his fine hymn of personal devotion, was written to the "Fairest Isle" tune of Purcell. Parry and Stanford composed alternatives; "Blaenwern" however is generally preferred now.

Interestingly the four most popular Welsh hymn-tunes were written by laymen. R.H.Prichard ("Hyfrydol", "Alleluia sing to Jesus") was a weaver's assistant; J.Hughes ("Cwm Rhondda", "Guide me O thou great Redeemer") was a railway official; & Joseph Parry ("Aberystwyth", "Jesu lover of my soul") was an ironmaster and musician.

1st April.   B R I E F   E N C O U N T E R.

The Famous Meeting of Geordie Muldoon (Jonty's Great-Grandfather) and the Bishop of Durham in the compartment of a 3rd-class railway carriage, April 1st.1887. Mr. Muldoon was unaware that his companion was a Man of the Cloth, as the bishop was travelling in mufti, without his distinctive dog-collar, plum-coloured shirt, and pectoral cross (it was his day off). Mr. Muldoon, wanting to appear polite, opened the conversation by remarking on the weather...

Geordie: Nice day the day, marra, are ye gannin' far?...

Bishop: Not very far, my good man, only as far as Durham City...

Geordie: By, thon's a bonny place, mind, the cathedral's better than wor church at Eppleton, I hev to admit, but mind, the bishop's a bit queer, like...

Bishop: Queer? What's queer about him then?...

Geordie: Wi man, 'e gans around like Lord Muck wearin' one o' them funny pointed hats like owld-fashioned soldiers' helmets, an' the same fella wears a long white bit o' clobber what luks like a night-gown, an' 'e has the cheek to tell us aal that we're sinners if we don't gan to church of a Sunday...if that's not queer, what is?...

Bishop: Now listen here, young man, I happen to be the bishop of Durham, and I don't take kindly to your remarks, not even on my day off...

Geordie: An' I'm Napoleon Bonaparte, marra...now try an' pull me other leg forra change...ye cannit kid me that the bishop o' Durham wud be sittin' in a 3rd-class railway carriage, bonny lad, so don't try...

Bishop: I shall be in touch with your vicar, young man, All Saints Eppleton I think you said...

(If you read the above this morning, April Fool; if later, may I say I'm not satisfied with its historicity. Today's folly may stem from several sources including the Roman Hilaria (25.3); the Indian Holi (31.3); the Celtic Lud, god of humour; & Venus. In Scotland it's Gowkie (Cuckoo) Day; in France, poisson d'Avril. Apprentices are sent, to their dismay, for strap-oil; TV producers reap spaghetti in Ticino; thrush-eggs are sought in hedges; tails & "Kick Me" signs are attached to coats. (Orkney holds Tailing Day tomorrow.)

2nd April. In 1996 this day was Tuesday in Holy Week, so I feel it's time to think about Hugh Montefiore's question in "The Probability of God" (SPCK, 1985) on why anyone should in this secular society be interested in Jesus...without a prior conviction about the reality of God. Many say religious feeling is a subjective enshrinement of inadequate individuals' needs; Christians reply that all humans are of themselves inadequate! Let me summarise the indications of God's reality (I don't say existence, which means standing out, for I and many believe the Sacred Mystery to be the Ground from which things stand out.)

1. Cosmological argument from creation; the Universe could not create itself, since nothing can come from nothing. "E Nihilo Nihil". Also since things move, motion must stem from a Prime Mover. See also 15.9.

2. Design argument; Nature contains some amazingly precise aspects, e.g. the masses and motions of suns, stars, planets, moons and comets are selfsustaining over aeons. This can't be chance.

3. Teleological argument; evolution implies that the Universe is developing. The appearance of life and consciousness cannot be accounted for by mechanical interactions of dead matter. Purpose is implicit (see T. de Chardin's essay: "Man's place in the Universe"; & articles on Anthropic Principle.")

4. Moral argument; in addition to consciousness we have a moral sense, however conditioned by our backgrounds it may be. Hastings Rashdall, late Dean of Carlisle, said "A moral ideal can exist only in a mind; and absolute moral ideal can exist only in a Mind from which is derived, or to which is related, all Creation." Beyond all local variations in morality there appears a general if vague absolute ideal that "right" is better than "wrong". As my late friend the Revd. Harry Fawcett remarked, "Our own highest values and aspirations are not simply underwritten by the individuals who express them or have witnessed to them." This links to

5. Spiritual Experience argument; Millions have testified to such direct contact with the Spiritual Reality, as stated in the language of their own traditions. These experiences cannot be fully communicated to people who haven't had them, although poets (7 February, 21 March), musicians, ministers and guides make valiant efforts, not without some success.

(6. Ontological argument; St Anselm held that "If we assert that God is 'something-then-which-nothing-greater-can-be-thought-of', then such a Thing cannot exist in human understanding alone, but must have objective existence." The validity of this has long been controverted. I think it testifies to our sense of the Ineffable.)

– – – – – – –

All this can seem "too clever by half" in the face of the evil and sorrow in the world; yet the indications cannot be gainsaid.

3rd April.   A R T I S T I C   I N T E R L U D E.

Governmental Spending on Arts &
Museums, £ per head in mid-1990s
(from an Arts Council report '98)

Finland	59.2
Germany	56.5
France	37.8
Holland	30.3
UK	16.6
Eire	5.6
USA	3.8

Picture: Sibelius at Lake Saima.

- - - - - - - - - - -

Cultural background needs considering when comparing these figures. In the USA there is generous private patronage for the arts, whereas public opinion in Europe tends to expect public authorities to ensure funding. Local factors operate between nations; Ireland until recently was poor, whereas Germany's strong musical tradition of leading composers and proud former states ensures its prominence. The UK appears to move towards a "mixed economy". But Finland excels even Germany! This nation only gained independence in 1919 and its culture has helped build national identity.

As Wordsworth is to the English Lake District, and Yeats to Sligo, so is Sibelius to Finland, which is immensely proud of numbering one of the world's very greatest symphonists among its sons. His _Finlandia_ rallied resistance to Tsarist oppression at the turn of the 19th century, and his works on themes from the _Kalevala_ epic have popularised the Finnish mythology.

- - - - - - - - - - -

"What is Romantic is imperishable. It always has been, and always will be, as long as people inhabit the earth."

"I am myself a man of the orchestra. You must judge me from my orchestral works...I am not legitimately married to the orchestra; I am its lover."

"The impressions of childhood form our most precious inheritance in life." (The call of the crane).."the Leitmotiv of my life."

"All great men - each in his own way - are deeply religious.. The essence of man's being is his striving for God."(Sibelius).

4th April. "YE PRESENCES OF NATURE in the sky
And on the earth! Ye visions of the hills!
And Souls of lonely places!" (Wordsworth, *Prelude* I)

("And the Lord answered me, and said, 'Write the vision and make it plain...For the vision is yet for an appointed time, But at the end it shall speak and not lie: Though it tarry, wait for it; because it shall surely come, it will not tarry.'" – Old Testament, Book of Habakkuk, chapter 2 verse 3.)

William Ralph Inge (Dean of St Paul's Cathedral 1911-34) wrote books on "Christian Mysticism" and "Mysticism in Religion", as well as many on other topics whereby he was nicknamed, fairly or otherwise, the Gloomy Dean. He distinguished between healthy yet ecstatic Vision in which we have waking thoughts which we know do not ourselves initiate, and poetic imagination in which our imagination is active, and hallucinations under organic disturbance. Vision "is, or claims to be, a temporary enhancement, not a partial disintegration, of the mental faculties...That perfectly sane people often experience such visions there is no manner of doubt."

Citing Plato's 7th Letter which testifies to the 'leaping spark' of divine inspiration, and which rues the silence of God which is and always has been a great trial to humanity, Inge concludes that genuine mystics are rightly or wrongly "convinced that they have been in touch with objective reality, with the supreme spiritual Power behind the world of our surface consciousness. If they are right, this intuition means that reality is spiritual." (Compare Tennyson: "Depend on it, the spiritual is the real"; see also "Religion" in "Six Tennyson Essays" by Charles Tennyson, 1972.)

– – – – –

It was formative of my thinking as a physical-science lecturer to read Dostoevsky's masterpiece "The Brothers Karamazov" which is a work of theology in the context of a Russian blockbuster-novel. After the trauma of Ivan's rebellion from orthodoxy by reason of children's suffering, which leads to Alyosha's claim that Jesus' universal love alone can bear fruit in universal forgiveness and harmony, we read Father Zossima's discourses in which the Russian monk is made to say that science handles only what is subject to the senses. The spiritual realm, the higher part of our nature, is scorned and dismissed, even with triumph and hatred. (Happily many scientists now go beyond the 19th-century mechanical views which F.W. Robertson in 1852 had derided as "the lifeless scepticism of science". Earlier in "Karamazov", in the Fr Ferapont chapter, another monk Fr Paissy holds that influential scientist had criticised divinity but had looked only at the parts, to the neglect of the whole, which stands firm as ever. (12.6 Pascal) Attempts to improve on Jesus' ideals have but yielded monstrosities.

Good Friday 5th April 1996. The evidence of Scripture plus the Roman historian Josephus establishes that Jesus was put to death on Pilate's reluctant orders to appease the then Jewish establishment which was threatened by his presence. (It cannot be over stressed that very many Jewish people have no part or lot in this!) A recent writer called Good Friday "The blackest day in the Christian calendar"; but it contains no black days (though there's a fair sprinkling in nearly all human lives). Yet "Joy cometh in the morning" (Psalm 30⁶). Risking a flippant analogy, Good Friday and Easter Day aren't like a two-leg football-match with the Devil winning 1-0 today only to lose 2-0 on the Day of Resurrection. Christians call today Good because the love of Jesus overcame the world's worst evil; he told the penitent thief on the next cross "Today thou shalt be in Paradise with me."

Kenneth Leech, in his 1994 Lent book "We preach Christ Crucified" (DLT), has pointed out that the older the Good Friday hymn, the stronger its portrayal of the Victory of the Cross. Venantius Fortunatus was a 6th-century Italian who ultimately became Bishop of Poitiers. His poems include two fine Latin hymns for a "Procession of a Relic of the True Cross". One is known in translation as "The Royal Banners Forward Go"; and here is the other as published in full in the Victorian "Old Standard Edition of 'Hymns Ancient and Modern'". Though it sets out the "Scheme of Salvation" in terms of "literal Adam and Eve", its power resides in the spiritual force of that tradition:

SING, my tongue, the glorious battle,
 Sing the last, the dread affray;
O'er the Cross, the Victor's trophy,
 Sound the high triumphal lay,
How, the pains of death enduring,
 Earth's Redeemer won the day.

He, our Maker, deeply grieving
 That the first-made Adam fell,
When he ate the fruit forbidden
 Whose reward was death and hell,
Mark'd e'en then this Tree the ruin
 Of the first tree to dispel.

Thus the work for our salvation
 He ordained to be done;
To the traitor's art opposing
 Art yet deeper than his own;
Thence the remedy procuring
 Whence the fatal wound begun.

Therefore, when at length the fulness
 Of the appointed time was come,
He was sent, the world's Creator,
 From the FATHER's heavenly home,
And was found in human fashion,
 Offspring of the Virgin's womb.

Lo! He lies, an Infant weeping,
 Where the narrow manger stands,

While the Mother-Maid His members
 Wraps in mean and lowly bands,
And the swaddling clothes is winding
 Round His helpless Feet and Hands.

PART 2.

Now the thirty years accomplish'd
 Which on earth He will'd to see,
Born for this, He meets His Passion,
 Gives Himself an Offering free;
On the Cross the LAMB is lifted,
 There the Sacrifice to be.

There the nails and spear He suffers,
 Vinegar, and gall, and reed;
From His sacred Body pierced
 Blood and Water both proceed;
Precious flood, which all creation
 From the stain of sin hath freed.

Faithful Cross, above all other
 One and only noble Tree,
None in foliage, none in blossom,
 None in fruit thy peer may be;
Sweetest wood, and sweetest iron;
 Sweetest weight is hung on thee.

Bend, O lofty Tree, thy branches,
 Thy too rigid sinews bend;
And awhile the stubborn hardness,
 Which thy birth bestow'd, suspend;
And the Limbs of Heav'n's high Monarch
 Gently on thine arms extend.

Thou alone wast counted worthy
 This world's ransom to sustain,
That a shipwreck'd race for ever
 Might a port of refuge gain,
With the sacred Blood anointed
 Of the LAMB for sinners slain.

Praise and honour to the FATHER,
 Praise and honour to the SON,
Praise and honour to the SPIRIT,
 Ever THREE and ever ONE,
One in might, and One in glory,
 While eternal ages run.

The "two tree" legend was developed in medieval times even to the point of suggesting that the Holy Cross was made of the wood of the old tree. Manchester City Art Gallery has a Flemish picture with Jesus' blood falling on to Adam's skull at the foot of the Cross. With wiser caution some old service-books have a "Preface" which addresses God "Who in the mystery of the Cross hast ordered the work of man's salvation, that where death had its origin, there life should find resurrection..."

98

6th April.   **Bridging The Gap.**

After Good Friday comes Holy Saturday or Easter Eve; often called Easter Saturday to the annoyance of pedants who say that comes a week later — but this battle is hardly worth fighting. The holiday-crowds hope for warm sun for their first long weekend since Christmastide, yet those who recalled the Crucifixion yesterday can find themselves in a spiritual state of "marking time". I and others who see Christianity as the underlying national faith which is not exclusive to organised churches can find ourselves in a muddle involving both aspects! After a death there comes a day of remembering, and we can end up by believing not in God but in yesterday; whereas the events of so long ago would by now be of no account if they were without present-day effect! But "We are justified" wrote Abelard in his Moral Theory of the Atonement, i.e. the healing of our alienations from self, society and God, "in that by the life and death of His Son He has so bound us to Himself that love so kindled will shrink from nothing for His sake". (cf.13.1])

The Creed says Jesus after burial "descended into hell" to rescue the perishing; and this has been the focus of Easter Eve observances. Icons of the Eastern Orthodox churches portray it. Is there such a harrowing of the hells of today's world? Sheila Cassiday's impressive book "Good Friday People" (DLT, 1991), written in the wake of her own ordeal in Pinochet's Chile, goes into this and expounds the faith that not only is God with us humans as we suffer, but also the divine presence is one of victory — see Isaiah 63.9 which Arthur Coxe versified to include:
"I, that of the raging heathen Trod the winepress all alone
Now in victor-garlands wreathen, Coming to redeem Mine own."
(English Hymnal, No. 108).

So, in the old language of 2 Peter 1.19, "We also have a more sure word of prophecy...take heed, as unto a light that shineth in a dark place, until the day dawn, and the day star arise in your hearts".

— — — — — —

(To avoid theological overkill I made no Palm Sunday entry. I hope nevertheless that this extract from the Wiltshire Gazette in Spring 1993 may please: "The donkey failed to arrive for the Palm Sunday procession at St Peter's Church, Chippenham. The procession was led by the Vicar, the Revd. Jeremy Bray.")

7th April 1996. **An Easter Greeting :-**

Joy to the World for Easter Sunday; Resurrexit!

Whereas Christmas is the most "popular" religious festival in Western Europe, Easter is the prime celebration in the "Eastern Orthodox" lands. Rimsky-Korsakov's "Russian Easter Festival Overture" or tone-poem of 1888 portrays not only the church festival but also the associated "pagan merrymaking". In his autobiography "My Musical Life" the composer wrote that "The rather slow start on the theme 'Let God Arise'...alternating with the churchy theme 'An Angel Wailed' appeared to me in its beginning as if it were the ancient prophecy of Isaiah concerning the resurrection of Christ." (He seems to refer to Isaiah chs. 53 & 63.) The gloomy colours "seemed to depict the holy sepulchre which had shone with ineffable light...In the transition to the allegro 'Let them also that hate Him flee before Him' (we recognise the) holiday mood of the Orthodox Church...In this overture were thus combined reminiscences of the ancient prophecy, of the Gospel narrative, and also a general picture of the Easter service with its...Easter loaves and twists and glowing tapers - how far a cry from the philosophic and socialistic teaching of Christ."

(Those last two adjectives were expunged by the Communist censors from the 4th and 5th editions in Russian, thus proving themselves less tolerant than their Tsarist predecessors who let the words stand! Was this materialism the Soviets' weakness?

On the flyleaf of the score is printed a quotation from the 'Let God Arise' psalm (R.C.67, Reformed 68), the resurrection story by St Mark, and some words of the composer himself: "And the joyful tidings were spread abroad over all the world, and they who hated Him fled before Him, vanishing like smoke. 'Resurrexit' sing the choirs of angels in heaven, to the sound of the archangels' trumpets and to the fluttering of the wings of the seraphim. 'Resurrexit' sing the priests in the temples, in the midst of clouds of incense, by the light of innumerable candles, to the chiming of triumphant bells." And in his book Rimsky-Korsakov writes that to appreciate the overture "the hearer should have attended Easter morning service at least once...in a cathedral thronged with people from all walks of life..."

His tomb of late the threefold guard
Of watch and stone and seal had barred;
But now, in pomp and triumph high,
He comes from death to victory.

(Hymn 126 Old Standard A&M)

8th April. **Tins, Cans, Kegs, Drums, and Pails.**

In 1943, whilst World War 2 ravaged much of the earth, the Ministry of Supply perpetrated "Statutory Rules and Orders 1943 No. 1216" which read, _inter alia_:

"1. The Control of Tins Cans Kegs Drums and Packaging Pails (No. 5) Order, 1942(a), as varied by the Control of Tins Cans Kegs Drums and Packaging Pails (No. 6) Order, 1942(b), the Control of Tins Cans Kegs Drums and Packaging Pails (No. 7) Order, 1942(c), the Control of Tins Cans Kegs Drums and Packaging Pails (No. 8) Order, 1942(d), and the Control of Tins Cans Kegs Drums and Packaging Pails (No. 9) Order, 1942(e), is hereby further varied in the Third Schedule thereto (which is printed at p.2 of the printed (No. 6) Order), in 'Part II, Commodities other than Food', by substituting for the reference '2A' therein, the reference '2A(1)'; and by deleting therefrom the reference '2B'."

I cite this from Sir Ernest Gowers' digression on Legal English, in "The Complete Plain Words" (HMSO 1954, Pelican 1962), stressing that legal draftsmen have a different job than do officials. Gowers quotes a correspondent of the _Spectator_, 17 September 1943, who comments on the Explanatory Note to the above, which reads: "The above Order enables tin-plate to be used for tobacco and snuff tins other than cutter-lid tobacco tins". The writer commends the "sound and time-honoured principle that a Government Department never explains", and adds "Do they suppose we can't read plain English?"

"Legal English" is, of course, a sub-species of the language which must elevate unambiguity above all other considerations, so that the "Rags (Wiping Rags)(Maximum Charges) Order 1943" had to tackle the question "What constitutes a Wiping Rag?" It declared that "'Rags' means any worn-out, disused, discarded or waste fabric or material made wholly or mainly from wool, cotton, silk, rayon or flax or from any mixture thereof. 'Wiping rags' means rags each one of which is not less than 144 square inches in size and has been trimmed and washed and is suitable for use as a wiping rag."

Gowers mentions that "In the summer of 1945, it appears, the President of the Board of Trade, moved perhaps by compassion for those who follow what must be a spiritually unsatisfying occupation, decided to increase the profit allowed for washing wiping-rags." An Amendment Order was accordingly made.

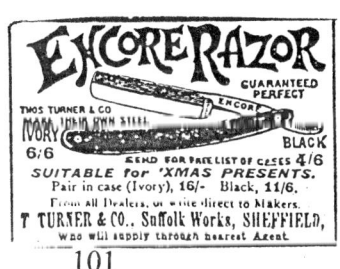

9th April. **God Save Great George Our King.**

So ran a version of the National Anthem in early Hanoverian days. Its danceable galliard-tune is perhaps the world's best-known melody, and is so overworked as to make unbiased assessment impossible. Rooted in phrases in that metre in popular airs, and in a John Bull piece for keyboard (1619) following Ravenscroft's carol (1611) "Remember O thou man" (which the famous fictional Mellstock Quire sang in Hardy's novel 'Under the Greenwood Tree'), it took definitive form by mid-18th century as a result of dissemination through the printing-press. Use by Beethoven, Brahms, Debussy, Haydn and Weber shows its ubiquity.

Similarly its words accrue from assorted watchwords - "God save the king" is biblical (1 Sam.10.24 as in Handel's anthem "Zadok the priest") - and although the supporters of the exiled James II and his son had drinking-glasses engraved "Send him victorious, Happy and glorious, Soon to reign over us, God save the king", it was the pro-Hanoverian English public that popularised it for their anti-Jacobite cause:

> "Lord grant that Marshal Wade
> May by Thy mighty aid
> Victory bring!
> May he sedition hush
> And like a torrent rush
> Rebellious Scots to crush:
> God save the king!"

(Wade is remembered for his roads and bridges that were built to help control the Stewart loyalists; but after the early victories of Bonnie Prince Charlie in 1745 he was replaced by "Butcher" Cumberland who won at Culloden.)

The 3-verse poem has received much criticism for its narrow sympathies, alleged bellicosity, and devotion to a particular constitutional system namely monarchy; but for good or ill it seems entrenched. Parodies are resented yet few can resist the version composed by the "Red Vicar of Thaxted", Conrad Noel:

"O Lord our God arise, Guard our securities, Don't let them fall! Confound all party hacks Save those my party backs; And let the Income Tax Be option-al."

The English Hymnal (No. 560) omits the standard second verse, but adds all three verses of W.E. Hickson's aspiring "God bless our native land". Songs of Praise (No. 318) gives the Privy Council's "Official Peace Version" - see foot opposite.

10th April.   "THAT DRIPPING MONARCH".

It is difficult to envisage a performance of the national anthem in more risible circumstances than when George III took to the sea during his stay in Weymouth at the time of the French Revolution, for health reasons. Fanny Burney noted that "The King bathes, and with great success; a machine follows the Royal one into the sea, filled with fiddlers who play 'God save the King' as His Majesty takes his plunge!

With the benefit of oral traditions in his native Dorset, the novelist Thomas Hardy enlarged on this in Chapter 33 of 'The Trumpet-Major'. "It was the 3rd of September", he stated, "but the King's watering-place still retained its summer aspect. The royal bathing-machine had been drawn out just as Bob reached Gloucester Buildings, and he waited a minute, in the lack of other distraction, to look on. Immediately that the King's machine had entered the water a group of florid men with fiddles, violoncellos, a trombone, and a drum came forward, packed themselves into another machine that was in waiting, and were drawn out into the waves in the King's rear. All that was to be heard for a few minutes were the slow pulsations of the sea; and then a deafening noise burst from the interior of the second machine, with power enough to split the boards asunder; it was the condensed mass of musicians inside, striking up the strains of 'God save the King', as his Majesty's head rose from the water. Bob took off his hat and waited till the end of the performance, which, intended as a pleasant surprise to George III by the loyal burghers, was possibly in the watery circumstances tolerated rather than desired by that dripping monarch."

(9th April, continued.)

E.H. 560: "God bless our native land,
May heaven's protecting hand
Still guard our shore;
May peace her power extend,
Foe be transformed to friend,
And Britain's rights depend
On war no more."

S.P. 318: "Of many a race & birth,
From utmost ends of earth,
God save us all!
Bid strife and hatred cease,
Bid hope & joy increase,
Spread universal peace,
God save us all!"

103

11th April. "Scots wha hae wi' Wallace bled":-

Robert Burns wrote his famous Ode in shock after the rebel Thomas Muir had been sentenced in 1793 to 14 years' transportation for sedition and distributing Thomas Paine's <u>The Rights of Man</u>. Certainly Scotland had long been colonised by the English; and the 1707 Treaty of Union was a very unequal affair, still resented by some Scots in spite of the recent devolution which stops short of total independence. Union was pressed on to the near-bankrupt (some would say financially-sabotaged) Scotland by the English who did not demur to bribe the Scottish negotiating commissioners. In 1704 the Scottish Parliament had insisted on choosing its own successor to Queen Anne, and this threat to the merged crowns was felt by the English establishment to put the "Protestant succession" at risk to the Stuarts who had won at Killiecrankie in 1689 and whose persistence led to the Jacobite risings in 1715 and 1745.

The remarkably youthful succession to the Crown of Scotland is little known south of the border, and may represent the relative **weakness** of that royal line. Prior to Robert Bruce (1306-29) Malcolm IV (1153-65) became king at age 11; Alexander III (1249-86) acceded at 8; and Margaret the Maid of Norway (1286-90) did likewise at 3. David II (1329-71) followed the Bruce at age 5 years; and in the 15th and 16th centuries there were seven child-monarchs in succession:-

James I	(1406-37)	at age	12.
James II	(1437-60)	" "	6.
James III	(1460-88)	" "	9.
James IV	(1488-1513)	" "	15.
James V	(1513-41)	" "	17 months.
Mary	(1542-67)	" "	6 days!
James VI	(1567-1625)	" "	3.

(The "financial sabotage" above took the from of a withdrawal of consent by the English Parliament to the Darien development-scheme for central America, fow which William III had granted a charter. This forced an English and Dutch withdrawal, whereupon practically all Scots liquid capital was lost, & Edinburgh rioted.)

"Bonnets of Bonny Dundee"-Daily Telegraph 27.7.1989

IN GLORIOUS REMEMBERANCE
of John Graham of Claverhouse, Viscount Dundee (Iain Dubh Nan Cath) & all those clansmen of the Royal army who gave thier lives for Scotland and King James during the victory over the rebel forces of the Dutch usurper in the Pass of Killiecrankie 27th July 1689. "Scotland and thou didst in each other live."

12th April.   By Loch Rannoch and Lochaber.

The West Highland Railway to Fort William and the fishing port of Mallaig is a single-track spur after leaving the Glasgow area suburban network at Craigendoran. It has lost some of its glory since the days of steam, when the old station[1] at Fort William, since replaced in order to ease traffic congestion in the town, was on the very bank of Loch Linnhe (pronounced Lynne). The visitor - and all should make the journey - will find Jacobite memorabilia in the town museum, including medallions struck for Henry Cardinal York, last of the Stuart line, calling himself Henry IX — but not by the will of the people. Another amazing artefact is a leather bag in which mail from St Kilda, when that island was populated, was put on the tide to be picked up from the shore of the Isle of Lewis. Fourth-class mail it would seem.

The passenger beyond "the Fort" can enjoy a generous half-day at Glenfinnan where the Jacobite standard was raised in 1745, to see the visitors' centre, the monument, the lochside hotel, the church, the rail-station museum, and the viaduct which gave its designer the nickname Concrete Bob (Macalpine.) Then there is Britain's most westerly station at Arisaig; Morar with silver sands, Scotland's deepest loch wherein hides shy Morag, sister to the Loch Ness monster, the lochside church where Eclipse Day 11 August 1999 was celebrated with a Creation Mass and garden-party, Tom McClean's museum of adventure - he rowed the Atlantic in the 60s, crossed it in a bubble-yacht around 1980, and is "King of Rockall" on which rocky outpost of the UK he spent 40 days in 1985, - and the stone in the cemetary a mile north of the village which reads "JOHN SAINT, HUSBAND OF GLADYS PERFECT" - (True!); and finally Mallaig itself, with famous views of the Small (or Cocktail) Isles which include Eigg and Rhum, and of the jagged Cuillins of Skye.

Such a railway through such a land inevitably has an old magic and many a rich tradition. John Thomas' book "The West Highland Railway" (David & Charles, 1984) says that on 18.7.53 two trains were scheduled to pass one another at Ardlui loops. At the last moment it was realised that both trains were too long for the loops; but the staff solved the problem by using the station siding. Actually two 12-vehicle trains (engine & tender being counted as a vehicle) could be got past each other using a loop that would hold 8 vehicles only, even if there is no siding. How can this be done? Answer overleaf.

B 6-car.   A   X   Y   H   K 6-car.

(1. see 21.10)

__13th April.__   __Trains passing at Ardlui, 13.8.59.__
(The engine on the right is heading south to Glasgow.)

Solution to problem: A moves to right, depositing B on X, and links to H. A & H go leftwards through Y leaving K there. A & H go through X pushing B well to right, then go thro' Y pushing K well to left. A runs to B. Trains reform via loop, & proceed.

Two true tales: When the SS 'Politician' was wrecked on rocks by Eriskay, and its cargo of whisky was looted, the railway was among the routes south for the contraband. Excisemen stopped a train "on suspicion" at Glenfinnan. Whilst they were searching the compartments, one of them saw a blinding flash from the engine. On asking the driver to explain, he was told "It must have been the spirits of our ancestors, Officer."

Then in the early days the 'Ghost' or night freight train to Fort William was coming off the moor at Corrour summit one dawn. The driver slowed down so that the fireman could collect the tablet which allowed the train to use the next stretch of "single line"; then he accelerated briskly down towards the Fort. As the couplings took up the slack caused by the speed-check, there was a great deal of jerking, so much that the rear-most link snapped. The guard in his brake-van had not cleared the summit, and the van slowed down, stopped, and ran backwards, gathering speed all the time, till the signalman at Rannoch saw the runaway vehicle, which the rulebook required him to divert into a siding and derail. Since he knew the guard would be on board and would be killed, he let the van continue. So did the Gorton signalman; and the vehicle ran on until stopped by a rising gradient south of Bridge of Orchy, a free run of 25 miles. The local stationmaster found the guard asleep and shook him awake!

<u>14th April.</u>   "I Do It."

That was Archbishop Michael Ramsey's reply when he was asked if he thought that it was appropriate to take political topics into the pulpit. On the other hand Tory M.P. Douglas (now Lord) Hurd told the Church of England's General Synod in February 1988 that "the Church's territory lies firmly within the realm of the maintenance and restoration of moral and spiritual values".

Kenneth Leech, commenting on this in his book "Care and Conflict" (DLT, 1990) notes that "'moral' tends to be restricted to the areas of sexuality, the family, and law and order, 'spiritual' to those of the inner world and life after death. Major issues such as peace, justice, the defence of the poor and oppressed, are labelled 'political'."

Leech adds, from his own experience as a vicar, that "one of the most damaging features of recent church life has been the reduction of pastoral ministry to a counselling role." "In our society the counsellor, the social worker and the therapist pick up the pieces, care for the casualties...They represent in secular form what has already happened to Christian pastoral ministry. My experience has been that it is because of its role as...gap-filler...that the church is valued in our society ...To (accept this role) would be a disastrous theological and political mistake."

<u>Long-lost Spire of Old St Paul's Cathedral London.</u>

Quoting Canon Widdrington who as long ago as 1913 said "The Church has been too long the Church Quiescent here on earth, content to serve as the scavenger of the capitalist system", Ken Leech stresses that Hurd's view, often called traditionalist, is anything but that! "If you had told any typical Christian thinker in any century from the 12th to the 16th that religion had nothing to do with economics...he would have regarded you as either a heretic or a lunatic". (M. Reckitt, 1935.) "The idea of a shepherd has nothing to do with clinical pastoral methods. It is a ministry of public care, defence, and leadership as in Ezekiel 34." Even the statement in "Faith in the City", p.55, is highly suspect theologically:- 'Christians can hardly be expected to propose a realistic alternative to the entire economic system'! - "For there is a persistent strain in Christian history which claims that the gospel is actually about an alternative vision/kingdom/world."

15th April. "What are schoolgirls for?"

When a young friend posed the mischievous question "If a schoolgirl can't be deliberativly provocative, what's the point of being one?" I found it hard to reply without sounding altogether too pompous. Cats, I guessed, exist to catch mice, and mice are there to feed cats; but that's a circle which begs the question "Why have either?" Short of entering the field of high theology, I can but seek such a circle which identifies the proper purpose and place for the girls in question. This must centre on the development of their powers via the meeting of their needs, alongside the fostering of the caring elements in their nature via the giving of love to them.

Exactly the same applies to schoolboys, but the competitive "macho" attitudes of the West make it difficult to apply such language. Of course deeds speak louder than words; also we should try and fortify young people to cope with life's difficulties and hard knocks.

This responsibility needs sharing by **family**, friends, community, church, and schools. Too much of it is being left to teachers, who in turn are "put upon" by national government which, seeking to correct predecessors' neglect, sets too much store on assessment-tests, "league tables", and bureaucratic documents. This is too mechanical - it smacks of Messrs Gradgrind & McChoakumchild in Dickens' "Hard Times" - and a suspicion lurks that pupils are having self-centred competitiveness built into them by the emphasis on marks and grades, to the detriment of valuing knowledge and wisdom for their own sakes. As Tennyson wrote in his first "Locksley Hall" poem: Knowledge comes, but wisdom lingers, and I linger on the shore,
     And the individual withers, and the world is more and more.

Justice to the young entails better support for all schools & pupils than hitherto, and a harmony of public and private sectors to foster equality of provision, due allowance being made for spending on musical instruments and other specialist items.

Did the senior girl who posed the question intend to do me the kindness of making me define my thoughts? I'd like to think so, but I have honest doubts. I should have set her a 500-word essay on her own topic!

16th April:

On this day in 1746 the Jacobite army of Bonnie Prince Charlie gathered for its last stand on Culloden Moor, away from Glenfinnan where his standard had been raised on 19 August 1745:

There is mist on the mountain, and night on the vale,
But more loud than the sleep of the sons of the Gael.
A stranger commanded—it sunk on the land,
It has frozen each heart, and benumb'd every hand!

The dirt and the target lie sordid with dust,
The bloodless claymore is but redden'd with rust;
On the hill or the glen if a gun should appear,
It is only to war with the heath-cock or deer.

The deeds of our sires if our bards should rehearse,
Let a blush or a blow be the meed of their verse!
Be mute every string, and be hush'd every tone,
That shall bid us remember the fame that is flown.

But the dark hours of night and of slumber are past,
The morn on our mountains is dawning at last;
Glenaladale's peaks are illumed with the rays,
And the streams of Glenfinnan leap bright in the blaze.

O high-minded Moray!—the exiled—the dear!—
In the blush of the dawning the Standard uprear!
Wide, wide on the winds of the north let it fly,
Like the sun's latest flash when the tempest is nigh!

So wrote Sir Walter Scott in his novel *Waverley*, in which the hero's sister Flora McIvor sang this ballad to the strains of an old Highland battle-song which she played on her harp as she sat on a "mossy fragment of rock" near a mountain stream with waterfall. Such romantic war-cries are no fruitful way forward, yet I cannot but enjoy Scott's evocation of the emotions of the Royal Stuart cause as it went down to defeat on the morrow of the 25th birthday of the victorious Duke of Cumberland,—"Sweet William" to the English, Butcher Cumberland to the Scots because of the brutal Harrying of the Glens after the battle.

Scott is still honoured for his undoubted good qualities which cohered with his respectable, reasonable, reconciling, yet not altogether well-informed loyalty to the Hanoverian monarchs:

BREATHES there the man, with soul so dead,
Who never to himself has said,
This is my own, my native land!....
The wretch, concentrated all in self,
Living, shall forfeit fair renown,
And, doubly dying, shall go down
To the vile dust, from whence he sprung,
Unwept, unhonour'd, and unsung.

Ye sons of the strong, when that dawning shall break,
Need the harp of the aged remind you to wake?
That dawn never beam'd on your forefather's eye,
But it roused each high chieftain to vanquish or die.

O, sprung from the Kings who in Islay kept state,
Proud chiefs of Clan Ranald, Glengarry, and Sleat!
Combine like three streams from one mountain of snow,
And resistless in union rush down on the foe!

True son of Sir Evan, undaunted Lochiel,
Place thy targe on thy shoulder and burnish thy steel!
Rough Keppoch, give breath to thy bugle's bold swell,
Till far Corryarick resound to the knell!

Stern son of Lord Kenneth, high chief of Kintail,
Let the stag in thy standard bound wild in the gale!
May the race of Clan Gillean, the fearless and free,
Remember Glenlivat, Harlaw, and Dundee!

Let the clan of grey Fingon, whose offspring has given
Such heroes to earth and such martyrs to heaven,
Unite with the race of renown'd Rorri More,
To launch the long galley, and stretch to the oar.

By Yarrow's streams still let me stray,
Though none should guide my feeble way;
Still feel the breeze down Ettrick break,
Although it chill my wither'd cheek;
Still lay my head by Teviot Stone,
Though there, forgotten and alone,
The bard may draw his parting groan.

which in 1832 he did; though neither forgotten nor alone.

O Caledonia! stern and wild,
Meet nurse for a poetic child!
Land of brown heath and shaggy wood,
Land of the mountain and the flood,
Land of my sires! what mortal hand
Can e'er untie the filial band
That knits me to thy rugged strand!...

How Mac-Shimei will joy when their chief shall display
The yew-crested bonnet o'er tresses of grey!
How the race of wrong'd Alpine and murder'd Glencoe
Shall shout for revenge when they pour on the foe!

Ye sons of brown Dermid, who slew the wild boar,
Resume the pure faith of the great Callum-More!
Mac-Neil of the Islands, and Moy of the Lake,
For honour, for freedom, for vengeance awake!

Awake on your hills, on your islands awake,
Brave sons of the mountain, the frith, and the lake!
'Tis the bugle—but not for the chase is the call;
'Tis the pibroch's shrill summons—but not to the hall.

'Tis the summons of heroes for conquest or death,
When the banners are blazing on mountain and heath:
They call to the dirk, the claymore, and the targe,
To the march and the muster, the line end the charge.

Be the brand of each Chieftain like Fin's in his ire!
May the blood through his veins flow like currents of fire!
Burst the base foreign yoke as your sires did of yore,
Or die like your sires, and endure it no more!

109

<u>17th April.</u>   <u>Prince In The Heather.</u>

It is strange that the battle of Culloden Moor took place at all; for when after his early victories Charles Edward Stuart failed to raise the hoped-for support and abandoned his march on London at Derby on the insistence of his field-commander Murray, his cause was lost. Dispersal would have obviated the rout achieved by English cannon and musketry, and also his amazing personal escape around the Rough Bounds of Knoydart. A £30,000 reward, the then equivalent of a major Lottery win, was put up for his capture, but not one of the impoverished Highlanders betrayed him. His quintessentially romantic escape to the Outer Isles then "over the sea to Skye" disguised as Betty Burke, servant of Flora Macdonald (24), was alas not matched by the clansmen's fate. The system sustained by crofting and cattle droving was broken as the chiefs sold out to English aristocrats who evicted the villagers in favour of sheep for profit. When that failed, the sheep were replaced by shooting-lodges.

Self aboard Calmac ferry, Mull to Oban, mid-90s.

Tourism and the Crofters' Acts have given some sort of life back to the North, and John Prebble's fine books have given Scotland back her history. The Western Highlands and Islands remain a "fantasy come true", save for the Gare Loch submarines and the overcrowded cities at the end of the rail-trip home. I have enjoyed superb views of Loch Lomond in the evening sun, calling to mind the Victorian ballad for the sorrowful lips of a condemned Jacobite awaiting death in Carlisle:

"The wee birdies sing and the wild flowers spring,
And in sunshine the waters are sleeping,
But the broken heart it kens nae second spring again   knows
Tho' the waeful may cease from their greeting; -   crying
O ye'll tak the high road and I'll tak the low road,
And I'll be in Scotland afore ye,
But me and my true love will never meet again
On the bonnie, bonnie banks of Loch Lomond."

Strongly Recommended! - the Pitkin illustrated guide "Bonnie Prince Charlie" - an amazing tale, told in full lucid detail.

<u>18th April.</u>　　　The　Pen　and　the　Press.

In these days of <u>paparazzi</u> - media-photographers and newshounds who stop at naught to secure merely-sensational material to gratify our prurient curiosity and engage our unrefined emotions with titbits that are of little or no consequence, it is refreshing to recall the Victorian verses which celebrated the profession of journalism. After all, reporting the facts of a situation is essential if public opinion is to assess it responsibly, and we owe deep respect to those who ferret them out and publicise them, especially when this is done at considerable personal risk:

> "The Press - the Press - the glorious Press,
>   It makes the nations free;
> Before it tyrants prostrate fall
>   And proud oppressors flee!"　　　(Anon.)

(But they don't! George Orwell rightly warned, in "1984", of the manipulative power possessed by those who control the media. They may and do subvert it for personal gain, or to promote evil social systems, or to divert an entertainment-minded public into the trivial pursuit of a distractive agenda built around "celebrities" who are of interest solely through being built up as such and lavished with "wealth" by the irresponsible money-system of the West.

> "They were made to exhort us, to teach us, to bless,
> Those invincible brothers, the Pen and the Press."
> 　　　　　　　　　　　　　　　　　　(J.C. Prince).

Again, they don't! But a proportion still do, and great honour is due to such uncorrupted wordsmiths and publishers, our debt to whom is greater than we acknowledge!)

The late Tom Driberg was a fine constituency M.P., first for Maldon and then for Barking; and he had a very felicitous pen which he devoted in the Sunday "Reynolds News" and in regular columns elsewhere, to advancing the socialism of Attlee and Bevan. His biography of the Press magnate Lord Beaverbrook contains a delightful frivolity based on "Indian" place-names, and those of the rivers Skookawaskooksis and Skoodawabskook, the latter serving as rhyme for the word "nook".

Before Attlee's days came the long slow "Making of the English Working Classes" (E.P. Thompson gave that title to his huge survey, more archive than book;, Gollancz 1963) within a radical culture, built and taught by writers in correspondence societies daring the bludgeon of an Establishment terrified by the French Revolution: Hazlitt, Montgomery (jailbird hymn-writer of the Sheffield <u>Iris</u>), Thelwall's <u>Champion</u>, the <u>Gorgon</u> &c. &c...

111

<u>19th April.</u>   "Hooked On Classics".

I love concert-going, though I find most 20th-century music uncongenial, with composers offering startling effects rather than structure and euphony. There are exceptions, yet I feel the grat symphonic tradition effectively ended with Sibelius (1865-1957) and Ralph (pronounced Rafe) Vaughan Williams (1872-1958), both of whom were more than capable of scoring for sensational sound in proper context. The "pop scene" does very little for me; a source of fun for many, it nevertheless is coarse by comparison with pre-commercial dance-band music.

The following letter from me appeared in the RVW Society's Journal for February 1996:

Having travelled from the Pennines to be thrilled by Sibelius's 6th and 5th symphonies in the 1992 "Tender is the North" festival at the Barbican Hall, I wondered if I dare miss the recent symphonic cycle of his English friend Vaughan Williams. When I found that the final concert would include the 9th and 2nd RVW symphonies in that order, I got myself a ticket and was not disappointed. *The Times* review (12 October) calls it "a pity that his unearthly farewell was not placed at the end"; but I don't agree. Sibelius, when asked how a particular bit of music should be played, replied that there was not a best way; and that each interpreter was free to use it as thought best. So on 9 October I wanted to hear the ninth again - the Hallé did it a couple of years ago, and I have the Everest recording - to see whether its strivings, after those of the '*Antarctica*', got RVW out of the 6th's "Slough of Despond" marooning (Gwyn Parry-Jones' term in your July number), to lead us "back to normality" if not to regain Paradise. They did; and we could feast on the much-loved *London Symphony* in the heart of the city it epitomises, with its lovely slow movement and superb march in its finale. "*The Ninth*", says *The Times*, "may not be a great symphony" - but it may; we still don't know it well enough, and I find it harder to get to know than even Sibelius's 4th was - "but it is a darkly impressive work often underrrted... an unmistakeable journey's end". RVW's symphonies are the most interrelated of any great composer, and may be appreciated *in toto*, so that the new experiences of one who has passed through the desolation of our stricken 20th century go beyond but do not destroy our earlier understandings. As Wordsworth wrote: "The form remains, the function never dies".

Incidentally, the *London Symphony* was given a warm and welcome performance by the Todmorden Orchestra in our town hall recently. It is good to find that some major works by RVW are not limited to use by the big professional orchestras. Nevertheless, all thanks must go to Richard Hickox and the Bournemouth Symphony Orchestra for their enterprise in giving us our long overdue complete cycle of Vaughan Williams Symphonies.

Frank McManus

Incidentally RVW at just 16 was a normal albeit able schoolboy, as shown by documentary evidence:

Excerpt of Charterhouse Detention Book showing entry for RVW at bottom

20th April. "What? after Bach?"

Perhaps those three words are the greatest tribute ever paid to the adored German composer, for they are the reported reply by Sibelius to someone who asked if he would be writing any sacred music. Other sayings of the Finnish master are given on 3 April; he is to Finland what Robert Burns is to Scotland & what Abraham Lincoln is to the U.S.A. which knows that it has fallen below the ideals of his vision. Sibelius though warmly human could hear the underlying harmonies of Nature and depicted them in his music.

The great Finn's "Kullervo Symphony" took his homeland by storm in 1892. It is a sombre tragedy of a youth who abducted a maiden only to be driven by remorse to suicide on finding she was his long-lost sister. His "Finlandia" inspired the Finns' opposition to their oppressive colonisation by Tsarist Russia, as did his first two numbered symphonies also. "Valse Triste" swept the salons of Europe; and the brilliant joy of his "Karelia Suite" assures its evergreen popularity.

Several of the tone-poems of Sibelius are based on scenes from the Kalevala, the Finnish mythology compiled from oral poetry and published by Lönnrot in 1849. The short and swift "Lemminkäinen's Return", one of his suite of "Four Legends", portrays how this Nordic Don Juan was rescued from literally fatal disaster. "Pohjola's daughter", i.e. the maiden of the Northland, whom he wooed, set him some impossible tasks, e.g. to kill the black "Swan of Tuonela" as it sang and swam on the river around the land of the dead. Himself killed in the attempt, he was saved by his mother who recovered the bits of his body with a huge rake, sewed them together, and rode south with him!

Then the lively Lemminkainen
From his cares constructed horses,
Reins from evil days he fashioned,
Saddles from his secret sorrows,
And he rode upon his journey.
 -(Kalevala, cantos 15 & 30)

Picture: Sibelius ca. age 80.

<u>21st April.</u>   <u>A Short Story of a Long Friendship.</u>

Rosa Newmarch (1859-1940) was the respected authoress of the programme-notes for concerts at the Queen's Hall, London, which housed the "Proms" until it was destroyed during World War 2. She first met Jean Sibelius around New Year 1906 when Granville Bantock, conductor of the Liverpool Orchestral Society, invited her to his house where the composer was staying. Her booklet "Jean Sibelius" (Goodwin & Tabb, 1945) carries the above subtitle. Of the Finn in his early 40s she writes that with "his well set-up figure, neat and admirably tailored, he presented a complete contrast to the unkempt <u>musikant</u> with whom one associates the apparition of a 'new genius'...we soon effected a compromise: a sort of sandwich between French and German, to which...we always adhered."

Sibelius when younger had been somewhat "Bohemian" in his behaviour, and he was always prone to get into debt — he never economised on restaurant meals — so that his dear and loyal wife had to supervise him. He knew that his whisky-drinking was a trial to her, but since he could not follow his vocation without it, he won and valued her sacrificial tolerance. Astonishingly tidy in his ways and immaculate in dress, he formed deep friendships whilst being elusively shy of mere callers. This copy of a letter to Bantock - the Colonel was a mutual friend - testifies to his warm courtesy.

Newmarch tells of his further visits to England - in 1907 to conduct his 3rd Symphony, & in 1909; then in spring 1910 she made a return visit to Jarvenpää to see the sights of Finland's capital & countryside. Meetings tailed off as years went by. Letters still came.

Järvenpää, Finland, 19/I 21.

My dear Friend,

Excuse my [that] I write to you in my "own" english.

I shall conduct in London at Queen's Hall 12/II, 19/II and 26/II. I would be very glad to see you if you have time to come to London.

I shall leave from Helsingfors 22/I and hope to be in London 28/I.

With the best greetings to you and mrs Colonel, I am

Yours old Sibelius

114

22nd April.   JENNIE LEE REMEMBERS.

Born during Edward VII's reign, into grinding poverty as the daughter of a Scottish miner, Jennie worked her way through to Edinburgh University and had a brilliant academic career. In her autobiography she confessed to succumbing to "small-town snobbery" on winning a secondary-school place. She bullied her very loving mother into clearing the china dogs and her wedding tea-service from the kitchen dresser, so that the shelves could be "arrogantly lined" with books. The children then derided their father for his socialist theories and his obstinate failure to make more money than his job as colliery-fireman paid him. But by 24 Jennie was the then youngest woman ever to be elected to Parliament; & she married Nye Bevan who became Attlee's Minister of Health. Recognising that he was a colossus whose abilities eclipsed her own, she repeated her parents' sacrifice by giving herself to sustaining him instead of seeking her own political fulfilment; but that followed after his death, for she was Wilson's Arts Minister, entrusted to set up the Open University.

Jennie told a typical story of injustice to a mining community such as has always marred the industry. An old lady was reminiscing about the struggle in Fife, 1880-1, for an eight-hour working day. Recalling her early days in the oil-lit house at Lochgelly, the lady said "I can remember my father coming in and saying to my mother, 'How many bowls of porridge can you make from a peck of meal? Don't lose heart, lass. If you can spin it out, we'll beat them yet.'"

The old lady spoke about a hewer in a narrow underground seam and every little while peering out anxiously to see if the hutches (small trucks) are arriving. None come...the coal company is out to break or starve him...Just before finishing time the hutches come hurtling through. He loads them like a man gone mad. It is bread he is shovelling, not coal ...bread for the wife and bairns (but) not so much as a single pebble after two o'clock, he promised that to his workmates...They're tempting us to betray one another, to go on working long past the eight hours, and if we do, what then? The life of a pit rat, starvation wages, never seeing the light of day.

The Franco-German war helped the miners to win. Coal prices soared. For quick profits the coal companies needed the pitmen to co-operate, so they conceded the eight-hour day.

115

23rd April. St George for England, even if too little is known about him so that the nation's first martyr Alban would be a better patron-saint to adopt. Our land is shamed by extremes of wealth and poverty as great as when Victorian labour-intensive capitalism polarised it into a cosily well-heeled "middle class" (which included a super-rich "aristocracy")- and a large "working class" below. The threat of workhouse-misery forced the people into factories to work for subsistence-wages, the amelioration of which was the central issue of public life for over a century.

Even so, the absence of external threats gave Britain a sense of security; the settled values and higher aspirations fostered a stability of life and hope that had yet to be eroded by the catastrophic 20th-century wars and rootlessness. Each stratum of society developed a domestic culture, and the prosperous had

PARLOUR POETRY

to share around the fireside many a winter afternoon or evening. "The boy stood on the burning deck Whence all but he had fled", declaimed many a child from memory; for the young and short-lived Felicia Hemans' true story from the Battle of the Nile was enjoyed for decades, and spawned many a parody. Hearts were (3.1) wrung by Mad Carew's fatal quest for the Green Eye of the Little Yellow God, and by the doom of Longfellow's "Schooner Hesperus":

"She struck where the white and fleecy waves
   Looked soft as carded wool,
But the cruel rocks they gored her side
   Like the horns of an angry bull."

(It is barely credible that the word "bull" was taboo in polite society in some parts of the 19th-century USA, so that a visiting lecturer had to modify that last line in her talk, and say "Like the horns of a gentleman cow"! True, but details elude me.)

Then there were the Lewis Carroll parodies and nonsense-poems; who now recalls "The Old Man's Comforts and How He Gained Them", by Robt. Southey?

"In the days of my youth,"
  Father William replied,
"I remembered that youth
  would fly fast,
And abused not my health and
  my vigour at first,
That I never might need them
           at last."

To Economical Mothers!
MAYPOLE SOAP DYES ANY COLOUR
No mess No Trouble — For Home Dyeing
A NEW BLOUSE for 4d.
MAYPOLE SOAP dyes CURTAINS FROCKS SILKS SATINS COTTONS & in fact EVERYTHING
COLOURS 4d. BLACK 6d.

How the children will have loved Carroll's subversion of such hyper-serious wisdom! More on this topic on 25 April.

24th April.   INDUSTRIALISM & THE LIFE OF THE PEOPLE.

For those less fortunate, life in Britain was miserable, as alas it still is for the deprived folk among us and overseas. Tennyson shocked educated opinion in 1886 by including this volcanic explosion in his wide-raging and integrative "Locksley Hall Sixty Years After":

> Is it well that while we range with Science, glorying in the Time,
> City children soak and blacken soul and sense in city slime?
>
> There among the glooming alleys Progress halts on palsied feet,
> Crime and hunger cast our maidens by the thousand on the street.
>
> There the Master scrimps his haggard sempstress of her daily bread,
> There a single sordid attic holds the living and the dead.
>
> There the smouldering fire of fever creeps across the rotted floor,
> And the crowded couch of incest in the warrens of the poor.

(as 28.2)

Queen Victoria's beloved Laureate, angrier than any Angry Brigade, had devoted his great powers to concentrate his social concern, little mentioned elsewhere (not even in *Maud*) into just eight lines on "London Labour and the London Poor".

The "music-hall" culture grew to give solidarity to cityfolk who were above turning for consolation to the gin-palace. Tear-jerking poems such as "She was poor but she was honest" found ready audiences in both the so-called middle and working classes. (see 26 April). The cultures of both groups are worth seeking on the shelves of public libraries. The "proles" were not tied to the level of "poverty poverty knock" songs in mill-districts. Aspirations could be high, aided by self-help classes and the more perceptive Christians who offered more than "a happy land, far far away". Miners' Institute libraries held works on Greek philosophy which served the enthusiasms of brilliant folk like Nye Bevan, founder of the National Health Service, before the greater postwar opportunities and contentment led them to gather dust prior to being discarded altogether.

Tennyson earlier in his poem had castigated the decadent elements in the late-Victorian literary and artistic world:

> Authors—essayist, atheist, novelist, realist, rhymester, play your part,
> Paint the mortal shame of nature with the living hues of Art.
>
> Rip your brothers' vices open, strip your own foul passions bare;
> Down with Reticence, down with Reverence—forward—naked—let them stare.
>
> Feed the budding rose of boyhood with the drainage of your sewer;
> Send the drain into the fountain, lest the stream should issue pure.
>
> Set the maiden fancies wallowing in the troughs of Zolaism,—
> Forward, forward, ay and backward, downward too into the abysm.

Wild words maybe — some have called them hysterical — yet I say their warning needs heeding once more, now that Georgian (V/VI) stuffiness and Reith's BBC have yielded to openly-prurient media.

25th April. "The little toy dog is covered with dust."

Thus splendidly did the "Childhood's Laureate" Eugene Field begin a poem with matchless sentimentality! Another poet who died young was Adelaide Anne Procter (1825-64) whose "Lost Chord" kept its popularity through the sound-broadcasting era: "It may be that Death's bright angel Will speak in that chord again,- It may be that only in Heaven I shall hear that grand Amen". The largely forgotten Ella Wheeler Wilcox, of "Laugh, and the world laughs with you", was frankly emotional: "She touches my cheek and I quiver - I tremble with exquisite pains..."! Lewis Carroll not only routed poor pedestrian Southey (23 April) but he also wrote two parodies of Isaac Watts, "How doth the little crocodile" (for "busy bee") and "'Tis the voice of the lobster" (for "sluggard"); and his "Speak roughly to your little boy", also in "Alice", is a rejoinder to David Bates' "Speak gently."

Other favourite recitations included Longfellow's "Excelsior", Kipling's "If", "Christmas Day in the Workhouse", "The Burial of Sir John Moore" at which no drum nor funeral note was heard, "Woodman, Spare that Tree", "The Stately Homes of England", "And Shall Trelawney Die?", and Thomas Bayley's song of a frustrated courtship, "Oh, no! we never mention her, her name is never heard..." But season follows season, and the 99-year _Pax Britannica_ (1815-1914) ended by showing we must "Wait a little longer" for Charles Mackay's "Good Time Coming". His song "There's a land, a dear land" was almost as popular, as was W.E.Henley's "England, my England: You with worlds to watch and ward", which of course can no longer be sung. Nor can Newbolt's _Vitae Lampada_ (Torches of Life) with its innocence of naive patriotism which perished in Flanders along with Rupert Brooke's doomed sonnet "Now God be Thanked", a posthumous disaster!

> "There's a breathless hush in the close tonight,
> Ten to get the match to win,
> A bumping pitch and a blinding light,
> An hour to bat and the last man in.....
>
> "The sand of the desert is sodden red -
> Red with the blood of a square that broke;
> The Gatling's jammed and the Colonel dead,
> And the Regiment blind with dust and smoke.
> The river of death has brimmed its banks,
> And England's far and Honour a name,
> But the voice of a schoolboy rallies the ranks:
> 'Play up, play up, and play the game!'"

Yet the sincerer of the middle-class folk doubtless needed their hearthside ease amid the lamplit streets of cabs & trams.

26th April.   *She was Poor, but She was Honest.*

She was poor, but she was honest,
   Victim of the squire's whim.
First he loved her, then he left her,
   And she lost her honest name.

Then she ran away to London,
   For to hide her grief and shame,
There she met another squire,
   And she lost her name again.

See her riding in her carriage,
   In the Park and all so gay,
All the nibs and nobby persons
   Come to pass the time of day,

See the little old-world village
   Where her aged parents live,
Drinking the champagne she sends them,
   But they never can forgive.

In the rich man's arms she flutters,
   Like a bird with broken wing,
First he loved her, then he left her,
   And she hasn't got a ring.

See him in the splendid mansion,
   Entertaining with the best,
While the girl that he has ruined,
   Entertains a sordid guest.

See him in the House of Commons,
   Making laws to put down crime,
While the victim of his passions
   Trails her way through mud and slime.

Standing on the bridge at midnight,
   She says: Farewell, blighted Love.
There's a scream, a splash—Good Heavens!
   What is she a-doing of?

Then they drag her from the river,
   Water from her clothes they wrang,
For they thought that she was drownded,
   But the corpse got up and sang:

It's the same the whole world over,
   It's the poor that gets the blame,
It's the rich that get the pleasure.
   Ain't it all a blooming shame?

27th April.   THE BLEAK AGE.

In August 2000 A.D. it was found that girls had excelled boys in the "GCSE" and "A-level" examinations. An article appeared in a broadsheet newspaper, saying that boys were not exerting themselves with academic schoolwork because they saw it as peripheral to "real life" and to "getting on in the world" moneywise. To the extent that this is correct, it seems that they have succumbed to the much-mooted "market values" that dominate the media, sport, and entertainment. Interestingly the sociologist couple J.L. & Barbara Hammond, in their 1934 book "The Bleak Age", say apropos the period around 1800 when landless people were forced into factory towns, that the then rulers of Manchester & Leeds taught that you could treat the desire to grow rich as the object of universal ambition. We have been here before! They wrote that "To make a society out of men that are sick is to make a sick society. Between the spirit of Athens and that of a goldfield, between a number of persons whose bond of union is their enjoyment of..beauty and amusement, and the same number of persons whose bond of unity is that each of them hopes to become a rich man, there is a difference which affects the depths and not merely the surface of social life."

In Roman days Cicero had said the worst of all institutions was that in which the richest was accounted the best. J.S. Mill added later that the best state is when no one is poor & no one desires to be rich. Wordsworth contrasted medieval towns which served as nurseries of civilised custom:

"...around those churches gathered towns,
Safe from the feudal castle's haughty frowns;
Peaceful abodes, where Justice might uphold
Her scales with even hand, and culture mould
The heart to pity."

Itinerary poem (1833) XI, verse 15.

with the new and very different industrial towns of the early 19th century:

"...there indeed
Love cannot be nor does it thrive with ease
Among the close and overcrowded haunts
Of cities, where the human heart is sick,
And the eye feeds it not and cannot feed."

"Prelude" (1850) bk 13, 201 - 205.

The Hammonds note, re cinema and radio (TV too I say), that civilisation stands or falls on choosing between their use and their misuse! Crude sensation destroys the beauty & peace of life

28th April.   "Sermons in Stones".

   I am reluctant to visit our large cities now except for special events or to meet old friends. With exceptions the architecture of the late 20th century is brash and ugly; and there is too much distress and poverty on the streets of a Britain that lacked the vigilance to sustain all the welfare services and full employment of the postwar period. We have recognised and curtailed some of the worst excesses of the 1960s, but too many fine buildings were lost and vistas ruined by steel-and-concrete structures that knew none of the traditional grace, elegance and proportion of public buildings.

   The great Town Halls survive as monuments to Victorian civic pride, from the days when Councils were allowed to run their own public utilities and services - water, gas, electricity, health, transport, education, parks and so forth. Manchester's fine Banqueting Hall has a set of Ford Madox Brown paintings of local historic scenes - expulsion of Danes, Dr Priestley collecting marsh-gas, Dr Chetham birch in hand before his pupils! - and a roof celebrating the world-wide places that were then reached by the city's industry. Leeds has a concert hall with baroque marble arches front and back, and texts all around[1] - perhaps supplied one per alderman as they don't form a related set. Halifax is smaller, with windows dedicated to the virtues and a mosaic floor with crest reminding the Labour group among others that their labour is vain unless the Lord builds and watches with them. Bradford's council meets under a skylight which proclaims, at times unavailingly, that "Labor Vincit Omnia"; and my home-town of Todmorden is favoured by a lovely Town Hall with sculpted cornices of industrial scenes both inside and outside.

Central Premises, Hetton Downs Amicable Industrial Society, 1910 (when shops too had dignity!)

1. see 21.10

29th April. At Peace in St Kentigern's, Crosthwaite, Keswick
rest the remains of Robert Southey, a generous man and voluminous writer who became Poet Laureate after Walter Scott had declined the honour in 1813. He lived from 1774 to 1843; and his play "Wat Tyler", which gave dramatic effect to his youthful radicalism, was refused publication in 1794. This was just as well, for twelve English radicals were that year spared the gallows by the treason-trial jury, and Southey would have been jailed at the very least by the Establishment which, in terror over the revolution in France, reacted by mounting its own campaign of repression. He changed his views following the French Terror, and by 1819 had condemned in the "Quarterly" magazine the agitators who were following his own youthful example of politicising the poor. For this he was attacked in Parliament by the Whig William Smith, and was cruelly lampooned by Byron, whose mock-dedication of Don Juan began thus:

"BOB SOUTHEY! - You're a poet - Poet-laureate
And representative of all the race;
Although 'tis true that you turned out a Tory
Last, - yours has lately been a common case;
And now, my Epic Renegade! what are ye at?
With all the Lakers, in and out of place?
A nest of tuneful persons, to my eye
Like 'four and twenty Blackbirds in a Pye.'"

THEATRE by the LAKE at KESWICK 017687.74411

With his Blenheim poem no longer in school anthologies (which have been 'sanitised' free from naval and military epics), Bob Southey is best remembered for first rendering in English the German fantasy-tale The Three Bears, and for his jingle on 'How does the water come down at Lodore?' (that being the waterfall on the Watendlath Beck below the hamlet which is said to have received its name from a lisping honeymooner who told his new bride "Watendlath blith in a plaith like thith" - but I don't think that's true!):

"And thumping and plumping and bumping and jumping
And dashing and flashing and splashing and clashing..."

Southey was embarrassed when a pirated version of "Wat Tyler" appeared in 1819. A "Collector's Edition", hand-sewn on acid-free paper, has been published at £18 by Woodstock Books, Spelsbury House, Oxford OX7 3JR - please state "through Wordsworth Trust" if ordering - and I'll lend on request. I think the first performance was given at Grasmere to the Wordsworth Winter School by the Readers' Theatre on 1 March 1990. I played the Tax-collector at an open-air performance shortly afterwards at an anti-polltax rally in Todmorden. Since the play begins with a maypole-dance, mention today is seasonal!

30th April.   **Eve of St Philip.**

Tomorrow is May-day, the Celtic "Beltane" in celebration of the returned warmth! - the season of lambs, blossoming trees, and new green fields - a nature-festival long enjoyed with maypole-dances such as we had when I attended St Philip's C.E. Primary and Infants' School in Southport. In the Church of England 1st May is the festival of St Philip and St James-the-Less; in the Church of Rome it is St Joseph's day. Famously it was designated "Labour Day" by the Socialist International in the late 19th century. Why then do I put these churchy notes first?

I do so because <u>social justice is too precarious to maintain by mechanical, materialistic means alone</u>; as witness the Thatcherite destruction of Britain's post-war social structure, with public assets clawed into private hands. <u>A spiritual element is indispensible!</u> This is implicit in some socialist classics such as William Morris's poems (3 May), but explicit in the Bible, e.g the Epistle of James which should tell church folk who steer clear of politics that "Faith without works is dead" (2.20) - indeed a truly-living faith is known by its works as a tree is known by its fruit (C.E. Article 12).

At primary school we enjoyed Percy Dearmer's May Carol which deserves to be better known, though it appears to err by quoting the above Epistle which was probably by James the Lord's brother who was <u>not</u> one of the two apostles called by the popular name James (= Jacobus, Jacob, Iago, Seamus).

1. THE winter's sleep was long and deep,
   But earth is awakened and gay;
   For the life ne'er dies that from God doth rise,
   And the green comes after the grey.

2.*So God doth bring the world to spring;
   And on their holy day
   Doth the Church proclaim her Apostles' fame,
   To welcome the first of May.

3. Two Saints of God went by the road
   That leadeth on to light;
   And they gave up all at their Master's call,
   To work in their Master's sight.

4. Would Philip's mind the Father find?
   Lo, he hath found the Way;
   For to know the Son is to know the One
   Whom the earth and the heavens obey.

5. And, James, 'twas thine by grace divine
   To preach the Christian life,
   Where our faith is shown by our works alone,
   And love overcometh strife.

6. Lord, grant that we may brethren be—
   As Christians live in deed;
   For it is but so we can learn to know
   The truth that to thee doth lead.

1st May. Our Hope For Years To Come.

(Some diviner force to guide us thro' the days I shall not see?)

So wrote Tennyson at 77 in his second Locksley Hall poem:

"When the schemes and all the systems, Kingdoms and Republics fall,
Something kindlier, higher, holier - all for each and each for all?..
Earth at last a warless world, a single race, a single tongue -
I have seen her far away for is not Earth as yet so young? -
Every tiger madness muzzled, every serpent passion kill'd,
Every grim ravine a garden, every blazing desert till'd,
Robed in universal harvest up to either pole she smiles,
Universal ocean softly washing all her warless Isles."

A SOUVENIR FOR MAY DAY 1907

Is that marvellous line in this marvellous poem realistic? Countless folk have yearned and worked for its fulfilment - the socialists overcame the subsistence-labour exploitation of the early industrial era, the best Tory insisted that justice be done in freedom so that we avoid the tentacles of bureaucracy - but the hope is elusive and now burns too low (Hardy wrote "After two thousand years of mass, We've got as far as poison gas".) Are the flaws of the human heart insurmountable? The prosperous West contains millions who are anything but prosperous, and individualism abounds, yet we can't give up the hope without also abandoning the Lord's Prayer - "Thy Kingdom Come...on earth as in heaven". Till then the hope needs to enter "within the veil" (Heb.6.19) as a "common salvation" that goes beyond individualism (Jude v.3). As Bishop Westcott of Durham said in 1890, "Individualism regards humanity as made up of disconnected or warring atoms; Socialism regards it as an organic whole". That goal is biblical! (Eph.4.11+, 1 Pet.2.4/5)

2nd May. "Old Labour, Old Integrity" - or so one may hope!

In late 1994, concerned with some aspects of the newly-elected Labour leadership, I, more "politically active" then than now, was able to have this short article published in the monthly newsletter of our local Constituency Labour Party for Calder Valley, which operates from Todmorden through Ellard to Brighouse - towns served by 3 MPs in the textile era:

"We must not change its colour now!"

"The Red Flag", by Jim Connell, written to the Jacobite tune "The White Cockade" but now sung to the German carol "Tannenbaum", is the official song of the Labour Party. Much parodied in lines such as: "By tax-adjustments we have planned To institute the Promised Land", it has a direct link with our constituency which is very little known. Chicago is mentioned in a verse which the Party Song Book omits. The reference is to the Haymarket Anarchists, seven of whom were convicted of murder there after a bomb had been thrown at an hour-of-work rally there. Four were executed who had no link with the incident, merely because they had referred in speeches to the idea that violence might be needed to overthrow capitalism. Among the reprieved was Samuel Fielden who was born in Todmorden, in a family distinguished by the radical M.P. John Fielden who got the Ten Hours Act through Parliament. (Thatcher had it repealed.) Other Fieldens financed the building of Tod. Town Hall from textile profits; others still may be found in Todmorden Labour Party to this day.

The song in full, from Chicago History Museum, runs:

The People's flag is deepest red,
  It shrouded oft our martyred dead;
And ere their limbs grew stiff and cold
  Their life-blood dyed its every fold.

Then raise the scarlet standard high
  Beneath its folds, we'll live and die,
Though cowards flinch and traitors sneer,
  We'll keep the red flag flying here.

Look 'round! the Frenchman loves its blaze,
  The sturdy German chants its praise;
In Moscow's vaults, its hymns are sung,
  Chicago swells its surging song.

It waved above our infant might
  When all ahead seemed dark as night;
It witnessed many a deed and vow,
  We will not change its color now.

It suits today the meek and base
  Whose minds are fixed on pelf and place;
To cringe beneath the rich man's frown,
  And haul that sacred emblem down.

With heads uncovered, swear we all,
  To bear it onward till we fall;
Come dungeons dark, or gallows grim,
  This song shall be our parting hymn!

The Haymarket tragedy of 4th May 1886 was an international *cause célèbre*. The travesty of a trial took place in 1887, and Samuel Fielden was in jail from then until a new State Governor quashed all the convictions in 1893.

- - - - -

(Happily the new Government restored the limitation of working hours by adopting the European Social Charter.)

3rd May.   "All For The Cause."

William Morris was a fine Victorian artist, with links to the Pre-Raphaelite movement; but it is unfair that some people are more aware of his wallpaper designs than his social commitment as a passionate Socialist - possibly a shade too romantic if he overstressed the "humanist" potential for turning the hearts of men and women into co-operative ways. This poem (I omit some verses) bears the above title, and celebrates the early pioneers who suffered in the struggle for justice and fair play for the common people:

> Nothing ancient is their story, e'en but yesterday they bled,
> Youngest they of earth's beloved, last of all the valiant dead.
>
> In the grave where tyrants thrust them, lies their labour and their pain,
> But undying from their sorrow springeth up the hope again.
>
> Mourn not therefore, nor lament it, that the world outlives their life;
> <u>Voice and vision</u> yet they give us, making strong our hands for strife.
>
> Some had name, and fame, and honour, learn'd they were, and wise and strong;
> Some were nameless, poor, unlettered, weak in all but grief and wrong.
>
> Named and nameless all live in us; one and all they lead us yet
> Every pain to count for nothing, every sorrow to forget.
>
> Some shall pause awhile and ponder on the bitter days of old,
> Ere the toil of strife and battle overthrew the curse of gold;
>
> Life or death then, who shall heed it, what we gain or what we lose?
> Fair flies life amid the struggle, and the Cause for each shall choose.
>
> Hear a word, a word in season, for the day is drawing nigh,
> When the Cause shall call upon us, some to live, and some to die!

- - - - - - - - -

Morris's "March of the Workers", written for the tune John Brown's Body, is stirring albeit idealised. In this verse he quotes the strictures of the Epistle of James 5.1 on the rich:

> O ye rich men hear and tremble! for with words the sound is rife:
> "Once for you and death we laboured; changed henceforward is the strife.
> We are men, and we shall battle for the world of men and life;
>   And our host is marching on."
>
>   Hark the rolling of the thunder!
>   Lo the sun! and lo thereunder
>   Riseth wrath, and hope, and wonder,
>   And the host comes marching on.

- - - - - - - -

"Behold the wages of the labourers who mowed your fields, which you kept back by fraud, cry out; and the cries of the <u>harvesters have reached the ears of the Lord of Hosts!</u>"(Jas. 5. 4).

Good Morning Mr. Quaker

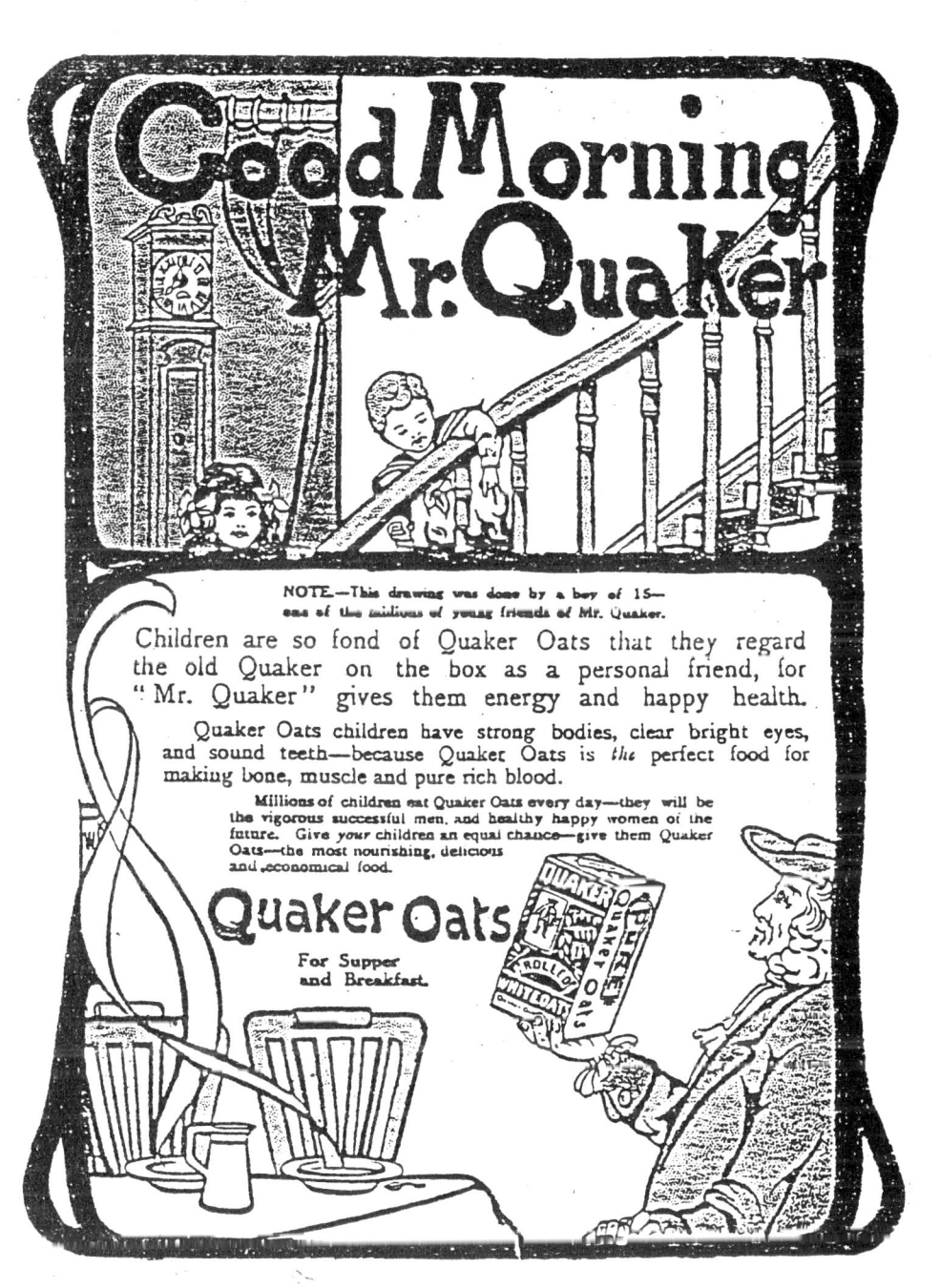

NOTE.—This drawing was done by a boy of 15—one of the millions of young friends of Mr. Quaker.

Children are so fond of Quaker Oats that they regard the old Quaker on the box as a personal friend, for "Mr. Quaker" gives them energy and happy health.

Quaker Oats children have strong bodies, clear bright eyes, and sound teeth—because Quaker Oats is *the* perfect food for making bone, muscle and pure rich blood.

Millions of children eat Quaker Oats every day—they will be the vigorous successful men, and healthy happy women of the future. Give *your* children an equal chance—give them Quaker Oats—the most nourishing, delicious and economical food.

Quaker Oats

For Supper and Breakfast.

1930s Advertisement

Summary of contents.

March:

1 - School Rhymes.
2 - Tarantella.
3 - Star-Spangled Banner.
4 - Gilbert Shaw Poem.
5 - Crossing The Bar.
6 - The Big Ship Sails.
7 - Miracle.
8 - Threadneedle Street.
9 - Pennies from Heaven.
10 - Friendly Greetings.
11 - English Hymnody Saved.
12 - Planetary Orbits.
13 - A Mirror of Faith.
14 - Joy of Music.
15 - Ides of March.
16 - Mousetail.
17 - Saint Patrick.
18 - Corslet of Faith.
19 - Jail for 33 Seconds.
20 - Co-Delinquents.
21 - A Young Man's Fancy.
22 - Tennyson (1). ⁕
23 - Fiddler of Dooney.
24 - Abp. Robert Runcie.
25 - Does Football Matter?
26 - Tennyson (2).
27 - More Limericks.
28 - Goliath Rehabilitation.
29 - The Baby's Opera.
30 - Yeats. (see also 23rd.)
31 - Blaenwern.

⁕ --- see also 5th.

April:

1 - Brief Encounter.
2 - Probability of God.
3 - Artistic Interlude.
4 - Presences of Nature.
5 - Good Friday.
6 - Bridging the Gap.
7 - Overture of Easter Joy.
8 - Tins, Cans, Kegs etc.
9 - God Save Great George.
10 - That Dripping Monarch.
11 - Royal Scots.
12 - West Highland Railway.
13 - Ardlui loop problem &c.
14 - Pulpit politics.
15 - Provocative schoolgirls.
16 - Scott on the Forty-Five.
17 - Prince in the Heather.
18 - Journalism.
19 - RVW in Detention.
20 - "What? after Bach?"
21 - Sibelius in England.
22 - Jennie Lee Remembers.
23 - Parlour Poetry (1).
24 - Industrialism.
25 - Parlour Poetry (2).
26 - Poor but Honest.
27 - Bleak Age.
28 - Architecture.
29 - Southey.
30 - Song for May-day.

May:

1 - Hope for future.
2 - Red Flag.
3 - William Morris.

"BELOW THE DARKSOME BOUGH"

"I WASTED MY TIME SADLY IN THOSE DAYS."

Girl's Own Paper, 29 May 1886.

A Summertime Book of Days
[4th May to 5th July]

"The March and the Muster" Part 3

Frank McManus

"The Ringing Grooves of Change." (foreword, "Below the Darksome Bough.")

Tennyson's 1830 rail-ride spawned his famous error of imagining that trains ran in grooves (20-21.6); yet if his prescience had been on target he could have claimed prophesy of the wonderfully-bizarre tramcars that rattled through our towns in the first half of the 20th century. His true platitude "The old order changeth, yielding place to new" (The Passing of Arthur) applies in all continents and centuries. The great poet was himself a prisoner of "Establishment" thinking, as witness his support of "strong measures" when UK settlement was threatened by rebellious horror in India, Jamaica &c. (see "The Victorians" by A.N.Wilson; Hutchinson 2002, £25) - support that begged the question of what right "we" had to be there in the first place. "Niggers are tigers" he whispered over the port at a dinner with friends, one of whom replied citing bad deeds by Englishmen too. But his sympathies grew with his years.

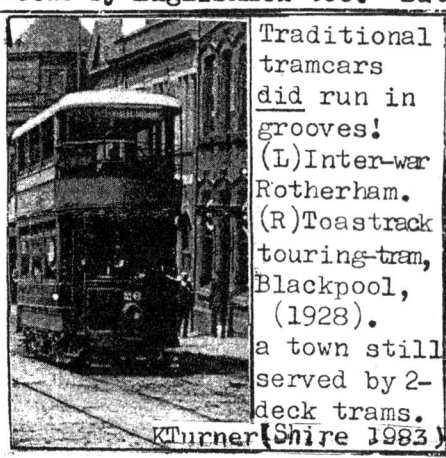

Traditional tramcars *did* run in grooves! (L)Inter-war Rotherham. (R)Toastrack touring-tram, Blackpool, (1928). a town still served by 2-deck trams. KTurner(Shire 1983)

England's Big Changes Down the Last Millennium include:

1066   — Norman Conquest, with baronial system established.
1215   — Magna Carta; royal autocracy reined in by barons.
1485   — "Modern Times" (!); nation pacified under Henry VII.
1536+ — Pilgrimage of Grace (our largest rising) just fails to unhorse Henry VIII the plunderer (11.1).
1571   — Usury law eased, decriminalising loans at interest.
1645   — This easement subverted the stable value of money, impoverishing the king whose taxes alienated support.
1780+ — "Bleak Age" (27.4) with scientific progress spawning industrial capitalism, with population-explosion.
1837   — Queen Victoria accedes as British enterprise expands her empire wider still and wider whilst battle is mounted for decent standards at home. (see ANWilson.)

4th May. **WHEN CATS RUN HOME.**

The first poem, not counting nursery-rhymes, that I memorised was "Song - The Owl" by Tennyson. This pleasant exercise was set to us 7-year-olds by our primary-school teacher who thus not only helped to train our memories but also gave us a source of lasting enjoyment which later campaigns against rote-learning, alas taken to excess, have denied to younger people.

SONG—THE OWL.

I.

WHEN cats run home and light is come,
  And dew is cold upon the ground,
And the far-off stream is dumb,
  And the whirring sail goes round,
  And the whirring sail goes round;
    Alone and warming his five wits,
    The white owl in the belfry sits.

II.

When merry milkmaids click the latch,
  And rarely smells the new-mown hay,
And the cock hath sung beneath the thatch
  Twice or thrice his roundelay,
  Twice or thrice his roundelay;
    Alone and warming his five wits,
    The white owl in the belfry sits,

Tennyson is in general not well understood, and serious doubts have been expressed about his devoting a decade to his Arthurian "Idylls of the King". Ruskin respected them but felt that the poet should have used his energies against real present evils rather than those of a romantic past. (see 1 June). But Tennyson was a polymath with a gift for phrasing, e.g "the murmuring of innumerable bees", who deserves wide-ranging attention.

Returning to my younger days, let me share the tale of my most embarrassing pedagogical moment from my teaching career!

WHO INVENTED TELEVISION?   131

From 1954 to 1968 I was a Chemistry lecturer in the Lancaster & Morecambe College of Further Education. My duties halfway through this spell included an hour-long class each week for secretarial day-release students, for it was decreed that such a course in "Science for the Citizen" would benefit them. It was a joy to teach about twenty smartly-dressed girls of 18 to 20! One week I surveyed the history of "Communication" from smoke and flag signalling through to the telegraph and into the 20th century, and asked them to study the topic for a test the following week. When we next met I asked them a dozen or so questions, and then they exchanged papers to mark one another's. "Who invented radio? - Marconi!" I said, whereupon a student remarked "Yes, and Yogi Bear invented television." "Don't be so silly", I scolded her, only to be indignantly advised by several voices that Logi Baird _had_ invented TV. Realising that my hearing was no longer sharp, I apologised profusely, much to the friendly amusement of the young ladies - yes and of myself.

5th May. THE MILLENNIAL VERSES.

When in 1980 a fellow-teacher and I came across a pupil called Debra, with the traditional Old-Testament spelling abandoned in favour of brevity, we proposed a limerick that began: "There was a young schoolgirl called Debra
   Who went for a ride on a zebra..."
Alas we got no further; but following the unplanned mating of a Shetland pony and a zebra in 2001 which resulted in a darkly-striped "shebra" - after all, crossbreeding of equines is nothing new, for horse with donkey yields mule - I tried again:

> The stroppy young schoolgirl called Debra,
> Who went for a ride on a shebra,
>   Said 'You'll think me an ass
>   To play truant from class,
> But I hate learning French and Algebra.

Also zoological is my "Song for Iris", another retired teacher, which also may be used for Quidenham folk, &c.:

> There was an old lady of Sydenham
> Whose dogs wondered why she had hidden 'em;
>   But her friends the Scott-Ferriers,
>   Who hated fox-terriers,
> Were coming, though she hadn't bidden 'em.

Here is my "Riposte to a 'Guardian' Critic" who claimed in Spring 2001 that Mr Eminem, then a pop-entertainer who could draw the crowds, was a modern great poet who expressed the feelings of contemporary society as did the literary lions of old. Considering that the start of the Third Christian Millennium deserved better, I wrote that

> The degenerate rapper called Eminem
> Uses diction too crude to be feminine;
>   After Milton and Dante
>   His vision seems scanty -
> Your critic is wrong to link them an' 'im.

and "One to a Writer of Distinction", George W. Target whose novels of the later 20th century, The Teachers, The Americans, The Patriots &c. are of lasting value, as are his devotional and other writings. In Tell it the way it is (Lutterworth 1970) he asks why he hasn't heard any Christian limericks. So:

> Precede us O Lord with Thy Grace
> As we travel in time and through space;
>   In all that we do
>   May we glorify You
> Our reward as we run the straight race.

(Contact F.McM for details of the George Target Society.)

6th May. Just a wee 'deoch an doruis'.

Sir Walter Scott, who lived from 1771 to 1832 (see 16th April), embellished his pioneer historical novel "Waverley" with copious notes, one of which refers to the old custom of the "stirrup-cup" of wine given to someone mounted for departure from a friend. In Scotland, however, "a company, after having taken leave of their host", often finished the evening at the village tavern. On their departure the landlord would by custom present them with 'deoch an doruis', the drink at the door, without charge.

Scott tells of a Bailie (magistrate) of Forfar who dealt with a case involving an ale-wife who had brewed her peck of malt and had left the large bucket outside her front door to cool. Her neighbour's cow, passing by, saw it, tasted it, liked it, drank it, and staggered around "under the influence". The landlady, finding her tub empty, recognised and belaboured the culprit, whose roaring attracted its owner. He remonstrated with the publican, only to be met with a demand for the value of the ale which the cow had consumed. This was refused, the case came to court, and the Bailie asked the landlady whether the animal had stood or sat to drink. She said she supposed the cow drank whilst standing on her feet, and added that if she'd been around she'd have made her use them to some purpose. "The Bailie", notes Scott, "on this admission, solemnly adjudged the cow's drink to be 'deoch an doruis', a stirrup-cup for which no charge could be made without violating the ancient hospitality of Scotland." Doubtless the Bailie presented his correct decision lightheartedly to soften it for the ale-wife.

I remember a popular song from my childhood days, before commercial material had eclipsed the simple songs from tradition, which included the lines "Just a wee 'deoch an doruis' / Afore ye gang awa'." Now to say this to a motorist would be utterly antisocial and all too possibly lethal. Mad cows too, alas, present graver problems than in pre-industrial Scotland, as we shall see tomorrow. In the meantime it is notable how tremendous a vogue attached itself to the name Waverley, a South-country surname chosen by Scott for his character so as not to identify him with any public figure. We have had a Waverly rail-station in Edinburgh and line thence to Carlisle; an express train thereon to London; a Waverley pen; a Waverley overture by Berlioz; the Waverley paddle-steamer which survives as the last of its kind in the world; the Waverley school in Peckham where I last taught before retirement; and many roads and hotels of the name in question. Alas the Scott novel is ponderous by modern standards, and not easy reading.

7th May.   Compassion in World Farming?
(CIWF, 5a Charles St, Petersfield, GU32 3EH; tel.(01730.264208 & 268863)

It is to be feared alas that mad cows have a much more serious aspect than in yesterday's pre-industrial Scotland. The "mad cow disease" of BSE, first diagnosed in 1980, was made notifiable in 1988, and 160,000 cases were observed in Britain over the next eight years. The then Government failed to ban the use of crushed infected carcases as food for other cattle, & big firms traded in it, until the public panic in spring 1996 over the claim that infected beef can damage the brains of humans who eat it. Europe imposed a blanket-ban on British beef, in excess of veterinery opinion's judgment and probably for commercial reasons; so that, whilst the lamentable export of live calves was fortuitously stopped, healthy cattle were culled.

Mother Teresa of Calcutta famously remarked that "I do not believe in the big way of doing things"; and our callousness to farm animals makes me concur. The foot-and-mouth-disease outbreaks of 1967 and 2001 each caused widespread culling of cattle, sheep and pigs, and traumatised the affected farmers who at least were compensated (unlike the hoteliers and "B & B" proprietors who received but little solace for loss of tourism in their areas). The Government was much criticised in spring 2001 for not opting for vaccination, though scientific opinion was divided, and EEC regulations prohibit this, partly for commercial reasons, except in emergency, as the European Court held in a case involving Holland. Actually this was of benefit to the animals, for they were spared the final misery of a 250-mile journey to southern abbatoirs - a fact that escaped public awareness in a nation whose agriculture has declined from acceptability in my younger days to present barbarity. Some farmers feel for their stock, but do we who buy supermarket-packed produce stop and think of its origin? Arable farming is big business too, with excessive use of chemicals.

134 European co-operation is fine but needs basing on ethics and human solidarity and not on impersonal profit-seeking. In 1983 the EEC farm-authorities destroyed 206,350 tonnes of apples in a starving world, and large amounts of vegetables and other fruit. This is obscene and disgraceful (though Europe takes ameliorative steps on occasion.)

8th May.   MAY PEACE PREVAIL.

I was Town Mayor 1994-5 and I promoted and went to some local events to mark the end of the war in Europe on 8 May 1945, my 172½th birthday 50 years be-fore. To celebrate 50 years without major European war I invited groups from our twin-towns to join us - those from Roncq in France could not come because of their legal duty to vote in the presidential election, but 32 German folk including Burgomaster Ewald Fisse and his wife Erika came from Bramsche.

On Saturday 6th we planted three trees given by our Town Twinning Society, our Greenpeace Group, and the Calderdale United Nations Association. In the evening my mayoress Mrs Julia Poulton and I enjoyed the 1940s-style supper-and-dance which the local Lions Club organised in Todmorden Town Hall. Then on Sunday 7th we made a civic attendance at the Peace Celebration of choral communion. Vicar Peter Calvert surprised everyone by greeting the overseas guests in German - "Wir alle haben guten Grund..." - and Herr Fisse responded through an interpreter. The first hymn was sung to Haydn's tune "Austria" which is also used for "For the heal-ing of the nations" and two Eastertide hymns. The contrast between this event and the service on 3rd September 1939 at which the outbreak of war was announced was most striking.

Our big Monday event began when at 1pm we let a surprisingly-large queue into the Town Hall. I found the settling-in problems stressful and was shooed by my invaluable volunteer-stewards to rest in the Parlour, to emerge presently to find that all was well, with the audience happy.

The Mayor of Todmorden
Councillor Frank McManus
invites you to his

Mayor's VE Anniversary Festival

Saturday 6th May, 3pm —
Tree Planting, Lobb Mill Garden

Peace Celebration,
Sunday 7th May, 11am —
St Mary's Church

Monday 8th May, 1pm to dusk* —
Music and Dance, Centre Vale Park*

1.00	Geoff Love recorded music
1.20	Todmorden High School Choir
1.50	Todmorden High School Pop Singers
2.05	Halifax Inst Dancers
2.30	Bramsche German Dancers
3.00	Todmorden Ukrainian Association Choir
3.30	Todmorden Choral Society
4.30	Bramsche German Dancers
5.00	Mad Susan rock band
5.45	Julia's Mayoressal Circle Dance — all join in!
6.45	Geoff Love "Manuel of the Mountains")
7.00	Todmorden Old Brass Band

*Town Hall if wet —alas it was!

With Bonfire lit at 8pm and Grand Finale —
"1812 Overture", with special percussion

Admission free,
with collection for
Mayoral Charities

Refreshments,
picnic areas, stalls,
bouncing castle

135

9th May. Growth of a Poet's Mind.

No, my poet is not this time Wordsworth, who used that phrase as sub-title for his long autobiographical "Prelude". He is Idris Davies (1905-53), a miner then teacher who drew from T.S. Eliot the tribute that his poems "are the best poetic document I know about a particular epoch in a particular place..." It is hard now to envisage the inter-war industrial Britain which formed their backcloth. Wages peaked in 1920; and by mid-decade the coalowners, angry that overseas competition had ended their unbridled Victorian enrichment, were demanding "longer hours and lower wages". (※) Baldwin's Tory Government temporised with a year's subsidy to 1st May 1926. All the big Trade Unions feared for their members' wage levels after that date; and, with the Government organising against challenge like Thatcher's in 1984, a well-planned National Strike ran from 3rd to 12th May when the TUC called it off on the basis of inadequate promises of negotiations. The miners themselves were forced back in November by hunger and hardship, not to recover their 1925 levels for a decade. The inhuman conditions thus inflicted were avenged when the coalowners were swept aside in the postwar nationalisation - only for this in turn to be reversed by Thatcherism from the 1980s!

A good book of social history should be consulted for the full story, e.g. Noreen Branson, "Britain in the 1920s" (Weidenfeld & Nicolson, 1975). A.J.P. Taylor's "English History, 1914-1945" (OUP, 1965) contains a useful summary; see also 'Celticus' (Aneurin Bevan), "Why not trust the Tories?" (Gollancz, 1944). The earlier social atmosphere of industrial Wales in the 19th century is preserved in Alexander Cordell's novels and in Richard Llewellyn's "How Green was my Valley".

IN GARDENS IN THE RHONDDA

(quoted by Michael Foot, opening the Labour Party General Election campaign in Carmarthen, 1983)

In gardens in the Rhondda
  The daffodils dance and shine
When tired men trudge homeward
  From factory and mine.

The daffodils dance in gardens
  Behind the grim brown row
Built among the slagheaps
  In a hurry long ago.

They dance as though in passion
  To shame and to indict
The brutes who built so basely
  In the long Victorian night.

XXXVI

In the places of my boyhood
  The pit-wheels turn no more,
Nor any furnace lightens
  The midnight as of yore.

The slopes of slag and cinder
  Are sulking in the rain,
And in derelict valleys
  The hope of youth is slain.

And yet I love to wander
  The early ways I went,
And watch from doors and bridges
  The hills and skies of Gwent.

Though blighted be the valleys
  Where man meets man with pain,
The things my boyhood cherished
  Stand firm, and shall remain.

[Gwalia Deserta]

Some of Davies' poems of earlier industry in South Wales.

XI

Dark gods of all our days,
  Have mercy upon us.

Dark gods, take away
  The shadows from our towns,
The hopeless streets, the hovels
  Behind the colliery sidings.
Dark gods of grime and grief,
  Soften the bitter day,
And give our children eyes
  To see somewhere a summer.

Dark gods, we beg you,
  Make us proud and angry,
That we shall rise from shame
  And imitate the torrent,
And scatter the high priests
  Who deal in blood and gold.
Dark gods of all our days,
  Dark gods of life and death,
Have mercy upon us
  Who wait in the shadow.

Davies in his twenties was a "humanist" with little or no time for the "service in the chapel to make us meek and mild"; and on Christmas Eve 1939, home in Rhymney (pron. Rumney), he wrote in his diary that "Christianity as we know it is indubitably one of the weeds of human history... And yet tomorrow morning...I will probably read again the second chapter of Luke for my childhood's sake! 'Hoping it might be so!'" But most interestingly, when the post-war sun shone on South Wales, and the pits were owned by the nation, Davies wrote some poems, including a hymn for Christmas Eve, in the faith and love of Jesus. Please see 11th May and later for more on Idris Davies.

10th May.

In her autobiography "THE YEARS THAT ARE PAST", David Lloyd George's second wife Frances wrote that "Sometimes LG would discuss the old Welsh preachers...a favourite topic with him. On page 248 of this book (Hutchinson, 1967) she stated that "One of the sermons which LG was most fond of was the sermon of The Little Lantern. It was preached by Herber Evans on the subject of the 'Higher Criticism' - the 'New Theology' which found fault with the Bible on the ground that its history was poor, its influence failing, its theology full of holes and its meaning in places very doubtful. To illustrate his story Herber Evans described an old preacher who had come a long way to address his congregation, and who had to return home that night along a dark road beset with danger and difficult to follow. As he was leaving, a woman in the congregation put a small lantern into his hands with the words: 'It is only a small lantern, Mr Evans bach, and it is full of holes and very old; but it will light you home, Mr Evans, it will light you home.' And lifting up the great Bible from the lectern, the preacher held it aloft and cried 'Thy word is a lantern unto my feet, and a light unto my paths!'

"As LG retold the story we could see the anxious face of the woman as she thrust the lantern into the man's hand, we could see the little flickering lantern itself; and when his voice rang out with the final words, the thrill which it produced brought the tears to our eyes.

"...these men had the power of bringing the Bible to life ..., LG would say, like a ship getting out of harbour...the Divine Spark". The best of them of course did <u>not</u> make people meek and mild, for the social gospel is an integral part of the Christian Faith!

11th May.   DAVIES' "PRELUDE".

Here then are verses from "I was born in Rhymney" when the "Valleys" held 250,000 miners and Barry was the world's energy-capital before the days of oil. Idris Davies' quasi-doggerel verses can hardly be further removed from Words-worth's expansive grandiloquence. Inelegantly trivial at times, the poetry deliberately aimed at the reader who had left school at 12 or 13; yet its <u>total</u> appeal was universal. The tabloids and coarse "literati" had yet to corrupt people, so everyone could follow his tale from when he "went to church and chapel/ Ere (he) could understand/ That Apollo rules the heavens/ And Mammon rules the land." "And there was my Uncle Edward", he adds, "Solemn and stern and grey,/A Calvinistic Methodist/ Who made me kneel and pray."

He would carry me on his shoulders
When I was six or seven
And tell me of the golden days
When chariots flew to heaven.

He was furious against Pharaoh
And scornful about Eve,
But his pathos about Joseph
Could always make me grieve.

And Moses was his hero
And Jehovah was his God.
And his stories were as magical
As Aaron's magic rod.

But sometimes from the Bible
He would turn to politics
And tell of Gladstone's glory
And Disraeli's little tricks.

But even William Ewart Gladstone
Of beloved memory
Would fade and be forgotten
When it came to D.L.G.

The little Celt from Criccieth,
The Liberal on fire,
He was the modern Merlin
And Moses and Isaiah !

The ghost of Uncle Edward
In a solemn bowler hat,
Does it haunt the plains of Moab
Or the slopes of Ararat ?

Or lurks it in the Gateway,
Where Peter holds the key,
To welcome on the harp strings
The ghost of D.L.G. ?

I lost my native language
For the one the Saxon spake
By going to school by order
For education's sake.

I learnt the use of decimals,
And where to place the dot,
Four or five lines from Shakespeare
And twelve from Walter Scott.

I learnt a little grammar,
And some geography,
Was frightened of perspective,
And detested poetry....

(then after he'd left school)

there were strikes and lock-outs
And meetings in the Square,
When Cook and Smith and Bevan
Electrified the air....

And I walked my native hillsides
In sunshine and in rain,
And learnt the poet's language
To ease me of my pain....

And there were dark and bitter morn
When the streets like coffins lay⁻ings
Between the winter mountains,
Long and bleak and grey.

But season followed season
And beauty never died
And there were days and hours
Of hope and faith and pride,...

(Davies moves on through college & workaday London to the advent of war.)

I saw the placards screaming
About Hitler and his crimes,
Especially on Saturdays —
That happened many times.

And I saw folk digging trenches
In 1938,
In the dismal autumn drizzle
When all things seemed too late.

And Chamberlain went to Munich,
An umbrella at his side,
And London lost her laughter
And almost lost her pride....

And crisis followed crisis
Until at last the line
Of battle roared to fire
In 1939,...

And the world is black with battle
In 1943,
And the hymn of hate triumphant
And loud from sea to sea.

And in this time of tumult
I can only hope and cry
That season shall follow season
And beauty shall not die.

To do justice to Davies read this & other poems in full (Collected Poems, Gomer, 1972 repr. 1984, £3.25).

138

DLG = David Lloyd George. Cook led 1926 pit-strike; Smith was Yorks official. Bevan founded NHS. ∅ see the valley-terraces.

12th May. <u>Tales of Tin Bath Terrace.</u>

(many such rows of miners' cottages dated from before pithead baths became the norm after 1947 and nationalisation.)

People still suffer depression during times of grey cold damp or wintry weather; but we get through in the knowledge that the order of nature is that "season follows season". Davies finished his proletarian epic on that note of hope; and his postwar verses express it in contrast to his embattled earlier work. "Heaviness may endure for a night, but joy cometh in the morning", as the Psalmist so deliciously states (Ps.30.5, C.of E. Book of Common Prayer version). It is the hope of life and Easter that it's this way round and not the other! - and Idris Davies was fortunate in that his later years excelled the early ones. I conclude with a small selection showing this trend.

Mrs. Evans fach, you want butter again.
How will you pay for it now, little woman
With your husband out on strike, and full
Of the fiery language? Ay, I know him,
His head is full of fire and brimstone
And a lot of palaver about communism,
And me, little Dan the Grocer
Depending so much on private enterprise.

What, depending on the miners and their
Money too? O yes, in a way, Mrs. Evans,
Yes, in a way I do, mind you.
Come tomorrow, little woman, and I'll tell you then
What I have decided overnight.
Go home now and tell that rash red husband of yours
That your grocer cannot afford to go on strike
Or what would happen to the butter from Carmarthen?
Good day for now, Mrs. Evans fach.

{The Angry Summer (1926)}

'Would that we two were living
  In a cottage by the sea,
Away from these blackened valleys
  And the towns of misery.'

'No. Better the days of battle
  And the days of sacrifice
Among our own warm people
  Who have honest hands and eyes.'

THE SOCIALIST VICTORY

(A majority Labour Government under Attlee was elected in 1945)

Blow on your morning bugles,
  Sons of the morning hills,
Stand on the graves of your fathers,
  See that your day fulfils
All that they bled and died for
  Who dreamed their blood should bring
A greater, prouder nation
  And a greater song to sing.

Blow on your morning bugles,
  Sons of the morning hills,
Awaken the slumbering warriors,
  Awaken the strength that wills
A world of lovelier nations
  And a surer ecstasy.
Blow on your morning bugles
  And shake the morning sea.

<u>Bevan Foretold?</u>

Verily out of Gwalia
  Shall come a soul on fire,
A prophet great in anger
  And mighty in desire.

His words shall move the mountain
  And make the floods rejoice,
And the people of his passion
  Shall lift the golden voice

A prophet out of Gwalia
  Shall rouse the heart again,
Give courage to the bosom
  And beauty to the brain.

High St. Byers Green (County Durham)

139

13th May. MAYORAL MOUNTAIN MASTERY.   140

They tell me that humility is a virtue, yet I have to admit to overweening pride in my inconsequential fell-walking as a "retiree"!

Picture: Scafell Pike summit, English Lake District, Saturday 13th May 1995, 1pm.

(Gary Muir, of Todmorden News.)

Foreground: (L to R) Bob Uttley, Frank McManus, Julia Poulton (Mayoress) (now Mercer)

The stony summit of Scafell Pike is England's highest ground. It is far from beautiful; but it offers fine panoramic views of central Lakeland including its neighbouring "giants" (by England's standards — its own 3210', not to be metricated in my lifetime please, falls well short of the heights reached by Ireland, Scotland and Wales). Having reached the summit five or six times in my twenties, I had the idea of a sponsored climb for our local "Calder Valley Moorland Search-and Rescue Team"; and a Town Mayor who undertakes such an event can hardly fail to accomplish it, for fear of loss of face!

So Julia drove us to Seathwaite at the head of Borrowdale, where at 9.20 or so we were met by Bob from our search-team; he is a strong walker, several years younger than I am. We took the easiest route up the mountain, turning left after crossing the stream at Stockley Bridge, for the long pull up Grain Ghyll to near Esk Hause. (Strong walkers might prefer the popular touristic path to the north, so as to see Styhead Tarn and Sprinkling Tarn. All should treat the mountains with respect, and carry enough clothing and rations for emergency, plus a torch and a whistle, if not a mobile telephone.)

Thereafter we had to fight for our victory over a wild fell that doesn't yield easily, for we had to cross some 150 yards of boulder-strewn terrain (good boots are essential), then lose height before regaining it in a short, steep, stony pull!

14th May. Folk Fiction from the great old days of the vast Durham Coalfield.

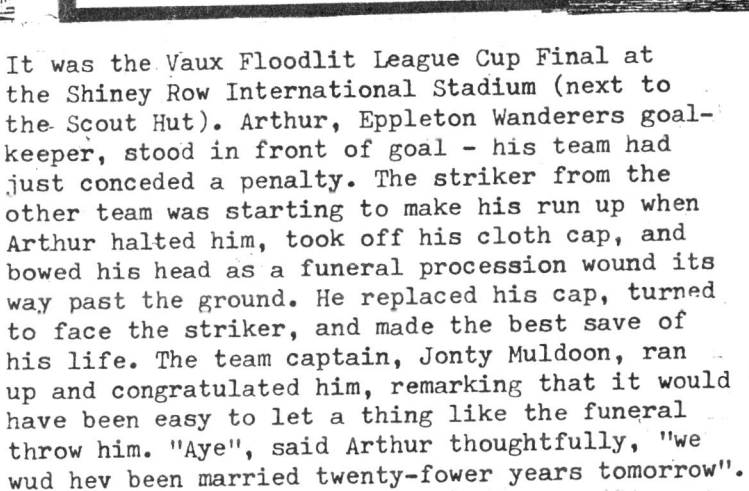

GOD SAVE THE POOR

It was the Vaux Floodlit League Cup Final at the Shiney Row International Stadium (next to the Scout Hut). Arthur, Eppleton Wanderers goal-keeper, stood in front of goal - his team had just conceded a penalty. The striker from the other team was starting to make his run up when Arthur halted him, took off his cloth cap, and bowed his head as a funeral procession wound its way past the ground. He replaced his cap, turned to face the striker, and made the best save of his life. The team captain, Jonty Muldoon, ran up and congratulated him, remarking that it would have been easy to let a thing like the funeral throw him. "Aye", said Arthur thoughtfully, "we wud hev been married twenty-fower years tomorrow".

15th May. Old Customs prior to Ascensiontide.

The three weekdays between Rogation Sunday and Ascension Day are Rogation (i.e. Asking) Days of prayer for the nation's economy and especially its agriculture. Processions to "beat the parish bounds" occur in some places, and were widespread in medieval England. Eamonn Duffy's monumental account "The Stripping of the Altars - Traditional Religion in England 1400-1580", Yale 1992 reports that all were expected to turn out for them. On each of these "Cross-days" or "gang-days" a great show was made of carrying all the parish banners and processional crosses around the boundary. with "stations" at wayside crosses for Gospel readings and prayers for harvest. A standard of a dragon was carried ahead on the first two of these days; then on the last day it was shorn of its cloth tail and carried last to symbolise the Devil's overthrow.

141 Norwich City Museum displays the dragons used in that
(to foot of next page

Thursday 16th May 1996, Ascension Day.

The Ascension doctrine causes trouble to some Christian enquirers, for it deals with the return of the risen Jesus in victory to the spiritual realm, and cannot readily be given a physical representation. Old pictures that show His feet protruding below a cloud are thought risible, and it seems more likely that the cloud which took Him up (Acts 1.9) was a mountain mist, by which the event was made intelligible.

Among the best celebratory Ascensiontide hymns are Charles Wesley's "Hail the day that sees Him rise", and Christopher Wordsworth's "See the Conqueror mounts in triumph", best seen in the full version (Old Standard Hymns A. & M 148) with the verse that prays to the Spirit to

> Lift us up from earth to Heaven, give us wings of faith and love,
> Gales of holy aspirations wafting us to realms above ;
> That, with hearts and minds uplifted, we with CHRIST our LORD may dwell,
> Where He sits enthroned in glory in His heavenly citadel.

Returning to Rogation hymns, this is Will O'Connor's new one:

1. For what is all our labour? -
   A mad pursuit of wealth? -
   A struggle with our neighbour? -
   A wearing down of health?
   This fate is forced upon those
   whose industry is cursed
   With false design and purpose
   Of profit-making first.

2. In wrongful competition
   Work bears the curse of Cain,
   And leads to our position -
   We all bear needless pain!
   How may a true vocation
   As artist-craftsman grow
   When modern automation
   Keeps mind and spirit low?

3. The hungry nations' pleading
   For food we could supply...
   Shall we pass by unheeding
   Whilst countless thousands die?
   Yet statesmen served by science
   Turn us to tools of war
   When peaceful world-alliance
   Should fill each harvest-store.

4. Shall East and West stay parted
   By fears which hatreds bring?
   Should nations use Apartheid
   When all folk have one King?
   Let Christ the Worker-Master
   Our pattern be for life,
   Our leader and our pastor
   To end our foolish strife.

Also strongly recommended are Chesterton's "O God of earth and altar" and Charles Dalmon's "Ye faithful saints of (England)" - his words being slightly modified - three verses of which can be seen on 14th January "above".

(15.5 concluded) area. In some localities the last procession was held on Ascension Day itself, i.e. the Thursday that falls 40 days after Easter Sunday; and sometimes the defeated dragon was not carried but was deflated and dragged along the ground at the tail of the procession. In the 20th century some such events were held in Stepney streets during a rent-strike, and around air-bases where there were nuclear weapons; not without success! (For Rogation homily see 27 June.)

17th May.   The Gunslinging Gambler of Govan.

That was the title which Ron Ferguson gave to his address at the memorial service for George MacLeod, the Lord MacLeod of Fuinary, who founded the Iona Community and led the restoration of the Abbey Buildings on the Inner Hebridean isle of Iona (the Abbey itself having been restored under the auspices of the 8th Duke of Argyll around the start of the 20th century). George was a passionate "nuclear disarmer" and indeed pacifist, but Ron called him a gunslinger because of his service with the "Agile and Suffering Highlanders" in World War 1. He won the Military Cross, but the sights of hardship and horror led him to change his views. He became a minister of the Kirk, then resigned his up-market Edinburgh parish to work in the poor and depressed Govan district of Glasgow. He there became acutely aware of the "distance" between daily life and overt Christian practice, and had the vision of restoring Iona as a centre where workers and ministers would share one another's concerns, so that a new generation of ministers would be better trained for mission in industrial Scotland. George thereupon made the great gamble of leaving Govan for an Iona venture which lacked assured funding. The gamble paid off, as Ron's biography of George shows.

I myself share the belief that it is wrong to compartmentalise life into "sacred" and "secular" zones. That heresy crept in at the Reformation alongside some good things; the whole of life is "sacred" except when we "desecrate" it! As a Christian Socialist I generally concur with George in saying I'd rather have churchfolk oppose me politically than have them apolitical or individualistically "pious"!

Nevertheless I commend the fictional dialogue in Studdert Kennedy's "Democracy and the Dog Collar" (1921) between "Mr Organised Labour", who accuses the Church of insufficient sincerity, and "Mr Organised Christianity", who accuses the Labour Movement of inadequate spirituality. Both are correct, I fear; so co-operation languishes and fruitfulness is lost. In "Lies" (1919) Kennedy wrote that "only new men(*), or men who are becoming new, can make a new world. Only new men.... could possibly work any other system than the capitalist system of industry.... No one wants to see it destroyed more than I do, but I have not the slightest faith in its being destroyed except to lead us in something worse, unless its destruction is carried out by new men." I say this can be achieved if we attain an ascending spiral of public and private morality! (27 June refers.)

(*) - Please forgive exclusive language; this was in 1919!

18th May. *In Time of 'The Breaking of Nations'* (Jer. li. 20.)

ONLY a man harrowing clods   Only thin smoke without flame   Yonder a maid and her wight
  In a slow silent walk   From the heaps of couch-grass;   Come whispering by:
With an old horse that stumbles and   Yet this will go onward the same   War's annals will cloud into night
  Half asleep as they stalk.   nods   Though Dynasties pass.   Ere their story die.

Thomas Hardy wrote this famous little poem in 1915, yet the idea had lain dormant in him since he watched the horse at work during the Franco-Prussian War of 1870.

I was a Chemistry lecturer at the Lancaster and Morecambe College of Further Education from 1954 to 1968. Norman Iles, Liberal Studies lecturer there, then wrote in a contemporary non-rhyming idiom; and he produced the following lines when it had occurred to him that Hardy had become outdated:

"ONLY A TRACTOR HARROWING CLODS."

Already the old horse has nodded
And stumbled into the silent past.
The smoke from burning couch-grass
Is rarer now, as, water-bodied,
Cancerous chemicals contort the weeds.
Our courting couples park in lanes,
Where, if they whisper, no one heeds.
And not one reader now remains
Conversant with that word "wight".

Dynasties have passed. There Hardy's right.
But, how many centuries?
The poet of the breaking of the nations
Did not foresee such transformations.
Or that war's annals might enshroud
Not individual love-stories,
But the time of the breaking of the world.

NONPAREIL
DE GUICHE
Parisian Polish.
FOR VARNISHING DRESS
BOOTS AND SHOES; IS MORE
ELASTIC AND EASIER TO USE
THAN ANY OTHER.

This in turn prompted me to venture a traditional and more hopeful "unauthorised variation on a theme by Norman Iles." My sixth line does not offer a serious opinion on modern farming.

Already the old horse has nodded and stumbled
    Into the silent past.
The world of the squire and the parson has crumbled,
    Too simple to last.

Though couch-grass is eaten by deadly white powder,
    Farming seems none the worse;
But Hardy's grave diction is vanquished by louder
    And angrier verse.   (to foot of next page.

144

19th May.   "Swing the Locksley shield."

By 1972 my family and I had moved south, but I was kindly invited to spend a few summer days with Norman Iles and his wife Mary in Morecambe. I mentioned my interest in Tennyson's two Locksley Hall poems, and was delighted when they gave me the Laureate's "Complete Poetical Works". For this I wrote my thanks in the Locksley metre which Longfellow had used in "The Belfry at Bruges", and Betjeman for "Huxley Hall" and some other wry poems:

Oh it's good to flee from teaching and from money and from care,
And be driven up to Kentmere for a breath of Lakeland air,
Walk the Garburn pass to Troutbeck thro' the campers' homely crowd
And to see the crags of Scafell rise o'er Langdale and the cloud;
Then the church with treasured prayer-sheets of the wars of old Queen Anne,
And a pint of bitter shandy at the deathless Mortal Man;
Then to travel back to Morecambe with its million-dollar view,
And to dine and talk and slumber with your family and you;
Send a letter to a Bishop and some cards to friends and home,
Browse amid the works of Poets, then among your music roam -
Hear the rage of Vaïnemoïnen at the Daughter of the North,
And the daemon of Beethoven bringing life from death to birth;;
Then a hasty ride by Arnside on the rare expensive trains,
And an hour with Harry Gregson (*), and there's nothing that remains
But to thank you for the kindness shown to me by one and all,
And the lovely book you gave me for the sake of Locksley Hall.
(* - then Principal, L&MCFE.) _____

18.5   Do young folk who yell about "luv" of their women
(concl.)   Still whisper their mirth?
         Will war-clouds engulf them and all that is human
            In judgment of earth?

         On gain and on loss in great change we may ponder,
            Nor yearn for the past -
         The old virtues stand! - to our fainthearted wonder,
            'Tis love will outlast.

- - - - - - -

(Norman Iles' publications include "Who Really Killed Cock Robin? Nursery Rhymes & Carols Restored to their Original Meanings" - Robert Hale 1986, and "The Restoration of Cock Robin" - ditto 1989. Percy Dearmer's interesting Preface to "The Oxford Book of Carols" (1928), whilst identifying carols as simple, hilarious, popular songs with a religious impulse, reminds us that the word Carol once meant to dance in a ring, e.g. The Holly & the Ivy, "probably of pagan origin" (p.81).)

20th May. "THIS ENGLAND."

The New Statesman magazine has for many years printed each week a few curious pieces which have appeared in the press. "England" is varied on occasion when the extracts hail from elsewhere. The older curiosities give an impression of the then climate of opinion; here are some from the 1930s:

"Silver Cigarette Case, engraved with map of Europe. British Isles inlaid in Gold." (Advertisement in Punch.)

"If the working classes do not provide the country with a stock of miners, scavengers, bus drivers, sewermen, fishermen, dock labourers etc., who is to do it?" (Letter, Daily Telegraph.)

"The bows of the Napier Star had ripped through the bows of the Laurentic just beneath one of the anchors...Three men were found dead in their bunks...How near disaster came to catastrophe was also evident. Had the Napier Star struck twenty yards further astern, she would have cut clean into the first-class staterooms." (Daily Mail.)

"There is no such thing as a household drudge in South Africa. Even in the poorest farms or in the meanest suburb, there is a native to do the work of the home. He will start at half-past five or six in the morning..."(D. Tel.)

"On Wednesday the Westminster Coroner referred to the suicide of ---, who shot himself within a few minutes of the time when his insurance policy lapsed, as a 'cold-blooded method to defraud the insurance company." (News Chronicle.)

"I do not know whether you are a knave or a fool if you thought you were going to corrupt a police officer with a paltry £5," said Mr ---, the Magistrate at Old-st."(D.Tel.)

"Complaints have been made that unnecessarily broad jokes and strong language have got past the microphone.... in future 'Damn', 'Hell!' and 'Blast' are to be excised from the plays." (Evening Standard.)

146

21st May.   CASTING A SPELL.   147

Some teachers and "educational advisers" minimise the importance of correct spelling (and, for that matter, of grammar), on the ground that it is an idol before which creativeness and spontaneity should not be sacrificed. Up to a point this is true. Tutors worth their salt don't apply too much red ink to students' scripts lest a message of destructive discouragement is given. But Melanie Phillips ("All must have Prizes", Warner 1996) reproduces a story written by Paul (10) in which an ant says to an anteater: "Eat me them but down throu me in that hole." A critical article in the *Guardian* brought letters from teachers who "dismissed his mistakes as unimportant and (gave the view) that mastery of the language was a bar to creativity". One English teacher wrote "The classroom teaching of spelling is a profligate waste of time...and is a source of frustration for the 'dyslexics'..." But surely any sensitive teacher would, whilst not harrying the pupils, least of all the dyslexics, try and raise the Pauls from the verbal indiscipline and slovenly speech that blurs "them" and "then", and renders "don't", meaning "do not", as "down"! Failure to demand good diction and correct spelling may in the short term free a pupil to be creative, but unless such freedom is countered by sufficient discipline, any such creativity will not be satisfactorily communicated to others.

After all a rabbet[1] is not a rabbit, nor is a manciple a maniple. But beware of pitfalls! (1-but see 10.11) The former Royal Institute of Chemistry, protesting against candidates' poor spelling, once all but misspelt the word "misspell" in a circular to colleges. Its printed report bore a handwritten correction. More happily, a Student Christian Movement booklet on 1970s feminist theology rendered an old phrase as "Barnished Daughters of Eve", which made readers wonder whether these damsels were banished, burnished, tarnished, or even varnished.

TO LADIES!
All the most beautiful women use
CREME SIMON.
Mme. ADELINA PATTI says: "Have found it very good indeed." For all irritations of the skin it is unequalled. CHAPS, REDNESS, ROUGHNESS disappear as if by magic. Paris: 13, Rue Grange Bateliere. London: Mertens, 64, Holborn Viaduct, E.C.; Chemists, Druggists, Perfumers, and Stores.

THE 'NEW GUINEA' SPRING BEDSTEAD.
Pillars, 1 in., Sides 1¼ in., strong Tubes, Double Woven Wire Mattress. Patent side fastenings to prevent Sagging. Bottom frame in 1 piece.
Please mention this Paper.

6 ft. 6 in. long, 3 ft. wide.
21s.
CARRIAGE PAID.

EVERY DESCRIPTION of Bedsteads, Bedding, Spring Mattresses, Bedroom Furniture, &c., direct from the manufacturer. To be had only direct from (where samples may be seen)

CHARLES RILEY, Albert St., BIRMINGHAM

A weakish candidate for Cambridge University's General Ordination examination is said to have "mugged up" the Kings of Israel and Judah since for several years the Old Testament paper had been focussed on them. When to his dismay he found the question before him read "Compare the life and work of the prophets Elijah and Elisha" he wrote in reply: "Far be it from me to compare the lives of these holy men – here is a list of the Kings of Israel and Judah."

22nd May. "When lovely woman stoops to folly.."

This enticing line from Oliver Goldsmith is grist to the mill to entrants in "composite-poem" competitions such as the New Statesman's No.3700 set by me in 2001, to the effect that "we'd like you to have another stab at verse with every line taken from a well-known poem of your choice...no nonsense verse, please." S.J. Kilmington's prizewinning entry on that previous occasion made merry with the follow-up line "In the happy fields of hay"; but I have failed to locate its source, and, so far as this topic is concerned, we'll go no more a-roving till all the seas gang dry.

A 1968 contest for "Hello Words", at the opposite end of life's span from "Famous Last Words", elicited Dr Spooner's "Now for a nab at the gripple" from Peter Peterson, and Romulus' "What big teeth you have, Grandma" from A. Macintyre.

An excruciating 1973 game called for questions with personal names as their answers. Abbreviating slightly, we had:
"How do you arrive at BST?" - Adenauer. (James Dowell)
"How did the Byrd avenge the cat?" - Claude Debussy.
"Are you working on your Gospel, Matthew?" - (S. Heek)
    Omar Khayyam. (Michael Grosvenor Myer)
"What noise does a French warhorse make?" - Marshal Ney.
                                                       (M. Yelsap)
Anagrams were sought in 1976 on the model of:
"Asa Briggs = Sir Gas Bag." From Joyce Johnson this drew "Florence Nightingale = Fight gore! Clean linen!" Emma Fisher offered "Simon Raven = Rains Venom"; and, slightly less fiercely, J. Harvey won with "Pam Ayres = Reams pay".

(In fact it is seldom difficult to produce an anagram. Karen Maloney noted "Tony Blair = Tory in Lab."! Be that as it may, I'm dumbfounded by the Guardian's crossword-compiler who in 2001 produced the clue: "Poetic scene with a surprisingly chaste Lord Archer vegetating. (3,3,8,12)" The answer, an exact anagram of the last four words, was "The Old Vicarage Grantchester".)

Occasionally the Statesman, or Staggers, set a more serios competition, such as the one which procured Robert Baird's poignant sonnet "Belfast: Autumn 1974". At the other end of the scale, definitions of sports failed to equal the example in the question: "Sumo wrestling: Survival of the fattest." I conclude lightheartedly with a verse from Stanley L. Sharpless' dumbed-down version, in words of four letters, of a favourite Tennyson lyric:
"Come into yard, Maud, / Wait near gate. / Come into yard, Maud, / Meet your fate./ Lips like wine, / Baby mine."

23rd May.   "When the Rudyards cease from kipling;
            (and the Haggards ride no more)".

That old frivolity was devised to denote the longed-for day when all earthly sorrows are swamped into a universal harmony. Kipling was a poet of note, and deserves to be honoured as such by those among us who may deride him for blind imperial support of the British Raj in India, "the brightest jewel in the crown".

Mentioning the Jungle Book and Kim in passing, I turn from his prose to his verse which included some famous aphorisms:

Oh, East is East, and West is West, and never the twain shall meet,
Till Earth and Sky meet presently at God's great Judgment Seat..."
(Kipling didn't anticipate the late writings of Bede Griffiths)
and
When the Himalayan peasant meets the he-bear in his pride,
He shouts to scare the monster, who will often turn aside.
But the she-bear thus accosted rends the peasant tooth and nail,
For the female of the species is more deadly than the male...

Mandalay was popular as a parlour-ballad until at least 1960:

By the old Moulmein Pagoda, lookin' lazy at the sea,
There's a Burma girl a-settin', and I know she thinks o' me!....
An' I seed her first a-smokin' of a whackin' white cheroot,
An' a-wastin' Christian kisses on an 'eathen idol's foot:
   Bloomin' idol made o' mud -
   Wot they called the Great Gawd Budd -
   Plucky lot she cared for idols when I kissed 'er
      where she stud!....
   On the road to Mandalay,
   Where the flyin'-fishes play,
   An' the dawn comes up like thunder outer China
      'crost the Bay!

(But the "ten-year soldier", back in London, hankers for his "neater, sweeter maiden in a cleaner, greener land" than ours where he feels that "the blasted English drizzle wakes the fever in my bones)

— — — — — — —

Famous too are the well-known "Recessional", and "If"; also items such as "Danegeld", "A Smuggler's Song" ("Watch the wall, my darling, while the Gentlemen go by"), "The Glory of the Garden", "The Gods of the Copybook Headings", and some which follow later in this volume, and "Eddi's Service" at Christmas. For today, however, here's Kipling's "Appeal":

"If I have given you delight / By aught that I have done,
 Let me lie quiet in that night / Which shall be yours anon!"

149

24th May. The Captains and the Kings depart. 150

Queen Victoria's birthday, kept as Empire Day in my childhood in the 1930s. The sun never set on the proud British Empire shown in red on large "Mercator's Projection" maps on classroom walls. Arctic Canada's icy mountains gave vastness to our presence. We heard of Clive and Wolfe, though happily little of Cecil Rhodes. We sang "It comes from the misty ages" from "The Banner of St George" (Elgar; words by S. Wensley), and of course Kipling's hymn "Land of our Birth", with its earnest innocence that raises it above mockery:

Land of our birth, we pledge to thee
Our love and toil in the years to be;
When we are grown and take our place
As men and women with our race.

FATHER in heaven who lovest all,
 O help thy children when they call,
That they may build from age to age
An undefilèd heritage.

Teach us to bear the yoke in youth,
With steadfastness and careful truth;
That in our time thy grace may give
The truth whereby the nations live.

Teach us to rule ourselves alway,
Controlled and cleanly night and day;
That we may bring, if need arise,
No maimed or worthless sacrifice.

Teach us to look in all our ends
On thee for judge, and not our friends;
That we, with thee, may walk uncowed
By fear or favour of the crowd.

Teach us the strength that cannot seek,
By deed or thought, to hurt the weak;
That, under thee, we may possess
Man's strength to comfort man's distress.

Teach us delight in simple things,
And mirth that has no bitter springs;
Forgiveness free of evil done,
And love to all men 'neath the sun.

Land of our birth, our faith, our pride,
For whose dear sake our fathers died;
O Motherland, we pledge to thee,
Head, heart, and hand through the years to be!

The "Great War" of 1914-18 was too recent for critical comment in schools - we were sold red poppies for Martinmas silence but didn't hear of the white peace-concern flowers of the Co-operative Women's Guild. A kind conspiracy of silence still spared us the worst horrors, such as the poets Sassoon and Owen drew upon in work that Yeats refused to anthologise on the questionable ground that passive suffering is not a suitable subject for poetry. These two by Owen include a famous sonnet:

The Parable of the Old Man and the Young

So Abram rose, and clave the wood, and went,
And took the fire with him, and a knife.
And as they sojourned both of them together,
Isaac the first-born spake and said, My Father,
Behold the preparations, fire and iron,
But where the lamb for this burnt-offering?
Then Abram bound the youth with belts and straps,
And builded parapets and trenches there,
And stretchèd forth the knife to slay his son.
When lo! an angel called him out of heaven,
Saying, Lay not thy hand upon the lad,
Neither do anything to him. Behold,
A ram, caught in a thicket by its horns;
Offer the Ram of Pride instead of him,
But the old man would not so, but slew his son,
And half the seed of Europe, one by one.

ANTHEM FOR DOOMED YOUTH

What passing bells for those who die as cattle?
 Only the monstrous anger of the guns.
 Only the stuttering rifles' rapid rattle
Can patter out their hasty orisons.
No mockeries for them from prayers or bells,
Nor any voice of mourning save the choirs,—
The shrill, demented choirs of wailing shells;
 And bugles calling for them from sad shires.

What candles may be held to speed them all?
 Not in the hands of boys, but in their eyes
Shall shine the holy glimmers of good-byes.
 The pallor of girls' brows shall be their pall;
Their flowers the tenderness of patient minds,
And each slow dusk a drawing-down of blinds.
                                    Wilfred Owen

[Sassoon: 16 June].

25th May. St Bede's day, so THE CATHEDRALS OF OUR LAND stand in testimony to his Faith as declared in the gilt text over his shrine in Durham's grand old Norman cathedral: "Christ is the Morning Star who when the night of this world is past brings to his saints the promise of the light of life and opens everlasting day". Bede (673-735) taught young people, without benefit of National Syllabus or Standard Tests, in monasteries at Jarrow and Monkwearmouth (Sunderland); and he wrote his "Ecclesiastical History" which shows regard for relics.

Architecture influences the "spirit of the age", as witness the impersonal towerblocks which 1960s architects thought good enough for industrial communities displaced by slum-clearance. The great medieval cathedrals testify to another order of things altogether - Cologne, Chartres, Seville, Paris.....in Scotland only Glasgow and Kirkwall escaped ruin at the Reformation, the latter being built in the sweetness of red stone by masons with Durham experience. Wales has St David's and Bangor; in Ireland Cork and the modern Galway and Killarney are perhaps her best. Alec Clifton-Taylor's guidebook "The Cathedrals of England" (Thames & Hudson, rev. 1986) is invaluable to those who don't want Pevsner's monumental volumes. It divides our 26 Anglican cathedrals (excluding those that were parish churches and the modern ones at Coventry, Guildford, Liverpool and Truro) into a First 13 which all lovers of great places of worship should see, and a very good 2nd 13:

1st in regional groups.	2nd.
Canterbury.(✱)	Bristol.
Salisbury.	Carlisle.(♭)
Winchester.	Chester
Exeter.	Chichester.
Wells.(✱)	Hereford.
Gloucester.	Lichfield.
Ely.	Oxford.
Norwich.(+)	Ripon.(∅)
Peterborough.	Rochester.
Lincoln.(✱)	St Alban's.
York.	Southwark.
Durham.(✱)	Southwell.
London.(@)	Worcester.

Old St Paul's: Chancel & E. Window.

(✱) = sure to be on shortlist for England's finest.
(♭) = a little gem! (∅) = Saxon crypt survives. (+) = see 28.5.
(@) = St Paul's, Wren's triumph(yet we should grieve for the loss of the huge Old St Paul's by fire in 1666)

Warning: some cathedrals charge for admission, which I think is wrong, and I won't pay though I will donate. One may of course ask free access for private prayer.

Whitsunday 26th May 1996. PENTECOST!

Often called the birthday of the Christian Church, this festival is observed on the 50th day of Eastertide, hence the second name above. It celebrates the coming of the Holy Spirit (Ghost) in power to the gathered apostles in Jerusalem, with tongues of fire and a sound like the rush of a mighty wind (Acts $2.^{2,3}$). The men, who at first had not believed the resurrection-message of Mary Magdalene and the other women (Luke 24.11), and even when persuaded had met timidly behind closed doors, were emboldened to proclaim it openly regardless of Establishment hostility! Clearly there had been a gift of energy from the spiritual realm. After two millennia this would now be inconsequential were it not still available today, as it has been down the ages, mainly "soul by soul and silently". As the prophet Habakkuk said: "The vision is yet for an appointed time...though it tarry, wait for it"! (2.3)

– – – – – – – – –

Now for two older poems in praise of women, lost though they be. (see tomorrow for Kipling's).

HESTER

When maidens such as Hester die,
Their place ye may not well supply,
Though ye among a thousand try
    With vain endeavour.
A month or more hath she been dead,
Yet cannot I by force be led
To think upon the wormy bed
    And her together.

A springy motion in her gait,
A rising step, did indicate
Of pride and joy no common rate
    That flush'd her spirit :
I know not by what name beside
I shall it call : if 'twas not pride,
It was a joy to that allied
    She did inherit.

Her parents held the Quaker rule,
Which doth the human feeling cool ;
But she was train'd in Nature's school,
    Nature had blest her.
A waking eye, a prying mind,
A heart that stirs, is hard to bind ;
A hawk's keen sight ye cannot blind,
    Ye could not Hester.

My sprightly neighbour ! gone before
To that unknown and silent shore,
Shall we not meet, as heretofore
    Some summer morning—
When from thy cheerful eyes a ray
Hath struck a bliss upon the day,
A bliss that would not go away,
    A sweet fore-warning ?

←–Chas. Lamb.
Wm. Barnes–→
(Dorset, for his Julia.)

MELTONIAN BLACKING.
(As used in the Royal Household.)
RENDERS THE BOOTS SOFT, DURABLE, AND WATERPROOF.

THE WIFE A-LOST

Since I noo mwore do zee your feäce,
    Up steärs or down below,
I'll zit me in the lwonesome pleäce,
    Where flat-bough'd beech do grow ;
Below the beeches' bough, my love,
    Where you did never come,
An' I don't look to meet ye now,
    As I do look at hwome.

Since you noo mwore be at my zide,
    In walks in zummer het,
I'll goo alwone where mist do ride,
    Droo trees a-drippèn wet ;
Below the rain-wet bough, my love,
    Where you did never come,
An' I don't grieve to miss ye now,
    As I do grieve at hwome.

Since now bezide my dinner-bwoard
    Your vaïce do never sound,
I'll eat the bit I can avword
    A-vield upon the ground ;
Below the darksome bough, my love,
    Where you did never dine,
An' I don't grieve to miss ye now,
    As I at hwome do pine.

Since I do miss your vaïce an' feäce
    In praÿer at eventide,
I'll praÿ wi' oone sad vaïce vor greäce
    To goo where you do bide ;
Above the tree an' bough, my love,
    Where you be gone avore,
An' be a-waitèn vor me now,
    To come vor evermwore.

"Work is the Curse of the Drinking Classes." – Oscar Wilde.

27th May. A *Kipling Trifle* with a surprise ending; and parts of three *Ballad-Poems*: short extracts from "The Law of the Jungle" and "The Gods of the Copybook Headings", plus eight verses of the poet at his best in a haunting elegy. For his cheery fantasy "The Last Chantey" please see 4 July.

---

from DIRGE OF DEAD SISTERS (1902)

(quoted in "Testament of Youth" by Vera Brittain, nurse on the Western Front in W.W.I) *see 1 July*

(For the Nurses who died in the South African War)

WHO recalls the twilight and the ranged tents in order
  (Violet peaks uplifted through the crystal evening air?)
And the clink of iron teacups and the piteous, noble laughter,
  And the faces of the Sisters with the dust upon their hair?

(Now and not hereafter, while the breath is in our nostrils,
  Now and not hereafter, ere the meaner years go by—
Let us now remember many honourable women,
  Such as bade us turn again when we were like to die.)

Who recalls the morning and the thunder through the foot-hills,
  (Tufts of fleecy shrapnel strung along the empty plains?)
And the sun-scarred Red-Cross coaches creeping guarded to the culvert,
  And the faces of the Sisters looking gravely from the trains?

(When the days were torment and the nights were clouded terror,
  When the Powers of Darkness had dominion on our soul—
When we fled consuming through the Seven Hells of Fever
  These put out their hands to us and healed and made us whole.)

Who recalls the midnight by the bridge's wrecked abutment
  (Autumn rain that rattled like a Maxim on the tin?)
And the lightning-dazzled levels and the streaming, straining wagons,
  And the faces of the Sisters as they bore the wounded in.

(Till the pain was merciful and stunned us into silence—
  When each nerve cried out on God that made the misused clay;
When the Body triumphed and the last poor shame departed—
  These abode our agonies and wiped the sweat away.) ...

— — — — — — —

Yet their graves are scattered and their names are clean for-gotten,
  Earth shall not remember, but the Waiting Angel knows
Them that died at Uitvlugt when the plague was on the city—
  Her that fell at Simon's Town¹ in service on our foes.
                                    [¹ — Mary Kingsley.

*Wherefore we they ransomed, while the breath is in our nostrils,
  Now and not hereafter—ere the meaner years go by—
Praise with love and worship many honourable women,
  Those that gave their lives for us when we were like to die!*

FOX-HUNTING
1933
(The Fox Meditates)

WHEN Samson set my brush afire
    To spoil the Timnites' barley,
I made my point for Leicestershire
    And left Philistia early.
Through Gath and Rankesborough Gorse I fled,
    And took the Coplow Road, sir!
And was a Gentleman in Red
    When all the Quorn wore woad, sir! ...

When William landed hot for blood,
    And Harold's hosts were smitten,
I lay at earth in Battle Wood
    While Domesday Book was written.
Whatever harm he did to man,
    I owe him pure affection;
For in his righteous reign began
    The first of Game Protection. . . . .

When men grew shy of hunting stag,
    For fear the Law might try 'em,
The Car put up an average bag
    Of twenty dead *per diem*.
Then every road was made a rink
    For Coroners to sit on;
And so began, in skid and stink,
    The real blood-sport of Britain!

153

The Lair of the Wolf is his refuge, and where he has made him his home,
Not even the Head Wolf may enter, not even the Council may come. /Man!/
Ye may kill for yourselves, and your mates, and your cubs as they need, and ye can;
But kill not for pleasure of killing, and even times never kill
Now these are the Laws of the Jungle, and many and mighty are they;
But the head and the hoof of the Law and the haunch and the hump is—Obey!

On the first Feminian Sandstones we were promised the Fuller Life
(Which started by loving our neighbour and ended by loving his wife)
Till our women had no more children and the men lost reason and faith,
And the Gods of the Copybook Headings said: "The Wages of Sin is Death."

28th May.   BISHOP POLLOCK'S FEMALE FRIEND

Visit Norwich Cathedral and you can hardly fail to be impressed by its fine proportions, graceful high spire, large lawn in the cloisters, and other architectural splendours. Go however into the far right corner of the north transept and you'll discover hidden treasure, in the form of Derwent Wood's dignified statue of Violet Morgan, whose marble form is often taken to denote a New Testament saint. But make your way behind it and you'll be surprised by the poignant fulsome inscription, cut in block capitals:

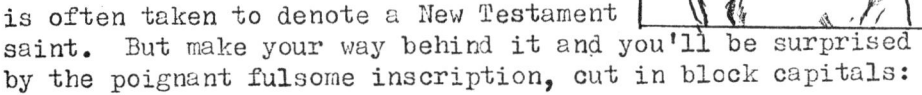

"In Caistor churchyard was laid to rest by Bertram bishop of Norwich all that could die of Violet the lovely and beloved only child of Penry and Evelyn Arden Vaughan Morgan Sweet Vi who on February 22 1919 at the age of twenty years passed from this life to the life eternal".

I discovered the sculpture after reading George W. Target's 1986 book "Holy Ground", in which the author writes that he is uneasy in cathedrals...the weight of all that dead grey stone, and doesn't need the military memorials to remind him of the pity of war. But then he adds "..this dead girl. Seems that she was the secretary of the then bishop, who was extremely fond of her, and terribly distressed at her tragically early death...and had this statue erected to her memory. 'Near the High Altar', said somebody, 'so that he could see her every time he officiated'. But it was moved when he died.'"

Now bishops are not in the habit of placing statues of their secretaries, however excellent, in their cathedrals; and here we have Violet's own lines on the plinth to her right:

"No voice shall break the glory of the stillness
Or touch the joy that our two souls fulfils
And we shall see the splendour of the morning
Dawn on the hills. V.V.M."

So clearly we have a "love-story", involving the bachelor bishop in his mid-fifties, and made sad by Violet's death at 20 before engagement, let alone marriage, ensued. A shy man, formal, aloof, reserved, perhaps awkward, Bertram Pollock was Bishop of Norwich from 1910 to 1942, without any parochial experience. Born on 6.12.1863 into a senior judicial family, and a scholar of Charterhouse and then Trinity, he taught in male enclaves at Marlborough then Wellington where he was an able and distinguished headmaster for 17 years. As bishop he opposed Prayer Book revision, then at 64 he married at last, to Joan Ryder one of Vi's successors. They had one daughter.

154

29th May. - "Oak Apple Day" in honour of the Restoration of Charles II on this his 30th birthday in 1660. The Wars of the Roses didn't reach Todmorden where I live (except peacefully in 1888 when the Yorkies won a boundary-change).

The well-known claim that it marks his escape after his defeat at Worcester in 1651, when he was hidden up the "royal oak" tree at Boscobel in Middle England by Richard Penderel, remains unproven. Nevertheless when I was a councillor in Grange-over-Sands in the 1960s our finance chairman was Cllr Dick Pendrill, whose birthday also fell on 29th May. He told me that ever since Boscobel there had been a Richard Pendrill in the family, and also a family birthday on 29th May.

I make no comment on the Roses' War save to say the Putney Debates of the Roundheads deal with issues still alive today.

(see 30/31 May re this Victorian mag.)

Vol. VII.—No. 335.]   MAY 29, 1886.   Price One Penny.

THE GIRL'S OWN PAPER

MY BROTHER'S FRIEND.

By EGLANTON THORNE, Author of "The Old Worcester Jug."

CHAPTER V.

BUSINESS WORRIES.

EDMUND did not throw off his cold so quickly as I had hoped he would. It clung to him for weeks, for when I fancied it was about to depart he would be sure to increase it by some act of imprudence. I do not think I was more anxious than other girls would have been, but I remember well how, sometimes, when I heard his cough sounding through the house in the stillness of the night, my heart would almost stand still in my agony of dread as I asked myself, was it possible that Salome's fears could be

155

30th May.   A G O N Y   I N   1 8 9 2.

The "Answers" column of the "Girl's Own Paper" was resolute for "traditional values", so that rebel teenagers got the shortest shrift. Why did they write in? To have their sense of duty upheld against their distractive desires?! I don't think the editors fabricated any of the questions; though some were hoaxes!

"CROCUS – Ask your mother's permission. You seem to fancy that you are quite your own mistress at seventeen years of age, yet only an infant in the eye of the law." (8.10.1892)

"STANLEY CAMERON – Yes, put up your back hair. At sixteen your wearing it down your back answers no good purpose, and is only a dirty practice, soiling the back of your dress or jacket."

And, crushingly "'IN LOVE' – The fancy of a little girl of fourteen could not be regarded in the light of the sobriquet she has chosen. Is there no 'amusement' for you but going out with a 'fellow'? Have you no girl companions approved of by your mother? Are there no interesting books, no indoor and outdoor games, no delightful pursuits for leisure-hours? You ought to be much occupied with your studies, so far as we can judge from your modes of expression...Trapesing about the streets with a 'fellow' at the age of fourteen is a deplorable beginning in life."
(17.12.1892)
So it can be! – but surely the next enquirer could have been given more selfconfidence instead of this scolding:

"TWENTY-ONE – If you be incompetent to read aloud well and agreeably, are a bad needlewoman, and are deficient in musical ability, you are ineligible for the situation of a companion, more especially if what you say of yourself be true – that you are also stupid and dense. You had better read our article on 'Occupations for Women and Girls'..." (10.12.1892)

Also put down, though less relentlessly, was

"AN IRISH GIRL – We thank you for your kind letter and pudding recipe, and are sorry that the one for which you ask is not of a kind that can be given in this paper. You ought to write small round handed copies daily, and use better pens and ink. The latter appears to be as thick as mud." (3.12.1892).

Well, there is a lot of mud in Ireland. Other answers were practical:
"S.W. – March 25th, 1874 was a Wednesday." (29.10.1892)

"A NEW SUBSCRIBER – The telephone between London and Paris is an accomplished fact." (19.11.1892)
(continued on next page.

31st May. "Kipper sur Toast" (from postwar Lyons' menu).   157

More quaintnesses cropped up in the era before television, when the printed word was supreme. This Corner-House menu maintained the strange English custom of menus in French. The Hayes News carried this "small ad.": "Dog for Sale, eats anything. Fond of children". And the Daily Mirror once had this report: "Opposing a proposal to name new roads in Great Yarmouth after Byron, Chaucer, Milton, Shakespeare and Tennyson, Mr R.F. Kerrison declared at Yarmouth Town Council today: 'In my opinion, the moral character of these people is not such that we should name new roads after them.' He suggested that the roads should be named after present councillors."

— — — — — —

Returning to the Girl's Own Paper "Answers to Correspondents", we may sympathise with the special problems in the life of:

"PUSSY — Keep your mouth shut, and use your handkerchief more frequently. Snoring in church is not permissible. At night you should tie up your chin to keep your mouth closed.." (15.10.1892)

The paper aimed up-market as shown by this avoidance of pen-name:

"DUCHESS OF DEVONSHIRE — Opinions vary as to the best colleges in our several Universities." (22.4.1893 — any other reply would surely have brought a hornet's nest down on the editor's head!)

— and also in the reply to

"BLUSH ROSE — In the upper ranks of life a girl ought not to be out of the schoolroom at seventeen, and in any case she would be far too young to think of marriage. Her growth is not finished,...her bones not hardened, her judgment very far from being matured...Five-and-twenty would be a more suitable age."(22.10.92)

Decorum in personal life is indispensible:

"TWO NICE GIRLS are far from 'nice' in permitting strange men to speak to and actually walk with them...the permission of your parents is essential." (24.6.1893)

But for sheer delinquency these young minxes were excelled in what looks like a surprising "April Fool"

"DOES YOUR MOTHER KNOW YOU'RE OUT? — "Alas...a pseudonym of so flippant a character at 15 & 17...it is sad to learn that you both climb out of your window every night"(1.4.93)

BLACKBURN CATHEDRAL

1st June.   Unpopular Opinions!

Tennyson spent many years and much effort on his "Idylls of the King", versifying the traditional Arthurian legends penned by Malory, which told of the King's building a civilised kingdom out of lawless chaos, followed by slow corruption of its noble ways of life, and then its disastrous disintegration — all too often a pattern for nations and empires on earth, as "The old order changeth, giving way to new". The poet's youthful Fragment, "Sir Launcelot and Queen Guinevere", contains the seeds of his concern that giving way to sexual attraction at the expense of loyalty can trigger "untold further evils in both the individual and society" (J.B. Steane, Tennyson, Evans 1966 - see 21 March). Later he developed in several books this theme, which the Victorians blew up above other moral matters but which is largely scorned now except when the prurient media take prominent people for a modern version of the skimmington-ride: (it is timely to mention this because Thomas Hardy was born on 2nd June 1840 and his "Mayor of Casterbridge" novel portrays such a hounding with "rough music" and effigies of ex-mayor Henchard and mistress!)

The theme is developed in several books through Geraint's testing of Enid, Vivien's distracting of Balin, the unrequited love of Elaine for Arthur's disloyal best friend Launcelot, & "Pelleas and Etarre" in a cynical disillusioned society, to the sorrowful rebuke of his fallen wife by the King who can no longer hold his own: "For thou hast spoilt the purpose of my life".

Ruskin respected the Idylls but felt that Tennyson should have railed more against real present evils than those of a romantic past. Sexual indiscipline is disintegrative, yes, as we see around us if not in ourselves today; but the poet can be charged with disproportion to the point of obsession even though he did recognise many other destructive developments.

More cheerfully, this having in 1996 been Trinity Eve, here is Reg. Heber's fine hymn which was Tennyson's favourite:

HOLY, Holy, Holy! (*mf*) LORD GOD Almighty!
   Early in the morning our song shall rise to Thee:
Holy, Holy, Holy! (*mf*) Merciful and Mighty!
   GOD in THREE Persons, Blessèd TRINITY!

Holy, Holy, Holy! (*mf*) all the Saints adore Thee,
   Casting down their golden crowns around the glassy sea:
Cherubim and Seraphim falling down before Thee,
   Which wert, and art, and evermore shalt be.

Holy, Holy, Holy! though the darkness hide Thee,
   Though the eye of sinful man Thy glory may not see,
Only Thou art Holy, there is none beside Thee
   Perfect in power, in love, and purity.

Holy, Holy, Holy! (*mf*) LORD GOD Almighty!
   All Thy works shall praise Thy Name, in earth, and sky, and sea:
Holy, Holy, Holy! Merciful and Mighty!
   GOD in THREE Persons, Blessèd TRINITY!

St Patrick's Breastplate

Trinity Sunday 2nd June 1996.

It is very arguable that today is the greatest of all Christian festivals, celebrating not just one historical event but the entire Sacred Mystery of the Divine Reality. Christmas, God made man in weakness, would be a cruel mockery but for Easter. Easter and Ascension would just be historical events were it not for Whitsun – Pentecost – and the presence of God's Holy Spirit here and now, which they effected.

1. I bind unto myself to-day
   The strong name of the Trinity,
   By invocation of the same
   The Three in One and One in Three.

2. I bind this day to me for ever
   By power of faith, Christ's incarnation;
   His baptism in Jordan river,
   His death on Cross for my salvation;
   His bursting from the spicèd tomb,
   His riding up the heavenly way,
   His coming at the day of doom
   I bind unto myself to-day.

3. I bind unto myself the power
   Of the great love of Cherubim;
   The sweet 'Well done' in judgment hour,
   The service of the Seraphim,
   Confessors' faith, Apostles' word,
   The Patriarchs' prayers, the prophets' scrolls,
   All good deeds done unto the Lord
   And purity of virgin souls.

4. I bind unto myself to-day
   The virtues of the star-lit heaven,
   The glorious sun's life-giving ray,
   The whiteness of the moon at even,
   The flashing of the lightning free,
   The whirling wind's tempestuous shocks,
   The stable earth, the deep salt sea
   Around the old eternal rocks.

5. I bind unto myself to-day
   The power of God to hold and lead,
   His eye to watch, his might to stay,
   His ear to hearken to my need.
   The wisdom of my God to teach,
   His hand to guide, his shield to ward;
   The word of God to give me speech,
   His heavenly host to be my guard.

6. Against the demon snares of sin,
   The vice that gives temptation force,
   The natural lusts that war within,
   The hostile men that mar my course;
   Or few or many, far or nigh,
   In every place and in all hours,
   Against their fierce hostility
   I bind to me those holy powers.

7. Against all satan's spells and wiles,
   Against false words of heresy,
   Against the knowledge that defiles,
   Against the heart's idolatry,
   Against the wizard's evil craft,
   Against the death-wound and the burning,
   The choking wave, the poisoned shaft,
   Protect me, Christ, till thy returning.

8. Christ be with me, Christ within me,
   Christ behind me, Christ before me,
   Christ beside me, Christ to win me,
   Christ to comfort and restore me.
   Christ beneath me, Christ above me,
   Christ in quiet, Christ in danger,
   Christ in hearts of all that love me,
   Christ in mouth of friend and stranger.

9. I bind unto myself the name,
   The strong name of the Trinity,
   By invocation of the same,
   The Three in One and One in Three.
   Of whom all nature hath creation,
   Eternal Father, Spirit, Word:
   Praise to the Lord of my salvation,
   Salvation is of Christ the Lord.

So God is not a monolith, but upholds us and the universe in many and various ways (Hebrews 1.1)! Lightheartedly I ask if I take one or three medicines when I solace my sore throat with Glycerine Lemon and Honey. (Hymn tr. Fanny Alexander.)

3rd June. "Words Worth Updating". 160

On this day in 1988 I was flattered when the following letter of mine to our local Hebden Bridge Times appeared under that heading — (see also 19th March, "Voice and Vision"). I sent my doggerel also to the paper which circulates in Patley Bridge where the woman in question appeared before the bench of magistrates, but I don't know whether it appeared.

Longfield Road, Todmorden.

ACCORDING to the "Hebden Bridge Times," Dr Linda Patterson of that town, has "reluctantly" paid a fine of £25, with £45 costs, for having placed a daffodil on the fence of the U.S. base at Menwith Hill, in April, 1987.

This fatuous fine has inspired the following lines which I hope will not sully the memory of William Wordsworth.

She wandered lonely as a cloud,
That floats on high o'er Menwith Hill,
Until she saw the fence of wire,
And thought it God-forsaken still —
"I'll brighten up this place," quoth she,
"And add my golden daffodil!"

"Hello, Hello," the p'liceman said,
"Our byelaws say 'Hands off that fence'!
You'll come along with me, my lass
For hazarding our sure defence;
You must be tried at Pateley Bridge —
This flower shall be our evidence!"

"Your Worships, please," dear Linda said,
"The Yankee base at Menwith Hill
Is putting all our lives at risk —
It's linked with bombs and overkill —
That's why I left, in hope of peace,
My single golden daffodil."

The magistrate looked very grave:
"Of politics we've had our fill.
The freedom of the USA
Hangs on the base upon that hill,
So ugly, yet too sacred for
Defilement by your daffodil."

Said Reagan unto Gorbachev,
"Let's stop these games and build for trust —
Let's sack our spies and ban our bombs
Ere Mother earth is turned to dust."
Quoth Mikhail — "Yes I quite agree —
And pay that girl's fine back we must!"

FRANK R. McMANUS

Will O'Connor's Satanic Verse to the H-bomb:
Hail the hell-born foe of peace, Hail the end of righteousness! Death for life to all it brings, Ris'n with murder in its wings. Veiled in steel the Monster see, Hail its fearful tyranny:— Might, by stupid men ador -ed, Might, their everlasting Lord: Hark, the demon angels howl, Glory to the Thing most foul!

I believe in God the Father,
I believe in God the Son,
I believe in God the Spirit
And the Church by Christ begun;
In His Church is grace abounding
Till in heav'n our rest is won.
God the Father, still creating
Things on earth and things above,
We adore Thee for Thy goodness,
Holiest wisdom, soft as dove
Circling round Thy humblest, Crea-
Source of life and truth and Love.
(&c. St Laurence Morecambe mag.)

PEACE

Also by W. O'Connor

n June.   REASON TO REFUSE.   (A Mystery of Horton-in-Ribblesdale, to be told now and over the next few days.)

Before the days of accurate surveying the inhabitants of the Craven district of Western Yorkshire celebrated the "3 Peaks" of their limestone countryside in a rhyme which, scorning the Lake District and Northern Pennines, states falsely that "Ingleborough, Whernside and Pen-y-Ghent / Are the highest hills between Scotland and Trent." Of these three the lowest and most easterly is Pen-y-Ghent, known as "the crouching lion of Craven" on account of its silhouette when viewed from the west where the still-small Ribble flows seaward towards Preston and Blackpool, with the famous Settle-Carlisle railway in its valley. The typical Dales Limestone church at Horton is easily reached by road, or on foot from Horton station. Dedicated to the ubiquitous St Oswald, it has a Norman doorway with chevron-mounting plus billet and cable ornamentation. Arrow-scratches to the porch testify to archery-practice with arrows from the churchyard yews. Enter the church and cross over to the north-west corner, and one may just make out the inscription on a metal plaque, unless bright sunlight falls thereon to ease the task.

(I have been factual so far; but because my tale henceforth is an imaginative invention with no known foundation in history, I make three changes of Christian name in what follows: Charles for David, William for Thomas, and Ann for Janet. RIP the real folk. The writing is indeterminate between Don- & Dowbiggin).

"Here rest the remains of the Reverend Charles Dowbiggin, BA, of Catharine Hall in the University of Cambridge. One worthy (Reader) of thy imitation. He was plain honest and sincere without moroseness. Sensible without arrogance. And learned above those of his age without pedantry. He had constancy of mind enough to be always diligent. And good humour enough to be always cheerful. He had the sensibility to love what he had the reason to refuse. But above all He had Religion enough to give him a reasonable hope thro the merits of his Saviour, Of rising to eternal Happiness. He dy'd ye Second day of April One Thousand Sevn Hundred fifty six in the twenty-third year of his Age.

"Here also was interred the remains of Mr. William Dowbiggin of Newlandhouse who departed this life September 28th 1774 in the 50th year of his Age. What has been said of the moral and religious Character of his learned Brother may with Justice and Propriety be applied to his Par nobile Fratrum.

"And also Mrs Ann Dowbiggin Widow of the said William Dowbiggin she died 7th day of march 1797 in the 65th year of her Age. For this lost friend a tear will trickle and a sigh ascend."

5th June. St Thomas' Eve 1745 and a cold starlit night as the carol-singers left Newlandhouse with a florin for their efforts. "Pity we couldn't sing some modern words and not just have 'Remember Adam's fall' wherever we go", said young Ann Dawson; "Charles there says 'While shepherds watched' is worth trying — d'ye know it?" "Hark at 'er — girls of fourteen should be in bed by now, and here she is, sweet on the young master!" "Oh just you shut up, Tommy Phillips, you're jealous of his voice and of all the songs and rhymes and tales he can tell." "That's about all 'e can do — knows nowt o't real world. Say have ye heard? — There's an army come down from Scotland and taken Carlisle and gone down Preston way to London. They say these Georges aren't proper kings and this Bonnie Prince Charlie says should be 'is father. You won't see our Charlie anywhere near that, will you, Ann?" "Got more sense I'd say", she chirped, and flounced away.

Pen-y-Ghent from Horton in Ribblesdale.

162

Visit Horton Church today and you may see, just outside the west end, a stone marking the resting-place of Ann Holden, vicar's wife, who died in 1794 at age 36. Her diary for the December before her tragically early death tells of a chat she had with Mrs. Dowbiggin, who had been living alone in Newlandhouse; her husband had died in 1774. This kindly old lady had invited the local carollers in for punch and mince-pies to warm them on their way; and Mrs. Holden had asked her if she had ever met her late husband's younger brother, who was said to have been drowned in Hull Pot on Pen-y-ghent at a time of flood, when (as happens "once in a blue moon" according to the caption of a picture now displayed in the local tea-room) the vast brick-shaped trough, large enough to hold an ocean-going ship, fills with water from rain and melting snow. "Yes, I do know the story," said Ann Dowbiggin, "but it isn't true! The skeleton they dug out of the caked mud in 1770 wasn't Charles, though they buried it in his name. We all thought it was, but it must have been a young wanderer of the same build. You see, Mrs. Holden, I *met* Charles four years later, and he was no ghost!" "What?! — why haven't you told anyone that, love?"

6th June.   ANN'S STORY.   163

"Ah, it's a long story, and a bit of a dark one, so you'll have to drop out of the carolling if you want to hear it; yes, do please listen, for I may not be around much longer, and I ought to get it off my chest.

"Charles and I were children together, though we didn't see much of each other - he wasn't robust enough then to go to school, so he had lessons at home. Then he went to Cambridge to study, and lived in Catharine Hall to work for his degree. Very taken by religion he was - a nice young man with a helping hand for everybody, and a real knowledge of the old tales from Greece and Rome; and of the Bible, the poets, and the historians. The bishop of Ely made him a deacon this time in '55 - a Reverend at just 23 - and he proposed to me that Boxing Day! He didn't seem to know I'd been going around with his older brother William - dinners and dances after work, him on his estate, me on my father's farm - and I didn't know what to say, 'cos I liked them both quite a lot, but that was all.

"Anyway Charles soon went back to Cambridge to translate a set of old Latin hymns, and we got on with our winter work here in Horton. But when he came home for the spring vacation he told me it was for the last time; he loved me too much but I couldn't be his Ann Dawson, for he didn't expect to live much longer, and someone like William would give me a much better life. I told him not to think that way; I hadn't made any decision so why not just give things a chance to work out? He made no reply, but he didn't come home one evening, and his footprints ended at Hull Pot. But there was no sign of him, and we gave him up as lost and washed underground. All we saw below where the footprints had stopped was a vast amount of slime. We were all so sad, but life had to go on, and I grew fonder of William as the years went by. We got married; and although no children came we were happy in Newlandhouse, which became his when the old squire died. Then that skeleton came up and was given burial and the plaque in memory of Charles was put in the church. William paid half the cost. So you can imagine how I felt when Charles came back, out of the blue, just before Michaelmas in 1774! William had ridden to Settle on business, and I was alone in the house as Charles told me the truth of what had happened.

"Back in Cambridge in '56 he'd pined for me as he forced himself to work on those hymns, and he'd decided he had to

7th June. "April is the Cruellest Month."

break away and find a new life. His best friend's father was the aging vicar of St. Hilary in Cornwall, no longer able to perform all his duties but not rich enough to resign or find a curate; so Charles took the job for bed, board, and a small allowance, provided he might first pay one more visit to me. Here he'd found a boat in Hull Pot, which had been used for fishing in shallow pools, and had paddled it to where it could be reached at the village end. Next morning (April 2nd), saying he was taking a walk, he'd gone to it, found the water was still high, paddled it to a snow-free slope at the far end, released it, and tramped via Litton and Arncliffe to an inn at Kettlewell. With plenty of money in his metal box and but few possessions in his budget - just a spare shirt and some socks and a bite of bread and cheese - he passed himself off as a holiday-visitor and took the coach south next morning, and settled into the curacy so successfully that the local bishop 'priested' him 'on the nod' at his advent ordinations. Some years later he succeeded to the incumbency of St. Hilary; but he couldn't forget Ann Dawson at Horton, or his brother William, and felt he could safely use his annual holiday to make touch there once more. Knowing how his sudden reappearance could cause a few shockwaves he'd stayed last night in the New Inn, and was booked there for another night in the name Charles Smith, a tourist on a visit from Cornwall. So I could tell William that he'd call on us both next day.

"It was dusk when William rode back that evening, and he was so astonished at the news that he insisted on hunting his brother out there and then, to treat him to a meal if he hadn't dined already. I stayed up till midnight and still they hadn't returned, so I imagined William had booked himself overnight at the inn, and I went to bed. But there was no sign of William when Charles came by himself at nine o'clock next morning; and there had been no sign of William at the inn the previous night - so you can guess how worried I was. I told Charles to stay in the house and keep the doors locked against all comers - it was our maid's day off - and to stay upstairs so that nobody might see him. Then I set off, deeply worried, to try and find what had happened to William. Nobody had seen him in the

164

CARDINAL VAUGHAN wrote :—
"I have always found **Proctor's** Pinelyptus Pastilles efficacious."

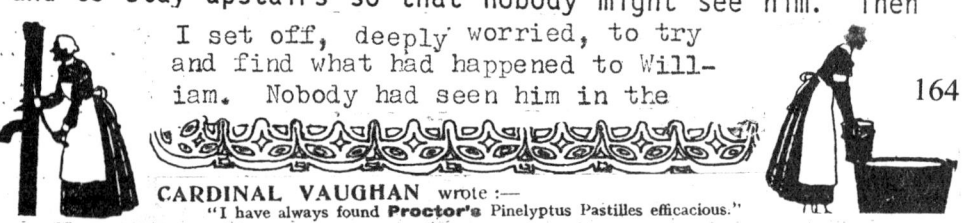

8th June.   **Bull and Bush?**   ....village, but I took the short cut home by the field-footpath, and there by the stile lay his dead body, and Phillips' bull quietly grazing in the far corner. Shouldn't've been there, but it was thought pretty safe, and there was no blood on it though William's head had a nasty gash - but the beast had been out in a heavy shower, so God alone knew what had happened. Anyway the old vicar took me in till he could send me home; I told Charles what had happened and I made him go back under cover of darkness to the New Inn and to leave next morning and I'd go to Cornwall and stay with him in the spring. It was an open verdict on poor William and a heavy fine for the farmer whose bull had pushed through a hedge. Everyone looked after me when the funeral was over, and I could say nothing when they added an inscription to the one about Charles whom we all thought had died in '56. Yet sometimes I did wonder about that bull - or if some passer-by had gone for William with a spike - and who? - and why?

"So I was Ann Dowbiggin, Widow, when I went south at Eastertide in '75, to stay with Charles for a month. He let it be known that I was his brother's widow; and though a few pussycat-tongues commented on our sharing the house, the bishop asked to be spared such tittle-tattle. It was a very emotional time, of course, with real grief and growing fondness, plus a tiny nagging doubt about William's death that I couldn't get rid of for all its unworthiness; it came back as often as I crushed it. Then Charles said he'd proposed to me once, had left Horton and Cambridge to get a new life without me, had returned incognito only to be caught up in William's tragic death, and wondered now if he dared think of proposing again. I replied that I thought he knew his Prayer Book from beginning to end, and had he forgotten the very last thing - 'A Table of Kindred and Affinity, wherein whosoever are related are forbidden in scripture and our laws to marry together'? Surely its silly start was well known: 'A Man may not marry his Grandmother'! - but it went on to add: 'A Woman may not marry with her... Husband's Brother'. He asked me what sense I thought there was in that, and all I could say was it must come from the Old Testament somewhere. 'Well, we're legally bound by it but is it morally binding?' he asked; 'the book says it is, see Article 7, but it's all so farfetched.' 'Look,' I replied, 'I'm going home till I can find a tenant, then I'll come back and stay with you, yes?' - And he nodded his agreement. We had twelve years together - you'll have to guess whether we ever slipped up! - Then he took ill with consumption and died and this time he really

9th June.   Reason to Refuse (conclusion).

was buried; so I moved the tenants on and settled into Newlandhouse again with a friendly community in this village to ease my loneliness a bit - though it sometimes hits me at night when I think of the days gone by."

- - - - - - - - - - - - - - - -

Mrs. Holden added in her diary that she gave Mrs. Dowbiggin a cup of tea to calm her after sharing such secrets, and had reassured her that when the previous vicar met her husband before handing over the parish documents, he had told him that, unknown to anyone else, he'd been walking on the lower slopes of Pen-y-Ghent the evening William had died, and yes it had been the bull. He'd kept his counsel on this because Tommy Phillips was a respected farmer and he didn't want to aggravate his punishment, or provoke a manslaughter charge when no one else was suspected.

Mrs. Dowbiggin then told her that the line would die with her and she wondered how to dispose of Newlandhouse. "I sometimes think," she said, "that a hospice for lonely women might be a good thing in our village, but I'm probably being ahead of our age." So she left it to the Church, and soon both Anns were laid to rest there, with their only memorials shaded by the old yew-trees.

166

(In the 20th century Horton old vicarage was given by its then owner to serve as a women's rest-house.)

BIRD'S CUSTARD POWDER

Sing a Song of Sixpence
a pocket full of Rye
A DISH of DAINTY CUSTARD
improves an APPLE PIE

10th June. THE DILLY SONG (NOT Burns' "Green grow the Rashes-O")

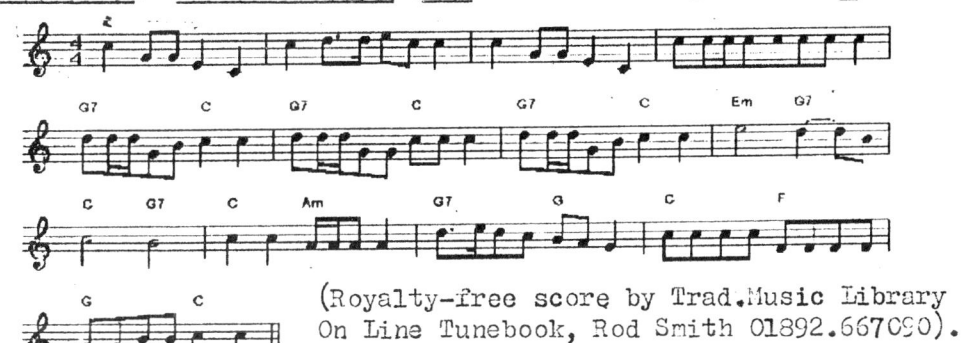

(Royalty-free score by Trad. Music Library On Line Tunebook, Rod Smith 01892.667090).

I'll sing you one O.
 Green grow the rushes O.
What is your one O?
 One is one and all alone
 And evermore shall be so. — etc. building up:
- - - - - - - - -
I'll sing you twelve O.
 Green grow the rushes O.
What is your twelve O?
 Twelve for the twelve apostles,
 Eleven for the eleven who went to heaven,
 Ten for the ten commandments,
 Nine for the nine bright shiners,
 Eight for the eight bold rangers,
 Seven for the seven stars in the sky,
 Six for the six proud walkers,
 Five for the symbol at your door,
 Four for the Gospel makers,
 Three for the rivals,
 Two, two, the lilywhite boys,
 Clothed all in green O,
 One is one and all alone
 And evermore shall be so.

This song was collected by Baring-Gould & Sheppard, "Songs of the West" (1892). The Faber Book of Popular Verse explains that it originates in the "middle ages" not as nonsense but as a school-pupils' aide-memoire or mnemonic to the heavenly orders. The "Digital Tradition Mirror" presents it, with minor alterations e.g. "Three, three, the rivals" as "a summary of postings to the internet." B.McC adds "I have always been intrigued by the mix of references to the Bible and to the constellations, and wonder if the verses are a blending of an astronomical and a biblical version." But since "The heavens declare the glory of God" (Ps.19.1), as those of us who are fortunate enough not to have them blotted out by urban lighting will confirm; so some overlap hardly surprises, especially in folklore where "official versions" seldom crystallise. Combination of my sources yields the following:

Nos. 4 (Matthew, Mark, Luke & John), 10 & 12 are self-evident. No. 1 is the Root: "One Lord, faith, baptism, God in and through all." 2 are the Testaments Old & New, denoted by John the Baptist (sic) and Jesus Christ, presumably because this John is a Prophet. 3 are the co-equal Persons of the Trinity, Father, Son & Holy Ghost, though the term "rivals" is unexplained.

"Mirror" says 5 denotes the Books of Moses (Genesis, Exodus, Leviticus, Numbers & Deuteronomy) or the pentagram motif found
(to foot of next page

11th June.   "W A S P I E S."

IZOD'S PATENT CORSETS Are the Best.
Prepared by a New and Special Scientific Process.
Medical opinion recommends them for THE HEALTH.
Public opinion all over the world unanimous that they are unsurpassed for COMFORT, STYLE, AND DURABILITY. Sold all over Europe, and everywhere in India and Colonies. Name and Trade Mark, Anchor, on every pair and box. Ask your Draper or Outfitter for IZOD'S make; take no other, and see you get them, as bad makes are often sold for sake of extra profit. Write for our sheet of Drawings.
E. IZOD & SON,
30, Milk St., London.
Manufactory: LANDPORT, HANTS.

Perceptions of beauty vary from culture to culture, and I doubt that many Westerners would wish our ladies to become giraffe-necked in the style favoured in parts of S. E. Asia, by having a series of brass rings fitted. Yet in less extreme fashion, women used to minimise their waistlines even to less than 17" (I'm too old to metricate this into meaninglessness) by torturous means.

In "Yesterday's Britain" (Reader's Digest 1998) an anonymous girl remembers having an overhead bar hung, by cords over pullies on her bedroom ceiling, to which bar she clung while her mother laced her. On special occasions she would have her hands strapped to the bar lest she fell or fainted when it was hoisted to raise her on tiptoe, with her body best placed for tight lacing.

10.6 (cont^d) on some doorposts. "Faber" however relates 5 to the "senses" of touch, taste, smell, sight & hearing, symbolised in a painting as at Longthorpe Tower, Northants, early 14th Century; and goes on to add that 6 in most poems of this type are <u>Workers</u>, the six working-days bar the Sabbath. "Mirror" however suggests "charming waiters" as an alternative, which makes confusion worse confounded, and that "walkers" may be a corruption of "waters", the six pots used in Jesus' water-to-wine miracle at Cana in Galilee.

"Faber" continues that 7 "stars" are sun, moon, Mercury, Venus, Mars, Jupiter & Saturn which were known to move relative to earth and "fixed stars", symbolising God's gift of the seven "Liberal Arts" (grammar, logic, rhetoric, music, arithmetic, geometry, astronomy). "Mirror" however favours the 7 stars in the constellation Ursa Major (Big Dipper, Plough, Great Bear), or visible in Pleiades (Catherine Yronwode, 1996); 8 then are "rainers" in the Hyades - but "Faber" prefers the survivors in Noah's Ark, or else the groups in the 8 Beatitudes of Matt.5.3+. with 9 orders of Angels, Archangels, Thrones, Dominations, Choirs, Princedoms, Powers, Cherubim and Seraphim, and 11 apostles-minus-Judas-Iscariot (or maybe the 11000 virgins of St Ursula.)

12th June. More LIMERICK FASCINATION.

A project to put in hand the reform of the House of Lords was begun by the British Government in 1999; eight years & 3 general elections later, we are no further than having debarred the hereditary peers from voting, save for a select 92 chosen by their fellows. New peers continue to be Prime Ministerial nominees, with no scheme for elective ones in the offing; so Britain's achievement at the time of writing is merely to

"Pluck the mighty from their seat, but set no meek ones in their place" (Tennyson, "Locksley Hall Sixty Years After".)

The move is retrograde unless and until a second phase of Lords' Reform is enacted, for the "hereditaries" were a random selection albeit mainly from one element in society, whilst State nominees are likely to form a compliant oligarchy.

On 16.12.1999 the Times published a letter deriding the Lord Chancellor's after-dinner claim that hereditary peers were as ridiculous as hereditary poets. The writer, Lord Limerick, ended thus: "The virtues of genes, I insist, / Should not be too lightly dismissed: / If a poll's on the cards / For hereditary bards - / My name will be found on the list."

"Christian Feminists" may pose the question:

> God made earth, sun, moon, stars and sea,
> Rat, tiger, bacillus and flea
> According to plan;
> But when God made man,
> God made a mistake, didn't She?

Scientists may commemorate the discoverer of radioactivity:

> When defeated at chess, Henri Becquerel
> Told his victor, who crowed like a cockerel,
> "The Queen's Bishop's gambit
> Is outside my ambit -
> I'd rather go fishing for mackerel!"

Another great scientist, Blaise Pascal, pioneer of computing and an invalid who employed workmen to take a barometer-tube up a mountain in his study of the laws of density and depth, gave up but did not disown science after having a religious experience, and went on to write notes for a spiritual classic - available as his "Pensées" or thoughts. His sister was a nun:

> Said Jacqueline Pascal to Blaise,
> "Are you making thee most of your days?
> Though science has its seasons,
> The heart has its reasons;
> Now sit down and write your Pensées."

13th June.   Wisdom of Ralph Vaughan Williams...(pron. 'Rafe').

"RVW" lived from 1872 to 1958 and is one of England's very greatest composers. He was great-nephew to Charles Darwin, whose "Origin of Species" caused intense debate in Victorian days. When he was 6 or 7 his mother said to him: "The Bible says that God made the world in six days. Great-Uncle Charles thinks it took longer — but we need not worry about it, for it is equally wonderful either way."

On liturgical dance in church, which many pewfolk fear, he declared that "The dance has always been connected with religious fervour. What are the great church ceremonies but a sublimation of that dance; what about the 150th Psalm?" (Its 4th verse states "Praise God in the cymbals and dances"—& see Ps.149.3)

Other RVW dicta include this to Swaffham Primary School, which had named a House after him: "Music will enable you to see past facts to the very essence of things in a way which science cannot do. The arts are the means by which we can look through the magic casements and see what lies beyond."

To Daily Telegraph 8.12.1955, the 90th birthday of Sibelius: "I do not count as civilised those mid-Europeans who ignore Sibelius."

To Michael Kennedy 22.1.1956 on a desolate wispy piece that concluded one of his nine symphonies (mostly written at 70+!): "With regard to the last movement of my No. 6, I do NOT BELIEVE in meanings and mottoes as you know, but I think we can get in words nearest to the substance of my last movement in 'We are such stuff as dreams are made of, and our little life is rounded in a sleep.'" (Shakespeare — Prospero in The Tempest.)

...and some snatches by other composers.

Berlioz on Berlioz: "I live in music like a fish in water. I write music as an apple tree produces apples."

Saint-Saens on Saint-Saens: "After my death they will forget me for twenty years, for more than twenty years. My work will have to defend itself alone. I have confidence in my writings. A new generation will know how to rediscover them."

Berlioz on Saint-Saens: "He knows everything but he lacks inexperience."

14th June. — The decisive battle of NASEBY (14.6.1645) saw the defeat of King Charles I in the English Civil War, and occasioned a redoubtable poem by Macauley, which was in most school-anthologies until the cultural change that began around 1960 banished such martial heroics. The poet's enthusiasm for his subject led him to unfairness, for the King had no part or lot in torture. The mention of Durham in the penultimate verse is also an unsubstantiated exercise in poetic licence.

THE BATTLE OF NASEBY
LORD MACAULAY

Oh! wherefore come ye forth, in triumph from the North,
   With your hands, and your feet, and your raiment all red?
And wherefore doth your rout sent forth a joyous shout?
   And whence be the grapes of the wine-press which ye tread?

Oh evil was the root, and bitter was the fruit,
   And crimson was the juice of the vintage that we trod;
For we trampled on the throng of the haughty and the strong,
   Who sate in the high places, and slew the saints of God.

It was about the noon of a glorious day in June,
   That we saw their banners dance, and their cuirasses shine,
And the Man of Blood was there, with his long essenced hair,
   And Astley, and Sir Marmaduke, and Rupert of the Rhine.

Like a servant of the Lord, with his Bible and his sword,
   The General rode along us to form us to the fight,
When a murmuring sound broke out, and swell'd into a shout,
   Among the godless horsemen upon the tyrant's right.

And hark! like the roar of the billows on the shore,
   The cry of battle rises along their charging line!
For God! for the Cause! for the Church, for the Laws!
   For Charles King of England, and Rupert of the Rhine!

The furious German comes, with his clarions and his drums,
   His bravoes of Alsatia, and pages of Whitehall;
They are bursting on our flanks. Grasp your pikes, close your ranks;
   For Rupert never comes but to conquer or to fall.

They are here! They rush on! We are broken! We are gone!
   Our left is borne before them like stubble on the blast.
O Lord, put forth thy might! O Lord, defend the right!
   Stand back to back, in God's name, and fight it to the last.

Stout Skippon hath a wound; the centre hath given ground;
   Hark! hark! — What means the trampling of horsemen on our rear?
Whose banner do I see, boys? 'Tis he, thank God! 'tis he, boys,
   Bear up another minute: brave Oliver is here.

Their heads all stooping low, their points all in a row,
   Like a whirlwind on the trees, like a deluge on the dykes,
Our cuirassiers have burst on the ranks of the accurst,
   And at a shock have scattered the forest of his pikes.

Fast, fast, the gallants ride, in some safe nook to hide
   Their coward heads, predestined to rot on Temple Bar:
And he — he turns, he flies: — shame on those cruel eyes
   That bore to look on torture, and dare not look on war.

Ho! comrades, scour the plain; and, ere ye strip the slain,
   First give another stab to make your search secure,
Then shake from sleeves and pockets their broadpieces and lockets,
   The tokens of the wanton, the plunder of the poor.

Fools, your doublets shone with gold, and your hearts were gay and bold,
   When you kissed your lily hands to your lemans to-day;
And to-morrow shall the fox, from her chambers in the rocks,
   Lead forth her tawny cubs to howl above the prey.

Where be your tongues that late mocked at heaven and hell and fate,
   And the fingers that once were so busy with your blades,
Your perfumed satin clothes, your catches and your oaths,
   Your stage-plays and your sonnets, your diamonds and your spades?

Down, down, for ever down with the mitre and the crown,
   With the Belial of the Court, and the Mammon of the Pope;
There is woe in Oxford Halls; there is wail in Durham's Stalls;
   The Jesuit smites his bosom; the Bishop rends his cope.

And She of the seven hills shall mourn her children's ills,
   And tremble when she thinks of the edge of England's sword;
And the Kings of earth in fear shall shudder when they hear
   What the hand of God hath wrought for the Houses and the Word.

Macauley (1800-59) was a noteworthy parliamentarian who won fame for his "History of England" — see the biographical article in Encyclopaedia Britannica, that "university on a shelf". I enjoy his emotional verse, e.g. "A Jacobite's Epitaph", and his popular poem about the beacon-chain warning of the Armada:

For swift to east and swift to west the ghastly warflame spread,
High on St Michael's Mount it shone; it shone on Beachey Head...
Till broad and fierce the star came forth on Ely's sainted fane
And tower and hamlet rose in arms o'er all the boundless plain...
Till Skiddaw saw the fire that burned on Gaunt's embattled pile,
And the red glare on Skiddaw roused the burghers of Carlisle.

(Fenland is flat, but the use of Ely lantern may be more poetic licence; seeing Lancaster from Skiddaw certainly is!)

15th June.   CURIOSITIES of the ENGLISH LANGUAGE.

Should rules of grammar be taught? and always obeyed? Some say "No" to the first question, rather than sacrifice spontaneity to structure. This, however, though fashionable among some "educationalists", is harmful in that it scorns our collective experience on avoiding ambiguity and achieving clarity and precision. Better to answer "Yes" to optimise communication and the subtlety of our language.

The second question is more open. The rule against "split infinitives" bans our saying "It started to heavily rain"; but Fowler's "Modern English Usage" rejects the rule in favour of common sense. The "deafening" split infinitive should be avoided since it is ungainly and confusing; for example there is too great a gap in "The book's main idea is <u>to</u> historically, even when events are maturing, and divinely, from the Divine point of view, <u>impeach</u> the European system of Church & States."

Yet even the "deafening" may rise in a glorious crescendo, as Bruce Fraser comments in his revision (Pelican 1973/77) of "The Complete Plain Words" by Sir Ernest Gowers. He cites:

"The tenant hereby agrees:
  (i) to pay the said rent;
  (ii) to properly clean all the windows;
  (iii) to at all times properly empty all closets;
  (iv) to immediately any litter or disorder shall have been made by him or for his purpose on the staircase or landing or any other part of the said building remove the same."

Fraser calls this "a museum piece. To improve it... would be to spoil it. Like some appallingly bad poem it acquires a weird beauty of its own, and every successive reading increases our awe for its creator."

Exercise! What if anything is wrong with these sentences?
(a) Ex-Tory Prime Minister Edward Heath spoke. (b) Hitler out-heroded Mussolini in barbarity. (c) The explorer saw a man-eating tiger. (d) The Church of England now ordains woman priests. (e) The caravan's dragomen trusted their talismen. (f) The Middle Temple is named after the Knights Templars. (g) The zoo was well stocked with rhinoceri, hippopotami, platypi, wayzgooses, mongeese and other exotic creatures. (h) The cream of the Russian army was tuned up to concert pitch. (i) Ravens are not black birds. (j) The data he sought was the height of Ben Nevis. (k) The choice is between glorious death or shameful life. (Answers tomorrow.)

16th June.   War-Poems by Siegfried Sassoon....
        but first here are answers to yesterday's test!

(a) is wrongly hyphenated and should be "Tory ex-PM". An excellent example of this blunder was provided in 2001 by a national broadsheet daily paper's headline: "Ex-woman police chief cleared on assault charge". A few days later the newspaper made a brave confession, saying Alison Halford "is still a woman. Apologies"! (b) only Herod can be out-Heroded. (c) Hyphenate man-eating! (e) plurals are "dragomans" and "talismans". (f) Avoid multiple plurals such as Alsatians dogs; spot the main noun and treat the others as adjectival. (g) not all Latin plurals end in "i", and only "hippopotami" is correct. "Wayzgoose is not an animal, but was a printers' outing, and the plural of "mongoose" is "mongooses". (h) is a wild "mixed metaphor". (j) "data" is plural and should not be used of a single fact. (k) between...and. (i) is a lie, (d) true – the endemic use "women priests" violates (f) above in its attempt to avoid the allegedly tainted word "priestesses". Better to say "female priests" – or "presbytresses" (with tresses)!

Dreamers.

Soldiers are citizens of death's grey land,
Drawing no dividends from time's to-morrows.
In the great hour of destiny they stand,
Each with his feuds and jealousies and sorrows.
Soldiers are sworn to action; they must win
Some flaming fatal climax with their lives.
Soldiers are dreamers; when the guns begin
They think of firelit homes, clean beds, and wives.
I see them in foul dug-outs, gnawed by rats,
And in the ruined trenches, lashed with rain,
Dreaming of things they did with balls and bats,
And mocked by hopeless longing to regain
Bank-holidays, and picture shows, and spats,
And going to the office in the train.

At the Cenotaph

I saw the Prince of Darkness, with his Staff,
Standing bare-headed by the Cenotaph:
Unostentatious and respectful, there
He stood, and offered up the following prayer.
  'Make them forget, O Lord, what this Memorial
    Means; their discredited ideas revive;
  Breed new belief that War is purgatorial
    Proof of the pride and power of being alive;
  Men's biologic urge to readjust
    The Map of Europe, Lord of Hosts, increase;
  Lift up their hearts in large destructive lust;
    And crown their heads with blind vindictive Peace.'
The Prince of Darkness to the Cenotaph
Bowed. As he walked away I heard him laugh.

from: *Memorial Tablet* [Great War]

("I died in hell – (They called it Passchendaele.)"

In sermon-time, while Squire is in his pew,
He gives my gilded name a thoughtful stare;
For though low down upon the list, I'm there:
"In proud and glorious memory"—that's my due.
Two bleeding years I fought in France for Squire;
I suffered anguish that he's never guessed;
Once I came home on leave, and then went west.
What greater glory could a man desire?

17th June.   "WAR CRY" and "PEACE NEWS".

The Christian Church appears to hedge her bets when members buy publications with such "contradictory" names. Clearly the Lambeth Conferences do well to say that "War as a means of settling international disputes is incompatible with the teaching and example of our Lord Jesus Christ." Whilst nations so often drive a coach and six through the old "just war" rules, pacifism is cogent and world government a desperate need. This entails a fight but a spiritual one; see Paul's letter to the Ephesians (6.10+), illustrated in the following "serious spoof" reproduced by kind permission of a clerical friend.

Last month our Young Wives Union and our Mothers Bible Fellowship combined to hear a talk by Mrs. Dorinda Dross of the Bible & Prayer Book Conservation Society. Mrs. Dross displayed a cardboard cut-out of a Roman soldier and expounded the passage from St. Paul's letter to the Christians at Ephesus relating to the Christian's armour. The meeting ended with the singing of the first verse of the well-known Lenten hymn:-

Christian dost thou see them on the holy ground,
How the troops of Midian prowl and prowl around?
Christian, up and smite them, counting gain but loss,
Smite them by the merit of the holy Cross.

- Helmet of Salvation
- Breastplate of Righteousness
- Shield of Faith
- Belt of Truth
- Sword of Spirit
- Gospel of Peace (Sandals)

"The weapons we fight with are not the weapons of the world." 2 Cor. 10.4)

"All who draw the sword will die by the sword." (Jesus, Matt. 26.52)

__18th June.__ "There's rosemary, that's for remembrance;..."
pray you love, remember." (Ophelia to Laertes, in
Shakespeare's _Hamlet_, Act IV, Scene V, 17 2-3.)

- - - - - - - -

The popular culinary herb Rosemary was used medicinally in Tudor and early Stuart times. In 1607 Roger Hackett D.D. wrote that it "helpeth the brain, strengtheneth the memorie and is very medicinal for the head. Another property of the rosemary is that it affects the heart. Let this rosemarinus, this flower of men, ensigne of your wisdom, love, and loyalty, be carried not only in your hands, but in your hearts and heads."

More down-to-earth was the _Crete Herbal_: "Rosemary – for weyknesse of ye brayne. Against weyknesse of the brayne and coldnesse thereof, sethe rosemaria in wyne and let the pacyent receye the smoke at his nose and keep his heed warme."

- - - - - - - -

__19th June.__   The Lost "Peace-Poems".

In the 1950s I had a flysheet with three poems, which to my great regret I failed to keep, so that I can't now recall source or authors. Help, please! One was a simple ditty which ran something like this:

"Ages end, new worlds begin;
H-bombs threaten – so does sin.
Sin brings Satan toppling down
On the fields and on the town,
On the trains and omnibus,
On the housetops and on us.

"Nothing can survive the heat
Save Father, Son and Paraclete;
Father, Paraclete and Son –
And the souls the Cross has won."

Another was a sonnet of some solemnity, with five of its lines held in my memory as follows:

"Against war's butchery we are unsteeled,
We come to seek the sepulchre of Christ;
And, banner'd by the never-conquer'd Cross,
We march till all unfaith is exorcised,
Directed by the commandants of God."

Were they part of a non rhyming sestet, or more dispersed?

- - - - - - - -

20th June. A FROLIC – or "LET DEANS DELIGHT".

(lines 1 & 2 are poached from "A Refusal" by Thomas Hardy.)
Moral: Thou Shalt Not Covet Thy Neighbour's House.

Said the grave Dean of Westminster
"Mine is the best minster........"
"But mine was once very
Much better" said Bury.
"Oh was it really?"
Mused the sad Dean of Ely.
"Hark! how they talk;
They should see mine!" cried York.
"<u>Mine</u> will be best ere
I'm sixty" said Chester.
"With bells and with smells?"
Asked his brother of Wells;
"And a carpeted aisle?"
Said the Dean of Carlisle.
("For people to trip on"
Was the murmur of Ripon.)

"It's all a big puthel"
Lisped the Provost of Southwell.
"There's so much to think on"
Quoth the bright Dean of Lincoln.
"Back where we began"
Sighed Sodor and Man,
"My fane is a ruin,
Though none of my doin';
I'm Lord Bishop too,
Which saves me much rue;
Though not advantageous
Regarding my wages,
My mind it engages."

Then the Dean of Gibralter
Said "We shall not falter;
We serve our Lord's altar."
And the old Dean of Truro
Vowed "I always use Douro";
But the Provost of Leicester
Warned: "Jealousies fester."
"Well, it matters not which field
I work in", claimed Lichfield,
"Provided, of course
That we hear due remorse
Over Hereford's horse."

Written in 1995, since when all Provosts have been redesignated as Deans. No reference is intended to any individual alive or dead, except the horse and the Dean mentioned in the last line regarding a tale of long ago in Aubrey's "Brief Lives".

Not in vain the distance beacons. Forward, forward let us range,
Let the great world spin for ever down the ringing grooves of change.

21st June.   ## Victoria's Unknown Laureate.

Following the Tennyson studies of and before 1 June, it is noteworthy that the poet in later life continued to profess belief in the spiritual realm about us. "Prayer", he said to Gladstone & Dr Symonds, "is like opening a sluice between the great ocean and our little channels". Then he told Mrs Bradley that "There are moments...when I feel and know the flesh to be the vision, God and the spiritual the only real and true." But "for the vast majority, man's highest duty is not deliberately to cultivate an extreme pietism, but to throw in his lot with his fellow-men and help them...to realise the spiritual kingdom on earth." (<u>Alfred Tennyson</u> by his grandson Charles, 1968, p.385)

In "De Profundis - The Two Greetings", dated 11.8.1852 the poet's son is welcomed first as a wonder of physical science and then as coming from the world of spirit (compare Wordsworth's ode "Intimations of Immortality") as a moral being.

"The Ancient Sage" is another most significant poem, with Browning as its dedicatee. It is a dialogue between an old man who has retired to the hill country and a young sceptical city author, who claims that life is ruled by "the Days and Hours that cancel weal with woe." The elder replies with the conviction of mystics and philosophers that time is a mystery and in some sense an illusion:

> "The days and hours are ever glancing by,
> And seem to flicker past, thro' Sun and Shade,
> Or short, or long, as Pleasure leads, or Pain;
> But with the Nameless is nor Day nor Hour;
> Tho' we, thin minds, who creep from thought to thought,
> Break into 'Thens' and 'Whens' the Eternal Now:
> This double seeming of the single world! ....
> But thou be wise in this dream-world of ours,
> Nor take thy dial for thy deity,
> But make the passing shadow serve thy will."

...And climb the Mount of Blessing", and see "The high-heaven dawn of more than mortal day Strike on the Mount of Vision!"

The poems "Vastness" and the great "Locksley Hall Sixty Years After" should be read in full also — see tomorrow — I have marked selected parts. Mighty epigrams express the poet's refusal, in the face of evil, to surrender to the all-too-prevalent cultural cynicism. Then in his final six years he was "ever looking upwards at the mysteries" (W.Ward), completing "<u>Faith</u>" & "<u>God and the Universe</u>" with days to spare! A brief mention of the exuberant youthful 1st "Locksley Hall": earlier books cite "For I dipt into the future" (28 February) & "Knowledge comes" (15 April). The poet's rail-ride in 1830 yielded an erroneous analogy! (see foot of previous page.)

22nd June. *LOCKSLEY HALL SIXTY YEARS AFTER.*

Tennyson was one of England's last polymaths, well read in all branches of knowledge and speculation in a way that the current "communications-explosion" precludes. His second Locksley Hall poem, written at 77, is a remarkable intertwined summation of his views on literature, science (he had been made a Fellow of the Royal Society in 1865), the arts, history, politics, society and religion, & needs reading in full; or at least in two parts, the first of which should appear in Part 4 of "The March and the Muster". Here is the second, in the mouth of the swashbuckling hero of the first Locksley poem, now a passionate and volatile 80-year-old as he welcomes his grandson who has succeeded to the Locksley lordship:

> Step by step we gain'd a freedom known to Europe, known to all;
> Step by step we rose to greatness,—thro' the tonguesters we may fall.
>
> You that woo the Voices—tell them 'old experience is a fool,'
> Teach your flatter'd kings that only those who cannot read can rule.
>
> Pluck the mighty from their seat, but set no meek ones in their place;
> Pillory Wisdom in your markets, pelt your offal at her face.
>
> Tumble Nature heel o'er head, and, yelling with the yelling street,
> Set the feet above the brain and swear the brain is in the feet.
>
> Bring the old dark ages back without the faith, without the hope,
> Break the State, the Church, the Throne, and roll their ruins down the slope.
>
> Authors—essayist, atheist, novelist, realist, rhymester, play your part,
> Paint the mortal shame of nature with the living hues of Art.
>
> Rip your brothers' vices open, strip your own foul passions bare;
> Down with Reticence, down with Reverence—forward—naked—let them stare.
>
> Feed the budding rose of boyhood with the drainage of your sewer;
> Send the drain into the fountain, lest the stream should issue pure.
>
> Set the maiden fancies wallowing in the troughs of Zolaism,—
> Forward, forward, ay and backward, downward too into the abysm.
>
> Do your best to charm the worst, to lower the rising race of men;
> Have we risen from out the beast, then back into the beast again?
>
> Only 'dust to dust' for me that sicken at your lawless din,
> Dust in wholesome old-world dust before the newer world begin.
>
> Heated am I? you—you wonder—well, it scarce becomes mine age—
> Patience! let the dying actor mouth his last upon the stage.
>
> Cries of unprogressive dotage ere the dotard fall asleep?
> Noises of a current narrowing, not the music of a deep?
>
> Ay, for doubtless I am old, and think gray thoughts, for I am gray:
> After all the stormy changes shall we find a changeless May?
>
> > After madness, after massacre, Jacobinism and Jacquerie,
> > Some diviner force to guide us thro' the days I shall not see?
> >
> > When the schemes and all the systems, Kingdoms and Republics fall,
> > Something kindlier, higher, holier—all for each and each for all?
>
> All the full-brain, half-brain races, led by Justice, Love, and Truth;
> All the millions one at length with all the visions of my youth?

22.vi
LH2
cont.d

"All the Boundless Heavens"

All diseases quench'd by Science, no man halt, or deaf or blind;
Stronger ever born of weaker, lustier body, larger mind?
Earth at last a warless world, a single race, a single tongue—
I have seen her far away—for is not Earth as yet so young?—

Every tiger madness muzzled, every serpent passion kill'd,
Every grim ravine a garden, every blazing desert till'd,

Robed in universal harvest up to either pole she smiles,
Universal ocean softly washing all her warless Isles.

Warless? when her tens are thousands, and her thousands millions, then—
All her harvest all too narrow—who can fancy warless men?

Warless? war will die out late then. Will it ever? late or soon?
Can it, till this outworn earth be dead as yon dead world the moon?

Dead the new astronomy calls her. . . . On this day and at this hour,
In this gap between the sandhills, whence you see the Locksley tower,

Here we met, our latest meeting—Amy—sixty years ago—
She and I—the moon was falling greenish thro' a rosy glow,

Just above the gateway tower, and even where you see her now—
Here we stood and claspt each other, swore the seeming-deathless vow. . . .

Dead, but how her living glory lights the hall, the dune, the grass!
Yet the moonlight is the sunlight, and the sun himself will pass.

Venus near her! smiling downward at this earthlier earth of ours,
Closer on the Sun, perhaps a world of never fading flowers.

Hesper, whom the poet call'd the Bringer home of all good things.
All good things may move in Hesper, perfect peoples, perfect kings.

Hesper—Venus—were we native to that splendour or in Mars,
We should see the Globe we groan in, fairest of their evening stars.

Could we dream of wars and carnage, craft and madness, lust and spite,
Roaring London, raving Paris, in that point of peaceful light?

Might we not in glancing heavenward on a star so silver-fair,
Yearn, and clasp the hands and murmur, 'Would to God that we were there'?

Forward, backward, backward, forward, in the immeasurable sea,
Sway'd by vaster ebbs and flows than can be known to you or me.

All the suns—are these but symbols of innumerable man,
Man or Mind that sees a shadow of the planner or the plan?

Is there evil but on earth? or pain in every peopled sphere?
Well be grateful for the sounding watchword 'Evolution' here,

Evolution ever climbing after some ideal good,
And Reversion ever dragging Evolution in the mud.

What are men that He should heed us? cried the king of sacred song;
Insects of an hour, that hourly work their brother insect wrong,
While the silent Heavens roll, and Suns along their fiery way,
All their planets whirling round them, flash a million miles a day.

Many an Æon moulded earth before her highest, man, was born,
Many an Æon too may pass when earth is manless and forlorn,
Earth so huge, and yet so bounded—pools of salt, and plots of land—
Shallow skin of green and azure—chains of mountain, grains of sand!

Only That which made us, meant us to be mightier by and by,
Set the sphere of all the boundless Heavens within the human eye,

Sent the shadow of Himself, the boundless, thro' the human soul;
Boundless inward, in the atom, boundless outward, in the Whole.

* * * * * * *

179

23rd June.   *LOCKSLEY HALL*   (Tennyson) – __conclusion__.
             SIXTY YEARS AFTER

Here is Locksley Hall, my grandson, here the lion-guarded gate,
Not to-night in Locksley Hall—to-morrow—you, you come so late.

Wreck'd—your train—or all but wreck'd? a shatter'd wheel? a vicious boy!
Good, this forward, you that preach it, is it well to wish you joy?

Is it well that while we range with Science, glorying in the Time,
City children soak and blacken soul and sense in city slime?

There among the gloooming alleys Progress halts on palsied feet,
Crime and hunger cast our maidens by the thousand on the street.

There the Master scrimps his haggard sempstress of her daily bread,
There a single sordid attic holds the living and the dead.

There the smouldering fire of fever creeps across the rotted floor,
And the crowded couch of incest in the warrens of the poor.

Nay, your pardon, cry your 'forward,' yours are hope and youth, but I—
Eighty winters leave the dog too lame to follow with the cry.

Lame and old, and past his time, and passing now into the night;
Yet I would the rising race were half as eager for the light.

Light the fading gleam of Even? light the glimmer of the dawn?
Aged eyes may take the growing glimmer for the gleam withdrawn.

Far away beyond her myriad coming changes earth will be
Something other than the wildest modern guess of you and me.

Earth may reach her earthly-worst, or if she gain her earthly-best,
Would she find her human offspring this ideal man at rest?

Forward then, but still remember how the course of Time will swerve,
Crook and turn upon itself in many a backward streaming curve.

Not to-night in Locksley Hall, my grandson! Death and Silence hold their own,
Leave the Master in the first dark hour of his last sleep alone.

Worthier soul was he than I am, sound and honest, rustic Squire,
Kindly landlord, boon companion—youthful jealousy is a liar.

Cast the poison from your bosom, oust the madness from your brain.
Let the trampled serpent show you that you have not lived in vain.

Youthful! youth and age are scholars yet but in the lower school,
Nor is he the wisest man who never proved himself a fool.

Yonder lies our young sea-village—Art and Grace are less and less:
Science grows and Beauty dwindles—roofs of slated hideousness!

There is one old Hostel left us where they swing the Locksley shield,
Till the peasant cow shall butt the 'Lion passant' from his field.

Poor old Heraldry, poor old History, poor old Poetry, passing hence,
In the common deluge drowning old political common-sense!

Poor old voice of eighty crying after voices that have fled!
All I loved are vanish'd voices, all my steps are on the dead.

All the world is ghost to me, and as the phantom disappears,
Forward far and far from here is all the hope of eighty years.

*   *   *   *   *   *

In this Hostel—I remember—I repent it o'er his grave—
Like a clown—by chance he met me—I refused the hand he gave.

From that casement where the trailer mantles all the mouldering bricks—
I was then in early boyhood, Edith but a child of six—

While I shelter'd in this archway from a day of driving showers—
Peept the winsome face of Edith like a flower among the flowers.

Here to-night! the Hall to-morrow, when they toll the Chapel bell!
Shall I hear in one dark room a wailing, 'I have loved thee well.'

Then a peal that shakes the portal—one has come to claim his bride,
Her that shrank, and put me from her, shriek'd, and started from my side—

Silent echoes! You, my Leonard, use and not abuse your day,
Move among your people, know them, follow them, follow him who led the way.

Strove for sixty widow'd years to help his homelier brother men,
Served the poor, and built the cottage, raised the school, and drain'd the fen.

Hears he now the Voice that wrong'd him? who shall swear it cannot be?
Earth would never touch her worst, were one in fifty such as he.

Ere she gain her Heavenly-best, a God must mingle with the game:
Nay, there may be those about us whom we neither see nor name,

Felt within us as ourselves, the Powers of Good, the Powers of Ill,
Strowing balm, or shedding poison in the fountains of the Will.

Follow you the Star that lights a desert pathway, yours or mine.
Forward, till you see the highest Human Nature is divine.

Follow Light, and do the Right—for man can half-control his doom—
Till you find the deathless Angel seated in the vacant tomb.

Forward, let the stormy moment fly and mingle with the Past.
I that loathed, have come to love him. Love will conquer at the last.

Gone at eighty, mine own age, and I and you will bear the pall;
Then I leave thee Lord and Master, latest Lord of Locksley Hall.

24th June. ("Midsummer Day")   "A SHROPSHIRE LAD":

This wistful cycle of poems by the lonesome classics-don A.E. Housman appeared in 1896 and to this day is evocative of the years before the "Great War" which was beginning to be anticipated by some sensitive souls. (Tennyson in 1886 spoke of "a mighty wave of evil passing over the world...some new and strange development...", and in 1887 he ended his Jubilee Ode for the Queen with a section beginning "Are there thunders moaning in the distance? Are there spectres moving in the darkness?..." By April 1914 we had Thomas Hardy's "Channel Firing" on "gunnery practice out at sea", with the lines:
   "All nations striving strong to make
   Red war yet redder. Mad as hatters...")
But things hadn't yet come to that in 1890s Ludlow:

(In this extract Terence replies to a critic of his melancholy verse.)

"Why, if 'tis dancing you would be,
There's brisker pipes than poetry.
Say, for what were hop-yards meant,
Or why was Burton built on Trent?...
And malt does more than Milton can
To justify God's ways to man.
Ale, man, ale's the stuff to drink

For fellows whom it hurts to think.
Look into the pewter pot
To see the world as the world's not...

— — — — — — —

'Tis true, the stuff I bring for sale
Is not so brisk a brew as ale...
But take it: if the smack is sour,
The better for the embittered hour...
And I will friend you, if I may,
In the dark and cloudy day.

Two favourite poems are presented earlier in Housman's cycle:

When I was one-and-twenty
I heard a wise man say,
"Give crowns and pounds and guineas
But not your heart away;
Give pearls away and rubies
But keep your fancy free."
But I was one-and-twenty,
No use to talk to me.

When I was one-and-twenty
I heard him say again,
"The heart out of the bosom
Was never given in vain;
'Tis paid with sighs a-plenty
And sold for endless rue."
And I am two-and-twenty,
And oh, 'tis true, 'tis true.

From far, from eve and morning
And yon twelve-winded sky,
The stuff of life to knit me
Blew hither: here am I.

Now — for a breath I tarry
Nor yet disperse apart —
Take my hand quick and tell me,
What have you in your heart.

Speak now, and I will answer;
How shall I help you, say;
Ere to the wind's twelve quarters
I take my endless way.

Another Housman volume contains this Easter prayer-of-an agnostic, sensible at that

If in that Syrian garden, ages slain,
You sleep, and know not you are dead in vain,
Nor even in dreams behold how dark and bright
Ascends in smoke and fire by day and night
The hate you died to quench and could but fan
Sleep well and see no morning, son of man.
But if, the grave rent and the stone rolled by
At the right hand of majesty on high
You sit, and sitting so remember yet
Your tears, your agony and bloody sweat,
Your cross and passion and the life you gave,
Bow hither out of heaven and see and save.

25th June. Short letters and News-snippets.

The Press can afford piquancy and amusement as well as knowledge, confusion, annoyance and so forth. On 19 June 1998 the *New Statesman* published a letter from Sadie Smith of Bognor Regis questioning a claim that Tony Blair should suppress dissent. "I was too young to vote...but I spent every hour God sent canvassing for new Labour in places where a 17-year-old girl should not be after 6pm, and got physically abused in my (highly Conservative) school for supporting the principles that I felt to be right. Is it too much to ask the party for which I made so many sacrifices to allow its MPs to do the same?"

It is of course all too easy to say something that isn't meant; and this may be amusing (16th June), intriguing, disastrous, or a combination of these:

TIMES 12-4-91

Final say *D.Tel. 12.7.96*

FROM the *South Wales Echo*: "God Will Judge the Earth Tomorrow (God Willing)."

FROM the *Yorkshire Post*: "British Bulldog Bitch wanted to sire litter."

D.Tel. 18-3-97
Edited by
David Rennie

Clearing up the House

From Mr Hartley Booth

Sir, As the issue of cash and MPs has recently raised some eyebrows, I was interested to receive a letter from the Finance Office of the House of Commons to MPs, dated April 2, stating that:

Due to the disillusionment of the House on Tuesday, 8th April 1997, we are endeavouring to clear all outstanding accounts.

Yours faithfully,
H. BOOTH
(Conservative MP for Finchley, 1992-97),
House of Commons.
April 8.

TIMES 15-4-97

In gear for Marathon

From Mr Mark Davies

Sir, Are there really 25 women planning to walk Sunday's London Marathon, as your Diary reports (April 10), "wearing nothing but a Wonderbra above the waist"? Or would it be fairer to say that they will be wearing nothing above the waist but a Wonderbra?

Yours faithfully,
MARK DAVIES,
91 Onslow Gardens, SW7.
April 10.

Many witticisms are of course intended. I liked the letter in the *Times* just before the 1997 General Election, from Roy Roebuck who was Labour MP for Harrow East, 1966-70:

"Sir, my former parliamentary colleague, Sir William van Straubenzee, who urges....that Members of Parliament should be accorded the title "MP Emeritus" on retirement has overlooked the benevolent provisions of the Rehabilitation of Offenders Act 1974. Has his proposal anything to do with Mr Michael Howard's plans for tagging offenders?"

SIR—The letter recalling London Transport's poetic Billy Brown of London Town (July 2) reminded me of the time when it nannied its passengers by posting the following notice at "request" bus stops: "Face the driver, raise your hand/You'll find that he will understand."

I can still recall my youthful shocked-but-tickled-pink reaction when I saw one such notice to which had been added: "Of course he'll understand, the cuss,/ But will he stop the ruddy bus?"
ROSEMARY LUCK
London N12

WHENEVER I see The Guide supplement in Saturday's Guardian along with your magazine, I think of the hymn, Be Thou My Guardian And My Guide. Is that the origin of its name?
Frank McManus
Todmorden, Lancs

Guardian magazine, 12.11.94

Marking the time

From Mr David Hallson

Sir: May I remind all other readers obsessed by trivia that at four seconds before 12.35 pm today (7 August), the time and date creates the perfect number sequence — 12:34:56 7/8/90.
Yours faithfully,
DAVID HALLSON
Purley, Surrey

Ind. 7.8.90

182

26th June.   MARRIAGE GUIDANCE - 1560s version!

During Elizabeth Tudor's first decade as Queen, the mild Archbishop Matthew Parker produced a Book of Homilies for use by clergy as an alternative to preaching their own sermons. The "35th Article" at the end of the Prayer Book commends the Homilies as "necessary for these times". It would however be a brave, not to say foolhardy, minister or counsellor who reiterated the one "Of the state of Matrimony" in our new 21st century! After saying that marriage is meant to enable man and woman to "live lawfully in perpetual friendship to bring forth fruit" avoiding fornication, it warns that the devil will try to "bring in most bitter and unpleasant discord" via "that wicked vice of stubborn will and self-love"! (This at least is still all too prevalent.)

"The husband", we read after being referred to 1 Peter 3.7, "ought to be the leader and author of love, in cherishing and increasing concord...if he yield something to the woman. For the woman is a weak creature, not endued with like strength and constancy of mind...and lighter they be, and more vain in their fantasies and opinions...he ought to wink at some things - Howbeit the common sort of man doth judge that such moderation...is a token of womanish cowardice, and therefore they think that it is a man's part to fume in anger to fight with fist and staff."

"Now concerning the wife's duty...a good wife by obeying her husband shall (accept his authority) so that he shall have a delight and a gladness the sooner at all times to return home to her...but when the wives be stubborn, froward, and malapert, their husbands thereby are compelled to abhor and flee from their own houses"..."the woman is the more frail party...let them acknowledge their follies and say, My husband, so it is, that by my anger I was compelled to do this or that; forgive it me and hereafter I will take better heed."

The Homily then discusses "the apparel of her head...so appointed, to declare her subjection"! Yet "Let either party be ready and willing to perform that which belongeth to themselves especially. For if we be bound to hold out our left cheek to strangers which will strike us on the right, how much more ought we to suffer an extreme and unkind husband! But yet I mean not that a man should beat his wife; God forbid that; for that is the   (to foot of next page.)

27th June. STANDARDS in COMMERCE and POLITICS.

Of more lasting value than the document noted yesterday is the Rogationtide homily that precedes it. Written for "beating the bounds" (see 15 May), it bids us to "consider the old ancient bounds and limits belonging to our own township, and to our other neighbours bordering about us, to the intent that we should be content with our own." It warns against the filching of land, and dispossessions, and oppression of the poor: "Let us flee, therefore, good people, all wrong practices in getting, maintaining, and defending our possessions..." And so forth, not fearing to teach that when those with power act unjustly they have a considerable responsibility for any rioting that this provokes; and that God brings down entire nations for injustice. All this may be thought rich, coming with the authority of a monarch whose father appropriated all the monastic lands; yet it is good to see it "in black and white", as official doctrine!

Today we need to correct the world's commercial system so that the Third World is not bled white by debt-interest (not to mention the deprived enclaves in the West). Usury, banned in the Old Testament (e.g. Exodus 22.25; Nehemiah 5.10; Psalm 15.6; Ezekiel 18.8+) and by Jesus ("Lend expecting no return", Luke 6.35), was defined by the 5th Lateran Council of the undivided Western Church including Britain, 1515, as "gaining benefit or increase from a thing, money, not in itself fruitful or fecund, without labour, cost or risk on the part of the lender". One person's unearned income is usually another's undeserved deprivation, and loan-charges should be limited to what is justified by "1515" (see 17.5)

(26.6 concl.) greatest shame that can be, not so much to her that is beaten, but to him that doth the deed....No, it is not to be borne with."

"Use oft prayer to (God) that he would continue concord and charity betwixt you.. whereby we may win His blessing....Amen."

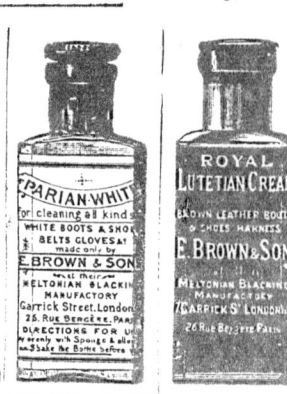

Indeed! Tudor women were doubtless "weak creatures", pregnant most of the time; but one needn't be feminist to be outraged by the unfair "womanish cowardice" - fruit of the then endemic male chauvinism. Yet the author (Abp. Parker or his nominee) clearly meant well and to promote harmony.

184

28th June. "Step by step we gained a freedom".

So wrote Tennyson in his "Locksley Hall Sixty Years After"; and so Britain did, industrially as well as politically, through the work and courage of the famous and the unknown alike. In 1830 Oastler wrote to the Leeds Mercury that in Bradford, "where anti-slavery fever rages most furiously", boys and especially girls from 7 to 14 years labour in the worsted mills from 6am to 7pm "with only 30 minutes allowed for eating and recreation", as "innocent victims of the accursed shrine of avarice", "half-dressed but not half-fed", without legislative protection.

Later that century the fiery Ruskin, in "Sesame and Lilies", reproduced in red print a report on a London inquest that had appeared in the Morning Post on 13.2.1865:

185

An inquiry was held on Friday by Mr. Richards deputy coroner, at the White Horse tavern, Christ Church, Spitalfields, respecting the death of Michael Collins, aged 58. Deceased was a "translator" of boots. Witness went out and bought old boots; deceased and his son made them into good ones, and then witness sold them for what she could get at the shops, which was very little indeed. Deceased and his son used to work night and day to try and get a little bread and tea, and pay for the room (2s. a week), so as to keep the home together. On Friday-night week deceased got up from his bench and began to shiver. He threw down the boots, saying, "Somebody else must finish them when I am gone, for I can do no more." There was no fire, and he said, "I would be better if I was warm." Witness therefore took two pairs of translated boots[1] to sell at the shop, but she could only get 14d. for the two pairs, for the people at the shop said, "We must have our profit." Witness got 14 lb. of coal, and a little tea and bread. Her son sat up the whole night to make the "translations," to get money, but deceased died on Saturday morning. The family never had enough to eat.—Coroner: "It seems to me deplorable that you did not go into the workhouse." Witness: "We wanted the comforts of our little home." A juror asked what the comforts were, for he only saw a little straw in the corner of the room, the windows of which were broken. The witness began to cry, and said that they had a quilt and other little things.

Witness: I could work now if I had food, for my sight would get better." Dr. G. P. Walker said deceased died from syncope, from exhaustion from want of food. The deceased had had no bedclothes. For four months he had had nothing but bread to eat. There was not a particle of fat in the body. There was no disease, but if there had been medical attendance, he might have survived the syncope or fainting. The coroner having remarked upon the painful nature of the case, the jury returned the following verdict, "That deceased died from exhaustion from want of food and the common necessaries of life; also through want of medical aid."

"Why would witness not go into the workhouse?" you ask. Well, the poor seem to have a prejudice against the workhouse which the rich have not; for of course every one who takes a pension from Government goes into the workhouse on a grand scale:[1] only the workhouses for the rich do not involve the idea of work, and should be called play-houses. But the poor like to die independently, it appears; perhaps if we made the play-houses for them pretty and pleasant enough, or gave them their pensions at home, and allowed them a little introductory peculation with the public money, their minds might be reconciled to the conditions. Meantime, here are the facts: we make our relief either so insulting to them, or so painful, that they rather die than take it.

Contrasting this tragedy with the menu of a Society banquet, Ruskin attacks the British for lack of compassion, and stresses that "a nation cannot last as a moneymaking mob." "It is our imaginary Christianity that helps us to commit these crimes.... You had better get rid of the smoke, and the organ pipes....and the painted glass....and look after Lazarus on the doorstep. For there is a true Church wherever one hand meets another helpfully, and that is the only holy or Mother Church which ever was, or ever shall be." This lesson was learnt slowly till by 1950 we had the finest social structure since the Reformation at least; but Tennyson went on to warn that "Through the tonguesters (spin doctors!) we may fall". We have done and must check this quick!

29th June.   ENGLAND'S SHAME.

The early 19th century was a dreadful time for our common people. The Enclosures Act of a landowners' Parliament had displaced many peasants into urban slums, and Oliver Goldsmith wrote his famous poem "The Deserted Village", saying:

> "Ill fares the land, to hastening ills a prey,
> Where wealth accumulates and men decay."

The Establishment feared revolution on the French model, and applied draconian laws including the Combination Acts in the hope of containing radicalism. The Chartist Movement for parliamentary democracy escalated until nearly all its demands were met in a succession of small concessions. Working conditions were usually abysmal. In 1842 Betty Harris (37) told a group of MPs making a Parliamentary enquiry that:

I was married at 23, and went into a colliery when I was married ... can neither read nor write.

I work for Andrew Knowles of Little Bolton (Lancashire) and make sometimes 7s (35p) a week, sometimes not so much. I am a drawer, and work from 6 in the morning to 6 at night. Stop about an hour at noon to eat my dinner: have bread and butter for dinner: I get no drink. I have two children, but they are too young to work. I worked at drawing when I was in the family way. I know a woman who has gone home and washed herself, taken to her bed, been delivered of a child and gone to work again under the week.

I have a belt around my waist, and a chain passing between my legs, and I go on my hands and feet. The road is very steep, and we have to hold by a rope, and when there is no rope, by anything we can catch hold of. There are six women and about six boys and girls in the pit I work in: it is very hard work for a woman. The pit is very wet where I work, and the water comes over our clog-tops always, and I have seen it up to my thighs. It rains in at the roof terribly. My clothes are wet through almost all day long. I never was ill in my life, but when I was lying in.

I am very tired when I get home at night. I fall asleep sometimes before I get washed. I am not so strong as I was, and cannot stand my work so well as I used to. I have drawn till the skin was off me: the belt and chain is worse when we are in the family way. My feller has beaten me many a time for not being ready. I were not used to it at first, and had little patience.

A law was passed in 1842 prohibiting the employment of women and young children below ground in the mines. Things were bad enough for the men, of course, especially in old coalfields such as Durham where the iniquitous Bond System tied men to one pit for a year even if no work was available at times. Miners were jailed for breach of bond, and evicted with their families for joining the Federation that Tommy Hepburn initiated.

186

30th June.   "Start the way you intend to continue."

Although the enclosures of common land around the year 1800, and the introduction of the new Poor Law, had produced an urban proletariat forced to live in squalor and deprivation, the accession of Queen Victoria in 1837 coincided with an amazingly swift change in the climate of opinion, from "Georgian licence" to moral rectitude in personal life. Here is the Queen's contribution; as a girl of 18 she'd been monarch for just 1 day

BY THE QUEEN.
A PROCLAMATION,
For the Encouragement of Piety and Virtue, and for the preventing and punishing of Vice, Profaneness, and Immorality.

(abbreviated)

VICTORIA R.

WE, most seriously and religiously considering that it is an indispensible duty on Us to be careful, above all other things, to preserve and advance the honor and service of Almighty God, and to discourage and suppress all vice, profaneness, debauchery, and immorality, which are highly displeasing to God, so great a reproach to Our Religion and Government, and (by means of the frequent ill examples of the practices thereof) have so fatal a tendency to the corruption of many of Our loving subjects, otherwise religiously and virtuously disposed, and which (if not timely remedied) may justly draw down the Divine vengeance on Us and Our Kingdom: We also humbly acknowledging that We can not expect the blessing and goodness of Almighty God (by whom Kings reign and on which We entirely rely) to make Our Reign happy and prosperous to Ourself and Our People, without a religious observance of God's holy laws..hereby declare Our Royal purpose..to punish all manner of vice, profaneness, and immorality..and prohibit all Our loving subjects..from playing on the Lord's Day at dice, cards, or any other game...and We do hereby strictly charge and command all Our Judges, Mayors, Sheriffs, Justices of the Peace, and all other Our officers.. (to punish) all persons who shall be guilty of excessive drinking, blasphemy, profane swearing and cursing, lewdness... and also to suppress and prevent all gaming..on the Lord's Day (and selling wine, coffee, ale or beer etc during service-time.)

Given at Our Court at St. James's, this Twenty-first Day of June, in the Year of Our Lord One thousand eight hundred and thirty-seven, and in the First Year of Our Reign.

GOD save the QUEEN.

187

DUBLIN :— PRINTED BY GEORGE AND JOHN GRIERSON,
PRINTERS TO THE QUEEN'S MOST EXCELLENT MAJESTY.

1st July.   A WESTERN EUROPEAN HOLOCAUST.

The Battle of the Somme was joined this day in 1916, and A.J.P. Taylor states ("English History 1914-45", OUP, 1965) that the British Army lost 19,000 killed and sustained 57,000 casualties on the first day. Total losses in the battle were 420,000 British, 280,000 French, and 465,000 German.

Vera Brittain, writing in New Clarion (30.9.1933) tells of her post-war visit on a perfect summer day to the Somme Valley, where French workers were gathering the harvest. She carried Beverley Nichols' book "Cry Havoc" through Hédauville, Thiepval with its memorial to 73,367 unnamed Britons who "fell on the Somme Battlefields July 1915 to February 1918...", Albert, Bapaume, and other small places whose names were burnt into the British consciousness as a result of the slaughter there.

Brittain writes that she was glad to have the book with her, for it helped her to "remain undeluded by those beautiful memorial acres".. It reminded her that the Somme battle need never have been fought at all. "'Germany...would have capitulated in 1915, its ironmasters have since admitted, if Briey had been bombarded.' For Briey, Mr Nichols tells us, was the region which furnished the material for the guns that slaughtered the French and British troops, and through the influence of the great metallurgical industry it remained immune from Allied attack all through the war." She goes on to warn the adults and children "who now play their games with such happy confidence in the world that politicians and generals and armament manufacturers have made for them" that further war will be destructive beyond recovery.

This shadow still falls across the world 80 years after my late father was wounded on the Somme and "discharged 100% disabled". He regained his health; others did not. It is our clear duty to be mistrustful of official justifications for war; I don't think conscription would now be tolerated, but we need to stop sanitised scientific killing of unseen victims!! Active dedication to serve peace is a universal human duty; and may peace prevail!

Tuesday 2nd July 1996. The television programmes yesterday featured the commemoration at Thiepval of the Somme battle on its 80th anniversary. Fifteen survivors, aged 97 to 103, attended what may be the final event of this type. The oldest veteran said when interviewed that "war achieves nothing" and is to be avoided at all cost.

3rd July.   A SAD CURIOSITY.

Many Englishfolk found themselves forced to beg in the days before an adequate social security system was put in place. Voluntary bodies sprang up to try to cope with the need.

City of Durham.

AT THE SIXTH
ANNUAL MEETING
OF THE SOCIETY FOR THE
SUPPRESSION OF
MENDICITY

Held in the TOWNHALL, January 21, 1834.

THE REVEREND
W. S. Gilly, D. D. Prebend of Durham,
PRESIDENT.

It was Reported—That the Number of Strangers, chiefly Trampers, but not applying at the Office of this Society for Relief, received into the Lodging Houses between January 1st and December 31st, 1833, were as under:

Framwellgate	2358
Gilesgate	4886
Elvet	1109
Claypath	4049
Total	12,402

Being an Increase on the preceding Year of 532.

It was Reported—That the Number of Applicants at the Office amounted to 2744.

Women	446		2416 were relieved and lodged.
Children	564		175 relieved but not lodged.
Labourers	597	of	36 lodged without other relief.
Seamen	162	these	117 dismissed without any relief, not being objects who were thought to require the Society's assistance.
Soldiers	1		
Mechanics	974		
	2744		2744

It was Reported—That the Number of Irish and Scotch were,

Irish........ 3341 the Increase upon the last Year being 647.
Scotch...... 1622 the Increase upon the last Year being 170.

Durham singled out Celtic immigrants from Ireland & Scotland, and was more motivated to suppress than help, as its title says.

<u>4th July</u>.   One Last Look at Kipling: THE LAST CHANTEY.
("And there was no more sea" - Revelation 21.1)

T HUS said the Lord in the Vault above the Cherubim,
Calling to the Angels and the Souls in their degree:
"Lo! Earth has passed away
On the smoke of Judgment Day.
That Our word may be established shall We gather up the sea?"

Loud sang the souls of the jolly, jolly mariners:
"Plague upon the hurricane that made us furl and flee!
But the war is done between us,
In the deep the Lord hath seen us—
Our bones we'll leave the barracout', and God may sink the sea!"

Then said the soul of Judas that betrayed Him:
"Lord, hast Thou forgotten Thy covenant with me?
How once a year I go
To cool me on the floe?
And Ye take my day of mercy if Ye take away the sea."

Then said the soul of the Angel of the Off-shore Wind:
(He that bits the thunder when the bull-mouthed breakers flee):
"I have watch and ward to keep
O'er Thy wonders on the deep,
And Ye take mine honour from me if Ye take away the sea!"

Loud sang the souls of the jolly, jolly mariners:
"Nay, but we were angry, and a hasty folk are we.
If we worked the ship together
Till she foundered in foul weather,
Are we babes that we should clamour for a vengeance on the sea?"

Then said the souls of the slaves that men threw overboard:
"Kennelled in the picaroon a weary band were we;
But Thy arm was strong to save,
And it touched us on the wave,
And we drowsed the long tides idle till Thy Trumpets tore the sea."

Then cried the soul of the stout Apostle Paul to God:
"Once we frapped a ship, and she laboured woundily.

There were fourteen score of these,
And they blessed Thee on their knees,
When they learned Thy Grace and Glory under Malta by the sea!"

Loud sang the souls of the jolly, jolly mariners,
Plucking at their harps, and they plucked unhandily:
"Our thumbs are rough and tarred,
And the tune is something hard—
May we lift a Deepsea Chantey such as seamen use at sea?"

Then said the souls of the gentlemen-adventurers—
Fettered wrist to bar all for red iniquity:
"Ho, we revel in our chains
O'er the sorrow that was Spain's!
Heave or sink it, leave or drink it, we were masters of the sea!"

Up spake the soul of a grey Gothavn 'speckshioner—
(He that led the flenching in the fleets of fair Dundee):
"Oh, the ice-blink white and near,
And the bowhead breaching clear!
Will Ye whelm them all for wantonness that wallow in the sea?"

Loud sang the souls of the jolly, jolly mariners,
Crying: "Under Heaven, here is neither lead nor lee!
Must we sing for evermore
On the windless, glassy floor?
Take back your golden fiddles and we'll beat to open sea!"

Then stooped the Lord, and He called the good sea up to Him,
And 'stablished its borders unto all eternity,
That such as have no pleasure
For to praise the Lord by measure,
They may enter into galleons and serve Him on the sea.

Sun, Wind, and Cloud shall fail no! from the face of it,
Stinging, ringing spindrift, nor the fulmar flying free;
And the ships shall go abroad
To the Glory of the Lord
Who heard the silly sailor-folk and gave them back their sea!

<u>5th July</u>.   ENVOI - with a picture of St Morwenna the parish dedicatee of clifftop Morwenstow in Cornwall where R.S. Hawker, author of the Western song "And Shall Trelawney Die?", ministered...and gave us the Harvest Festival (see 1.8). Also this Poetic Précis from Gray's Elegy:
   "Night drops; Cows moo; Work stops; Me too............

MORWENNA 5 July (Shirley Toulson: "The Celtic Year".)

An unusual version of the sacred head theme occurs in the story of the sixth-century Morwenna, a descendant of Brychan (6 April). When she came into Cornwall from Wales, she climbed up a cliff carrying on her head a stone that she wanted to use to build her church. The stone fell to the ground and where it struck a rock a spring gushed forth. I think that this stone, like many others that saints are reported to have carried with them, may well be taken to represent the small portable altars that accompanied the saints on their travels.

Summary of contents.

ZUBES Cough Mixture

May:
- 4 — When Cats Run Home.
- 5 — The Millennial Verses.
- 6 — Deoch an Doruis.
- 7 — Compassion in Farming.
- 8 — VE Anniversary Peace.
- 9 — Idris Davies, Poet.
- 10 — "Years that are Past."
- 11 — A Rhymney "Prelude."
- 12 — Tin Bath Terrace.
- 13 — Mayor Masters Mountain.
- 14 — Durham Folk Fiction.
- 15 — Beating the Bounds.
- 16 — Ascensiontide.
- 17 — The Gambler of Govan.
- 18 — Harrowing after Hardy.
- 19 — A Locksley Greeting.
- 20 — This England.
- 21 — Casting a Spell.
- 22 — Anagrams & Competitions.
- 23 — Kipling (1).
- 24 — Kipling (2) & Owen.
- 25 — Cathedrals of our Land.
- 26 — Whitsun; praise of women.
- 27 — Kipling (3).
- 28 — Bp Pollock's girl friend.
- 29 — Oak Apple Day.
- 30 — Agony in 1892.
- 31 — "Kipper sur Toast."

June:
- 1 — Tennyson's Idylls.
- 2 — Trinity; St Pat's Hymn.
- 3 — Wordsworth/Wesley parodies.
- 4 — Reason to Refuse – also on following days to
- 10 — The Dilly Song.
- 11 — "Waspies."
- 12 — Lord Limerick's Limerick.
- 13 — Vaughan Williams' sayings.
- 14 — The Battle of Naseby.
- 15 — Linguistic oddities.
- 16 — Sassoon war-poems.
- 17 — Divine armoury & arsenal.
- 18 — Rosemary for remembrance &c.
- 19 — Lost Peace-Poems.
- 20 — Let Deans Delight.
- 21 — Tennyson; little-known aspects.
- 22)
- 23) — Locksley Hall 60 yrs after.
- 24 — Housman & "Shropshire Lad".
- 25 — Press-snippets.
- 26 — Marriage Guidance in 1560s.
- 27 — Standards in Public Life.
- 28 — Victorian destitution.
- 29 — England's Shame.
- 30 — Vicky's determined start.

July.
- 1 & 2 — Holocaust of WW1.
- 3 — Durham mendicants of 1834.
- 4 — Kipling (4): Last Chantey.
- 5 — Envoi (Gray, abbreviated.)

192

"SUMMER SUNS ARE GLOWING"

Lake Mascardi, Rio Negro, S. Argentina.   Silvia Duarte.

A Dog-Daybook
(6th July to 5th September)

"The March and the Muster" Part 4

Frank McManus

"The Times They Are A'Changing." (foreword, "Summer Suns Are Glowing.")

This well-known title of a Bob Dylan song repeats the message from our last section's foreword: "The old order changeth, yielding place to new". This comes from Tennyson's Idylls; cf. "Here we have no continuing city" (Heb.13^{14}).

Britain in the 20th century failed to ward off "The darkness of that battle in the West" against which the Idylls' last lines warned, "Where all of high and holy dies away." Two wars separated by decades of slump and fear put paid to the Empire; but the peaceful revolution of the Attlee years 1945-51 worked a transformation of the social structure, setting up a cradle-to-grave welfare system, with a free comprehensive National Health Service as its crowning glory, and taking the utilities into public ownership. Alas, and perhaps inevitably, the vision faded, so that during the 1959 election the 'NHS architect' Aneurin Bevan told a journalist friend that history had given the common people of Britain their chance "and they didn't take it". They had opted for the hope of quick personal gain and the comfort of the television armchair, in a <u>Spectatorial Age</u>!

A concerned minority made their views known on many late-20th-Century issues: US/Soviet rivalry; WMDs; EEC & EU; privatisation; wars including Vietnam & Iraq; intensive farming; global warming/market/so-called village; information technology (IT); but few gained the overview needed to sustain democracy.

K.Shelton (detail)

Thus our agricultural nation where York's mercers had built this fine Great Hall by 1360 - their "Gild of the Holy Trinity" was significantly renamed Merchant Adventurers' Gild after the Reformation - has changed to one of isolated persons, as shown by the disappearance of local names from shop-fronts. Money is far too dominant, so that the ethics of the game Monopoly (if such they be) have captured large sections of our serious-life agendas, in particular the buying and selling of houses. Yet the awakening to the iniquities of Third World Debt show that all is not lost. We need, however, to be tough not only on debt but also on the causes of debt; in particular to control the financiers' stranglehold on money-creation which holds us in Mortgage, (French for Death-grip!)

6th July.   **A SONG FOR ALL TO SING.**

Near to Banbridge Town in the County Down one morning in July
Down a bohreen green came a sweet colleen and she smiled as she passed me by;
She looked so neat from her two white feet to the sheen of her nut-brown hair,
Sure the coaxing elf I'd to shake myself to make sure I was standing there.

(CHORUS) From Bantry Bay up to Derry Quay and from Galway to Dublin Town
    No maid I've seen like the sweet colleen
    that I met in the County Down.

As she onward sped I shook my head,
and I gazed with a feeling quare,
And I said, says I, to a passer-by,
"Who's the maid with the nut-brown hair?"
Oh, he smiled at me, and with pride says he, "That's the gem of Ireland's crown,
She's young Rosie McCann from the banks of the Bann;
she's the STAR OF THE COUNTY DOWN."

195

(CHORUS) From Bantry Bay, etc.   (continued at foot overleaf.

7th July. "DIVES AND LAZARUS". (pronounced Die-vees.)

The same tune, or at least a closely-similar one, is used for a few other folk-songs, especially for this rhyming version of Jesus' stern warning to us rich folk in a hungry world (Luke 16.19+). The name of the man condemned for indifference to the plight of his poor neighbour is rendered Diverus for ease of singing:

Extract from Dives and Lazarus

Vaughan Williams wrote a lush orchestral work called "Five Variants on 'Dives and Lazarus'"; and interestingly he had the bright idea, as musical editor of the 1906 "English Hymnal", of setting Horatius Bonar's hymn "I heard the voice of Jesus say" to it as No. 574. The hymnal names the tune "Kingsfold. From an English Traditional Melody"; yet it has equal Irish origins.

(From 6 July:

I've travelled a bit, but never was hit
Since my roving career began;
But fair and square I surrendered there
To the charms of young Rosie McCann.
With a heart to let no tenant yet
Did I meet with in shawl or gown,
But in she went and I asked no rent
From the Star of the County Down.

At the cross roads fair I'll be surely there
And I'll dress in my Sunday clothes,
And I'll try sheep's eyes, and deludhering
On the heart of the nut-brown Rose.]cries
No pipe I'll smoke, no horse I'll yoke,
Though my plough with rust turns brown,
Till a smiling bride by my own fireside,
Sits the Star of the County Down.

(CHORUS) From Bantry Bay up to Derry Quay and from Galway to Dublin Town
No maid I've seen like the sweet colleen that I met in the County Down.

8th July.   "A TASTE OF HONEY".

Shelagh Delaney's youthful play of this title, filmed in 1961 (see 6 March), was followed by her gleeful citation, in a later work, of the critic whose response to the play was: "It is an unhappy thing that a young girl of 20 years of age should have such a low thought-structure". I use the title here, however, to present my bee-like search through Arthur Marshall's "Salome dear, Not in the fridge!" (George Allen & Unwin, 1968), an earlier anthology from New Statesman competitions than the one which yielded the anagrams &c of 20 May. Marion Hill's "Salome dear.." led the field for "Gruesomes".

Even W.G. Daish's 1958 "Ode to Rain" brought better cheer:

"..Thou midwife who, at birth, drown'st all my seeds,
Yet givest safe delivery to weeds;
Thou washerwoman of the ocean strand,
Who clearest fronts of kids and stops the band...
    Sixteen lines done; I'll write '&c' –
    Too bad; the weather has got wetterer!"

Peter Veale won in 1964 with his entry about the contents of a coloured section to a paper which then had none. Choosing the Church Times he proposed "The Archbishop of Canterbury at home", with verses "specially written by John Betjeman", who was always a delight to imitate:

"Large in the rose garden looms Dr Ramsay,
Patriarch, leader and chum to us all."

I love Peter Rowlett's up-to-date Cautionary Tale that year:

At sixteen Jayne was at her Best,
With Smiling Buttocks, Beaming Breast,
A modern Girl, right in the Swing,
Who'd scream at Almost Anything.
The Group that served her Cultural Needs
Was called the Swinging Centipedes.

Jayne loved the Lead Guitarist, Frank,
Whose Hair hung down his Shoulders, Lank.
And followed him both Near and Far
To hear him play his Lead Guitar.
A Dream come True it was, no doubt,
The night her Hero asked her Out.

Come 2014, fifty years after, I'll be asking the "Staggers" to seek a more fruitful sequel than Peter's, maybe ending:

"At sixty-six Jayne teems with Life,
For Frank's a Baron, she his Wife
With ample Bosom, Buttocks broad,
And loving Heart by all adored.
Their Crest of Arms a smile may bring:
Five Centipedes upon a Swing."

PBS
Prayer Book Society

197

9th July.   "Far I Hear The Steady Drummer".

Autumn 2001 was less merry, even though England's "Foot and Mouth" epidemic was ending. The lugubrious lines in a 1976 New Statesman competition for "meaningful verse made up of lines from well-known poems" had felt apposite for the days of mass-slaughter of healthy animals rather than vaccination:

> "The curfew tolls the knell of parting day.
> The hungry sheep look up and are not fed.
> Ill fares the land, to hastening ills a prey.
> I would that I were dead."   (Gray/Milton/Goldsmith/Tennyson)

In suggesting the re-run which the magazine set on 28.9.2002 I had hoped for cheerier lines; but alas our relief that the "F & M" had abated was submerged in grief for the 3000 or so victims of the suicidal terror-outrage at New York's World Trade (Usury!) Centre...And for the threat of airstrikes to the civil population of Afghanistan which in the event took a still larger toll of life, not counting the deaths from hunger and exposure which awaited too many displaced refugees in and from that unhappy land.

"War on terrorism" is, strictly speaking, a contradiction in terms, for both nouns denote an anarchistic dispensation from law and ethics. (This is not to deny the usefulness of military metaphors in everyday speech, for human life bears the stamp of self-discipline and spiritual conflict e.g. "War on Want".) Pending the overdue establishment of an adequate system of world government, with minimum human rights upheld by an international police service, criminal court and judiciary, the response to terrorism should involve policing and spying, and not war. Indeed as a winner of "my" Staggers competition movingly warned:

> Far I hear the steady drummer,
> Ancestral voices prophesying war.
> The Assyrian came down like the wolf on the fold
> Once more unto the breach, dear friends, once more;
> Lest we forget – lest we forget,
> So long as men can breathe or eyes can see.
> I heard a voice within the tavern cry,
> "Dulce et decorum est pro patria mori".
> Swept with confused alarms of struggle and flight
> I think it better that in times like these
> Rage, rage against the dying of the light.
> Tears from the depths of some divine despair
> But when the days of golden dreams had perished
> What passing bells for those who die as cattle?
> Do you hear the children weeping, oh my brothers?
> Down the foggy ruins of time, far past the frozen leaves –
> Better by far you should forget and smile
> Ring in the thousand years of peace.
>   SARA WILLIAMS
>
> (A E Housman, Coleridge, Byron, Shakespeare, Kipling, Edward FitzGerald, Shakespeare, Wilfred Owen, Emily Brontë, Wilfred Owen, Elizabeth Barrett Browning, Matthew Arnold, Yeats, Dylan Thomas, Bob Dylan, Christina Rossetti, Tennyson)

10th July. Last Lines for England?

Around 1970 I wrote the following verse for a school magazine

> "They come as a boon and a blessing to men:
> The Pickwick, the Owl, and the Waverley Pen" -
> This old-fashioned jingle's excessively long
> For brash television and popular song!
> The people may stray from their forefathers' church,
> The State has abolished the rod, pole or perch;
> And in two years' time we shall cease to enjoy
> The bushel, the peck, and the pennyweight Troy.

And so it was, as part of the dulling of the variety of life resulting from "rationalisation". Some changes are of course benign; I would not now use the "exclusive language" of "men" and "forefathers", though I baulk at its removal from old and familiar contexts and from words such as "workmanlike". The drive for metrication is still upon us, and it won me two bottles of wine from Corney and Barrow, the London vintners who sponsor the "New Statesman" Letter-of-the-Week award.

The workers' kilo is deepest red

Did the ancient Romans, as their empire declined, cling stubbornly to their ridiculous numbering system, which made anything beyond the simplest addition sums almost impossible? Did they hold out for their heritage of Ls, Cs and Vs? Did they have their numeral martyrs as we have our metric martyrs? History does not record, but the *Daily Mail* columnist Melanie Phillips explains that we should resist metrication lest we are seduced by the "abstract thinking" of Continental revolutionaries. The English, she writes, prefer "the familiar and the useful"; the yard, for example, being "the distance from the nose to the outstretched fingertip of King Henry I". Even in the most elevated circles, it is not easy now to find a monarch on hand as one goes about, say, designing a garden. But the logic is clear: measurement, to her, is a privilege that should be confined to the elite. Ms Phillips has illuminated the battle between imperial and metric measurements: like most things in life, it is a class issue.

New Statesman 2nd Editorial 25/2/2002

Letter of the week

I FEAR that in your editorial attack on Melanie Phillips ("The workers' kilo i deepest red", 25 February) you have left your back unguarded. Since *Whitaker's Almanack* defines the metric alternative to Henry I's arm, the metre, as "the length travelled by light in a vacuum during a time interval of 1/299,792,458 of a second", it is even more elitist, arcane and remote from us poor déclassé proles than its royal alternative, the yard.

NS 11.3.2002   FRANK McMANU
                  Todmorden, West Yorkshir

(A later correspondent wrote that scientists had superseded Whitaker!)

Metrication assists computerised calculation but as a teacher I found that this was at the expense of popular numeracy. Pupils lost their skills of say dividing by 8 (to get from pints to gallons) and multiplying by 12 (for shillings to pence); and in some cases their grasp of magnitude - where to put the decimal-dot. George Orwell pointed out that our old units had evolved from everyday experience and gave information in immediate ways, e.g. "Tom's height is four foot nine" - not 1.47 metres!

<u>11th July.</u>   <u>Milton, Tennyson, Wordsworth</u> – England's Trinity
　　　　　　　　of poets, hard pressed by Blake, Byron, Shelley..!

Having masked my preferences under alphabetical order, may I look at John Milton (1608-74, the earliest of those named), who was ardent for the Commonwealth cause in the English Civil War. His sonnets appear in good anthologies: Impassioned against the religious massacre of French Huguenots ("Avenge O Lord thy slaughtered saints..."); Poignant "On his Blindness" and "On his Deceased Wife"; and socially Commonsensical against over-lavish living ("To Mr Lawrence") and showy Workoholism in "To Cyriack Skinner" which ends with this "sextet":

> To measure life learn thou betimes, and know　(in good time
> Toward solid good what leads the nearest way;
> For other things mild Heaven a time ordains,
> And disapproves that care, though wise in show,
> That with superfluous burdens loads the day,
> And, when God sends a cheerful hour, refrains.

Milton's hymn "Let us with a gladsome mind" is sung at harvest festivals, and choral societies sing Parry's settings of "Blest Pair of Sirens.."; but his odes, mood-poems and epics are now mainly the province of scholars. Thrice married, the unhappiness of his first (1643-52) affected his views on women. An anonymous schoolteacher has noted that "Everyone is very hard on Mrs Milton – It was hard on her to be married to a stern old puritan who wrote Divorce tracts during the honeymoon!"

Wordsworth believed that it was his vocation to succeed Milton as the poet in contemporary terms of the loss and recovery of Paradise; and <u>his</u> work is not marred by Miltonic misogyny. The earlier poet's "Paradise Lost" struggles to expound "literal Adam and Eve"; and in its Book XI makes the Archangel Michael tell Adam that earth's sorrows from the murder of Abel onward depict "What misery the inabstinence of Eve/ Shall bring on men." (lines 476-7). Adam submits to the "justice" of this Fall (515+) and Michael counsels him to austere living. Another vision follows in which hillsmen descend to a plain only to be "caught in the amorous net" of "a bevy of fair women, richly gay / In gems and wanton dress!" These "fair atheists"(!) though blithe are "Yet empty of all good wherein consists/ Woman's domestic honour and chief praise". Husbands "yield up all their virtue" to their blandishments, in ways not specified, and a "world of tears" ensues. Adam says he sees Man's woe begin from Woman; but Michael retorts that "From Man's effeminate slackness it begins"! Yet these lines (573+) have a power of diction which is justly celebrated, even though Wordsworth's <u>Prelude</u> renders the Fall as Alienation and Loss of Vision – a worthier stance!

　　　　－　－　－　－　－　－

<u>12th July</u>. # Bands to the banner born
(9.7.1990 <u>Northern Echo</u>.)

On the march: banners flying in Durham on the big day.

201

Following the first Miners' Procession at Wharton Park in 1871 the Gala (pron. "gayla" in the north-east!) was moved in 1872 to Durham Racecourses, where it has outlived the mining industry and is held each second Saturday in July (but check with the tourist office, 0191.384.3720). All should go to the event at least once, for it remains one of Britain's largest community-rooted events, if not <u>the</u> largest. At the peak in the early 1900s of County Durham's centuries-old industry, entire communities would leave their villages by train or bus to join the "big meeting" to hear the passionate speeches or ignore them in favour of the fun of the fair. Best of all were the post-war years when hopes ran high that the nationalised pits would serve the nation not the few.

Nine o'clock and the bus leaves West Auckland, with the New Inn its first and last stop. No other choice, anyway. All traffic's banned beyond there. The banner's out now and the band's ready — nothing else left but to follow behind to the racecourse.

Twice apiece at the fish 'n' chip van, and on to the boxing booth. Five pounds in your pocket if you beat the pro, and that's what we earn in a week. A Newcastle lad steps forward. Plenty to drink's made him brave. One round later and they're picking him up, so we all chip in the collection. Fifteen bob and he's happy. Worth a few pints is that!

Our banner's lifting at half-past two,

Shildon, one stop before home, and preparing to march where the old miners' cottages are. Not long to wait, the band strikes up, and we're off. The old man's deaf, well nearly, but he hears the music all right. His legs aren't what they were either, but he'll make it as far as the window.

A peep through the curtain and the tip of a banner riding the crest of the hill Turned a hundred banners that day, but this one's special for him.

He breathes in gasps, lungs crippled by the pit. Ever so slowly it unfurls through the glass. Tears welling up in his eyes...

(1946, told by NL Banks to B. Wedgwood)

15th July.   HOPE BETRAYED.

At the peak of British coal-mining there were a quarter of a million miners in South Wales (where the industry was a mere Victorian creation). Barry Port was the energy capital – the "Persian Gulf" – of the pre-war world! Some decline may have been unavoidable as other sources of energy became available; but the British industry was "helped on its way" by deliberate felony, culminating in the early 1990s' massacre which put paid to all but a handful of the pits that had survived the 1984/5 trauma. Calling for an independent inquiry into the decision to close 31 pits at a time of deepening recession, the Guardian newspaper editorialised thus on 14 October 1992:

Whitehall claims these closures are the result of post-privatisation market forces. Nothing of the sort. The energy market is a byzantine stitch-up. While subsidies have been progressively withdrawn from coal, the nuclear industry receives £1.2 billion a year, equivalent to £50 per tonne of coal — and enough to show coal imports the way home. Even if UK coal was the cheapest in the world, it could not displace nuclear stations, which have to be run 24 hours on "base load". Amazingly, this is also happening to gas-fired stations. Gas has been purchased on 15-year contracts where the generating authorities agree to pay for it even if they don't use it — so that (imported) gas, too, is being burned on base load displacing coal. A straight case for the Monopolies Commission.

It is often claimed that in spite of politicians' words, money is the god which rules commerce. This generalisation does not account for the subsidising of other fuels but not of coal. Concurring with the Guardian, David Lunn (then bishop of Sheffield) wrote in his December 1994 newsletter that

Most of the battles I fight I seem to lose! But the battle for Coal had to be fought; I am still proud to have been able to join in and I am sure that the wrong side lost! Even on economic grounds, future historians will be unable to understand why we simply abandoned an infinite source of home-based energy in favour of uncertain imports and that temporary supply of North Sea Gas. And the heartless way in which the livelihood of the coalfield communities was suddenly cut off will leave permanent question marks about the judgement and commonsense of those responsible.

The offending Government was removed in 1997 but the damage was done, and a Herculean effort of reconstruction is needed!

Detailed literature obtainable from Durham NUM, Miners' Hall, Red Hills, Durham tells the story of the betrayal of post-war hope by unsatisfactory Ministers and Coal Board appointees; by overgenerous compensation to coalowners and interest-charges on money borrowed to provide it; and by the closure of far-from-exhausted pits for no satisfactory reason. Of course the miners benefited from pithead baths and improved safety. But alas by 1980 a world slump aggravated the loss of demand that the run-down of British steel and engineering had caused in the wake of Governmental refusal to protect our industrial base against cheap imports of the products of subsistence-labour in Columbia and elsewhere. The moneyfolk of the world united to obstruct workers' unity across the frontiers of nations and industries; and desolation followed the '84/5 strike and the 90s massacre.

<u>14th July.</u>   "Edward, bring me a glass of lemonade."   203

   Feelings ran high during the 1984/5 coal-strike just as they did in its 1926 forerunner. The miners on each occasion felt that they were the milch-cows of capitalism; and so they were, even though they may not always have seen that particular employers also were at the mercy of impersonal forces. There was alas governmental dishonesty each time. The Trade Union Congress called off the 1926 general strike through trusting assurances that were not honoured; and in October 1984 the pit foremen's union NACODS, which had voted 83% to join the NUM's strike, pulled out when given a useless promise of an independent review of pit closures. "We were told lies" says its then secretary. It seems however that no one industry can be freed from monetarist predation; so the global market needs replacement, or transforming by a world-wide ban on usurious interest.

   Much folklore surrounds the "Big Meeting". The most sensational tale relates to a lamentable episode of 1926 when Dean Welldon of Durham Cathedral, arriving to speak at a temperance meeting following the main one, was mistaken by a group of angry miners for Bishop Henson, an East Anglian whom Lloyd George had moved from Hereford to Durham some years before - unwisely since Henson, unlike Bishop Westcott in 1892 and David Jenkins in 1984, didn't understand the Trade Union movement and had publicly criticised it. The cry went up: "Here's the Bishop - Hoy him i' the river!", and the 70-year-old Dean was hustled down and tripped by a riverside bush. The miners held back and the Dean was picked up by a passing launch.

   Met by a friend at the landing he was helped back to the Deanery, where his butler served his lemonade on a silver salver. An hour later he preached at the Cathedral gala-service with no mention of this.

The Years of Victory, Durham Miners Gala, in post-nationalisation fervour hears Nye Bevan speak.

15th July.   T H E   D E L U G E.

If this St Swithin's Day is wet, tradition has it that we're in for forty wet days; a very rainy summer, that is. North Country folk shrug that off as "nowt unusual". Being one myself I believe that the world suffers all the time from a different sort of deluge. We are swamped and damaged by consumerist urges! "Getting and spending, we lay waste our powers" (Wordsworth)!

> The people still flock to the poll
> And think they have final control,
>   But really they dance
>   To the tunes of Finance,
> And solace themselves with the dole.

(C.M.Hattersley, original version 1937.)

Experience shows that coalmining and other mighty industries are vulnerable to the rogue forces of human vengefulness and pride of power, as well as to technical changes and shifts in world commerce. Something more is needed; and William Temple's words in mid-20th-century seem wise: "Economic conditions are among the forces moulding the moral tendencies of those who are subjected to them; far more deeply is it true that those conditions themselves are rooted in a moral state and outlook, which must therefore be the first object of attack". He may overdo things when he says "attack" and "far more deeply", but he is substantially correct. Centuries of general connivance have seen the slow development of the usury-based system into a "global market", and Ruskin was right in predicting that the usurer would deceive himself and think he's a benefactor!

International finance now performs a greater Money Trick than the one portrayed in Tressall's "Ragged Trousered Philanthropists" to depict the local-level exploitation of workers by too many employers. Let us "Leave Off This Usury" (Nehemiah 5.10), with usury defined as by the major ethical religions. The 5th Lateran Council 1515 of the undivided Western Church including England banned it as "The attempt to draw benefit or increase from a thing, money, not in itself fruitful, without labour, cost or risk on the lender's part". Only the charges justified by such 'extrinsic titles', and costs of administration, are ethical.

— — — — —

To end on a lighter note this visit to the story of coal: I was guest of the Hetton Lodge at the 1983 Gala; and as we were alighting from the coach at Durham, a vehicle drew up and some VIPs from the Nigerian miners' association got out, dressed in resplendent robes, and with coal-black complexions! - whereupon a Hetton miner remarked with glorious political incorrectness: "Them's just coom up from pit!"

<u>16th July.</u> <u>Downing Street Austerity.</u>

Humphrey the cat-in-residence at 10 Downing Street absented himself for a while after the 1997 General Election, giving rise to false rumours that the new tenants had evicted him. In fact the Blair family had a more cordial welcome to their much-desired residence than was enjoyed in 1924 by their first Labour predecessor, the widower James Ramsay Macdonald. Terence Feely, in "Number 10" (Sidgwick & Jackson, 1982), notes that Macdonald's eldest daughter Ishbel (20) had run the family home for two years before she met Mrs Baldwin, the jolly wife of the previous Prime Minister. It was explained that the Baldwins owned all the crockery, cutlery and linen, and would also take all the furniture bar a few items provided by the Board of Works. Ishbel was sent to the Co-op to buy such essentials, having first been advised not to "go mad"!

An unusual sight in Downing Street was the Co-op grocery van; another was the two younger daughters walking in their green uniforms to school in Camden Town to save bus fares. Instead of eating in their own unheated private part of the house, the family used the official dining room, which was heated by the State.

THE SUBSIDISED MINEOWNER — 1920s cartoon capitalist!

The Board's snobbish civil servant was so unhelpful that Ishbel had to "pull rank" and say she was the P.M's political hostess (shades of Margot Asquith) and his social secretary and his daughter, and that he wasn't prepared to put up with the mean sur- but wants good carpets ...pictures... In these days of pampered professional politicians it is difficult to imagine such top-level working class poverty!

For 1926 "Industrial politics" please see 9.5 & the <u>Angry Summer</u> poems (12.5), & book of that title, J. McIlroy (Univ. of Wales 2004).

17th July.   " T R O U G H S ! "

In the golden age of the steam railway-locomotive the problem arose of maintaining an adequate supply of water for the engines of long-distance expresses which made too few stops for filling their tenders from water-towers at stations. The difficulty was solved by providing long water-troughs between the rails, and fitting the engines with scoops whereby they could take up water at speed, albeit with some splashing.

In his book "Rail Tales of the Unexpected" (RCA, 1992), Kenneth Westcott Jones tells of travelling in a group of 6 or 7 businessmen returning from Ireland one evening in 1961. They were dining in the front coach of the Heysham-to-London boat-train, when a railway-executive among them realised that they were speeding towards the troughs at Brock just north of Preston, and that the fanlight-windows were open. Hastily he shut the sliding pane over his table, and then leaned over the gangway pointing to the open window opposite, whilst exclaiming "Troughs!" anxiously to his colleagues opposite. Unfortunately his wineglass was in his raised hand; and the nearest man took this as an exotic greeting, and rose with his glass saying "Troughs!" in return - just as water poured in through the still-open top window, to the immense chagrin of the waiters. Dining-cars were not normally put next to engines, nor were trains allowed to pass one another at troughs after coal was dislodged from the Silver Jubilee's tender at Northallerton.

BR 46121 at Dillicar - Bp. Eric Treacy (detail)

Another railway curiosity was the Port Carlisle Dandy, now preserved in York Railway Museum. Third class passengers were supposed to perch on its sides. When the horse-drawn vehicle was replaced by steam in 1914, the mare persisted in walking between tramlines when drawing a van along the road.

"THERE HATH PASS'D AWAY A GLORY FROM THE EARTH" - many rail-lovers appropriate Wordsworth's line in memory of the most elegant machines ever to move on earth. The "Golden Age" of Steam" (1890-1914) was followed by an inter-war "Silver Age" and a 1950s Bronze Age. Comfort ranged from palatial to dire, whilst services were more reliable than now, if slow for long-distance journeys.

18th July.   WORDSWORTH'S BLENDED MIND. (see 8.2)   207

In later years Wordsworth advanced in grandiloquence, and has mischievously been deemed a walking definition of that word. Granted that we may not be so cavalier in all moods as to rely on his Somerset lines in "The Tables Turned":

> "One impulse of a vernal wood
> May teach you more of man,
> Of moral evil and of good,
> Than all the sages can"...

his successive revisions of his "Prelude", an extended study of "the growth of a poet's mind", expanded it from the short two-part work of 1799 to the thirteen-book version of 1805. This in turn was continually revised at Rydal Mount in the direction of orthodox gravity, to appear posthumously in fourteen "books" in 1850. Among long biographical passages are invocations of

> "Ye presences of Nature, in the sky
> Or on the earth; ye visions of the hills
> And souls of lonely places" (1805, Book I) -

and the assertion that "an auxiliar light
> Came from my mind, which on the setting sun
> Bestowed new splendour" (1799, II, lines 417-9).

-Thus the poet's mind, influenced externally and internally,

> "Even as an agent for the one great mind[*],   (* God;
> Creates, creator and receiver both,   (cf. Psalms)
> Working but in alliance with the works   (104, 148.)
> Which it beholds." (1799, II, 302-5).

Wordsworth amplifies this in "1805, VI, lines 525-548" or, less vividly, "1850, VI, lines 592-616". Also towards the end of "Home at Grasmere", a work recently compiled by editors from various manuscripts so that it does not appear in standard collections of his poems, Wordsworth declares his wish to proclaim ...how exquisitely the individual mind (is fitted) to the external world...and how exquisitely the external world is fitted to the mind"; and also to proclaim "the creation which they with blended might accomplish". The "Prelude" ends with a moving declaration that even if a Dark Age should return, the "Prophets of Nature" may yet teach people to love "the good, the true, the pure, the just" (Tennyson, "Locksley Hall Sixty Years After" - for it is the human mind that can become "a thousand times more beautiful than the earth...of quality and fabric more
                                                        divine."

19th July. "Tit For Tat Down Mammary Lane!"

This "New Statesman" headline from the early 1970s celebrated the first nipple-portrayal in the "Daily Mirror" in response to those by its commercial rival the "Sun". Lacking both the resources and the inclination to challenge these "tabloids", I can but offer two germane titbits!

"Council officials at Southend have been ordered to make sure that there is no cover-up among topless dancers in seaside pubs. Complaints have been received that the girls are not topless and acting under the Trade Descriptions Act consumer protection officers are attending sessions to make sure everything is on view" - Evening Standard (Leonard Skevington) - in This England 25.7.75.

"Four bikini-clad guys, who packed 400 women into a Dundalk bar last Sunday, have been ordered by a Baltimore liquor board to cover their bare breasts...Joseph J. Hess, chairman of the liquor board, ruled yesterday that male dancers must adhere to the same rules as female dancers and conceal the entire nipple area and lower breast". - Evening Sun (Alan Drinnan) - in This America 12.12.75 (Both these items come from "New Statesman" magazine.)

"I don't mind some peace, but a just and lasting peace puts us out of the picture entirely."

(Works-manager to director) "OK, it shouldn't have leaked into the Calder; but it won't matter to us so long as it doesn't leak into the Press."

- - - - - -

20th July. GEORGE ORWELL.

Eric Blair, who wrote under this pseudonym, is justly famed for his trenchant attacks on all tyranny. His "1984", written in 1948, is the direst of warnings against a world locked in warring power-blocs and manipulating public opinion by skilled perversions of honest speech. Sadly "1984" seems to exist in some corner or other of the world pretty-well all the time.

The more readable and indeed delightful fable "Animal Farm" portrays the corruption of a movement for social justice when trusted leaders act selfishly; a warning for his namesake Prime Minister?! In correspondence following (to foot opposite

21st July.   Dilettantalistic Dabblings.

E.B. Alletson's cricket-century for Notts against Sussex in May 1911 is all-but-forgotten. Although he rattled up 189 runs in 90 minutes his failure to reach 200 keeps his innings out of most compilations. It was a sensation at the time, for at No. 11 he was "last man in" at Hove, and his admirable 47 in 50 minutes before lunch was satisfying. But "the devil then seemed to enter him", and with safe and furious hitting he ran up another 142 in the 40 minutes from 2.15 to 2.55pm. Never again did he achieve anything memorable.

> ❏ I should love to help you. But I am Philosophy. Religion has gone to lunch.
> – *a Foyle's bookshop worker, apologising being unable to assist a caller.* Star 22.4.2002

Michael Wescott (18) of Vicarage Road, Birmingham, said: "I plead for peace in a world of war, love in a world of hate, free speech for all, and an end to politically-motivated trials in this country". Judge Neil McKinnon, who directed that pleas of not guilty be entered in each ccase, told Mr Wescott: "I will have to have a medical report on you if you are not careful." - Guardian (M.Kant) - in This England, NS, 10.10.75.

Personal advertisement in "New Statesman" 7.11.75:
"I wish there was a man who knew / a femme fatale is feeling
Such varied trends her leisure takes / as travel, plays blue
Who is 30, Jewish too / with honesty, wit and baking cakes.
(Box 2128.) Will she please contact F.McM if she sees this!

20.7   Orwell's "Animal Farm" radio-broadcast on the BBC
(concl.)   Third Programme in 1946 he wrote that he meant the moral of his tale to be that the effect of a revolution is bound to be transitory unless there exists what Eisenhower called "an alert and intelligent citizenry" that will throw out their leaders when their jobs are done. The turning point was when the pigs kept the milk and fruit. As Lord Acton rightly said, "Power tends to corrupt; absolute power corrupts absolutely" - and should always be refused, I add.

It is almost "not done" to criticise Orwell! - yet the idea has been broached that in thus addressing itself to a people who had borne great hardship in World War 2, he overstressed the dark side of human nature and undervalued our potential for good.

22nd July.   **Vastness - the Long and Short of it!**

Until the Renaissance nobody thought of questioning that we and our world are at the centre of creation. Then Bruno's speculations and Galileo's telescopic observations disturbed this confidence. Victorian conflicts on evolution were felt as a further threat to our status, and Tennyson in 1892 asked:

> "Will my tiny spark of being wholly vanish in your deeps and heights?
> Must my day be dark by reason, O ye Heavens, of your boundless nights,
> Rush of suns, and roll of systems, and your fiery clash of meteorites?"

The Open University has shown a film "Powers of Ten" at some of its science Summer-schools. Photographs taken at distances from earth which increase tenfold from one to the next are shown or simulated. They draw attention to the mind-boggling "infinities" of size and of smallness. Great thinkers have struggled with their consequences for Physics; but no coherent unity was reached in the 20th century to link giant-scale Relativity and subatomic Quantum Theory. I was therefore fascinated by Teilhard de Chardin's chapter "Man's Place in the Universe" in his 1966 book "The Vision of the Past" (tr. J.M. Cohen, publ. Collins).

The famous palaeontologist offers an original view of "man as an element of special...interest in a world of movement". First of all he reviews the physicists' Universe of Two Infinities, foreseen by Pascal in Pensee 72. (The "Powers of Ten" notation shows e.g. 1000 or 10 x 10 x 10 as 10^3; and 1/1000 as 10^{-3}.)

10^{25} metres	-	"boundary of Universe".
10^{20}	-	Milky Way diameter.
10^{0} (or 1)	-	Human dimensions.
10^{-10}	-	Atomic size.
10^{-16}	-	Nucleon separation in atom.

Only our good "middle zone", said Chardin, is Newtonian in Physics and Euclidean in Geometry! On the vast side time seems to break up into local versions; on the infinitesimal side particles seem to lose their individuality. The extremes differ in quality from one another and from our everyday world; but we need not think this puts our grasp on reality and life at risk.

Chardin accordingly asserts the need to preserve the "value of the spirit in face of matter, and the value of physics in face of spiritual phenomena" His method is to stress a "third infinity", of <u>complexity</u>, in which life emerges:- in numbers of atoms 10^2 - inorganic molecule; 10^6 - virus; 10^{10} animal cell; 10^{22} man

(continued on 20th August.

23rd July.   QUIRKS OF THE ENGLISH LANGUAGE.

On 9th July 1996 the following letter appeared in The Times:

Sir, Re Mr Page's letter (July 4):
"Mrs Mary Lock, head of English at Queen Anne's (girls') school in York, has been transferred to Archbishop Holgate's School to be Head of English. She will be addressed by boys as 'Sir', and referred to by all as 'Lady Master'."
My mother found this notice, signed by the Headmaster, in the masters' common room, on her arrival at Archbishop Holgate's early in the war.   Yours faithfully, BRIAN LOCKE.....

That's an extreme example of diehard insistence upon what schoolmasters used to love to teach, namely that "the masculine embraces the feminine". Nowadays chairpersons replace chairmen, and are often turned into chairs when they might be chairfolk. Why not, we may wonder, when many who ✱ t to "chair" as inanimate will themselves on occasion speak of Black Rod without expanding him into the Gentleman Usher thereof, or his poor relation the Yeoman Usher. One may say "Meet Tom, he's the first trombone in the LSO", but hardly "This is Jane, she's the organ at the Ritz". Language evolves and may then settle down, yet problems arise when terms are proposed such as milkperson or the somewhat ludicrous personhole. I think we should defer to those who dislike exclusive language, by which English is more dogged than most other tongues, except in old contexts or where it would be distractive.

Information Technology has led to linguistic change and to some solecisms; laps, unlike desks, have no underside and are all top, therefore the term "laptop computer" stems from false analogy with "desktop computer". We don't speak of laptopdogs. Pedantic classicists - and there is pleasure to be found in some pedantry - insist that "homophobia" means not hatred of homosexual people as is often thought, but hatred of similar people, (compare homocentric, having the same centre). "Television" is a Greek-Latin hybrid and would have been "telescope" had another instrument not already taken that name. More annoying is forced evolution, e.g. the over-use of "gay" for homosexual to the detriment of its long-standing meaning. (Wordsworth wrote of the Ullswater daffodils that "A poet could not but be gay / In such a jocund company.")

Are there male Lesbians? Yes, born on Lesbos. For 3rd Women see 29 August.

Falling Hair PREVENTED BY CUTICURA

Cleanse the scalp and hair with warm shampoos of CUTICURA SOAP, dry, and apply a light dressing of CUTICURA, purest of emollient skin cures. This treatment will clear the scalp and hair of crusts and dandruff, soothe itching, irritated surfaces, supply the roots with energy and nourishment, and make the hair grow, when all else fails.

24th July. **SMALL IS BEAUTIFUL:- The Hospice of Hampsfell.**

Cumbria's mountains offer many glorious panoramic views; the High Stile – Red Pike ridge-walk above Buttermere lets five major lakes be seen, a number which I don't think is exceeded elsewhere. Yet lower vantage-points should not be scorned. Black Combe in the far south-west fails to reach 2000' above Silecroft's seashore, yet Scotland, Snowdonia and the Isle of Man are visible from its summit on a clear day, along with the Cumberland coast stretched out like a map to the north below. As for hospitality, that of Hampsfell's limestone-pavement near Grange-over-Sands, a mere 727' high, far excels the doubtful welcome of England's highest area atop Scafell Pike (3210', 13.5)

Hampsfell's shelter has notices on its four inside walls, with quaintnesses of punctuation and (mis)spelling. On the roof there is a rotating pointer on a disc identifying the nearby tops. The landowner G.Remington who provided the facility in 1846 to the delight of generations of ramblers displayed the sardonic <u>Take Notice</u> board which reads: "All persons visiting this Hospice by permission of the owner, are requested to respect private property, and not by acts of wanton mischief and destruction show that they possess more muscle than brain. I have no hope that this request will be attended to for as Solomon says 'Though thou shouldst bray a fool in a mortar among wheat with a pestle yet will not his foolishness depart from him'." (Prov.27^{22})

Nevertheless Remington declared on another board that:
"This hospice as an open door, Alike to shelter rich and poor;
A roomy seat for young and old Where they may screen them from the cold...
A lengthened chain holds guard around To keep the cattle from the ground;
Kind reader freely take you pleasure But do no mischief to my treasure."

The door-lintel bears the Greek phrase by Homer, carved into the stone: ΡΟΔΟΔΑΚΤΥΛΟΣ ΗΩΣ – (Rosy-fingered dawn).

The facing wall includes a response by an imagined guest:
"Then (turning to the West) is seen Dear Cartmel's peaceful valley green,
Mid waving woods and verdant lands The fine old church of Cartmel stands...
For no good man would think it pleasure
To climb the fell to spoil your treasure..."

And indoor, over the exit:
"O God! O good beyond compare!
If this Thy meaner works be fair,
If thus Thy beauty gild the span
Of faded earth and fallen Man,
How glorious must those mansions be
Where Thy redeemed dwell with Thee."

25th July.   Silver Links and Golden Goals.

Books giving Vocational Guidance abound on library shelves. Parents are advised on choice of schools, teenagers on exam. subjects, students on colleges and courses, young adults on career-choice, 30- & 40-somethings on career-promotion and development. People who have notched up their half-century are helped to prepare for retirement. Young pensioners receive guidance on enjoying a fruitful life.

> If thou indeed derive thy light from Heaven,
> Then, to the measure of that heaven-born light,
> Shine, Poet! in thy place, and be content:—
> The stars pre-eminent in magnitude,
> And they that from the zenith dart their beams,
> (Visible though they be to half the earth,
> Though half a sphere be conscious of their brightness)
> Are yet of no diviner origin,
> No purer essence, than the one that burns,
> Like an untended watch-fire, on the ridge
> Of some dark mountain; or than those which seem
> Humbly to hang, like twinkling winter lamps,
> Among the branches of the leafless trees;
> All are the undying offspring of one Sire:
> Then, to the measure of the light vouchsafed,
> Shine, Poet! in thy place, and be content.

I've never, however, seen or heard any Vocational Guidance, with the sole exception of these lines by Wordsworth, which is applicable to those like myself who are probably, or at least very possibly, in the second half of their retirement. "Can this void be filled"? I wonder, and I venture a few tips — (you'll need none on family life)!

1. Pace yourself, for energy inevitably diminishes; think of when you were 25, and wonder where all the energy has gone!

2. Replace more arduous activities by less exacting ones when you need to - golf by bowls perhaps, or fell-walking by valley-walking - but 'work to limit' from time to time, and think nothing of it when in due course the valley-walks give way to rides (by train, bus or car as appropriate).

3. Watch your weight and health, don't forget the autumn flu-jab and other occasional measures, eat and drink enough not too much, dress not "old" or "young" but neatly with a dab of daring, and be "on the town" a few times each week.

4. Be outgoing and look out for new friends, for we have to part with some old ones; but don't move house unnecessarily, for "fresh starts" can be lonely for a few years.

5. Keep one or more cats and/or dogs; link with your local church or faithgroup or social group, and help in its work.

6. Have enough toys (radio, TV, CD-player or Ipod, IT, books) but not too many, and ration your time in the TV armchair. Follow the news and maybe send your views in letters to newspapers, especially regional ones ("nationals" get lots). Maintain and even expand your creative work and hobbies.

26th July.   "What Went Wrong?"

The 1960s were seen by many as a time of great social change. Susan Howatch in one of her compelling Starbridge Novels made a character call it "the Devil's Decade". Philip Larkin famously wrote that "Sexual intercourse began in 1963 / Between the end of the Chatterley ban and the Beatles' first LP." Be that as it may — permissiveness is a serious topic but not my present one — "the Devil never rests" and has a field-day somewhere in many a decade!

Our "teenage rebellion" involved some rejection of traditional family loyalties and scorning of parental experience and practicality. In a word, ageism! Jeremy Seabrook, in his books such as "City Close-up", "What Went Wrong?" and in 1987 "Working-Class Childhood", sheds light upon adult bewilderments. In the last-named (p.143) he claims that young folks' search for self-expression and fulfilment stems from social and economic changes, a fact that we don't like to face. "It is as though... society, when it ceases to intervene in our lives through poverty and scarcity, ceases to exist...whereas, of course, it extends its influence in more subtle but no less stringent ways than...through the old coercive disciplines, hunger & poverty."

Seabrook adds that "the control and disciplining of children at the earliest point in living memory in this book (Mr Baines, a child of the early 1890s) was a reflection of their future role as labour. The parents had to collude with the loveless disciplines of mine, mill and factory." Yet within the changed context of the 1980s "the same collusion is there with the external forces that shape our lives." The change has been from "a complex of crippling restraints" to "a state of disabling licence", because a mutation in the money-system of global capitalism has changed the West from a labour-intensive productive economy to a consumer-society parasitic on the Third World. The "fact that the change appears to be a complete reversal effectively conceals what remains constant through time — the lasting impotence and debilitation".

"In the 1890s the cruel conditions...created solidarity between generations... The collusion is still there, in that parents feel their primary function is to give their children access to the material riches on offer; but at the same time the defensive closeness that united them has been broken"; and "Love ...has a hard passage through the materialism of the world of the young... Dependency on the market-place has been created", and children grow up within it in isolation and without self-knowledge, for they scorn to attend to life's big questions. Mechanising our schools with tests and league-tables and over-emphasis on IT is no substitute for Faith, Hope and Love!

27th July.   **"It's The Economy, Stupid!"**

Mr Thomas Gradgrind, a retired wholesale hardware merchant of Coketown (based on Preston in Charles Dickens' 1854 novel Hard Times), was a ponderous local worthy in contrast with his whelp-of-a-similarly-named son (shown in an original drawing) who had failed to absorb wisdom or reliability from his ruthless father's training and restraint. The older man still advanced his "Nothing but Facts" viewpoint on the pupils at his 'model school', in which Mr McChoakumchild the teacher conscientiously plodded through the prescribed syllabus. Here we have a lesson in the presence of the then equivalent to OFSTED in the form of a government officer:

'Girl number twenty', said Mr Gradgrind, squarely pointing with his square finger, 'I don't know that girl. Who is (she)?'

'Sissy Jupe, Sir', explained number twenty, blushing, standing up, and curtseying.....

'Give me your definition of a horse.' (Sissy Jupe thrown into the greatest alarm by this demand.) 'Girl number twenty possessed of no facts, in reference to one of the commonest of animals! Some boy's definition of a horse. Bitzer, yours.'

'Quadruped. Graminivorous. Forty teeth, namely twenty-four grinders, four eye-teeth, and twelve incisive. Sheds coat in the spring; in marshy countries, sheds hoofs, too. Hoofs hard, but requiring to be shod with iron...' Thus (& much more) Bitzer.

'Now girl number twenty', said Mr Gradgrind. 'You know what a horse is.' She curtseyed again, and would have blushed deeper, if she could have blushed deeper than she had blushed all this time.

- - - - - - - -

We can but hope that today's teachers will resist the temptation to offer lifeless rote-learning as their response to special assessment tests, league tables, and pressures to "achieve"!

Later we read (Chapter LX) that poor Jupe, "after eight weeks of induction into the elements of Political Economy" had given to the question "What is the first principle of this science?" the absurd answer from the Prayer-book Catechism, "To do unto others as I would that they should do unto me."

Dickens adds that 'Mr Gradgrind, observed, shaking his head, that all this was very bad; that it showed the necessity of infinite grinding at the mill of knowledge, as per system, blue-book, report...and that Jupe must be kept to it.' (to foot overlf)

28th July.   "THE BELOVED ENEMY". (see also 16.1 & 14.2).

* Men are essentially dogs and women are essentially cats... Women are <u>sleeker</u>. (Martin Mull).

* Fighting is essentially a masculine idea; a woman's weapon is her tongue, which neither rusts nor rests. (after H. Gingold).

* Belles Dames sans Percy. (Shelley's discarded female friends).

* A woman may be as wicked as she likes, but if she isn't pretty it won't do her much good. (Somerset Maugham).

* Sex is the soft centre of the Newbury fruit of friendship. (Jilly Cooper).

* To actual women, being one is merely a good excuse not to play football. (Fran Lebowitz, but becoming out-of-date!)

* There are seven ages of womanhood; baby, child, young miss, young woman, young woman, young woman, young woman. (Anon.)

* Women do not like timid men. Cats do not like prudent mice. H.L. Mencken).

* Women represent the triumph of matter over mind, just as men represent the triumph of mind over morals. (Oscar Wilde).

* A woman is a mystery wrapped up in an enigma, (Maurice Darwin, after Churchill on Russia).

27.7 Then came the night when Gradgrind's daughter Louisa, **(concl.)** a kindly older girl of 16 or so, tried to help Sissy in preparation for school next day. When Sissy said tearfully that she was always making mistakes, Louisa asked for some:

'I am almost ashamed,' said Sissy, with reluctance. 'But to-day, for instance, Mr. M'Choakumchild was explaining to us about Natural Prosperity.'

'National, I think it must have been,' observed Louisa.

'Yes, it was.—But isn't it the same?' she timidly asked.

'You had better say, National, as he said so,' returned Louisa, with her dry reserve.

'National Prosperity. And he said, Now, this schoolroom is a Nation. And in this nation, there are fifty millions of money. Isn't this a prosperous nation? Girl number twenty, isn't this a prosperous nation, and a'n't you in a thriving state?'

'What did you say?' asked Louisa.

'Miss Louisa, I said I didn't know. I thought I couldn't know whether it was a prosperous nation or not, and whether I was in a thriving state or not, unless I knew who had got the money, and whether any of it was mine. But that had nothing to do with it. It was not in the figures at all,' said Sissy, wiping her eyes.

'That was a great mistake of yours,' observed Louisa.

Ang:Blackpool/Newcastle/Oxford/Doncaster/Leeds/Coventry/Carlisle/egnill/Cambridge/Newark/Torquay/Wakefield/Maidstone/Darlington/Haltwhistle.

29th July.   Guess the Town or City.

1. A dark puddle. *Blackpool*
2. Not an old fortress. *Newcastle*
3. Horned ruminant over the river. *Oxford*
4. Learned man moves furniture easily. *Doncaster*
5. Keep dogs in control. *Leeds*
6. Malicious boy sent there. *Coventry*
7. Vehicle plus partner in food firm. *Carlisle*
8. Part of a ship. *Hull*
9. They "entered" - spans the way. *Cambridge*
10. Noah needed a fresh one. *Newark*
11. A hill in Devon - a jetty. *Torquay*
12. To end sleep, a meadow. *Wakefield*
13. Girl with a rock. *Maidstone*
14. Sweetheart with a heavy weight. *Darlington*
15. Stop and hoot. *Haltwhistle*

(Answers opposite.)

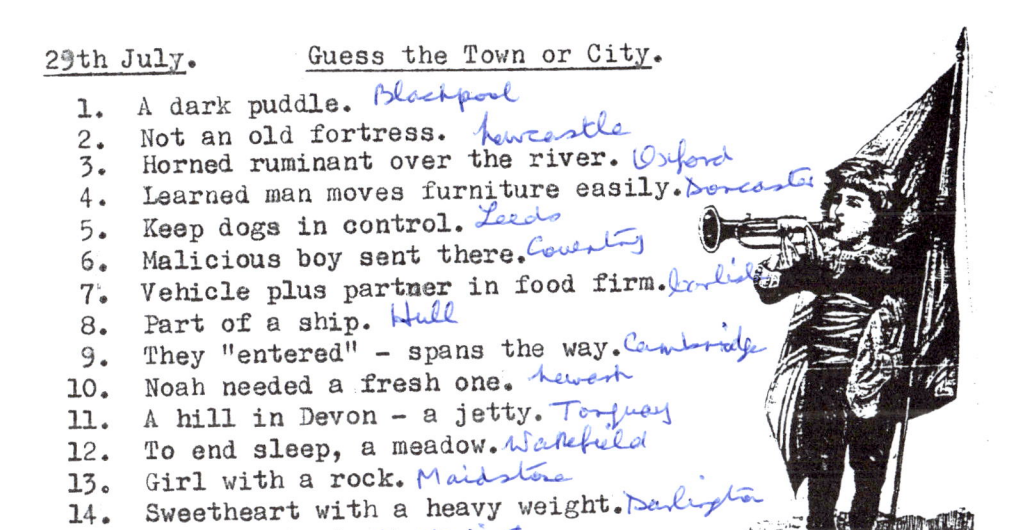

"Sir - The following is an extract from a recent CV we received with an application for a vacancy within the company: 'Personal Profile: I am innovative, artistic and very much gaol oriented.' Just as well the vacancy was not in our accounts department. - Bob Duncan, Maidenhead, Berks,"
(Daily Telegraph, 2002).

A South Lakeland curiosity: Interior of St Anthony's Church, Cartmel Fell (in hills some distance from Cartmel town); with three-decker pulpit & Burblethwaite Hall canopied box-pew.

__30th July.__   Publishers' Rejection-Letters.

One of George W. Target's novels tells with laughter and many tears of an embryo story-teller's rocky road to publication. I hope that his first episode doesn't follow his own experience too closely; the novelist hands his parcelled manuscript to the receptionist just before Christmas, whereupon they promptly mislay it as the office is prepared for the Christmas party. Some months later the author enquires after it. A desperate search locates it, and it is returned with a courteous letter testifying to its virtues but saying that after careful consideration it is feared that it is not quite attuned to their needs.

The New Statesman (18.1.1974) printed M.K. Cheeseman's prize-winning "rejection-note" to Charles Darwin for his "Origin of Species":

Dear Mr Darwin, We have been very interested to read your excellent manuscript. However, we fear that your book would not fit in with our list in its present form, being too liable to misunderstanding.

However, it is clear that your interesting experiences as a naturalist in the remoter corners of the globe would provide the basis of a book. We suggest a re-working of the material on the lines of Bishop Candlewick's popular *With Gun and Bible Up the Umbopopo* or *With Line and Prayer-Book, Across the Kakajari Desert.*

We are also looking for authors for our series 'Peeps at Nature for Wee Folk', and wonder whether you would be interested in contributing one on monkeys.

M. K. CHEESEMAN

DATE AS POSTMARK

Thank you for your esteemed communication of   ult/inst/prox

Regrettably, owing to unprecedented accumulation of documentation there will be a delay of ...... weeks/months/years pending a resumption of this correspondence.

Ultimately, however, you may rest assured that this will be dealt with without fear or favour, in due course and in strict rotation, D.V.

YOURS AS EVER

Your ref: Cross ref:

This acknowledgement-card covers all situations; I have on occasion inflicted it on close friends, but not yet on a hostile correspondent.

31st July. "SUMMER SUNS ARE GLOWING".

Bishop William Walsham How (1823-97) is best known now for his All-Saints-tide hymn "For all the saints", the popularity of which is further enhanced by Vaughan Williams' magnificently memorable tune "Sine Nomine" which Wilfrid Mellers in his book "Vaughan Williams and the Vision of Albion" (Pimlico 1991) claims has entered into the popular consciousness. Certainly the girls in the Fulham secondary comprehensive school where I taught in the late 1970s would sing all eight verses in assembly without lapsing into near-silence as was their wont; "hoping it might be so" (Hardy)! Less well known is How's song for high summer, which deserves its place in the hymnbooks and the repertoire, even though the minister needs to have a second choice in reserve against the possibility of bad weather!

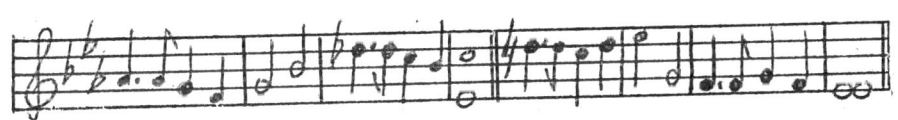

Tune: "Ruth".

1. Summer suns are glowing
   Over land and sea,
   Happy light is flowing
   Bountiful and free.
   Everything rejoices
   In the mellow rays,
   All earth's thousand voices
   Swell the psalm of praise.

2. God's free mercy streameth
   Over all the world,
   And his banner gleameth
   Everywhere unfurled.
   Broad and deep and glorious
   As the heaven above,
   Shines in might victorious
   His eternal love.

3. Lord, upon our blindness
   Thy pure radiance pour;
   For thy loving-kindness
   Make us love thee more,
   And when clouds are drifting
   Dark across our sky,
   Then, the veil uplifting,
   Father, be thou nigh.

4. We will never doubt thee,
   Though thou veil thy light;
   Life is dark without thee;
   Death with thee is bright.
   Light of light! shine o'er us
   On our pilgrim way,
   Go thou still before us
   To the endless day.

1st August. "Corny Lammas."

The only person I know of who has used the word "corny" in a literal sense rather than as slang is Tennyson. His short poem "Mine Host", which has seldom been printed, contains the line: "The creaming horn of corny ale"; and elsewhere he denotes 1 August as "corny Lammas", i.e. Loaf-mass, the medieval harvest festival when bread made from the "first-fruits" of he harvest-cornfields was used at Holy Communion. This custom faded after the agricultural age, but the festival was revived as an autumn thanksgiving by R.S. Hawker of Morwenstow, a Victorian vicar best known for his song "And shall Trelawney die?" Lammas, unlike the Dog Days (opposite), is to this day still listed in the "Book of Common Prayer" (BCP), but is little heeded, except perhaps in Scotland where, as befits the Celtic Fringe, it is a Quarter-Day when I suppose solicitors send out bills.

The old pagan customs, also nature-related, recognised the day as Lughnasadh in honour of Lud, the god after whom the fortress of Luguvalium, now Carlisle, was named by the Romans. It marks the death of the sun which alas begins to bow out by setting noticeably sooner in our northern latitudes. There may of course be fierce heat before the autumn sets in; if I had to choose, I'd opt for very cold weather as being that bit more bearable, even though we think little in high summer of the prospect of the next big

FREEZE

which we trust will be less bitter than before our climate eased. 1895 when a fair was held on the ice of Derwentwater is now out of living memory, though not 1947 when prolonged Arctic weather - two full months without a thaw - exacerbated the rigours of postwar austerity affecting Britain and much of Europe.

"Shiver with Shinwell and Starve with Strachey" was then an effective albeit somewhat unfair slogan of the Opposition in attacking the U.K. Government which included the named Ministers of Fuel and Power and of Food respectively! In his booklet "The Eppleton Seam" John Stephenson writes: "Bread Ration May Be Cut", "Beer Supplies to be Halved Immediately" - these were the newspaper headlines...no discotheques, no mass motoring, no drug problems....grimy steam trains, sooty towns". Shinwell touring the Commons switching lights off...

2nd August.   DOG DAYS.

The following notice appeared in Preston in the 19th century:

PUBLIC NOTICE.

I the undersigned Richard James Rawlinson, age 16, of 83 Friargate, Preston, acknowledge that I am guilty of having thrown a Dog with a stone attached to it into the Lancaster Canal, in the Borough of Preston, on Monday afternoon 31st July 1882.

Dog in a Manger from Bewick's Aesop's Fables

I am sorry that I committed such offence, and I promise that I will not, in future, do that or any other act to the prejudice of the said Navigation.

For the leniency shown to me in this matter by the Police and the Canal Company I express my thanks, and undertake to pay for printing fifty copies of this notice.

Date 1st August 1882.   RICHARD JAMES RAWLINSON.

Witness: CHRISTOPHER SUTTON. Police Constable 1.

— — — — — — —

(Notice copied by me at Todmorden Canalside Show, 25.9.94. F.McM I fear the dog may have been alive, and that it was very callous to make the young culprit promise to be kind to canals not dogs!

During heat-wave weather some people may think that the Dog Days are when "mad dogs and Englishmen go out in the mid-day sun - but they aren't that at all. They are when the brightest star excluding planets, Sirius the Dog Star, the hunter's dog by the constellation Orion, rises along with the sun and is eclipsed by its brightness. Sailing ships were liable to becalming in the tropics at that time of year, so its dates were listed in almanacs to remind seafarers to be prepared for that risk. Cranmer's prayer-book (1552 version) shows them as 7 July to 5 September (on the "old reckoning").

The chapel windows at Auckland Castle where the Bishops of Durham live illustrate the coming of Christianity to the North; there are Bible scenes too, and one window shows the only pet animal in Scripture, namely Tobias' dog from the Book of Tobit in the Apocrypha. Most dogs in the Bible are scavengers, and the word "cat" doesn't appear at all!

3rd August.   Shaggy Doggs and a Watery Bier.

I once lunched with Herbert Dingle, London University's professor of the History of Science, who in later life was a voluble critic of Special Relativity theory. I asked him if he attended his local Quaker Meeting; and he said he did when a car-lift was available, then added that the Purley Meeting had become small as members had departed. He then told of another meeting that dwindled to 4, 3, 2 through deaths, then down to just one blind man who came alone each Sunday to sit in silence for the hour. Then he died; but his guide-dog took itself in next Sunday and every Sunday for the hour (I presume it could push the swing-door, but it didn't occur to me to ask.) This was noticed by young people nearby, and some of them took to attending themselves, thus reviving the Meeting. Professor Dingle was serious-minded and not one to fabricate stories!

I found a parallel story in a book at the Royal Oak Hotel at Rosthwaite in the Borrowdale Valley south of Keswick in Cumbria. Sarah Youdell (1768 - 1869) lived there, and told of Joss Hardy who used to come over the 1100' pass from Watendlath each Sunday "blaw high or blaw low" with his dog. Joss died, yet the dog still came weekly to Borrowdale Church to sit by its master's grave. (Round about 1950 the yarn was popular that Joss's hamlet, popularised in Hugh Walpole's 'Herries' novels, gained its name from a lisping honeymooner's eulogy: Watendlath blith in a plaith like thith!)

Yet another churchgoing animal stars in Wordsworth's "White Doe of Rylstone", a Tudor saga of Bolton Priory in Wharfedale.

– – – – – – –

The Pre-Raphaelite redhead
    Liz Siddal
Liked to listen to lute and
    to fiddle
  Whilst she, richly gowned
  As "Ophelia, drowned",
In the bathtub lay up to
    her middle.

(True save for the musical second line!
With acknowledgement to a non-limerick rhyme by Christopher Morley.)

Millais was so intent on his Ophelia painting that he let the candles which heated the water that December night go out. Alas his stunningly-beautiful model Lizzie - if in Scarborough do see the pulpit-painting in St Martin's Church of her as Our Lady - caught a severe cold, and her father made Millais pay the doctor's bill. Liz, an artist herself and Rossetti's wife, died at

4th August.   The Day The World Changed For Ever - in 1914.

Nobody foresaw the stalemate of trench-warfare, the holocaust of the young men of Britain, France and Germany, and the long-term consequence of World War 2 which would follow the enthusiastic response to the call to arms which ended Europe's 99-year peace. Many have portayed the tragedy of disillusion as Byron and Hardy had done previously for the Napoleonic carnage. The "Rhymes of a Red-Cross Man" and Canadian balladeer Robert Service fall short of poetic fame, yet deserve mention as displaying the simple disenchantment of soldiers. Here's an infantryman in <u>The Red Retreat</u> from Mons which damped the hopes of the British Establishment and Expeditionary Force:

"Tramp, tramp, the bad road, the bits o' kiddies crying there,
The fell birds a-flyin' there, the 'ouses all aflame;
Tramp, tramp, the sad road, the pals I left a-lyin' there,
Red there, and dead there...Oh blimy, it's a shame!

"A-singin' 'Oo's Yer Lady Friend?' we started out from 'Arver,
A-singin till our froats was dry - we didn't care a hang;
The Frenchies 'ow they lined the way, and slung us their palaver,
And all we knowed to arnser was the one word 'vang',
They gave us booze and caporal, and cheered for us like crazy,
And all the pretty gels was out to kiss us as we passed;
And 'ow they all went dotty when we 'owled the Marcelaisey!
Oh, Gawd! Them was the 'appy days, the days too good to last...

"We wondered where the 'Uns was - we wasn't long a-wonderin',
For down a scruff of 'ill-side they rushes like a flood;
Then oh! 'twas music 'eavenly, our batteries a-thunderin',
And arms and legs went soarin' in the fountain of their blood...
But though we mowed 'em down like grass, like grass was they a-springin....
And 'ow we cussed and wondered when the word came: 'Retreat!'...,

"Tramp, tramp, the dread road, the Boches all a-comin' (&c. &c).

Even the tough old mercenary from Arctic Canada, with his "brag of bear and beaver" said "Enough of war" as does Pope John Paul II, (Baku)
"For I've had my fill of fighting, and I've seen a nation scattered, (2002)
And an army swung to slaughter, and a river red with gore,
And a city all a-smoulder, and...as if it really mattered,
For the lake is yonder dreaming, and my cabin's on the shore;
And the dogs are leaping madly, and the wife is singing gladly,
And I'll rest in Athabasca, and I'll leave it nevermore."

Amen; so be it! _ _ _ _ _ _ _ _ _ _

223

5th August.

The Selkirk Grace

The small county town of Selkirk in Scotland's border country is well worth visiting to see the courtroom of Sir Walter Scott's sheriffship (1799-1832), and his house at nearby Abbotsford which houses his vast library and large collection of old weaponry and memorabilia — Bonnie Prince Charlie's hair, the key of Mary Queen of Scots' island prison, a pouch sewn by Flora Macdonald, & so on.

Yielding to Byron as versifier (16.4) & balladeer:
"Come fill up my cup,
　come fill up my can,
Come saddle your horses,
　and call out your men,
Unlock the West Port,
　and let us gae free,
And it's up wi' the bonnets
　o' Bonnie Dundee":—
he turned to novels, wrote over 30 including such classics as Rob Roy & __The Heart of Midlothian__, and did his court-work conscientiously:

"The people of Selkirk must have justice as well as the people of England books", he noted on arrival home tired and famished after an $8\frac{1}{2}$-hour hearing.

COME TO SELKIRK

this December for

Scott's Selkirk

Saturday 2ⁿᵈ & Sunday 3ʳᵈ December 2006

"Heap on more wood! - the wind is chill
But let it whistle as it will,
We'll keep our Christmas merry still ...
While music, mirth and social cheer
Speed on their wings the passing year."

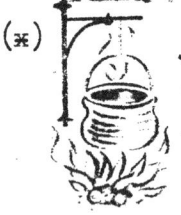

Marmion, Sir Walter Scott

(∗) *Some hae meat an' canna eat*
an' some wad eat that want it.
But we hae meat an' we can eat
an' sae the Lord be thankit.

Robert Burns

6th August.   Blue Bonnets Over The Border.   225

Most visitors to Scotland enter by a coastal route, East or West, but John Prebble the historian likes the Borders way down Teviotdale at dawn, knowing he can be in Kintail by dusk. This lovely approach takes the pilgrim-cum-tourist through lands now peaceful that once were a cockpit of Balkans-type battle and pillage for long centuries. A phone-call to the Selkirk tourist-office and town museum (01750.20054) secures a B&B base for exploring the district, where the surviving shells of once-fine abbeys, Dryburgh Jedburgh and Melrose, cry out against the overblown bigotry of the Scottish Reformation.

Selkirk itself is happier, with its Scott memorabilia. I saw the town library in the old jail, where the condemned cell enjoys benign use as a store for children's books & toys. Yet past sadness has its markers in the 1913 statue for the fallen in the Scots' defeat at Flodden - four centuries before, but still mourned in folk memory. The intriguing "POETS' CORNER" provided by the white front wall of a High Street shop quotes:

```
We'll hear nae more lilting, at the ewe-milking
Women and bairns are heartless and wae              woeful
Sighing and moaning on lika green loaning           farm-lane
The flowers of the forest are a' wede awae.         withered
                         (Jean Elliot).
```

Other poems of course are more cheerful. The balladeer allows himself the naughtiness of Janet in the cautionary tale of "The Young Tamlane":

```
Janet has kilted her green kirtle A little abune her knee,
And she has braided her yellow hair A little abune her bree.
```

There is an "accidental poem" too in the text by the display:

```
Sponsored by New Ways...Lindsay and Gilmour
Lothian Angus  &  Borders Co-op.
```

I am reminded of a footnote in a 1930s railway timetable for a branch line in another borderland, that of the Welsh marches:

```
Passengers joining at Wooferton must
Obtain their tickets at Tenbury Wells.
```

It is a pity that John Betjeman seems not to have hit on this; for the prophet did well to warn us not to despise the day of small things (Zechariah 4.10), as did St Augustine in saying it is better to kill wars with words than men with weapons. All in all the Blue Bonnets of Ettrick and Teviotdale, and Bonnie Dundee for that matter, are excelled by the Borders Co-op, and by Janet's kirtle to boot. "Soldiers of all lands, go home!"

7th August.   **Prelude to The Silent Symphony.**

Hector Berlioz the most famous of France's composers lived from 1803 to 1869, thus being spared the grief of seeing his beloved Paris fall to the Germans in 1870. He wrote four symphonies: the famous 'Fantastique'; 'Harold in Italy' with viola obbligato; 'Romeo and Juliette', a 'dramatic symphony, with choruses'; and the impressive Funeral and Truimphal Symphony, a large-scale work designed for open-air performance by a large military band, and one which deserves to be far better known, not least for its long processional movement which never loses its momentum and would provide exalted music for a venturesome small-town band.

Still less well-known is the 1852 story in Berlioz' memoirs about the symphony which he dreamt. Next morning he recalled "nearly the whole of the first movement"; but en route to his desk to write it down he suddenly realised that if he lost the income from some months' journalism in order to write and produce the work, he would be unable to provide for his poor invalid separated wife who as the young Shakespearean actress Harriet Smithson had inspired the "Fantastique". The dream recurred next night, and the allegro theme pleased him exceedingly when he woke; but he steeled himself against temptation. The 5th symphony was lost! Yet maybe its silence was more loving than the glories of many resplendent works.

My play-prologue starts however at 11.30am on 23rd September 1864 and is set in Lyons, in a simply-furnished room with plain table, chairs and dresser; piano; spinning-wheel; and two or three comfortable chairs by a fire of coal or wood. Oil-lamps and candles remain unlit; tapestries and curtains give warmth. To the strains of say the overture "Les Francs-Juges", played live by a band if possible, Mme ESTELLE FORNIER (67 or so) is seen arranging her table with wine, bread, cheese, salad, and fruit. She is a bespectacled widow of some 20 years. The clock strikes the half-hour and ticks on as the doorbell rings and a MAID enters with a letter and a card. Estelle leaves her fireside coffee-things, takes them from the maid, looks at the card, and nods. She rises as the maid admits M. HECTOR BERLIOZ, age 61 but old for his years, with his fine hair turned grey-white, "a little white bird with pince-nez", who walks with difficulty because of intestinal neuralgia. He smiles and bows in silence, she smiles back, they embrace shoulders, and she draws him by the arm towards the fire. They converse slowly and carefully, with pauses. (The drama is set out over a few days as follows:)

8th August.   A Scene from the "Memoirs".

Estelle: We are very old acquaintances, you and I, M. Berlioz...we were children together... (They sit gravely, silently.)

Hector: (quietly): The letter, madam, if you would be so kind as to read it, will explain my visit. I ought not to have given your maid my card, but just the letter, so that you could have read it in my absence and made up your mind if you wanted to meet me. (She opens and reads it.)

Estelle: "Madam, I come once again from Meylan, where I visited the house where you lived 49 years ago. I ask you to receive me, and I shan't get carried away. I promise. Do let me see you, again." (She puts the letter on the mantelpiece.) Was it a chance visit you made to Meylan?

Hector: No, no, I have wanted to revisit there for a long time.

Estelle: You have had an eventful life, M. Berlioz.

Hector: How do you know that, Madam?

Estelle: I have read your biography by Méry. I bought it a few years ago.

Hector: Oh no, if it's the one I think, don't call it Méry's. He's my friend and an intelligent artist, and I'm sure he didn't write all those absurdities. The publisher must have used a ghost. But I'm going to have a proper biography, one that I've written myself. I'll put in all I feel about you, without mentioning your name. (*)

Estelle: (more easily now they are reassured of one another's friendship): Yes I'm sure you write so well. My life has been more ordinary, though quite sad, for I lost several of my children, and my husband before I was 50, so I've done my best to look after the family by myself. I'm touched by your feelings, M. Berlioz, and grateful too! (Hector moves to take her hand which she offers to him to kiss.)

Hector: Madam, will you allow me to write sometimes and very occasionally to call?

Estelle: Oh yes indeed, but one of my sons is getting married and I shall live with him in Geneva. Would you like coffee? (She pours and they drink.) (∅)

                                                  (continued overleaf.

(*) Berlioz kept his word.
(∅) To this point the Berlioz Memoirs have been followed closely. In fact Berlioz left without taking coffee. Other ideas, from letters etc., will be worked into this sketch from this point on.

9th August. "A Smile as you Pass" - Prologue continued - 228
"The Last Symphony".
Hector: Many thanks, madam...
I wonder if you are free this evening, and, if so, would you like to come and hear Adelina Patti sing in The Barber of Seville at the Grand Theatre? I met her brother-in-law last night and he said Adelina would be so pleased if I could come. Mlle Patti is such a nice young woman! - once I had dinner with her family. She said I must try and be happy, and she kept paying me coaxing attentions; then the exquisite creature insisted on coming to the railway station with her brother-in-law and a female friend. And when the whistle blew she hugged and kissed me and made me promise to come again in a week. Oh I do like women, but a girl of 22 can't help me very much, however good and charming she is. I lived with one called Amélie last year, but we hurt one another, for she realy cared for me; and now she's dead. Oh the time comes when old friends are best. Do you happen to be free tonight, Estelle?

Estelle: I'm so sorry but I'm not, though I would have loved to hear Mlle Patti with you. I am expected in the country tomorrow, quite a long way from here, and I have to leave at twelve. But I agree with you about old friends. I know very little about art or music, but I did buy some settings of folksongs from Scotland that Beethoven once wrote, and there's one you might like to see, though I'm sure you know it already. (She goes and rummages in the stool by the piano.)

Hector: Actually I don't. I've heard about the songs, but very few people know they exist; he must have set them when he went to Britain, and, things being what they are between France and England, nobody sings them here.

Estelle: Yes indeed Sir; now look at this! (She shows him some sheet-music.) Can you play it?

Hector: No I never did learn the piano, my father wouldn't let me; he said pianists are ten-a-penny, and he was right. If you can play it I'll try and sing. Here, let me see the words. (She hands him the sheets.)

"Oh sweet were the hours when in mirth's frolic throng
I led up the revels with dance & with song!
When brisk from the fountain and bright as the day,
My spirits o'erflowed & ran sparkling away!
"Return ye sweet hours! Once again let me see
Your airly light forms of enchantment & glee;
Come give an old friend while he crowns his gay glass
A nod as you part & a smile as you pass."
(Estelle goes to the piano, tries out the melody;

...then she plays as he sings):
"I cannot forget you, I would not resign
There's health in my pulse & a spell in my wine;
And sunshine in Autumn, tho' passing too soon,
Is sweeter & dearer than sunshine in June;
"Wine, come wine, come bring me wine to cheer me,
Friend of my heart, come pledge me high!
Wine, till the dreams of youth again are near me,
Why must they leave me, tell me, why?"

(They laugh, she leads him to the table, and they pour wine. They drink as they take the food.)

10th August. "Simple...Romantic...Emotional."

(Hector continues): There, madam, I who have filled great halls and cathedrals with wave upon wave of sound, and the Place de la Bastille with the Funeral & Triumphal Symphony in the open air, can't sing decently in an old friend's drawing-room!
Estelle: And I play like an incompetent schoolgirl! - never mind, they'll still be playing your Fantastic Symphony 100, 200, 300 years hence, everywhere too, Paris, London, Moscow, New York!
Hector: Never! They'll all be forgotten when I'm around no more to promote them - even now they won't listen to Faust or Trojans
Estelle: Ah but they're so huge! I've only heard bits of them myself, because I'm not a serious musician. What people want is simpler and romantic and emotional; and that's where you win!
Hector: Well maybe, and it does cheer me to hear you say so. It would make my life worth while after all - but it can't happen - why, remember the growls when Beethoven wrote his gruff new music.
Estelle: He'll last too! - I've heard some of his nine symphonies - Why, you didn't even write five, Hector.
Hector: I nearly did, but it's a long story for another day. (They drink, and eat.) Madam! - I would like to try and gain all your affection even now, and surround you with deep and tender care.
Estelle: Alas I am an old woman, six years older than you, and my heart is heavy with past afflictions, and free from illusions about the delights of this world. I live in emotional seclusion with my family, and I dare not risk the peace of mind which this brings. I cannot dream of beginning the sort of relationship which needs to grow from close friendship in the happy (cont'd
-and A MUSICAL DISCOVERY!   overleaf.)

The church of St Roch, Paris, where Berlioz' "Messe Sollenelle" (not the Requiem) was first performed in 1825 after difficulties of performance, as detailed in his Memoirs, had been surmounted. The impressive "apprentice work" was performed again soon after; but the self critical composer then withdrew it and burned it except for the Resurrexit which he liked and revised. Both versions are well worth hearing.

Amazingly a copy of the work was located in 1991 in the music library of the church of St Charles Borromeus, Antwerp. In 1993 the Mass received a third performance (in Westminster Cathedral), and was recorded.

11th August.   "Carry on, my son, carry on!"

days of one's youth. It would be cut down too soon and would store up fresh sorrows, but I don't disparage your memories of me, for I treasure them; and I _will_ meet you, and write to you when I can overcome my lazy mind and my stiff fingers. I shall give you my portrait from my room, and I shall ask my son to meet you in Paris with his bride. (Exit.)

Hector: Ah, perhaps as time goes on, despite her dread of new friendships, little by little she may find her feelings growing warmer towards me. My sky is black no longer; she doesn't love me (why should she?) but she knows I adore her, and she is kind. Which power is the greater to lift the human heart: love or music? Well, love cannot give an idea of music, but music can of love. Yet why separate them? They are the two wings of the soul. Alas that some people have such ideas of love and music that they remind me of pigs snuffling for truffles under mighty oaks and among lovely flowers...O, Stella!

(Enter Estelle with the portrait which she gives him.)

Estelle: Were you speaking to me, Sir?

Hector: I wonder if you know what Shakespeare wrote in _Macbeth_?
  "Life's but a walking shadow, a poor player
  That struts and frets his hour upon the stage,
  And then is heard no more; it is a tale
  Told by an idiot, full of sound and fury,
  Signifying nothing."
That's how I often feel, and I shall put it in my Memoirs.

Estelle: I know the feeling; but what about your Requiem? How can you give up your hopes and high thoughts after writing _that_? It's so sure and devout that it _can't_ "signify nothing"!

Hector: (after a pause.) You have me there, Estelle! I don't know. But I've always said I'd choose _it_ if I could save one composition only from oblivion. My brain felt as if it would boil and explode with the pressure of ideas in the text. I was afraid of forgetting the musical ideas which flooded my mind, and I had to invent a sort of shorthand, especially for the _Lachrymosa_. Then Habeneck almost spoiled it by bad conducting – and then they tried to dodge paying me. You know I was brought up in the Roman Catholic church – a charming religion once it gave up burning people. If I'd been born a Lutheran or a Calvinist I'd've left that drabness for the poetic bosom of Rome as soon as I could. I was a saint! Mass every day for several years, Communion every Sunday. I went regularly to Confession in order to say: "Father, I have done _nothing wrong_!" and he had to answer: "Carry on, my son, carry on". But now I'm nearly 61, past hopes, illusions and lofty visions. I'm alone, I hate the horrible cruelty of the world, and every hour I ask Death to come. Why does he tarry?   (concluded at foot opposite

12th August. VILLAGE CRICKET WHIMSY, from John Hadfield's novel "Love on a Branch Line" (Pan, 1959, repr. 1974) that pleased P.G.Wodehouse but may now seem too innocently charming!

Beyond help

FROM the *Cumbrian Gazette*: "Central Clinic. Family planning, Youth Cancelling."
D.Telegraph 14.8.96

During the dreadful days of American slavery this girl of 20 had the misfortune to be 2nd prize in a raffle; 1st prize - a horse.

RAFFLE

DARK BAY HORSE, "STAR,"
MULATTO GIRL, "SARAH"
Will be Raffled for
CHANCES AT ONE DOLLAR EACH.

JOSEPH JENNINGS.

... he flung the ball towards me, straight, very fast, and at perfect length.

I timed it to a nicety, hit it plumb in the middle of the bat, and drove it, a shade too high perhaps, over the bowler's head.

'Come on!' I called to Jones.

We took a fast single, but as I reached the farther crease I saw, with a pang of dismay, that the ball was falling from the sky straight into the hands of the Flaxfield captain. He stood quite still on the edge of the boundary, just in front of the pavilion, waiting to take the catch.

I turned to take a second run, in desperate hopes that he might possibly err in his judgment. At that moment, into the dead hush with which everyone present, players and spectators, awaited the descent of the ball, there broke a weird, unearthly cackling sound – something between the staccato rattle of a bren-gun and a chorus of witches on a blasted heath.

From amongst the cars parked beside the pavilion there rose into the air a huge winged shape, trailing a long, iridescent tail.

The fielder made every effort to disregard this wholly unforeseen intrusion; but the peacock passed, with ponderous wing-beats, just above his outstretched hands as the ball dropped into them, bounced out, and fell gently amongst the spectators beyond the boundary line.

Hats, sticks, eye-shades, handkerchiefs, ginger-beer bottles, and ice-cream cornets were flung into the air as the inhabitants of Arcady hailed a boundary hit for six, a grand total of 105 runs, and victory over their ancient opponents in the centenary match.

Above the babel I could just hear the *diminuendo* of the eldritch flight-cry as the peacock winged his way over the oak trees by the edge of the park towards the battlemented turrets of the Hall.

11.8 Estelle: Perhaps there's a job or two that only you can
(concl.) do - a young musician to establish, a country that has not heard Beethoven's music - or yours - and the autobiography which you must write. Don't give way to gloom; believe in your own work, the day may come when the world will need it! (Silence - she pours wine and they drink.) Now be happy - go and enjoy the opera and get some flowers for your young friend. You matter to young musicians, they adore you for your work - I'll write and tell you my address in Geneva when I know it, and you must come every summer. And in the meantime we'll write.

Hector: (taking his coat.) An angel will reward you Madam for the good you have done me! (They go out through the door, and his voice is being lost as he says:)...After all these years - why, I still remember when I first met you as a boy of twelve...

(Curtain.)

<u>13th August.</u>   <u>Hiroshima and Nagasaki - Never Again!</u>

Some will defend the use of atom-bombs against those Japanese cities in 1945 by claiming that they shortened World War Two. The question arises, however: Since the U.S. and allies agreed to a conditional surrender in August 1945 sparing the Japanese Emperor, why was a similar offer refused in July 1945?

"The taproot of violence is our readiness to use nuclear weapons. Once we are agreed to that, all other evils are minor by comparison. Until we squarely face the question of our consent to nuclear weapons, any hope of large-scale improvement of public morality is doomed to failure." - Richard McSorley S.J.

"Failure to face the problem of war in its modern manifestations of diabolical horror may well be seen by some future historian of our times as one of the principal causes of the collapse of organised Christianity. I believe this is so."
 - Glyn Simon, Bishop of Llandaff, 1966 (later Abp. of Wales).
(see also Canon Prof. Charles E. Raven, F.O.R. 1952 - 1963)

"Mankind's ultimate blasphemy against the Creator would be to blow the world up." - Peter K. Walker, Bishop of Ely, 1983.
           (writing in his Diocesan Magazine.)
"We didn't need to hit them with that awful thing!" - Dwight D. Eisenhower, U.S. President, 1959.

(Advertisement, Pictorial Weekly, 22.6.1929)

SINGER HAND-TREADLE OR ELECTRIC **SEWING MACHINES**

Cash Prices from £5 5 0

Easiest of easy terms can be arranged where desired. Learn the fascination of Singer Sewing by having FREE LESSONS at the Local Singer Shop or in your own home—there is no obligation to buy.
SINGER SEWING MACHINE CO. LTD.
Shops in every Town

To Singer Sewing Machine Co. Ltd., 42/43 St. Paul's Churchyard, London, E.C.4. Please send me FREE and without obligation, a copy of the new book "SEWING SIMPLIFIED" by Ada Partington, the needlework Authority.
(Mention Dept. O.)
Name.................
Address..............
Cut out this Coupon! Send in unsealed envelope ½d. stamp

FROM FIRST STITCH TO FINISHING TOUCH - ON A SINGER

232

14th August.   A Thousand Years of Folly.

The Limerick verse-form has a long history of fascination. My "earliest example" comes from an 11th-century manuscript:

>   The lion is wondrous strong
>   And full of the wiles of wo;
>   And whether he pleye
>   Or take his preye
>   He cannot do but slo.   slay

Recent versions rhyme more effectively, with exceptions:

>   There was an old man of St Bees
>   Who was stung on his nose by a wasp.
>   When asked "Did it hurt?"
>   He replied "It did not –
>   I'm glad that it wasn't a hornet!" –   (Trad.)

and near failures:

>   There was a young man of Calcutta
>   Who spoke with a terrible stutter,
>   Saying: "Pass the h...ham
>   And the j...j...j...jam
>   And the b...b...b...b...b...b...butter." (Anon.)

Literary pièces abound; from Hardy's "Madding Crowd" we have

>   With devotion as strong as his name,
>   Shepherd Oak kept his life's love aflame.
>   Dashing Troy bowled her over;
>   Boldwood killed him; Oak grew bolder,
>   And his mistress his Mrs became. – (D.A. Nicholls)

& from over the pond; from James Joyce's "Portrait of the Artist as a Young Man" we learn that

>   When Ireland was bloody and leaderless,
>   The tedious, garrulous Daedalus,
>   Having failed both as priest
>   And as Glorious Beast,
>   Sailed away to write books that are readerless. –
>   (Gina Berkeley).

also:

>   There once were two cats of Kilkenny,
>   Each thought that was one cat too many,
>   So they quarrelled and fit,
>   They scratched and they bit,
>   Till, barring their nails
>   And the tips of their tails,
>   Instead of two cats, there weren't any.   (Anon.)

233

15th August.   Demon Lover and Dowie Dens.   234

   Beautiful Scotland has a history of much horror, not least in
the Border Country as excellently surveyed by Nigel Tranter in
his "Portrait" volume (Hale, 1972). At the level of personal
romance there was the Douglas Tragedy at Blackhouse Tower in
Ettrick Forest, whence Margaret Douglas eloped with her neighbour Lord William. Pursued by Margaret's father and seven tall
brothers, William took on and slew them all, presumably in chivalrous single combat. But he was wounded, and died soon after
riding back to the tower. This tale is told in one of many similar Border Ballads; another, "The Dowie — (sorrowful) — Dens O'
Yarrow" depicts a nine-to-one fight which leaves "ten slain men/
On the dowie banks o' Yarrow. Whereupon "She kissed his cheek,
she kaimed his hair, / She searched his wounds all thorough. /
She kissed them, till her lips grew red, / On the dowie houms o'
                                                         Yarrow."
   The young Scottish composer Hamish McCunn (1868-1916) wrote
three concert-overtures or tone-poems when he was a student at
the new Royal Academy of Music in London. Alas he was insufficiently appreciated by Grove its founder whose dictionary deals
unenthusiastically with him, and by teachers including Parry who
was unable to be hospitable because of domestic factors. I fear
that his confident brilliance fell foul of the Victorian English
school, and I wish he had spent time with the Northern masters
Grieg and Sibelius. At 18 he completed his best-known work "The
Land of the Mountain and the Flood", popularised in the 1980s TV
series "Sutherland's Law"; it depicts the beauty of his homeland untouched by shadows of industrialism or its grim history.
The title is taken from Scott's "Lay of the Last Minstrel" as
quoted on 16 April, which he set as a dramatic cantata in 1888.
"The Dowie Dens O' Yarrow" was the third, perhaps a shade least
gripping, of the overtures, also written that year.

Between the two tone-poems he at 19 wrote the astonishing "Ship o' the Fiend", based on the old "Demon Lover" ballad of the suitor who returns after a 7-year desertion to find his betrothed had married another. He woos her on to his ship, where she finds to her horror that he is cloven-footed and has no crew. Then "He struck the topmast wi' his hand, / The foremast with his knee;/ He split the gallant ship in twain/ And sank her in the sea."

Waverley paddles 'up the watter' to Glasgow. McCunn, a shipper's son, uses steamer-sound in "Ship"!   (McCunn CD: Hyperion A66815)

16th August. LARKS ASCENDING

Examination-howlers by school pupils include the following:
* A virginal is a piano that has never been played on.
* Wagner wrote "Tristan and Essoldo".
* Vaughan Williams was fond of folk music in queer keys.

Ralph Vaughan Williams reported that he had received many congratulatory letters on the first performances of his 7th (Antarctic) symphony in Manchester in January 1953, but also a critical one from a 9-year old boy who said how much he had enjoyed the Haydn symphony which preceded it, and how little he had liked the Antartica! To this the composer responded with a gem of a letter: "Dear Tommy, Thank you for your letter. Haydn was a very great composer and he wrote some wonderful tunes. One day I must try and write a tune that you will like. Yours.."

Sir Thomas Beecham's wit was legendary albeit cruel at times. When his second wife Betty Humby had given a less-than-superb performance of the Delius piano-concerto under his baton, he was asked during the interval if the piano should be taken off the platform for the second half of the concert. "Just leave the bl--dy thing alone", he replied, "it'll slink off by itself."

Beecham stories abound. He said he didn't approve of women in orchestras: "If they're unattractive they distract the other musicians; if they're attractive they distract me". He managed to crush Hitler when, after a concert during a late-1930s tour of Germany, the Fuhrer said to him "I'd've come to your Coronation but for the inconvenience it would have caused." To this Beecham replied "There'd have been no inconvenience."

Sir Thomas however was bested in his turn, by a receptionist at Manchester's Midland Hotel of all people. Reaching the city to conduct a concert, he asked for his favourite suite there, only to be told that another guest had taken it. He said he was Sir Thomas Beecham and would they please move the guest elsewhere - only to be told "Even if you were Sir Hamilton Harty we would not do that". (Harty was the then conductor of the Hallé Orchestra.)

During World War 2 the RAF Central Band under Wing Commander O'Donnell sought to expand its repertoire for the daily concerts in the National Gallery, London. When a violinist was engaged for the Beethoven concerto, the conductor's inadequate knowledge of the score came to light; for when he gave the opening beat in expectation that the wood-wind would enter with the melody he was surprised by the drummer's five quiet taps which Beethoven had prescribed. "I don't need you to give me the tempo", he said!

<u>17th August.</u>   "The Darkies' Sunday-School".   236

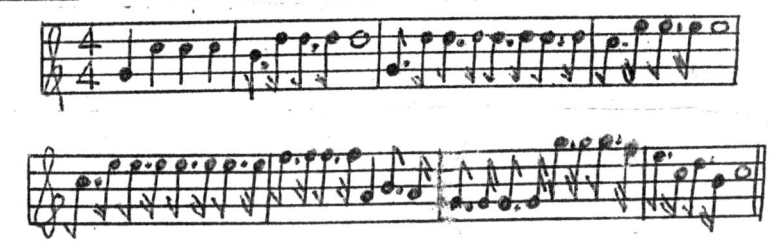

Here are some verses from one version of a once-popular song that was frowned on by the ultra-pietistic, yet which served the cause of the Bible by enhancing folks' awareness!

<u>Chorus</u>:   Young folk, old folk, everybody come,
       Join the Darkies' Sunday-School and make yourself at home.
       Bring your toffee-apples and sit down upon the floor
       And you'll hear some Bible stories that you've never heard before.

- - - -

Now Adam was the first man and he lived all alone
Till Eve was manufactured out of Adam's funny-bone.
They settled outside Eden and they lived with might and main
And built a little bungalow and started raising Cain.

- - - -

Now Cain he was a wicked lad, so big and strong and rude;
He hit his brother with a stick as any brother would.
Abel didn't like it and he asked him to refrain,
But Cain he wasn't able and so Abel got the cane.

- - - -

Now Pharaoh had a daughter with a most bewitching smile;
She found the infant Moses in some rushes by the Nile.
She took him home to Pharaoh, said "I found him by the shore",
But Pharaoh only laughed and said "I've heard that one before."

- - - -

Now Samson was a strong man with a head of pretty curls,
He did a bit of weightlifting and flirting with the girls;
But then Delilah changed him from a man into a mouse -
Till his last Command Performance came and brought down the house.

- - - -

Now Issy was a prophet and a visionary man,
Who, when he heard the seraphim and saw their six-winged span,
Said "Looking forward through the smoke I tell you what remains:
I see Southampton station; it's a temple filled with trains."

- - - -

<u>18th August.</u>   The Golden Age of Chemistry.

Before returning in two days' time to the vastnesses of physical science mentioned on 22 July, I recall the "homelier" side of the systematic study of the materials of nature, which afforded me my career-vocation as a chemistry lecturer and teacher at the chalkface for $33\frac{1}{2}$ years. For centuries the alchemists had sought to produce an "elixir of life" conveying eternal youth, and a "philosopher's stone" the touch of which would turn base metals into gold. Some thought that they had manufactured gold by the prolonged heating of tin with sulphur; but the substance had looks which deceived, and was known as "mosaic gold".

English experiments in the late 18th century replaced speculations by well-founded theories. At the Warrington Academy Joseph Priestley subjected the calx, formed on mercury when heated, to stronger heating, and found that it emitted a gas, now called oxygen, in which inflammable materials would burn more fiercely than in air. Chemical Elements were defined as materials which cannot be split into simpler ones; and another northerner John Dalton advanced his Atomic Theory to the effect that matter is built of submicroscopic indivisible particles called Atoms (Gr. a-tomos, unsplittable), all atoms of a given element being alike in all respects. Everything in the previous sentence has now been modified by detailed studies which ushered in nuclear physics; yet Dalton's broad depictions sufficed for his day & age.

Careful studies in the early 19th century yielded the "Laws of Chemical Combination by Weight", e.g. a given chemical compound always contains the same elements combined together in the same fixed proportions by weight. This led to the evaluation of "atomic weights" - now masses - specifying the number of times an atom of an element is as heavy as an atom of hydrogen (the lightest element); and to the allocation of "valencies" - combining powers of elements. (e.g. 1 for hydrogen, 2 for oxygen, 4 for carbon; so that the molecules or smallest particles of the compound carbon dioxide are O= =C= =O or CO_2, and of water are H- -O- -H or H_2O). Fixed "formulae" yield fixed proportions by weight; thus since oxygen's A.W.= 16, water with molecular weight 1 + 1 for the two H-atoms plus 16 = 18 and is $\underline{16}$ or 88.%
oxygen by weight.   18

An early crucial development was the recognition by the German chemist Döbereiner that "families" of elements with similar properties exist, in which the middle member's A.W. is the average of those of the other two. For example the very reactive non-metals chlorine, bromine and iodine have A.W.s 35.5, 80 and 127 respectively, and the mean of 35.5 & 127 is 81.25 - near 80.
                    (continued at foot overleaf.

19th August. **UNSPEAKABLY UNEATABLE!**

On 18 February 2002 the Church Times published my letter thus:

From Cllr Frank McManus

Sir, — I question Toddy Hoare's claim (Letters, 11 February) that "Hunting is . . . a satisfactory method of controlling numbers" of foxes.

The number of foxes in a given rural habitat is limited by the availability of food. The killing of an adult fox enables a cub to reach maturity.

The hunt therefore does not reduce the number of foxes in the specified area, but merely their average age. As a method of fox-control, it is futile.

FRANK McMANUS

It passed unchallenged, as did similar letters elsewhere; and I make bold to say I find the argument decisive for the banning of hunting with dogs! It leaves the pursuit of pleasure as the only opposing argument, and there comes a time when this must give way to the avoidance of cruelty to animals. For that reason we deny the freedom to promote bear-baiting or cock-fighting; and we long for Spain to abolish the bull-fight.

I reject the argument that a ban will cause unemployment. All it needs to avoid this is the encouragement of the drag-hunt, with prizes for the first riders home. Nobody in their senses wants to deny countryfolk the colourful excitement of the chase. It may be tempting to allow a compromise, but I feel that the sooner the issue is settled once and for all, the sooner the required cultural change to the drag-hunt will occur & satisfy.

18.8 Newlands followed this observation by noting that just
(concl.) as similar musical notes occur in octaves, so elements with similar chemical properties occur in octaves, e.g. lithium, sodium & potassium; carbon & silicon; oxygen & sulphur. Then Dmitri Mendeleev, 14th child of a Tobolsk schoolmaster, in Russia, linked with the chemists of western Europe and built a "Periodic Table of the Elements". This included the newly-discovered "inert gas" family so that the octaves became nonaves, and used various subterfuges to deal with anomalies. Yet the periodicity-law held, and led to a search for missing elements during the later 19th century, in what were exciting days for chemists. After the two lightweight elements H and He (helium) the table ran: Li Be B C N O F Ne
                                Na Mg Al Si P S Cl A....
One of the later gaps was filled when strontium was extracted from the carbonate mineral strontianite near Strontian, Argyll - the only element named for a place in Great Britain. Then in the 20th century the table was interpreted via subatomic-particle arrangement, & the "nuclear age" was upon us!

20th August.   **Big Fleas Have Little Fleas**
                   upon thir backs to bite 'em; and
little fleas have lesser fleas, and so ad infinitum. And the
big fleas themselves have greater ones to go on; and these in
turn have greater still...then greater still, and so on.

Linking this old nonsense with Chardin's stress on complexity (22 July), let us recognise, in the words of the late Dr Joseph Needham, that "Different levels of organisation occur one within the other. The ultimate particles build atoms, atoms build molecules, molecules build up the parts which are organised into living cells. Above that level the cells form tissues and organs, these combine into the living body, and the bodies form social communities." Chardin draws this curve and notes its shape:

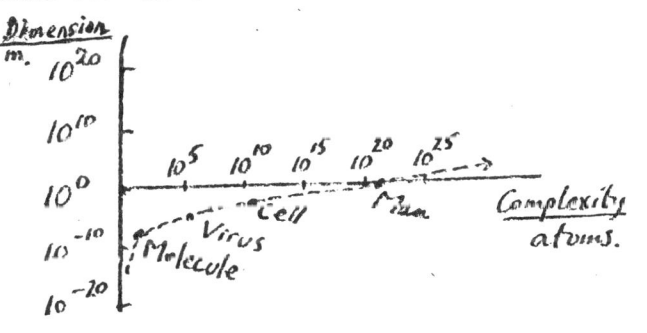

Higher beings such as humans are not situated between extremes, but are atop the branch of complexity. We form an extreme, "by the same right as a galaxy or an electron". And this extreme has its special properties too, namely consciousness and freedom. There is no such thing as absolutely dead matter, but the properties of life are imperceptible until they become more and more important as successive thresholds of complexity are crossed. Thus Chardin claimed that:

"Just as in the infinitely small, great numbers explain the determinism of physical laws; and just as in immensity, the curvature of space explains the forces of gravity; so, in the third infinite, complexity (and the 'centredness' resulting from it) gives rise to our freedom. Thus everything in the universe around us surely becomes clearer". Yet "number of atoms" doesn't ensure but merely permits complexity. Our brains excel the elephant's in organisation; and the vast stars aren't complex - they "repeat this line symmetrically on the side of the very great". They are nuclear reactors for producing atoms, and must become relatively small and cold for complexity to appear. Life is a "good middle zone" event, and our commonsense understanding is saved! Life arises wherever possible, in defiance of the destructive trend of thermodynamics towards randomness. We are at the forefront of the immensities. and Tennyson rightly finished his 22 July poem:

"Spirit, nearing yon dark portal at the limit of thy human state,
Fear not thou the hidden purpose of that Power which alone is great,
Nor the myriad world, His shadow, nor the silent Opener of the Gate."

21st August. "When Brahms Marches Onward."

[musical notation]

This "big tune" from Brahms' 1st Symphony, in the opinion of his majestic biographer Jan Swafford (Borzoi 1997, Macmillan 1998, 0 333 59662 5, £30), whose assessments strike me as being word-perfect, was "written to conquer the world" at the end of the long, "darkness-into-light" epic work. Used by a Party in the UK general election of 1987, albeit without such success, it has been supplied with bathetic words by one or two devotees; e.g. "When Brahms marches onward each loyal heart keeps time". One encounters worse in many pop-songs!

The work begins bleakly over a continuing drum-beat; and a "chilly wind" is noted by Swafford (S, at p.476) in the Alto Rhapsody too, and in the Songs of Destiny and of Fate (<u>Parzenlied</u>) which negates the Handelian <u>Triumphlied</u>. On Brahms' remaining three symphonies, all gloriously orchestrated, S comments (p.484): "The second had been a sigh of pleasure and relief, completed perhaps a touch too fast and too easily. Apparently also done in a summer, the third shows Brahms at the height of his mastery, confidence and concentration." (I, having heard all four many times, agree; indeed I regard No. 3 as one of the world's finest symphonies.)

Yet even the joyful 2nd is shadowed by the "gloomy lugubrious tones" (S, p.441) of the trombones in its first movement. Criticised on this by his older admirer Lachmer, Brahms wrote: "I can't get along without...I am...a severely melancholic person...black wings are constantly flapping above us..." So especially with the "dark well" (Hanslick) of the 4th symphony which "gives tragedy the last word" (S, p.526). A broadcaster recently hinted that bright stars lurked in the dark well. For myself I'm content to let its unusual finale speak for itself as a self-expression like that of Sibelius in <u>his</u> "fourth". Swafford calls the Brahms No.4 "his funeral song for his heritage, for world at peace...for the sweet Vienna he knew"; and certainly the master feared for music after his death, first viewing Richard Strauss as its undertaker then Mahler! ("Ours is a century of death, and Mahler is its spiritual prophet."- Leonard Bernstein - S, p.629). But Brahms followed his last symphony with the Double Concerto, 1888, for violin, viola and orchestra; and there is the German Requiem to assess too.

- - - - - - - -

22nd August.   FLAPPING WINGS & JACOB'S LADDERS.   241

The great German Requiem of Johannes Brahms is not a setting of the traditional Latin liturgy. It uses a selection of texts close to those of the Anglican Book of Common Prayer, though of course it is in the reformed Lutheran tradition of the composer's homeland. Yet the devout Antonin Dvorak said that "Brahms believed in nothing"! (1), and the conductor Furtwängler said that Brahms held "that there can be no development without man, beyond man..." (2). The Deutches Requiem however is so impressive that matters can't be left at that. Swafford's biography, p.27, asks "Why were there doors in Brahms that he never opened for anyone?" Some light may be shed by an exchange between Brahms and Reinthaler, who conducted the first rehearsals of the work.

"The second movement", wrote Reinthaler, "touches on the prophecy of the Lord's return, and in the penultimate movement the mystery of the resurrection of the dead...But what is lacking, at least for a Christian consciousness, is the pivotal point: the salvation in the death of our Lord...Now it would be easy to find, near 'O death, where is thy sting?', a suitable place." Brahms responded politely yet firmly that he would omit even German for Human and dispense with "places like John 3.16...I can't delete or dispute anything. But I had better stop before I say too much." (3)

At the first performance composer and conductor compromised by following the work by Handel's "I know that my Redeemer liveth", sung by Amelie Joachim. I am not alone in wondering whether the seventh section of the work adds anything after the triumphant sixth, though the response that it adds symmetry may suffice. In his analysis of the fugal exposition of Revelation 4.11 which concludes part 6, Donald Tovey notes the two "Jacob's-ladder sequences of 27 rising steps. (4)

Was Dvorak right in assessing the reserved Brahms as faithless? Not if Brahms' words in Autumn 1896, shortly before dying in 1897, to the American musical writer Arthur Abell are authentic: "All true inspiration comes from God. There is no great composer who has ever been an atheist, and there never will be." (See also 23 August.)

(1) Clapham, Musical Quarterly 57/2, 1971.
(2) Macdonald, "Brahms" (Schrimer 1990, p.417)
(3) Gal, "Johannes Brahms" (Greenwood 1977, pp177/8) & the above cited by Swafford, loc. cit. 21.3.
(4) Essays in Musical Analysis, V.p223, 1937.

23 August.   "God and the Composers".

It may seem odd that Abell's account of his interview with Brahms, secured through the master's violinist friend Joachim, has not settled the matter of the composer's faith. The explanation may well be that Abell's book "Talks with Great Composers", in which it appears, was embargoed till half a century after the interviewee's death, and then published by the Psychic Book Club, 48 Old Bailey, London EC4, apparently in 1955. This may have been an eccentric route which failed to reach concerned musicians in general; yet the 1972 book "Sibelius", by that composer's live-in secretary of his later years Santeri Levas, published by Dent, draws upon it in respect of Brahms and several other composers.

Sibelius himself claimed that "Music is on a higher plane than anything else in this world". "It is brought to life by means of the Logos, the divine in art."

(Sketches of Brahms conducting are by W. von Beckerath.)

Beethoven famously declared that "There is nothing higher than to approach nearer to the Godhead than other men, and from here to diffuse the rays of the Godhead among mankind." And Puccini claimed regarding Madam Butterfly: "God dictated this music to me." Thus there is a formidable consensus for the great days of music.

- - - - - - - -

It may be possible, if desired, to check that Abell met Brahms in Vienna because he reports having secured through the American Embassy in Vienna a bilingual stenographer to record what was said. Certainly the visit of Joachim, who also was present at the meeting, to Tennyson at Aldworth in Surrey is credible, for the biography[1] of the poet by his grandson Charles, who lived there as a small boy in the 1880s, mentions their growing friendship.   (1 - see 24 August for details.)

Towards the end of the discussion Brahms sat at the piano and improvised a companion-piece to his Cradle Song, then said to Joachim: "Joseph, it is a great comfort to me to learn that so profound a scientific thinker as Tennyson was convinced that we shall have in that future life, about which Jesus so often talked, real material bodies which will enable us to be distinct, separate, individual personalities." It appears that Brahms had kept doors within him closed because of his defensive reticence, yet did open them to Abell and Joachim. The Requiem texts said what he wanted to say, in widely acceptable words.

24th August.   The Poet's Grandson expounds "Locksley Hall 2".

Tennyson's "Locksley Hall Sixty Years After" is long, and its first part which follows is to be read before its concluding couplets (see "Darksome Bough", 22/23 June). In it the old hero returns for the funeral of the one who bested him in love for Amy (cf Tennyson's for Rosa Baring ("Maud")). I urge every effort to read Sir Charles Tennyson's assessment in "Six Tennyson Essays" (pp.102ff, SR Publishers 1972) and in the biography "Alfred Tennyson" (p491+, Macmillan 1949/68). CT's insights penetrate!

In particular the starred verse "Truth for truth..." holds that we 'should pursue truth and virtue for their own sakes and not in the hope of future reward, but...unless the human spirit is to survive, such a pursuit becomes meaningless, because the result of it is annihilated.' A fine point, very well put!

Late, my grandson! half the morning have I paced these sandy tracts,
Watch'd again the hollow ridges roaring into cataracts,

Wander'd back to living boyhood while I heard the curlews call,
I myself so close on death, and death itself in Locksley Hall.

So—your happy suit was blasted—she the faultless, the divine,
And you liken—boyish babble—this boy-love of yours with mine.

I myself have often babbled doubtless of a foolish past;
Babble, babble; our old England may go down in babble at last.

'Curse him!' curse your fellow-victim? call him dotard in your rage?
Eyes that lured a doting boyhood well might fool a dotard's age.

Jilted for a wealthier! wealthier? yet perhaps she was not wise;
I remember how you kiss'd the miniature with those sweet eyes.

In the hall there hangs a painting—Amy's arms about my neck—
Happy children in a sunbeam sitting on the ribs of wreck.

In my life there was a picture, she that clasp'd my neck had flown;
Yours has been a slighter ailment, will you sicken for her sake?
You, not you! your modern amourist is of easier, earthlier make.

Amy loved me, Amy fail'd me, Amy was a timid child
But your Judith—but your worldling—she had never driven me wild.

She that holds the diamond necklace dearer than the golden ring,
She that finds a winter sunset fairer than a morn of Spring.

She that in her heart is brooding on his briefer lease of life,
While she vows 'till death shall part us,' she the would-be-widow wife.

She the worldling born of worldlings—father, mother—be content,
Ev'n the homely farm can teach us there is something in descent.

Yonder in that chapel, slowly sinking now into the ground,
Lies the warrior, my forefather, with his feet upon the hound.

Cross'd! for once he sail'd the sea to crush the Moslem in his pride;
Dead the warrior, dead his glory, dead the cause in which he died.

There again I stood to-day, and where of old we knelt in prayer,
Gazing for one pensive moment on that founder of our blood.

Yet how often I and Amy in the mouldering aisle have stood,
Close beneath the casement crimson with the shield of Locksley—there,

All in white Italian marble, looking still as if she smiled,
Lies my Amy dead in child-birth, dead the mother, dead the child.

Dead—and sixty years ago, and dead her aged husband now—
I this old white-headed dreamer stoopt and kiss'd her marble brow.

Gone the fires of youth, the follies, furies, curses, passionate tears,
Gone like fires and floods and earthquakes of the planets dawning years.

Fires that shook me once, but now to silent ashes fall'n away,
Cold upon the dead volcano sleeps the gleam of dying day.

Gone the tyrant of my youth, and mute below the chancel stones,
All his virtues—I forgive them—black in white above his bones.

Gone the comrades of my bivouac, some in fight against the foe,
Some thro' age and slow diseases, gone as all on earth will go.

Gone with whom for forty years my life in golden sequence ran,
She with all the charm of woman, she with all the breadth of man.

Strong in will and rich in wisdom, Edith, yet so lowly-sweet,
Woman to her inmost heart, and woman to her tender feet.

Very woman of very woman, nurse of ailing body and mind,
She that link'd again the broken chain that bound me to my kind.

Here to-day was Amy with me, while I wander'd down the coast,
Near us Edith's holy shadow, smiling at the slighter ghost.

Gone our sailor son thy father, Leonard early lost at sea;
Thou alone, my boy, of Amy's kin and mine art left to me.

(continued)

25th August. _Cruelties and Terrors._ The poet continues:

Gone thy tender-natured mother, wearying to be left alone,
Pining for the stronger heart that once had beat beside her own.

Truth, for Truth is Truth, he worship, being true as he was brave;
Good, for Good is Good, he follow'd, yet he look'd beyond the grave,

Wiser there than you, that crowning barren Death as lord of all,
Deem this over-tragic drama's closing curtain is the pall?

Beautiful was death in him, who saw the death, but kept the deck,
Saving women and their babes, and sinking with the sinking wreck,

Gone for ever! Ever? no—for since our dying race began,
Ever, ever, and for ever was the leading light of man.

Those that in barbarian burials kill'd the slave, and slew the wife
Felt within themselves the sacred passion of the second life.

Indian warriors dream of ampler hunting grounds beyond the night;
Ev'n the black Australian dying hopes he shall return, a white.

Truth for truth, and good for good! The Good, the True, the Pure, the just—
Take the charm 'For ever' from them, and they crumble into dust.

Gone the cry of 'Forward, Forward,' lost within a growing gloom;
Lost, or only heard in silence from the silence of a tomb.

Half the marvels of my morning, triumphs over time and space,
Staled by frequence, shrunk by usage into commonest commonplace!

'Forward' rang the voices then, and of the many mine was one.
Let us hush this cry of 'Forward' till ten thousand years have gone.

Far among the vanish'd races, old Assyrian kings would flay
Captives whom they caught in battle—iron-hearted victors they.

Ages after, while in Asia, he that led the wild Moguls,
Timur built his ghastly tower of eighty thousand human skulls,

Then, and here in Edward's time, an age of noblest English names,
Christian conquerors took and flung the conquer'd Christian into flames.

Love your enemy, bless your haters, said the Greatest of the great;
Christian love among the Churches look'd the twin of heathen hate.

From the golden alms of Blessing man had coin'd himself a curse:
Rome of Cæsar, Rome of Peter, which was crueller? which was worse?

France had shown a light to all men, preach'd a Gospel, all men's good;
Celtic Demos rose a Demon, shriek'd and slaked the light with blood.

Hope was ever on her mountain, watching till the day begun—
Crown'd with sunlight—over darkness—from the still unrisen sun.

Have we grown at last beyond the passions of the primal clan?
'Kill your enemy, for you hate him,' still, 'your enemy' was a man.

Have we sunk below them? peasants maim'd the helpless horse, and drive
Innocent cattle under thatch, and burn the kindlier brutes alive.

Brutes, the brutes are not your wrongers—burnt at midnight, found at morn,
Twisted hard in mortal agony with their offspring, born-unborn,

Clinging to the silent mother! Are we devils? are we men?
Sweet St. Francis of Assisi, would that he were here again,

He that in his Catholic wholeness used to call the very flowers
Sisters, brothers—and the beasts—whose pains are hardly less than ours!

Chaos, Cosmos! Cosmos, Chaos! who can tell how all will end?
Read the wide world's annals, you, and take their wisdom for your friend.

Hope the best, but hold the Present fatal daughter of the Past,
Shape your heart to front the hour, but dream not that the hour will last.

Ay, if dynamite and revolver leave you courage to be wise:
When was age so cramm'd with menace? madness? written, spoken lies?

Envy wears the mask of Love, and, laughing sober fact to scorn,
Cries to Weakest as to Strongest, 'Ye are equals, equal-born.'

Equal-born? O yes, if yonder hill be level with the flat.
Charm us, Orator, till the Lion look no larger than the Cat,

Till the Cat thro' that mirage of overheated language loom
Larger than the Lion,—Demos end in working its own doom.

Russia bursts our Indian barrier, shall we fight her? shall we yield?
Pause! before you sound the trumpet, hear the voices from the field.

Those three hundred millions under one Imperial sceptre now,
Shall we loose them? take the suffrage of the plow.

Nay, but these would feel and follow Truth if only you and you,
Rivals of realm-ruining party, when you speak were wholly true.

Plowmen, Shepherds, have I found, and more than once, and still could
Sons of God, and kings of men in utter nobleness of mind,   find

Truthful, trustful, looking upward to the practised hustings-liar;
So the Higher wields the Lower, while the Lower is the Higher.

Here and there a cotter's babe is royal-born by right divine;
Here and there my lord is lower than his oxen or his swine.

Chaos, Cosmos, Cosmos, Chaos! once again the sickening game;
Freedom, free to slay herself, and dying while they shout her name.

(concluded 22/23 June.)

26th August.   (*) LOOK BEFORE YOU LEAP.

The early 1970s were vintage years for small advertisements in the "Personal" columns of "New Statesman" magazine! It is almost certainly too late for responses to these items:

"London Newcomer, MP's PA, seeks: fairly recent 'Who's Who?'; used ladies' (sic!) bicycle; cheap viola da gamba; many new friends. 352 0261 early or late." (31.8.1973)

"A blonde in her 40s, alone Seeks a well-meaning man all her own. He must have a flair, And be very aware; Then as soon as he likes he can phone. Box 944." (3.7.1973)

"Any Papua Niuginians in London please contact Elaine 01 385 8940." (5.9.1975)

"Formation of Society for the Abolition of Money. All interested write Box 422." (6.7.1973)

"Is there a London girl kind enough to type next year's best seller for published but penniless young author? Sorry, no pay. David. Box 1170." (24.8.73)

"Gentle lady, 34, has worked for two Royal families. Dark, attractive, lovely figure, 5ft 2½". Artistic. Alto voice. Seeks marriage companion, interests to include music, art, archaeology, ornithology; 6ft 4ins tall. Public school. Oxford, Cambridge, Harvard, Yale, Princeton. 25 to 40. Box 467." (4.7.75)

"Anecdotes...resulting from jury service...Box 1169." (17.8.73)

"How were you punished as a schoolgirl? Reminiscences and anecdotes with dates please. Box 1849." (17.10.1975)

"Male flautist, amateur, normal, London, seeks girl with piano for Baroque evenings. Box 2216." (21.11.1975)

"At Easter CND is undertaking a sponsored march from Aldermaston to London to demonstrate against Britain's expensive and dangerous nuclear force. To prepare CND needs now a good quality second hand office typewriter. All offers, information etc. to CND, 14 Grays Inn Rd., WC1 or ring Steve at 01-242 3872. (25.1.1974)

"Blue Stocking sea nymph wanted for weekend sail crewing. Box 5471." (24.5.1974)

(*) "Sappho magazine for homosexual women 30p incl. postage. c/o BCM/Petrel, London WC1V 6XX." (27.7.1973)

27th August. Delusions and Magnetic Mockeries.

Professor Richard Dawkins of New College Oxford drew a fair amount of attention in 2006 by his broadcasts on atheism and his book "The God Delusion", which contains some good sense and is worth a peep. His main concern is to oppose the Bible-Literalist "Creationism" of the "Religious Right, arguing that the variety of species on earth stems from evolution which is self-directive rather than led by Intelligent Design. I wonder how he would view the question posed by Henry Thoreau, an early-19th-century US author:

"With all your science can you tell me how it is, and whence it is, that light comes into the soul?"

In 1651 Gerard Winstanley the Leveller published an address to "his Excellency Oliver Cromwell" entitled "The Law of Freedom". In it he wrote: "And if you would know spiritual things, it is to know how the spirit or power of wisdom and life, causing both motion and growth, dwells within and governs both the several bodies of the earth below, as grass, plants, fishes, beasts, birds and man.

This concurs with W. Chalmers Smith's well-known hymn "Immortal, invisible..." which declares that God lives in all life as "the true life of all". On this basis any evolution is neither a fortuitous rattling-about of atoms nor just a mechano-electrical process of physical science, but involves creative direction overall. To deny purpose in matters of life is the Science Delusion that would reduce us to meritless automata. Canto CXX of Tennyson's "In Memoriam" includes the lines:

"I trust I have not wasted breath:/ I think we are not wholly brain, Magnetic mockeries..."

Please refer also to 13.6 (Vaughan Williams & Evolution, and the theological items on 4.2 and 15.9.

"Not till the loom is silent And the shuttles cease to fly
Shall God unroll the pattern And explain the reason why
The dark threads are as needful In the weaver's skilful hand
As the threads of gold and silver In the pattern He has planned."

(Patience Strong.)

28th August. Eminent Victorians.

John Henry Newman (1801-90) took part in the Oxford movement for reviving English Christianity. He is now best remembered for his devotional poetry. Elgar set his "Dream of Gerontius" as an oratorio; and "Lead Kindly Light" is second only to "Guide Me O Thou Great Redeemer" as a popular song for times of trouble:

> So long thy power hath blessed me, sure it still
>   Will lead me on,
> O'er moor and fen, o'er crag and torrent, till
>   The night is gone;
> And with the morn those angel faces smile,
> Which I have loved long since, and lost awhile.

All Lakeland fell-walkers will appreciate this third and final verse! A moor can be bleak and windswept; a fen is where one can become bogfast - avoid Floutern Pass between Crummock Water and Ennerdale! On a crag one hangs on by the fingertips for dear life; and the whole thing comes down on your ears in a torrent. Newman hid the secret of his ending.

Famous also is the 5-verse hymn extracted from "Gerontius"; but the lines "Holy Church as (Christ's) creation, / And her teachings as his own" needs varying to end "And his teachings as her own", since he warned against leaving our first love - (Revelation ch. 2 v. 5). Shiela Cassidy's book on hospice-care contains Jim Cotter's fine variant on Newman's "Firmly I believe and truly", and I have adapted this for general use:

1. Barely I believe yet truly
God is One and God is Three,
God is Love and seen mostly
Hanging from the wintry Tree;

2. And I trust Creator Spirit
In and through our common life,
Weaving threads all torn and broken,
Shaping justice out of strife.

3. So we cherish, with long patience
In the love of God alone,
Words and Folk of inspiration,
Jesus' teachings as our own.

4. And we own the Law of Loving,
Dying to possessive greed,
Ris'n with Christ, through joy and travail,
In His Realm for ever freed.

Augustus Donaldson can hardly be claimed as an Eminent Victorian; his name appears only, so far as can be ascertained, below Hymn 744 in the Old Standard "Hymns Ancient & Modern" (Clowes, 1916) - see 30th August. Yet his aspirational processional-hymn, based on the messages to the Church in the final book of the Bible (Rev. chs. 2 & 3) testify to the pre-war sincerity alongside the callous hypocrisy!

29th August.   **THIRD WOMEN.**

No! – this description lacks the pejorative overtones of "Other Women". The ladies in question are fieldsgirls in the cricketing position of Third Man. Fanatics for inclusive language might prefer Third Person(s), just as a 1982 letter to The Times wrote of Batpersons, eliciting a response that the term suggested a mixed XI, which was not the case. Just as Chair seems preferred to Chairperson, so Bat may displace Batperson. Did not Wilfred Rhodes from the glory-days of Yorkshire cricket say of Ranjitsinghji "'E were good bat"?

From the same paper's Letters page come quaintnesses, e.g.

* "Sir, I am the organist at a local crematorium, and at a recent ceremony I was asked to play Bach's 'Sheep may safely graze', which I dutifully did. I discovered later that the lamented deceased had been a New Zealand lamb-importer!
  Yours faithfully, George E. Hill." (8.5.82)

* "Last October I had my hair done in a glamorama in the state of North Carolina. Yours faithfully, Joyce Grenfell." (16.1.1971)

And from the "New Statesman":

* "Mr John McGlennon, prosecuting, asked 'Why did you hide? It is not illegal to have sexual relations in the Howard Bedding Company.' Bevan replied 'It is embarrassing when you are caught by an alsatian.'" D.Tel. (T. Philpot) – in This England 14.11.1975.

* "An advertisement they will discontinue is the one on a blank background saying 'I thought the Kama Sutra was an Indian restaurant until I discovered Smirnoff'. Mr Ambler explained: 'We made a survey and found 60% of people did think it was an Indian restaurant'." Evg. Standard (Mrs J. LeFrere) – in This America 14.11.1975.

* "Seven 'streakers' brought traffic to a standstill yesterday as they dashed in the nude across Kingston Bridge, Surrey. Police arrested a woman, aged 21, whose occupation was given as display artist." Kingston Times (G.J. Paterson) – in This England 22.3.1974.

* "The Mayor, Cllr Arthur Alcock, said it was unfortunate that the Queen's Silver Jubilee coincided with the bicentenary celebrations in January of Richmond Bridge." Richmond & Twickenham Times (E.M. O'Dea) – in This England 24.9.1976.

30th August. For a Street-procession such as a Whit Walk in the high industrial era, long hymns were used which said a lot more than some modern worship-songs! This versificat- of New Testament scripture may appeal as a very good example:

"*He that hath an ear, let him hear what the Spirit saith unto the churches.*"

Unison.

f   GLORY to the First-begotten,
    Risen CHRIST, Incarnate WORD!
Glory to the Faithful Witness,
  Over all dominion LORD,
Who hath loved us, Who hath wash'd us
  In His precious Blood outpour'd!

Harmony.

*Glory unto Him Who gave us
  Heritage of priest and king!
That for ever in His presence
  We our Eucharist may sing,
All our crowns cast down before Him,
  To His shrine our incense bring.

Harmony.

*Glory to the LORD ALMIGHTY!
  Every foe beneath Him cast,
High He reigns in splendour seated,
  He the First and He the Last.
He both Alpha and Omega,
  LORD of future, present, past.

Unison.

Glory unto Him Who holdeth
  Mystic stars in His right hand!
Glory unto Him Who walketh
  'Midst the lamps that gleaming stand!
Every Church and every pastor
  Subject to His dread command.

Harmony.

mf Thou Who knowest how we labour'd,
  Fainting not when foemen strove,
Raise once more our fallen courage,
  Stir again our early love:
Quench not all the light within us,
  Nor our candlestick remove.

Unison.

*From all subtle evil guard us,
  False apostles, deeds of ill;
Grant us every lie to conquer,
  Every hateful lust to kill:
By the Tree of Life sustain us,
  And our hungry spirits fill.

Harmony.

If, wherever Satan dwelleth,
  We confess Thee as our LORD,
Bid us fear not Satan's malice,
  Tribulation, fire, or sword.
Crown Thy faithful patient servants
  With the Martyr's bright reward.

Harmony.

p By Thy HOLY SPIRIT cleanse us,
  Pure in heart Thy law to own;
Grant to us the hidden manna,
  Grant to us the fair white stone,
And the new name newly written,
  Only to Thy servants known.

Unison.

f Thou hast once for our salvation
  On the raging Dragon trod,
Keep us steadfast, faithful, loving,
  Smite our foes with iron rod,
Scatter all the depths of Satan,
  Bright and Morning Star of GOD.

Harmony.

mf Save us from the name of living
  While the soul within is dead;
Wash our garments from defilement
  In the Blood that Thou hast shed;
cr Then confess us in Thy glory,
  Members worthy of their Head.

Unison.

f Thou Who hast the key of David,
  Set for us an open door,
Refuge in the Great Temptation
  When the testing tempests roar;
Plant us in Thy FATHER'S temple,
  Pillars firm for evermore.

Harmony.

p We are wretched, cold, and naked,
  Needing all things, poor and blind;
Thou hast raiment, riches, healing,
  Meet for body, soul, and mind.
Humbled, shamefast, we approach Thee,
  All our store in Thee to find.

PART 2.

Harmony.

mf Come, in love rebuke and chasten,
  At our hearts' door come and stand;
Knock once more, and bid us open,
  Knock with Thine own pierced hand.
We will hear Thee, we will open,
  Sup with Thee at Thy command.

Unison.

Grant to us that overcoming
  By a virtue not our own,
We may with Thee in Thy glory
  Be Thy crowned brothers shown,
Even as Thou, overcoming,
  Sittest on Thy FATHER'S throne.

Unison.

ff Glory unto Him that reigneth
  On th' eternal throne on high!
Glory to the LAMB that suffer'd,
  Living now no more to die!
Glory to the Blessed SPIRIT,
  One with Both eternally!

Processional.

AUG. G. DONALDSON.

* *These verses may be omitted.*

31st August. Cornish Cliffhanger. 250

From Father Bryan Storey

Sir, When a holiday promotions' company telephoned offering me a free holiday I was questioned about my status. Having established that I am not married I was then asked if I had a partner. When I replied that that is against God's Law, a shocked voice terminated the conversation.

Have I said something I ought not to say?

Yours truly,
BRYAN STOREY,
Tintagel Catholic Church,
Bossiney Road,
Tintagel, Cornwall PL34 0AQ.
July 15.

"TIMES" 16.7.2002

Tintagel Castle is a romantic medieval stately home and was much loved by Tennyson for its Arthurian feel which alas stems from touristic speculations. Yet the local people take holidays, as this press letter implies. I wrote in response thus:

"Pace Bryan Storey, it surely is not always against God's will to have a partner! These exist in many contexts; there can be partners in bridge, business, crime, dancing, golf, sex, tennis and so forth. I recall enjoying the company of a score of female partners one evening; does the Tintagel Catholic Church frown on the progressive barn-dance, I wonder?"

Alas the good parish-priest risks being hoist by his own petard (in a venial matter, I hasten to add); for it seems to be against God's will to accept the title "Father" (Matt.23.9). S.J.Forrest wrote:

"I cannot call you 'Father', because I'm C. of E.,
With such un-English customs I strongly disagree,
I can't forget a precept that I was taught at birth:
'Call nobody your father', the Bible says, 'on earth'."

(Parson replies) "'And be ye not called masters' the text announces too,
So do not call me 'Mister', which also is taboo.
Such narrow exegesis will one day drive you mad;
If 'Father' is forbidden, what do you call your Dad?"

"I cannot call you 'Father', it strongly smacks of Rome;
But I have found a title which brings us nearer home.
I think I'll call you 'Padre', as normally is done
Throughout our British forces, approved by everyone."

"But still you call me 'Father', which 'Padre' signifies;
Your quaint circumlocution deserves a special prize.
For 'Padre' is Italian, and papal, through and through,
So why use foreign language, when English words will do?"

"I cannot call you 'Father' in spite of what you say;
No argument will move me although you talk all day,
Yet I have found a label with which I can concur,
And, with your kind permission, I'm going to call you 'Sir'."

"Of course you're only leaping from frying-pan to fire;
Your 'Sir' is also 'Father', for 'Sir' is simply 'Sire';
So how you will address me I'm sure I do not know —
But as my name is Joseph you'd better call me Joe."

(A Baptist minister friend of mine got called "Pop" by the members of his church youth club; a variant of "Pope"!)

1st September. The Case of the Leaping Lizard?
(from the Guardian – Spring 2002)

Igwig the hurled iguana has his day in court

Martin Wainwright

Britain's first known case of common assault by iguana-throwing went to court yesterday, with the alleged offensive weapon himself watching beadily from a tank beside the dock.

The reptile, known as Igwig, and almost a metre long, curled up below magistrates at Newport, Isle of Wight, as his owner Susan Wallace, locally nicknamed the Lizard Lady, denied the attack and two charges of animal cruelty.

She admitted smashing a window, although not with Igwig. The court heard she upset customers at the Anchor pub in Cowes by putting the iguana on their heads and then hurled him at a doorman. With Igwig round her neck, she then went to the town's police station where officers thought she was wearing "a very brightly coloured scarf", until she took it off and threw it at them as well.

As Igwig dozed next to a water bottle and a selection of edible leaves, the court heard that Wallace, 47 and a former

air steward, launched her first attack when she became "extremely drunk" and Anchor doorman John Rosenthal showed her the door. Igwig flew through the air at him twice while Wallace hacked at his shins, he said, adding: "I was startled but I don't lose my calm easily."

Wallace then weaved off to the police station to register a protest with PC David Harry, who told the court that after his scarf mistake he ended up with Igwig clinging to his back. He used his radio to call a colleague, PC Richard Van Arendonk, who told the court he arrived to find "a rather unusual situation."

"PC Harry looked up and said, 'I'm glad you've arrived. Would you mind getting this off my back,'" he said. "I walked up to him and saw a lizard in a vertical position by his ear.

"Then Wallace ran past, shouting obscenities at me and screaming, 'My Iggy, my Iggy.' She tried to cuddle the iguana but ended up falling over and nearly squashing it." Wallace said at she would never throw Igwig and claimed

that he must have jumped. She told the magistrates: "He's my friend. He probably jumped in defence of me — he's done that before. When we went to the pub, I asked for extra vegetables for Igwig. I've had him for 3½ years and he sleeps in a rolled-up towel on my bed."

The bench, which heard that Igwig turned brown with unhappiness after his evening out, either because of the throwing or because he missed his owner after being confiscated, found Wallace guilty.

But the chairwoman Sally Crocker, told her: "We don't consider that in normal circumstances your care of Igwig is in any way wrong. It was taking him into licensed premises which was inappropriate behaviour."

Wallace will be sentenced in April, but meanwhile, o her delight, the iguana was returned to her care.

She told Mrs Crocker: "Oh thank you, thank you, thank you," before hoisting him out of his tank and on to her shoulders as she left the court.

(The court sentenced the defendant to 6 months' community-counselling.)

Copyright Guardian Newspapers Limited 2002.

251

2nd September. WILL THEY MARRY? IS IT SPECIAL OR WORTHWHILE?

Clearly it isn't an "open sesame" password to living "happily ever after". Conflicts arise which are overcome, if at all, by a lot of hard work and give-and-take. We are well rid of the "doll's house" diminution of wives; yet the loss of sexual restraint and discipline from public concern has led to poorer male behaviour in general.

Does not the weakening of the institution of marriage damage many men by the removal of the social constraints that urge them to be loyal to their wives and families? Dads — yes and mums — who hive off are liable to harm their children by so doing. Endemic family-breakdown robs children not only of settled parenting, but also of stable "extended families" with aunts and uncles and cousins to give longstop security against the risks of parental accident, illness, job-loss, and yes such marital upsets as may occur. Today's "free fall" is baleful!

Too many children run wild in home, street and school; and too much weight of child-care is falling on grandparents who'll be in short supply in a decade unless social and media attitudes harden against permissiveness among "celebrities" and others.

The contrast with the past is marked! Iona Abbey library has the Argyll kirk-sessions minute-book for mid-17th-century. One parish was rebuked for slack discipline, and was ordered to buy a new record-book and to be properly vigilant, e.g. re a named local worthy "anent fornication"! E.S. Turner's "History of Courting" (Michael Joseph, 1954) reports that Scots parishes in general were less laid-back, and shaved, ducked and expelled culprits in the hope of having fewer children "on the rates"! Todmorden south of the border rebuked man and woman at morning prayer on separate Sundays; but stern Gloucester made it 50 lashes, which alas is on the slippery slope to the outrageously excessive punishments (stonings etc.) where Sharia-law prevails.

"Hate the sin and love the sinner" entails a constructive admonition "We'll do our best for you and yours, but yours is the responsibility for child-care OR Else.."; certainly not the evil regime of some "magdalen-convents". The poet Burns accepted public scolding to regain his local standing, then made light of it it, on one occasion administering a mock rebuke to a pal of his in an empty church. In 20th-century England the distinguished theologian Professor F.F. Bruce was nicknamed by his colleagues "Flee Fornication" (1 Cor. 6.18) for his initials and dourness.

- - - - -

3rd September.   "In Meadow and Wood".

John Julius Norwich (Lord Norwich) has for many years sent his friends Christmas Crackers of collected literary items instead of cards, and to 2002 three bound volumes have been published. In 1995 he recalled the late Canon J.M.C. Crum of Canterbury, whose remarkable hymns included this gently startling celebration of birds and beasts and flowers:

O once in a while we obey with a smile
   And are ever so modest and prudent;
But it's not very long before something is wrong,
   And somebody's done what he shouldn't.

In meadow and wood the cattle are good,
   And the rabbits are thinking no evil,
The anemones white are refined and polite,
   And all the primroses are civil.

O Saviour, look down when we sulk or we frown,
   And smooth into kindness our quarrels;
Till our heart is as light as a little bird's flight
   And our life is as free as a squirrel's.

LESSER ARIZONA COTTONTAIL

This led to many letters to the anthologist. From Michael Gill:

> Growing up as a boy in Canterbury in the 1930s, it was impossible not to know Canon Crum. Quite apart from the violet and purple magnificence of Cosmo Lang – more like a Renaissance cardinal than an Anglican archbishop – the authority of the living cathedral was made manifest to the town by two opposing figures: the tall-striding, tightly gaitered and imperiously profiled Red Dean, Hewlett Johnson; and the fluttering, wavering, indecisive progress of the saintly canon, sicklied o'er with the pale cast of thought and incapable of the half dozen steps needed to cross the busy Mercery Lane.

and from an earlier Dean's daughter Peggy Richardson:

> He was wonderfully unworldly, very wise, very charming, and above everything else he was a scholar. His sermons were a delight, erudite and poetical. He said to us once 'I sit here in my study and read and read and read, and no one is any the wiser.'

      —   —   —   —   —   —

A Right Royal Problem for Elizabeth II.

In mid-February 2002 there was a power-fault at the Governor-General's residence in Kingston, Jamaica from just before the State Dinner until during the sweet. "It's so difficult, getting dressed in the dark", the Queen said as she stepped into the half-light of headlamps, torch and paraffin lamp. "I was just putting on my tiara when the lights went out."

4th September.   NECTAR WHERE THE BEE SUCKS.   254

Tastes in commonplace-books vary, but overlap is inevitable, and is good when not so overdone as to amount to copycat poaching. I would like to draw further on John Julius Norwich's "Still More Christmas Crackers - 1990-9" (Viking, 2000) for a few more little delights. He cites Tony Quinton's frolic of a letter from one Heather Clavering-Thorpe to the St Hilda's (Oxford) Annual Report, regaling her fellow alumnae with new of her career as a minor harem-wife of the sultan who had swept her off her feet. Lord Norwich also includes some intriguing verses, e.g.

"It was Hester up in Chester, it was Jenny down in Kent;
Up and down the motorways, the same where'er he went.
In Luton it was Sally, quite the nicest of the bunch,
But down on his expenses they were petrol, oil and lunch." (Anon.)

& "A lady from the Bosphorus with eyes as black as phosphorus
Once wed the wealthy bailiff of the Caliph of Kelat;
Though diligent and zealous, he soon fell a prey to jealousy -
Considering her beauty, 'twas his duty to do that." (also anon.)

Then there is Rossini's note to a pupil: "I wrote the overture to La Gazza Ladra (*) on the day of the first performance in the theatre itself, where I was imprisoned by the director and watched over by four stage-hands, who had instructions to throw my manuscript out of the window page by page to the copyists who were waiting to transcribe it below. In the absence of pages, they were to throw me." (* - The Thievish Magpie.)

From another source, the 1956 competition in the New Statesman, comes the Poem Against Children, after Masefield, by Stanley J. Sharpless. (I am varying the underlined letter.)

"Crocodile from Grey Towers, Ancient Seat of Learning,
Trailing down the avenue, pair by snooty pair,
With a cargo of snobbery, hauteur, prejudice,
Exaggerated accents and upper-class stare.

"Arnold-haunted small fry from the local Grammar,
Standing in a huddle, waiting for the bus,
With a cargo of sniggers, spectacles, horseplay,
Brashness and angst, stemming from Eleven-plus.

"Hordes of little dastards from the Secondary Modern,
Gadarining home to the Children's Hour and News,
With a cargo of comics, candy floss, ice cream,
Hollywood values and low I.Q.s."

(Teenagers and takeaways had yet to be invented!)

        - - - - - - -

5th September. "NO SADNESS OF FAREWELL".

A single rogue-letter may devastate, turning the police force into a farce, our Parish Council into a Pariah Council (which I fear it became through erosion of powers in 1974), and a Lonely Hearts plea for a lady with experience of other cultures into one for a girl who has encountered other vultures. Other Press howlers include:

> THE HUNGRY NEED BREAD
> NOT BOMBS
> From a Quaker poster
> For a free pack of QUACKERS their beliefs and their social concerns please fill in the form below. Obs:

&: Roman Catholic Archdiocese of New York has joined a group of Orthodox rabbits in condemning the "Life of Brian," a movie that they say is bigoted, blasphemous and a crime. *Caracas Daily Journal*

Archbishop Michael Ramsey on his "secret vice": "You should enjoy it surreptitiously, the way a secret drinker enjoys his gin."

Toastmaster: "Speak into the microphone, the agnostics here are terrible". (related by Archbishop Donald Coggan).

Tam O'Shanter, in Burns' comic epic, flies drunkenly to Brig o' Doon from the Kirk Alloway sabbath of witches that can't cross running water. (Painting in the "Cutty Sark" at Greenwich.)

Proverbs: Overlong sacrifices make stony hearts. (trad.)

Where there are no horses, donkeys must be used. (Pope John 23)

"Money's a good egg, and if you have money to leave behind you, lay it in a warm nest." - (George Eliot, Middlemarch, ch.12).

"Government and Co-operation are in all things and eternally the laws of life. Anarchy and Competition, eternally, and in all things, the laws of death." also: "There is no wealth but life." (Ruskin).

The profit of the earth is for all. (Ecclesiastes 5.9)

The land shall not be sold for ever. (Leviticus 25.23)

Rejoinder: from Bryan Storey to whom I copied my 31.8 entry: "It would mean that we mustn't call our fathers father or teachers, teacher. Surely it's the ego that has to be tackled." Well put, and in a nutshell too!

Summary of contents.

July:
6 - Across the Pond.
7 - Dives & Lazarus.
8 - A Taste of Honey.
9 - The Steady Drummer.
10 - England's Farewell.
11 - Poetic Trinity.
12 - To the Banner Born.
13 - Hope Betrayed.
14 - Glass of Lemonade.
15 - The Deluge.
16 - Downing Street poverty.
17 - Troughs!
18 - Poet's Blended Mind.
19 - Down Mammary Lane.
20 - The Other Blair.
21 - Dilettantalism.
22 - Vastness, Long & Short.
23 - Quirks of Language.
24 - Lakeland's sweet summit.
25 - Golden Goals for Life.
26 - 1960s Ageism.
27 - Girl number Twenty.
28 - The Beloved Enemy.
29 - Guess the Town or City.
30 - Rejection-Letters.
31 - Summer Suns are Glowing.

August:
1 - Corny Lammas.
2 - Dog Days.
3 - Watery Bier.
4 - August 1914.
5 - The Selkirk Grace.
6 - Blue Bonnets, &c.
7 - Silent Symphony.
8 - Scene from Berlioz' Memoirs, also each day to
12 - Village Whimsy.
13 - Never Again!
14 - 1000 years of Limericks.
15 - Hamish McCunn.
16 - Larks Ascending.
17 - Darkies' Sunday-School.
18 - Chemistry's Golden Age.
19 - Unspeakably Uneatable.
20 - Chardin on Complexity.
21 - When Brahms Marches On.
22 - Flapping Wings &c.
23 - God & the Composers.
24) - The Poet's Grandson ex-
25) - pounds 2nd Locksley poem.
26 - Look Before You Leap.
27 - Delusions & Mockeries.
28 - Eminent Victorians.
29 - Third Women.
30 - Procession for Whitsun.
31 - Cornish Cliffhanger.

September:
1 - Leaping Lizard.
2 - Is Marriage Worthwhile?
3 - In Meadow and Wood.
4 - Where the Bee Sucks.
5 - No Sadness of Farewell.

Thievish Magpie from Landbirds by Thomas Bewick (see 4th September).

"Ah, did you once see Shelley plain..?"
(Browning, Memorabilia. - Pl. see 19.10)

256

ENGLAND ARISE,
THE LONG, LONG NIGHT IS OVER

Suffragists on Nelson station, 1911.

England Arise, the long, long night is over,
Faint in the east behold the dawn appears
Out of your evil dream of toil and sorrow
Arise, O England, for the day is here.

Edward Carpenter

A Book of Autumn Days
[6th September to 6th November]
"The March and the Muster" Part 5
Frank McManus

"Arise! ye starvlings from your slumbers." - (Sectional foreword).
258

I recall from 1941 that when Russia was attacked by Nazi Germany and was welcomed as an ally by Churchill, the BBC refused to include in its weekly broadcast of national anthems the Soviet one quoted above, and substituted another ditty. I hold no brief for Leninism yet agreed with many that the ban was fatuous, for the struggles of slaves, serfs and "proles" cut across the world's boundaries of space and time. Here in Britain our landless industrial masses were pinned down for over a century to subsistence-wages (24.2, 22-23.10) before trade union activity and people-power in politics achieved a perhaps-precarious correction of the social framework. The "urban deprivation" consequent upon 1980s unemployment is a serious matter, but its poverty is more a matter of de-skilling than of bitter lack of nearly all property and money. For today's Starvlings of Pottier's 1880 "International" song, we need but look mainly at the undeveloped southern world, where a child dies every 3 or 4 seconds of hunger or curable illness.

Debt-cancellation is great, but in itself is not enough. "The overall arrangements of a world dominated by the 'Christian' West must change, or the poor will die in "the gutters..for all time!" (Ron Ferguson, former leader Iona Community.)

Summoning miners' wives to a mass meeting in Boldon 1879

So: Let's be TOUGH ON DEBT, TOUGH ON THE CAUSES OF DEBT!

World Bank Data Tables show an enormous escalation of Third World Debt - in $UStrillion 0.3 in 1980, 0.8 in 1986, 1.6 in 1992, 2.1 in 1998. This is owed (sic) mainly not to nations but to banks and the IMF (International Monetary Fund). Borrower-lands spend their loans in our "developed" world, but find it hard to export, in the teeth of powerful Western competition, the products of their industry which this spending makes possible. They can't redeem their debt, especially since interest is claimed and free trade enforced. Assets are seized, and big business dominates nations. Money needs to be created by Governments not finance-houses, and spent or placed into circulation rather than lent at interest. As the prophet said,- "LEAVE OFF THIS USURY" (Nehemiah $5.^{10}$).

6th September.   JUROR OF THE YEAR, 2002.   259

   David Pannick Q.C. wrote in The Times (T2, page 23) for
17 December 2002 that 'In the competition for juror of the
past 12 months the prize goes to Barnabas Miller, of Califor-
nia. The letter applying for him to be excused from jury
service stated: "I have a short attention span. I have to
go to the bathroom quite often. And I'm a dog." Barnabas'
owner was fined $250 for registering the poodle as a voter.
He says he did it to protest against lax registration rules.'

— — — — — — — — — —

Awake! February 8, 2003

Decoy Alligators

Cormorants, birds that can apparently eat about two pounds of fish daily, "are often the bane of recreational fishermen's lives," says Canada's *Calgary Herald*. The paper reports that to ward off cormorants and other fish-eating birds, North American farmers and fish-farm managers are using a new tool — plastic alligators. The 13-foot-long alligators "have two large luminous reflectors for eyes, simulating alert gators in the wild," explains the *Herald*. One biologist found that a plastic alligator floating on the surface of the water worked for about a month. After that, the birds began to catch on, and one blue heron actually "was seen perched atop the decoy." But when the decoy was moved to another location, it once again scared the fish-eating birds away.

— — — — — — — — — —

A "Clerihew" (see 25.2) by Norah Bone (1958):
"That Narcissus / Should acquire a missus /
Was an idea that he rejected / After he'd reflected."

   And my variant on Roger McGough's limerick set in the
most westerly town in Europe-excluding-Iceland:
"A tuneful young lady from Dingle / Liked music that set
her a-tingle. / She really did rave / At the song of the
cave - / The Mendelssohn one about Fingal."

7th September. CHATLINES ADVERTISEMENTS.

    Typical of the display-notices in weekend supplements to newspapers is one which read:
"The New Phone Bar. No. 1 for over 5 Years! Even more genuine women online now..." (24.5.2003) But if she isn't genuine she isn't a woman at all!

"Soulmates" advertising wasn't tolerated in Victorian days - The Young Ladies' Journal for April 1869 told "Rosebud & Lily" that "We do not insert matrimonial advertisements; we look upon them as exceedingly degrading." Other enquirers were told: "A Constant Subscriber - Yes, parents have control until you are of age"; and "Lilian Livingstone - You would, in introducing a gentleman to a lady, mention first the gentleman's name, otherwise you would be introducing the lady to the gentleman, which is not etiquette, unless the gentleman be of much higher rank than the lady." (Feby. & Jany. 1869).

Spanish Library Notice. ✠ It merely threatens exclusion for rulebreaking!

HAI EXCOMUNION
RESERVADA A SU SANTIDAD
CONTRA QUALESQUIERA PERSONAS,
QUE QUITAREN, DISTRAXEREN, O DE OTRO QUALQUIER MODO
ENAGENAREN ALGUN LIBRO,
PERGAMINO, O PAPEL
DE ESTA BIBLIOTHECA,
SIN QUE PUEDAN SER ABSUELTAS
HASTA QUE ESTA ESTÉ PERFECTAMENTE REINTEGRADA.

Famous first sentences of novels include of course Jane Eyre: "There was no possibility of taking a walk that day." - and A Tale of Two Cities: "It was the best of times, it was the worst of times..." I, however, join the many who opt for The Towers of Trebizond by Rose Macauley: "'Take my camel, dear,' said my aunt Dot, as she climbed down from this animal on her return from High Mass." Incongruity par excellence must win!

8th September. MOONLIT ROMANCE! (see 11.2 for Juan & Julia's!)

No Shakespearean myself, to my shame, I love some of the bard's episodes; <u>The Merchant of Venice</u> has this heady piece!

Lorenzo	The moon shines bright. In such a night as this,
	When the sweet wind did gently kiss the trees,
	And they did make no noise, in such a night
	Troilus methinks mounted the Trojan walls,
	And sigh'd his soul toward the Grecian tents
	Where Cressid lay that night.
Jessica	In such a night
	Did Thisbe fearfully o'ertrip the dew,
	And saw the lion's shadow ere himself,
	And ran dismayed away.
Lorenzo	In such a night
	Stood Dido with a willow in her hand
	Upon the wild sea banks, and waft her love
	To come again to Carthage.
Jessica	In such a night
	Medea gathered the enchanged herbs
	That did renew Old Aeson.
Lorenzo	In such a night
	Did Jessica steal from the wealthy Jew
	And with an unthrift love did run from Venice
	As far as Belmont.
Jessica	In such a night
	Did young Lorenzo swear he loved her well,
	Stealing her soul with many vows of faith
	And ne'er a true one.
Lorenzo	In such a night
	Did pretty Jessica (like a little shrew)
	Slander her love, and he forgave it her...

Then we have "the most wondrous passage in English verse concerned with the equation between love sacred and profane – Lorenzo's speech about music, from the last Act...the sensuous delight of love...both fulfils and, with the help of music, liberates us from the flesh." (Wilfrid Mellers,[*] on Vaughan Williams' <u>Serenade to Music</u> for orchestra and sixteen solo voices, written for Henry Wood's Jubilee concert in 1938.)

How sweet the moonlight sits upon this bank!
Here will we sit, and let the sounds of music
Creep in our ears – soft stillness and the night
Become the touches of sweet harmony;
Sit Jessica – look how the floor of heaven
Is thick inlaid with patens of bright gold.

There's not the smallest orb which thou behold'st
But in his motion like an angel sings,
Still quiring to the young-ey'd cherubims;
Such harmony is in immortal souls,
But whilst this muddy vesture of decay
Doth grossly close it in, we cannot hear it.

([*] see 11.1)

9th September.   FIRST AND LAST LOVES.

In his book of that title, published by Murray in 1952, the then Poet Laureate John Betjeman argues that love has been lost from England via "the killing of local communities, the stamping out of local rivalries, and the supplying of everything by lorry from industrial towns". This depersonalisation has now gone very much further, with the industrial towns themselves robbed of individuality. My favourite quotation from the book relates however to the dumbing-down of touristic descriptions.

Betjeman contrasts a fictional extract from The Guide, 1901 with the corresponding mid-20th-century one in Mr Sussex Tankard's "Hiking down the Valleys Wild". The old Guide reads:

"Tickleby Tomcat. (Station: West Lincolnshire Light Railway – $1\frac{1}{4}$ miles.) – The manor of Tuckoldbury is mentioned in Domesday Book as being worth XVIII pence, and held by one Lanfranc de Tuckoldbury, its glebes, messuages and pottages for all time. Thence the manor of Tuckoldbury seems to have had that of Tommecutte added to it by Bill of Attainder from Simon de Montfort... At the dissolution of the monasteries the estates passed to one Edward Stronghorn, doubtless a relative of our abbot, in whose family it remained until comparatively modern times (1682). Tomcat Park is modern. The Church, Norm., E.E., Dec..."

The vicar's wife much prefers Mr Tankard's account, writes Betjeman: "First to the right after Claxby...and you are in Tickleby Tomcat. There's something of a good Lincolnshire ring about a name like Tickleby Tomcat...imagine that Norman Barons and monks of old took...pleasure in leaning over picturesque Tickleby Bridge...watching the beautiful Tickold wind its way to the North Sea. The ancient church has a fine double piscina in the porch on the North side."

But, adds Betjeman, the bridge is a concrete structure of the Horncastle Rural District Council, 1920; the village has fifty grey limestone cottages and a line of fancy bungalows connected with the sugar-beet industry; bow-windowed shops distinguish the main street; and the church is uninteresting... Apart from Tomcat Park the only objects of interest in Tickleby Tomcat are the people; and antiquarians are not interested in people.

- - - - - -

(By 2003 there has been further change. All but two of the shops have gone; and so has the vicar, though the church has a service each Sunday taken by the priestess who is Rector of the local group of several churches, or by one of the two local Readers. The bus service to Horncastle runs on Weds. & Sats.)

10th September.   Happy Families and National Hubris.   263

The Chief Librarian of Calderdale Metropolitan Borough Council is a Mr Gary Borrows, a most appropriate name which reminds me of the parlour-game in which the players strove to collect sets of picture cards — "Mr & Mrs Simonious and old Pa Simonious"; "Mr Haddock the fishmonger..." and so forth. In real life I note too that the General Secretary of NASUWT (National Association of Schoolmasters and Union of Woman Teachers) is Mr O'Kane (O dear!); and the daughter of Gertrude Bugler, the actress who inspired Hardy's "Tess" and played her part on the stage, is a Mrs Toms who runs the Beaminster cattery.

— — — — — — — —

Julie Burchill (Gdn Bad Girl) 25.1.200?

" IT'S 40 YEARS OF DUMB-ASS YOUNGSTERS 'BELIEVING' IN MUSIC, WHEN THEY SHOULD HAVE BEEN INVOLVED IN POLITICS THAT'S BROUGHT ABOUT THE SOCIAL STAGNATION WE ARE WITNESSING TODAY " Guardian Weekend.

The music which engages a society provides a key to popular attitudes, and I'm delighted to find that journalist Burchill concurs with what I thought was an unpopular opinion of mine, namely that rock music (that of the 1950s vintage, not that of the Lakeland petrophone in Keswick museum) is escapist in tendency. Did the fomented "Cold War", and the failure to achieve nuclear disarmament, push young folk into an excess of escapism? (But "Say not the struggle naught availeth" against the arms-trade and the warmongers.)

At least we have learned from the horrors of the 20th century not to exult in songs like G.A.Macdermott's 1870's ditty that brought music-hall audiences to their feet:

"The dogs of war" are loose and the rugged Russian Bear, Full bent on blood and robber has crawled out of his lair....
It seems a thrashing now and then will never help to tame That brute and so he's out upon "the same old game"....
Chorus: We don't want to fight but by jingo if we do, We've got the ships, we've got the men, and got the money too!
We've fought the Bear before, and while we're Britons true, the Russians shall not have Constantinople.

(In the event the Russians withdrew their threat to invade Turkey and challenge "our" naval superiority in the Mediterranean. The Congress of Berlin gained "Peace with Honour" and the Turks were enabled to prolong World War 1.)

11th September.   "Lift up your Gates and Sing."   264

Not only did our Victorian forebears develop and join in a repertoire of music-hall songs, of which "Oh! Mr Porter" with verses sung by Marie Lloyd had a chorus even more popular than yesterday's bellicose example; but also they delighted in a range of <u>Parlour Songs</u> for the "middle-class drawing-room soiree" to enjoy alongside their Parlour Poetry (see 23,25,26.4) Many of these songs remained much-loved popular favourites till well after World War 2, and it is a great loss that they are now but seldom broadcast on radio or TV, or taught in schools:

> "Once in the dear dead days beyond recall,
> When on the world the mists began to fall,
> Out of the dreams that rose in happy throng
> Low to our hearts Love sang an old sweet song;
> And in the dusk where fell the firelight glow
> Softly it wove itself into our dream:
> Just a song at twilight, when the lights are low,
> And the flick'ring shadows softly come and go,
> Tho' the heart be weary, sad the day and long,
> Still to us at twilight comes Love's old song,
>   Comes Love's old sweet song."   (C.C. Bingham)

Life's losses and sorrows played their full part in these lyrics - here for instance is the conclusion of T. Oliphant's English words for a well-known Welsh tune:

> "Still glows the bright sunshine o'er valley and mountain,
> Still warbles the blackbird its note from the tree;
> Still trembles the moonbeam on streamlet and fountain,
> But what are the beauties of nature to me?
> With sorrow, deep sorrow my bosom is laden,
> All day I go mourning in search of my love;
> Ye echoes, Oh! tell me where is the dear maiden?
> 'She sleeps 'neath the green turf down by the Ash Grove.'"

Yet faith stronger than today's bade them desire "a better country, that is, an heavenly" (Hebrews 11.16) and dream of a Holy City, heavenly Jerusalem with angels calling to earth-bound citizens, as in the 24th psalm: "Jerusalem, Jerusalem, Lift up your gates and sing, Hosanna in the Highest, Hosanna to your King."   ——————————————————— (F.E. Weatherly)

<u>12th September.</u> <u>Bishop Ailbe and the Wolf.</u> 265

   The Irish legend is that Ailbe, left at birth by his slave-
girl mother on a hillside to die, was found by a she-wolf who
carried him to her lair and suckled him along with her cubs.
Soon he was found and adopted by a hunter. Years later, as
Christian bishop in Munster in the early 6th century, he saved
the life of his wolf foster-mother when she was being hunted.
"Thereafter she came every day to the hall where he was dining;
and in his turn he fed her." (S. Toulson, <u>The Celtic Year</u> —
Artist: B. Partridge.   see also 1.2 and 5.7)

13th September.   OLD ENGLAND - PRISON for Stealing a Turnip.

An ill-clad, half-starved man, named Goonricke, was charged at Scarborough with the theft of a turnip. When the farmer accosted him he was hungrily eating half of the turnip, and carrying the other half under his arm. He pleaded to the North Riding magistrates that he took the turnip because he was very hungry, but the Bench ordered him to pay 7s. 6d. or go to jail for a week. Goonricke asked for time to pay, but this was refused. It was the man's first appearance before the Court. He was at one time a prosperous tradesman in Scarborough.
(Teesdale Mercury, 18th November 1903.)

COW CLUBS.

Alford: The half-yearly meeting of the Society was held in the Windmill Inn on Friday evening last, when it was reported that 201 cows were insured; that more than £60 had been paid since the last meeting as compensation to the owners for the loss of four cows, at the rate of three fourths of their value; and that there had been 13 cows newly-entered during the half-year... (Lincolnshire Chronicle 11th June 1879.
One such club lasted until 1980.)

PUB LUNCH FOR ELEPHANT.

Two elephants were being taken to water at the river at Bishop's Stortford (Essex), when one of them entered the tap-room of the Old Bull's Head Inn, emptied all the beer-mugs in sight, and ate the bread and cheese of the customers. There was considerable excitement, but no damage was done, and the keeper enticed the animal away. (Ledbury Reporter, 8 May 1926. Circuses travelled by special train prior to the "BeechingAxe" of the early 1960s; I remember a street-parade of the animals.

ROUGH MUSIC - A PLEASANT CUSTOM?

Farnham: The quiet of this town was again disturbed...by one of those exhibitions...popularly known as "skimmingtons" or rough bands...A woman, who it was said had proved faithless to her marriage vow, and a man who was said to have won an undue share of her favour...a numerous number of lads met...and for a long time assailed the inmates with discordant noises, the instruments being old kettles, pots, pans, rattles etc... a large number of persons assembled to witness the finale. (2 nights later) Fireworks continued till 8.30pm when the offending couple were burnt in effigy on a bonfire! (Middlesex and Herts. Courier, 24th October 1863; compare the Dorset "skimmity-ride in Hardy's "Mayor of Casterbridge".)

14th September. THE LOST LEADER - by Robert Browning.

Just for a handful of silver he left us,
   Just for a riband to stick in his coat,
Found the one gift of which fortune bereft us,
   Lost all the others she lets us devote.
They, with the gold to give, doled him out silver,
   So much was theirs who so little allowed :
How all our copper had gone for his service !
   Rags—were they purple, his heart had been proud.
We that had loved him so, followed him, honoured him,
   Lived in his mild and magnificent eye,
Learned his great language, caught his clear accents,
   Made him our pattern to live and to die !
Shakespeare was of us, Milton was for us,
   Burns, Shelley, were with us—they watch from their graves.
He alone breaks from the van and the freemen,
He alone sinks to the rear and the slaves.

We shall march prospering—not through his presence;
   Songs may inspirit us—not from his lyre ;
Deeds will be done—while he boasts his quiescence,
   Still bidding crouch whom the rest bade aspire.
Blot out his name, then, record one lost soul more,
   One task more declined, one more footpath untrod,
One more devils'-triumph and sorrow for angels,
   One wrong more to man, one more insult to God.
Life's night begins : let him never come back to us ;
   There would be doubt, hesitation, and pain,
Forced praise on our part—the glimmer of twilight,
   Never glad confident morning again.
Best fight on well, for we taught him—strike gallantly,
   Menace our heart ere we master his own ;
Then let him receive the new knowledge and wait us,
   Pardoned in heaven, the first by the throne.

The idea for this poem was suggested to Browning by Wordsworth's "regentrification" from his youthful radicalism, which was shattered by his disappointment with the aftermath of the French Revolution. Browning made it clear he did not impute to Wordsworth the base motives of too many political leaders who allow themselves to be corrupted by power and/or seduced by the purple plums of wealth and adulation. The famous phrase "Never glad confident morning again" seems over-pessimistic, for the hope and possibility of spiritual revival are undying. (Isaiah 65.17; Revelation 21.1.)

15th September. "Understanding Space and Time". 268

In the 1970s the Open University gave this optimistic title to its course on Relativity Physics – the Special Theory which Herbert Dingle and Bertrand Russell faulted for internal contradictions, and the General Theory setting out Einstein's final vision. (He said he couldn't understand most of the books which seek to interpret it, but he trusted the Polish schoolteacher L. Infeld to the extent of accepting joint authorship of "The Evolution of Physics", which is a good read for the scientifically-minded.) Einstein's work was a major factor in the discovery that nuclear energy can be released from atoms (18.8); and this advance, comparable with the discovery of fire in primitive times, has authenticated relativity in the public mind. Observations however can on occasion be explained on more than one basis, e.g. Jupiter's orbiting by the Newtonian and Einsteinian theories of gravitation; so we need to be wary of Pascal's Two Infinities of size and of smallness (22.7), the mystery of which underlies Tennyson's <u>Voice & Peak</u>

"A deep below the deep, And a height beyond the height!
Our hearing is not hearing, And our seeing is not sight."

Stephen Hawking's "A Brief History of Time" (Guild, 1990) is another excellent read, even if one may balk at "imaginary time" and "virtual photons" and wonder whether such concepts are "names given to difficulties"! Hawking's final pages pose some intriguing questions, e.g. Einstein's "How much choice did God have in constructing the universe?" Even if there is only one possible unified theory linking quantum-mechanics and relativity, "it is just a set of rules and equations. What is it that breathes fire into the equations and makes a universe for them to describe?...Is the unified theory so compelling that it brings about its own existence? Or does it need a Creator...and who created him?"

These are old questions! Ideas can only exist in a Mind or minds. St Thomas Aquinas (1227-1274) deemed it immaterial whether or not the universe had a beginning in time; and Faber wrote of God in his hymn "Most ancient of all mysteries" (159, A&M Re

When heaven and earth were yet unmade,
  When time was yet unknown,
Thou in thy bliss and majesty
  Didst live and love alone.

Thou wast not born; there was no fount
  From which thy being flowed;
There is no end which thou canst reach
  But thou art simply God.

Compare E. Brontë's penultimate verse (7.1). The alternative to creation, i.e. universe existing from eternity, falls foul of the unknowability of things in the absence of a conscious Knower, and of the 2nd Law of Thermodynamics, which if true entails a start!

Topic continues 16.10

16th September. "IONA OF MY HEART".

The ageing Wordsworth wrote four rather gloomy sonnets after visiting the Hebridean isle of Iona where St Columba had come from Ireland to set up a Christian cell in 563AD. His monks were martyred by Nordic marauders in 890; then Benedictine monks built the fine abbey-church and lived by it till weakened by the Reformation. Thereafter the buildings lapsed into ruin till the 8th Duke of Argyll promoted church-restoration in the 1890s, and George Macleod ("the gunslinging gambler[1] of Govan") founded the Iona Community which refurbished the abbey-buildings in mid-20th-century as centres of applied Christianity. To book a stay there ring 01681.700343; or sample the isle by daytrip from Oban.

Iona Abbey.   **Old Nunnery, Iona.**

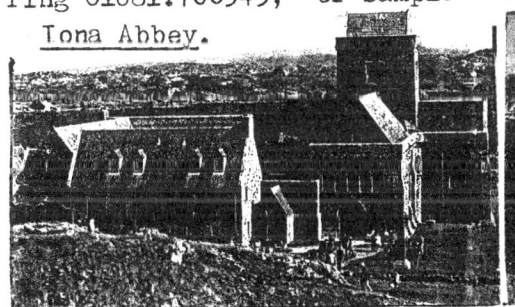

Wordsworth's "How sad a welcome" sonnet drew a response from me, entitled "Iona Christmas Celebration, 22-29.12.1989":

"How *glad* our welcome at the Church Restored,
When from the storm-tost boat we made our way
To join the Island Christians of *our* day
And celebrate the Coming of the Lord!
This latter house, made new by George Macleod   Haggai 2⁹.
And Glasgow youths in Scotland's hungry years
Her greater glory to the West declares
With cloisters, bell and Celtic crosses proud.
We danc'd, we sang *Messiah*, 'King of Kings';
We hail'd the sun rise bright o'er Mull's high hill;
We caroll'd through the village to its Kirk
Where happy children told of Him Who brings   Newell;
Redeeming grace. So Alison and Phil   Wardens,
And many friends renew Iona's work."   1989.

(Strongly Recommended: biography "George Macleod" by Ronald Ferguson - Fount 1990, £7.99; also his "Love your Crooked Neighbour"- St Andrew)

1. see 17.5.   Macleod Centre, Iona.

17th September. "The Fire of Love and the Meaning of Life".

Meet Richard Rolle, 14th-century spiritual mystic writer. His book of the above title shows that he felt threatened by women but tried to be fair to them! Here are some extracts, taken from Methuen's 1914 reprint.

Page 104. Truly it is the manner of women that when they feel themselves loved out of measure by men, they beguile men's hearts by cherishing flattery; and they draw to those things that their wicked will stirred up, the which before they assayed by open speech. Solomon...afterward, for the too muckle love by which he drew to women, he failed most foully in stedfastness and in the commandments of God...he, set in great wisdom, suffered himself to be overcome by a fond woman.

Page 126. Truly the beauty of women beguiles many men, through desire whereof the hearts of the righteous also are some time overturned, so that they that began in spirit end in the flesh. Therefore beware and...keep no speech with women's fairness...flee women wisely and alway keep thy thoughts far from them, because, though a woman be good, yet the fiend by pricking and moving, and also by their cherishing (alluring) beauty, thy will can be over-mickle delighted in them, because of frailty of flesh. But...if thou despise them as japes or trifles ("sawdust and nonsense") as they are - no marvel that thou shouldst have the more joy of God's love.

Pages 174/176. (Rolle has granted that _controlled_ love of men and women is natural, and "this love also has its pleasures as in speech and touching and goodly dwelling together...") Certain, _that_ friendship and companionship of men and women is unlawful and forbidden in which they accord to fulfil all their desire of covetous and foul lust; and putting the everlasting behind they seek to flourish in temporal solace and bodily love

Next the women of our time are worthy of reproof that in such marvellous vanity have found new array for head and body. Not only against the sentence of the apostle (1 Peter 3.3) in gold and dressing of the hair, in pride and wantonness, they go serving, but also...they set broad horns upon their heads, and a horrible greatness of wrought hair that grew not there, some of whom...with painting of beguiling adultery they colour and whiten their faces. Newly carven clothing also men and women use full fondly...

— — — — — — —

So, ladies and gentlemen, now you know; you have been warned. For the medieval subjection of women see 24.9; for the story of Hildegard of Bingen, to this day the most famous female classical composer, see 26.9

18th September. A HEADY SUNDAY IN 1927.

RHONDDA MINERS' DISTRICT & COUNCIL OF ACTION
RED SUNDAY IN RHONDDA VALLEY

Campaign Against BALDWIN & COALOWNERS

MONSTRE RHONDDA
DEMONSTRATION
ON PENRHYS MOUNTAIN
On SUNDAY, SEPTEMBER 18th, at 3 o'clock.

The following Speakers will positively attend

A. J. COOK
General Secretary, M.F.G.B.
WALL HANNINGTON
National Unemployed, London

David Lewis,   Arthur Horner,   W. H. Mainwaring
Miners District Secretary   E.C. M.F.G.B   Miners Agent

Chairman: T. THOMAS, Treherbert.

WORKERS, AROUSE! Line Up! Join in the Revolt Against the Coalowners' Government. NOW we want the 1914 Spirit in the Workers' Fight   Organise Your Grumbles and Fight Your Oppressors.

READ THIS TIME TABLE (Men and Women and Join Your Contingent in this Great March, by falling in behind your Band and Banners.

RHONDDA FACH Depart from Mardy 1.30 p.m. Ferndale Workmen's Hall 2 p.m. Queen's Square, Tylorstown 2.40 p.m. Porth Square, Porth 1.30 Workmen's Hall Ynyshir 2 p.m.

RHONDDA FAWR. Depart from Blaenrhondda Station 1.6 m. Bute Square Treherbert 1.15 p.m. Star Square Treorchy 1.15 p.m. Ystrad Station 2.15. Bowlers Arms, Penycraig 1.30 p.m. Pandy Square Tonypandy. 2 p.m. Partridge Road, Treslaw 2.15 p.m.

SPECIAL ATTRACTION! The Mid-Rhondda Section YOUNG COMRADES' LEAGUE and Bands will render Working Class Music and Songs and lead Mass singing

Down with Baldwin!   On for Workers' Government!

(The first great national clash on coal, not then displaced by oil as the world's staple fuel, had its climax in the 1926 strike which followed the Governmental failure to nationalise as recommended by the 1919 Sankey Report. Defeat bred fury!)

19th September. "Beulah-land, In Beulah-land..." – so ran an early Methodistic hymn quoting Isaiah 62.4, and so ran the steam trains over the high Beulah or Belah viaduct. Now dismantled, it was the crowning glory of the transpennine Stainmore line from Barnard Castle to Tebay, which conveyed coal in vast quantities from the Durham mines to the West Cumbrian iron and steel furnaces; also some passenger traffic – local and, at weekends, from the North-East to breezy Blackpool.

I myself crossed the deep valley on this viaduct (not to be confused with that at Bela near Arnside) before I found that it had been designed by the ill-fated Sir Thomas Bouch whose Tay Bridge fell during the storm in late December 1879, taking a train and 75 persons into the river. He was scapegoated and died of grief as victim number 76. The design & build were flawed; but the 150mph gale probably blew the the train off and against the side girders with immense force. The staff should not have attempted the crossing, which is vividly reconstructed, using models and a water-tank, in the film of A. J. Cronin's novel "Hatter's Castle".

20th September. Two Favourite Chess Problems.

In each case White to move and mate in 3 against any defence!

D. McIntyre, 1924.
N.B. The black K has no move.

H. von Gottschall, 1926.
N.B. The black R is pinned.

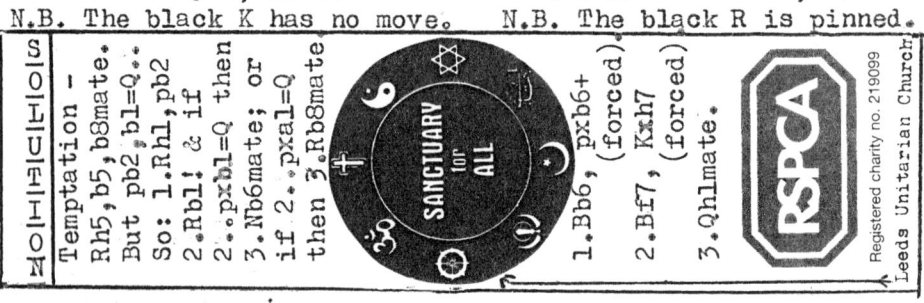

272

SOLUTIONS

Temptation –
Rh5, b5, b8mate.
But pb2, bl=Q.
So: 1.Rh1, pb2
2.Rb1! & if
2..pxb1=Q then
3.Nb6mate; or
if 2..pxa1=Q
then 3.Rb8mate

1.Bb6, pxb6+ (forced)
2.Bf7, Kxh7 (forced)
3.Qh1mate.

Registered charity no. 219099
Leeds Unitarian Church

21st September. "LET THEM GUESS AWAY!" (A Tchaikovsky Essay.)

Pyotr Ilyich Tchaikovsky (1840-1893) was dogged by hypochondria throughout his life, and was at times on the brink of madness. Shy and unable to relate adequately to women because of a peculiarity which he referred to as "Z" in his diaries - most likely involving latent homosexuality - he lived for his work. His early masterpiece the "Romeo and Juliet" overture, written and performed when he was 29, revealed his power to render the emotions of the human heart. Having recovered from a broken flirtatious half-engagement to the singer Désirée Arnot, he avoided further tangles until in 1877 he was foolish enough to marry Antonina Milyukova, an infatuated 28-year-old admirer who had sent him love-letters "out of the blue", threatening suicide if he wouldn't meet her. He told his platonic penfriend Nadezhda von Meck that he didn't love Antonina. Did he marry to mask "Z" - or out of an inept sense of destiny? Antonina's naive hope that her feminine charms would stabilise him proved false. He fled after twenty days; returned after a few weeks for the start of the Moscow Conservatoire term; but left again a fortnight later, after a half-hearted attempt at suicide. He then suffered a frightening nervous breakdown, which was contained by visiting Western Europe with his brother Anatol. Poor Antonina also suffered from unrecognised mental disorder which kept her in hospital for her last 20 years or so.

Nadezhda von Meck was a rich widow, seven years Tchaikovsky's senior, who admired his music. In 1876 on hearing that he was in financial difficulties, she commissioned him to make some violin-and-piano settings for her. Presently she settled a 6000-rouble annuity on him so that he could devote all his energies to composing. In 13 years of patronage (sic) she wrote him some 1100 letters, but by tacit aggreement they never met except trivially and fortuitously. Soon he was telling her that he was working on a new symphony, his Fourth, which would portray his feelings about Life and Fate. In April 1877, a few days after Antonina's first letter, he told Nadezhda that he would have to delay writing a violin-and-piano piece called "The Reproach" for her, because the symphony was taking all his energies, and would be dedicated to her.

This would-be commission was very strange, for in a fresh request in May 1877 she wrote that "my reproach must express an unbearable state of mind...in it one must find a broken heart, a trampled faith, principles insulted, happiness torn away, all that is dear and precious to man pitilessly torn away...."(continues

22nd September.   Tchaikovsky essay continued.

"...the despairing moment of anguish, the impossibility to endure any longer, exhaustion, and if possible death, so that at least in music one could find the appeasement which life does not always procure." Artists do of course sometimes try and portray desolation, but Nadezhda's background seems significant. She had not long been widowed; and, according to Edward Garden, her husband had died of a heart attack on discovering her infidelity. As on a later occasion, she may have felt the need for penance to enable her to forgive herself. Pyotr again declined the task but added that he would fulfil it one day. But no such item is listed among his works — or is it?

Amazingly Tchaikovsky worked on his symphony during his first separation from his wife, and had it posted to Western Europe for completion by the end of 1877. It is a well-known masterpiece and a popular favourite, but does it have a programme? Can music be rendered in words? Tchaikovsky wrote to Nadezhda that his long letter of 1 March 1878 to her was "a true echo of my feelings at the time" (of writing the symphony) "but only an echo..." Previously on 6 November 1877 he told her that "our symphony will be finished by December at the latest...May this music, which is so closely bound up with the thought of you, speak to you and tell you that I love you with all my heart and incomparable soul, my best incomparable friend..."

Although to the world he was vague, saying the programme should be obvious to everyone, was the same as Beethoven used for his 5th symphony, and so on, he mapped it out more fully in his letter to his patroness: "...I will tell you, and you alone, the meaning of this entire work and of its separate movements. The introduction is the germ...this is Fate, that inevitable force which checks our aspirations towards happiness before they reach the goal...which, like the sword of Damocles, hangs perpetually over our heads and is always embittering the soul...There is no other course but to submit and inwardly lament."

Andante sostenuto. Horns and Bassoons, unis. col 8va.

(the 'Fate' theme which recurs throughout the symphony, especially in its long first movement when it recurs with immense weight, impairing the ease of listening!)

(continues

23rd September. <u>Where Words Leave Off.</u>

The wistfully lovely second movement "expresses...the melancholy which steals over us when at evening we sit indoors alone, tired out after work...old memories fill the mind. There were moments when young blood pulsed warm through our veins...moments of sorrow, irreparable loss, all so far in the past." The fanciful patterns of the third movement "express no definite feelings. We have...intangible figures that enter the head when one has been drinking wine...a tipsy peasant, a drinking song, a military band." All this is dispelled in the festive fourth movement: "If you find no happiness in yourself, look around you, go to the people, see them enjoy life." The Fate motto intrudes at the end but is overcome by the general zest. "Be glad in the joy of others."

"I can tell you no more, dear friend" concluded Tchaikovsky - "there lies the peculiarity of music, we cannot analyse it. 'Where words leave off, music begins'..." Elsewhere he wrote: "I should have gone mad but for music...the most beautiful of all Heaven's gifts to humanity wandering in darkness. Alone it calms, enlightens and stills our souls...a true friend, refuge, and comforter."

Ten years passed before Tchaikovsky published his next numbered symphony, the popular Fifth which also begins with a motive, albeit less strident, for Fate, Destiny, or Providence - and incidentally ends with that of the Beethoven Fifth. The composer lost his initial liking for it, in spite of its great popularity and structural unity. Its warmth is less personal, Nadezhda's correspondence having lost some of its volume. Tchaikovsky left a jotted programme for the first movement. It reads: "Introduction. Complete resignation before Fate, or, which is the same, before the inscrutable predestination of Providence. Allegro (I) Murmurs, doubts, lamentations, reproaches against XXX (II) Shall I throw myself into the embraces of Faith???" (He never could solve his "contradictions". He refused the dogma of the Church whilst setting its liturgy, and denied personal immortality whilst "calling on God in his grief and thanking Him in his happiness".) The symphony ends in a triumph which, deliberately or otherwise, seems vulnerable; yet its <u>joy</u> brings content.

(narrative contd. 2.11

WIMBORNE MINSTER
An Ancient and Lovely Building.

__24th September.__ "My dearest Dick, Oh yes, yes, YES!..."

Thus did Foulsham's "The Complete Letter Writer" encourage a girl to write her acceptance of a cabled proposal of marriage. E.S. Turner's book "A History of Courting" (Michael Joseph, 1954) is choc-a-bloc with quaintnesses and delights from the dear dead days beyond recall when courting was courting as it so seldom is in the West today. Today's teenage sexual mating is too often taken for granted by adults who would do well by counselling against it, for it should be a celebration of achieving across-the-board commitment rather than a short-cut to it, a means of avoiding selfgiving in love. By contrast the Scottish Reformers had a jolly good try to suppress extramarital sex (see 2.9), and the medieval West was kept on the "straight and narrow" by the Church - "especially women"!! I shall not dwell on the cruelty of the methods used, and alas still used in some countries where "the punishment is a worse crime than the crime."

Old England enforced celibacy in various ways. The widow of a manorial tenant was granted "free bench" of her husband's lands for her lifetime so long as she did not marry and "remained chaste". In a strange blend of kindness and prurience, a very few places allowed widows "detected in inconstancy" to retain their rights on "riding the black ram". In Enborne near Newbury the unfortunate delinquent lady had to appear at the Court Leet riding backwards holding the beast's tail, and solemnly repeat the words some of which are sheer nonsense:

"Here I am
Riding upon a black ram
Like a whore I am
And for my crincum crancum
Have lost my bincum bancum
And for my tail's game
Am brought to this worldly shame.
Therefore, good Master Steward,
Let me have my lands again."

She got them back; but the effort must have all but choked her, poor thing.

Child-marriages, to ward off calf-love intrigues, lasted to Elizabethan times. Chaste betrothals of child to adult included Katherine Stonor's at 12 to the merchant Thomas Betson. In 1478 he sent her a ring from France, writing:

"And if ye would be a good eater of your meat alway, that ye might wax and grow fast to be a woman, ye should make me the gladdest man of the world, by my troth...And Almighty Jesu make you a good woman, and send you many good years and long to live ...At great Calais on this side of the sea, the first day of June, and the clock smote nine, and all our household cried after me ...come down to dinner at once! and what answer I gave them ye know it of old. By your faithful cousin and lover Thos. Betson.

25th September.   Well-a-day! (Curses & Verses).

An enjoyable chance-meeting with a girl on a train prompted me to play on her name with a non-rhyming limerick:
> The charming young lady called Dex
> Had friends who delighted to vex
>   Her by sending her verses
>   That called forth her curses
> Because they'd all end without rhyme.

Many people, perhaps nearly everyone, will respond with interjections of dismay or wrath if suddenly pained or frustrated. Alas-and-alack! Well-a-day! Ah me! are among the genteel interjections of grief which may fall short as expressions of feeling; and I'm not so mealy-mouthed as to limit myself to them. "Bl--dy h-ll" I say, with little compunction now that "bloody" has lost its meaning as the elided oath "by Our Lady", which made its use scandalous in the first half of the 1900s.

Denis Healey's expounded anthology "My Secret Planet" (Penguin, 1994) shows him to be far more widely-read than me. He offers a 32-line poem by an anonymous WW2 soldier from which I quote:

"Sheffield in the Blitz."

1. This bloody town's a bloody cuss
    No bloody trains no bloody bus
    And no one cares for bloody us
    Oh bloody bloody woe.

7. No bloody sport no bloody games
    No bloody fun with bloody dames
    Wont even give their bloody names
    Oh bloody bloody woe.

I think it's a moot point whether this expresses desolation or whether it bores by tedious repetition, which is no more meaningful than the barking of a dog. (Those fond of contemporary expletives please note!)

Lord Healey notes also the moving poems by young women who had the heartbreak of separation from their loved ones and also the panic of "being thrown into barracks with other girls from totally different backgrounds." (continues on 30 Sept.)

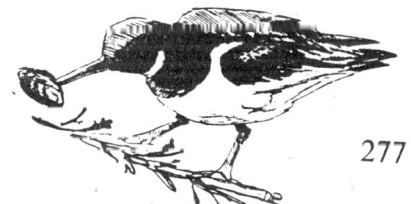

LEAD ME FROM DEATH to LIFE, from FALSEHOOD to TRUTH

26th September. **Hildegard of Bingen (1098-1179).**

We in England think of the Tudor composers Byrd and Tallis, their predecessor Taverner, and the continentals Palestrina and Victoria, as "ancient". The revival of interest in Abbess Hildegard's sweet ascending melodic phrases is intriguing, pointing to the existence of Gothic music alongside church-plainsong. Perhaps the best-known female composer before the 19th and 20th centuries in spite of her early date, Hildegard was a most versatile, brilliant and doubtless attractive woman of spiritual strength and distinction. Her noble parents put her with Jutta the anchoress and other young women at Disebodenberg. She became abbess at 38, and after some 15 years moved with a score of nuns to set up a new community at St Rupertsberg down the Rhine valley. She regaled with advice many authority-figures in church and state, arguing vigorously with the help of her visions.

At 42 she wrote in Scivias, a book-title meaning "Know Thy Ways", that "Heaven was opened and a fiery light of exceeding brilliance came and permeated my whole brain...not like a burning but like a warming flame, as the sun warms anything its rays touch. Then in Book of Divine Works she claimed that "All living creatures are sparks from the radiance of God's brilliance..." Elsewhere in these books and in her Book of Life's Merits she celebrates "viridatis (the greening power)" and uses "greenness" as a metaphor for life's vibrant energy: "the soul is the green life-force of the flesh, giving vitality to...the whole body, as the tree from its root gives sap and greenness to all the branches." But if we give up on these virtues and "surrender to the drought of indolence, so that we do not have the sap of life and the greening power of good deeds, then the power of our very soul will...dry up".

Prominent in propounding "Interconnectedness", Hildegard claimed that "everything...is penetrated with relatedness". Her paintings and those of her school show the winds and light that connect the unity. She anticipated physical science by noting patterns in nature. Humans are central, but humanity depends on our relationships with other creatures, and they will punish us if we abuse our dominance. (A lesson for today!)

As for individual humans, she saw body and soul as a single reality, needing to co-operate in their different roles. Our drives need discipline from the soul, and for wisdom we need to use all our powers in right proportion. "If our thoughts grow opinionated and obdurate, the powers of virtue will be weakened and desiccated within us"; but wherever soul & body live together in proper agreement, they attain...mutual joy.

Source, Hildegard essay by Eileen Conn in "Visions of Creation" (Godsfield, 1995).

27th September. "Home-Thoughts, From Abroad".

With our autumnal equinox four days gone, and Michaelmas yet to follow, our northern gloom is balanced by southern comfort, no more so than at the South Pole itself, to which the sun returns after its six-month absence. The Times' most distant reader had this tale of spiritual uplift published on 23.9.96:

At around the time of the autumnal equinox Dr Hart reported:

FOR most *Times* readers the end of summer is no cause for celebration. But for those of us stranded at the most southerly spot on Earth, Thursday was a day we had looked forward to. It was when our long, dark winter ended and we saw the sun for the first time in six months.

As the clouds cleared we could see the top of the sun peeking over the horizon. Although it was late at night, most of the personnel at the Amundsen-Scott Base gathered to witness the event. It was a surprisingly quiet affair, most people just standing around displaying big grins, basking in the first rays of light at the end of what had been a very long, dark tunnel. When you are restricted to one sunrise a year it is a moment to savour and, despite the cold, I stood watching for almost an hour as the snow surface turned a wonderful shade of lilac.

This quiet contemplation did not last long and on Saturday we celebrated with a wild party. Everyone sang along to the Beatles' *Here Comes The Sun* while drinking tequila sunrises.

Life here is one of extremes. During our summer the sun never sets and the glare of sunlight off the snow can be blinding. Towards midsummer the temperature soars to a balmy 0 fahrenheit. Military transport planes bring us food and fuel almost daily and the station population swells to near 150; life is hectic and crowded. The station is under a 50-metre-wide aluminium dome, but most people sleep outside in long black tents. Our only water supply is from melted ice, and fuel is limited, so we make do with two two-minute showers a week.

As winter approaches, the sun gradually sinks lower and the temperature drops to the point where flying becomes too risky. The last plane left on February 22. Since then we have had no mail and the last of our fresh fruit ran out months ago. We celebrate the end of each month with a formal dinner and, despite the reliance on frozen food, our cook has prepared some excellent dishes. A hydroponic greenhouse produces enough for a small salad each week, and we have even managed to create some authentic-tasting sushi. With the sun gone, the night sky during clear periods is astonishing. The Milky Way and the Southern Lights are visible in their full glory.

But it can also become very dark and dangerous. I once lost my way outside and had to radio for help. It was -70F and, while trying to retrace my steps, which were becoming obscured by blowing snow, I suddenly became very cold. I was rescued by colleagues waving torches to guide me back. I realised I had been heading in completely the wrong direction.

We find strange ways to pass the time in winter. When the weather first dropped below -100F, we climbed into the sauna, waited for it to heat up to 200F, then stripped naked and raced outside to the South Pole marker. It is a station tradition, and those who do it are enrolled into the exclusive 300 Club.

As one of only two Britons on the station, I would miss news of home were it not for the excellent *Times* Internet edition. It is particularly exciting to read the football results only hours after the games have been played. What a difference from a very few years ago, when the only communication with the outside world was by infrequent radio link.

Our collective mood follows the angle of the sun. Our low point was midwinter, but our spirits are now brightening with the sky.

Simon Hart beside the South Pole marker

(Topic continues 28.9 overleaf.)

28th September.   THE SOUTH POLAR TIMES.

My response on reading Simon Hart's account of Antarctic life was to write to him as follows — mainly out of mischief to see how the postal services would cope with such an address. They deal each winter with many letters to Father Christmas at the North Pole, so I thought they'd manage — and they did!

Councillor Frank R. McManus
Langfield Ward Todmorden Town Council

Locksley House.
97 Longfield Rd
TODMORDEN
OL14 6ND

Simon Hart, Esq.,
Amundsen-Scott Base,
South Pole,
Antarctica.

24.9.96

Dear Dr. Hart,

I was interested indeed to read your article in The Times today. At first I was puzzled by the sun's return to you last Thursday the 19th rather than at the equinox three days later, for the poet Hood wrote that "He never came a wink too soon". But this stems from the diameter of his disc, yes?

I imagine that the time o'clock varies greatly when you move eastward or westward; that you move from one time-zone to another and may cross the International Date Line during a walk; and that at the pole there is uncertainty of date and no time o'clock. Do these facts affect life at the Base, please?

I confess to writing partly in the hope of finding how and when this letter reaches you (if it does) — but I send it also in appreciation of your article and with my best wishes to all at the Base. I may publish a copy in my diary, as also any reply unless you say No.

Yours sincerely,
Frank R. McManus

29th September. (Michaelmas Day).

Michaelmas daisies are few and far between in my Pennine home-town of Todmorden, and must find it difficult to grow here, as (only more so) in

A N T A R C T I C A

(sketch on photo © Jody Forster: 50m dome, South Pole Station.)

Early in 1997 I was honoured and delighted to receive a postcard with the above picture, postmarked South Pole Antarctica FPO and dated Jan 6 1997, which read as follows:

"Dear Frank,
   Many thanks for your kind letter. It arrived after a tortuous route. It was misdirected to Warsaw, Poland. Obviously the postman thought South Pole was Southern Poland! Anyway it arrived in mid-December. Regarding your questions: The Sun appeared 3 days early due to refraction of its light rays by the atmosphere. All 24 time zones meet here but we operate on New Zealand time since that is where we fly 'south' from. The weather today is very warm (−23°C) as we have just passed midsummers day. I leave the pole in a couple of hours to return to England for the first time in 15 months.
   Best wishes.   Simon Hart."

(The picture, 27.9, of Simon Hart shows very little of him - he peeps through the protective clothing needed to survive the cold.)

− − − − − − − −

The Thomas Hood poem quoted in my letter (28.9) is called "Past and Present" and runs:

1. I remember, I remember
   The house where I was born,
   The little window where the sun
   Came peeping in at morn;
   He never came a wink too soon
   Nor brought too long a day;
   But now, I often wish the night
   Had borne my breath away.

4. I remember, I remember
   The fir trees dark and high;
   I used to think their slender tops
   Were close against the sky:
   It was a childish ignorance,
   But now 'tis little joy
   To know I'm farther off from Heaven
   Than when I was a boy.

(An evolutionist's parody rued that he "found it funky / To know (he's) farther off from Heaven / Than when (he) was a monkey.")

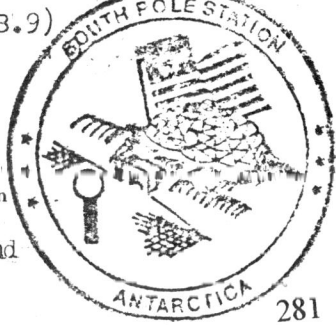

281

__30th September.__ More from the Secret Planet (25.9).

Joy Corfield's verses on her first night in WW2 barracks:
"Don't cry, young woman, / In your badly made bed; / Pull the grey blanket / Over your head. // Your mother cries, too, / On your first night from home, / Fearing your safety / Now you're on your own. // Take comfort, young woman, / If only you knew / Most of the others / Are crying, too."

Yeats died on a "dark cold day" at the start of the hard year 1939 — four centuries on from England's cruel 1539 — and the considerable poet Wystan Auden celebrated him in a 3-part poem which ends in Yeatsian hope. Here are parts 2 and 3:

You were silly like us; your gift survived it all:
The parish of rich women, physical decay,
Yourself. Mad Ireland hurt you into poetry.
Now Ireland has her madness and her weather still,
For poetry makes nothing happen: it survives
In the valley of its making where executives
Would never want to tamper, flows on south
From ranches of isolation and the busy griefs,
Raw towns that we believe and die in: it survives,
A way of happening, a mouth.

  Earth, receive an honoured guest:
  William Yeats is laid to rest
  Let the Irish vessel lie
  Emptied of its poetry.

  In the nightmare of the dark
  All the dogs of Europe bark,
  And the living nations wait,
  Each sequestered in its hate;

Intellectual disgrace
Stares from every human face,
And the seas of pity lie
Locked and frozen in each eye.

Follow, poet, follow right
To the bottom of the night,
With your unconstraining voice
Still persuade us to rejoice;

With the farming of a verse
Make a vineyard of the curse,
Sing of human unsuccess
In a rapture of distress;

In the deserts of the heart
Let the healing fountain start,
In the prison of his days
Teach the free man how to praise.

G.K. Chesterton's poems contain golden nuggets though he lacked clarity at times; not, however, in his little "Elegy in a Country Churchyard" which I quote in the wake of the 2nd Gulf War (2003) my mood during which was that of the Psalmist who wrote (60.3): "Thou hast given us a drink of deadly wine".

1. THE men that worked for England
 They have their graves at home:
 And bees and birds of England
 About the cross can roam......

3. And they that rule in England,
 In stately conclave met,
 Alas, alas for England
 They have no graves as yet.

(Happier autumnal poems will follow on 19th October.)

1st October.   Creationism and its Alternatives.

Charles Darwin's "Theory of Evolution" disturbed the "fundamentalist" view, which held that the Book of Genesis set out the literal historic "timetable of creation"; and it wounded the pride of those who wanted to regard humans as a special creation unconnected with animals and other "lower life". The theory substituted for our honour of having been made in God's image in His crowning creative act the doubtful privilege of being a "fortuitous" product of blind forces working competitively in a "Nature red in tooth and claw" (Tennyson, In Memoriam 56 - see also 54 & 55). That the evil in Nature, from the mousing cat to Auschwitz, presents difficulties of theodicy (justification of God) cannot be denied. Life is an "over-tragic drama", yet Christians including Tennyson go on to deny that "the closing curtain is the pall". The Christian Socialist Charles Kingsley asserted that now people had "got rid of an interfering God - a master-magician as I call it - they have to choose between the absolute empire of accident and a living, immanent, ever-working God". (A booklet entitled "Evolution and the Existence of God" was published by Catholic Truth Society.) To this, Frederick Denison Maurice added "Christianity if true must be expressed not only as a righteous social order but in terms consistent with the whole cosmic process", and Professor W. Sanday in his 1893 Bampton Lectures developed the idea of "progressive revelation".

This idea of "Cosmic Evolution", set out famously by St Paul: "...in the dispensation of the fulness of times (God) might gather together in one all things in Christ, both which are in heaven, and which are on earth..." (Ephesians 1.10), and touched on by Tennyson who looked for "one far-off divine event to which the whole creation moves" (In Memoriam, final verse), was wonderfully developed by the Jesuit palaeontologist Pierre Teilhard de Chardin (1881-1955), and endorsed by England's own Joseph Needham (1900-1994) who was president of the "Teilhard Centre for the Future of Man". (1 Cromwell Place, SW7 2JE).

Teilhard held that the evolutionary process had produced human beings and conscious thought, and that a collective mental evolution, in a "noosphere", would continue to an "omega-point" or final uniqueness of the Universe. He viewed human wisdom not merely as "seeing God from outside" as a telescope allows us to perceive the stars, but as being the actual process of divinisation itself...Science is an aspect of salvation! (Jn.8.32)

- - - - - - - - -

283

(Final quotation from Martin Counihan's essay in "Visions of Creation", Godsfield 1995, mentioned marginally on 26.9.)

2nd October. "Once More The Sheaves Are Gathered."

In the days before big "agribusiness" and supermarket food-shops had begun to stifle small farms and shops and replace the seasonal variation of goods on offer by an all-year-round availability of edibles, the local harvest was a major festival in agricultural communities. To this day the church festival (or its school alternative) and harvest supper takes place in a fair proportion of parishes; and it is a pretty safe bet that the hymns in church will include three favourites in the order: "Come ye thankful people, come" by H.Alford, "To thee O Lord our hearts we raise" by W.Dix who neatly ranges forward to the final "harvest of souls", and "We plough the fields and scatter" by M.Claudius. Fourth will be Milton's "Let us with a gladsome mind", or a variant on it, or a modern song.

The harvest supper in Thomas Hardy's much-loved novel "Far from the madding crowd" lacks a church service to match it, and the stated menu is 100% liquid with no matching food - an omission corrected by film-producers. The thrilling scene in which Gabriel Oak leaves the besotted roisterers, "in every conceivable attitude", to help Bathsheba cover the ricks of wheat and barley which faced ruin by the imminent thunderstorm, follows.

In the 1970s the divinity-mistress at the Fulham girls' comprehensive school where I was Head of Science wrote this beautiful hymn for assembly, to the tune "The Carnival is Over":

1. In the hard streets of the city
   Dreaming of the golden grain,
   Of the springtime and the summer
   And the harvest once again,
   Lord we thank you for our blessings;
   Let us take our daily bread,
   And make our harvest-offering
   So that others may be fed.

2. In the hard streets of the city
   Where there are no harvest-fields
   We thank you still our Father
   For the gifts that nature yields -
   For food and drink and clothing,
   For sun and wind and rain,
   For the winter, spring and summer
   And the harvest once again.

@ Ceres Squires
(pron. hard "C".

3rd October. MORE MILLENNIAL VERSES...   285

(unlike those of 5.5 these provide a serious celebration. They delineate some 2000 years of English church history, and may be sung to 'Thornbury' - 'Thy hand O God has guided', commencing with its first verse, with others interpolated later if a longer hymn is desired.)

Thy Prophets made a highway
For Thy triumphant Son.
By whose supreme oblation
The realm of Heav'n is won;
The Spirit sped Thy faithful
To die at Nero's court,
Ere some unknown evangel
The Truth to Britain brought.

Augustine came as Primate
To Canterbury's see,
With Cross and banners gleaming
In peaceful victory;
Then after Whitby's Synod
Saint Theodore went forth
To join the English bishops
With Celts from west and north.

Saint Alban hid a Christian
Who won him for the Church.
He wore that hunted priest's robes
When soldiers came to search.
For friend and Faith he suffer'd
As for their life he stood
And first endors'd in England
Thy covenant in blood.

Saint Bede the Church Historian
Was skill'd in word and song
And gave us John's great Gospel
In England's native tongue.
With joy was Wyclif's Bible
Transcribed and preach'd and heard,
Then Coverdale and Tyndale
Bestowed the printed Word.

Other verses may be added <u>ad lib</u>, there being no copyright! Northerners may wish for a Paulinus verse before that of the "apostolic succession" of Bible-translators (Bede, Wyclif, Tyndale, Coverdale); and Prayer-Book Society members may use one in honour of their author and editor-in-chief:

Paulinus met King Edwin
At banquet with his Thanes;
A sparrow flutter'd past them
Then out into the rains.
"Man's life is like that bird", said
An Elder, "Whence come <u>we</u>,
Where go? Let's heed this preacher.
He lights that mystery!"

Archbishop Thomas Cranmer
For many years complied,
Yet wrote our noble Prayer Book
By old King Henry's side;
But under Mary Tudor,
When Oxford flames leapt high,
He purged his life's confusions
And showed us how to die!

So far so good - the Church has documented the Deposit of Faith; but can we continue into the traumas of the modern world?

The Cross has always been a banner of triumph. Joy has always been the characteristic of Christianity. The miracle of the Resurrection has been to many Christians both a triumph and a power of salvation. One could trace in poetry, rude and rough, all the history of the triumph of the Resurrection; and although the history of the Christian Church fills one with shame and dismay, we must remember that only the history of prominent people and striking movements is written, but that the real history of the Christian Church is written in Christian homes.

(from "The New Life In Christ" - a Retreat Address by Geoffrey A. Studdert Kennedy.)

So:
Our Church down two millennia
Has earned dismay and shame;
Crusades and Inquisitions
Traduced God's Holy Name;

Yet deathless is her Triumph -
(Not most in fanes and domes) -
Her history is written
In countless Christian homes. <u>Now</u>:

I combine the verses contributed by Philip Reynolds and Rebecca Hodel to finish the processional hymn (see 20.10 foot.

4th October. Animals – An Ethical Overview.

This being my name-saint Francis of Assisi's day (though my given-name, unusually, is Frank not Francis), my topic chooses itself. What are the main animal questions of our day? There are the homely ones of care for one's animal-friends; of dog wardens; of spaying; and of hygiene. Here consensus rules.

There's the vegetarian and vegan challenge which has become more powerful in my lifetime because of the scarcely-credible acceptance of intensive rearing, especially of pigs and poultry. It is strange that so few people put their money where there minds are, and to seek "Freedom Food" products along with fairly-traded tea and coffee. Too often we leave our consciences at the door of the supermarket or grocery! We all should review our shopping-habits especially those formed before the sad development of crating and battery-raising. We can discriminate against meat, for example, by reviving the Friday Fast tradition; and we can enjoy vegetarian meals, at least occasionally even if we aren't in the vegetarian community that sets such a good example. Personally I see this as an open question; sheep for instance are brought into being for the market, and death comes to all in any event. Humane slaughtering is a paramount issue, however.

Animal experiments have, I think, been curtailed in recent years. Certainly those for luxury purposes like cosmetic-testing, for non-specific research, and for vague "purposes" should be banned. Dissection should not be compulsory in Biology examinations. In the controversial area of medical research there should at least be proportion between pain and gain. C.S. Lewis opposed all vivisection on the ground that it puts us on a slippery slope down to exploiting all creatures over which we have power, at the foot of which are outrages such as the Nazis' experiments on camp-prisoners. (See essay in "First and Last Things" (Fount 1985).)

Finally animals should not be killed for fun or humiliated for entertainment. For hunting with dogs see 19.8. Rotters no longer may kill otters. Genesis 1.26 on "dominion" gives a duty of care, not exploitative control. Animals give us pleasure and we can give them some in return. Those who say all animals are soulless, without notions of right and wrong, cannot have related to animals like some I've known. Dogs have given their lives for humans, as have humans for dogs. Keep things in proportion; DOG isn't spelt GOD. We frown on those who leave vast fortunes to pamper their pets, and on those who denounce cruelty to animals not children. But balance can rul

5th October. GREEN WITCHES AND DEAD CATS.   287

Further to the student-howlers noted on 16.8, my own favourite from 33 years at the chalkface, barring an accidental salacity which I demur to reproduce, came early in the day. I had discussed with an O-level Chemistry class at the Wigan further-education college the difference between elements, mixtures and compounds. (18.8 refers). I then set a homework to classify various materials under these headings. One answer read: "Meat is a mixture because it contains several separate substances such as blood, bone and grissole" - spelt thus, with a "g" in front of "rissole", a formed-meat-&-grain savoury now Americanised to "burger".

In August 1996 the <u>Guardian</u> reproduced from the <u>New Statesman</u> a collection of "howlers" including those which follow:

* Three kinds of blood-vessels are arteries, vanes & caterpillars.
* The moon is a planet, just like the earth only even deader.
* To collect fumes of sulphur, hold a deacon over a flame.
* The tides are a fight between the earth and the moon. All water tends towards the moon and nature absorbs a vacuum. I forget where the sun joins in the fight.
* Rhubarb is a kind of celery gone bloodshot.
* A magnet is something you find crawling over a dead cat.
* H_2O is hot water and CO_2 is cold water.
* Artificial insemination is when the farmer does it to the cow instead of the bull.
* A vacuum is a large empty space where the Pope lives.
* Mushrooms always grow in damp places so they look like umbrellas.
* The pistol of a flower is its only protection against insects.

To these I add from my own schooldays, in Geography tests:

* A prime meridian is a green witch.   (= Greenwich).
* There is a lot of disease in the tropics where there is a shortage of doctrine.   (= doctoring).

- - - - -

> Janice loves animals and can often be seen walking her west highland terrorist around the ward.
> *Morecambe Labour Party newsletter*

<u>Private Eye</u>, late April 2003.
I was parliamentary Labour candidate for Morecambe & Lonsdale 1958 (by-election), 1959 when we got a 2.6% swing our way when the nation went the other way to incur the Beeching axe on rail transport, & 1964. Unlucky -or was I?!

6th October.   Sweetie the Rat, and other Oddities.

The star of a new television series has been abducted. Sweetie the rat was stolen by burglars at the Gibson Group film production house in Wellington, New Zealand. Sweetie stars in the latest instalments of Mirror Mirror, a children's fantasy series. The rat had recently been depressed, a company spokeswoman said, adding: "Something like this could devastate her." AP - Wellington. (August 1997.)

Honorary Cat: A Cambridge college has found a way to get round a medieval statute without the cost of repeal. Feline fanatics at Queens' were enraged when a dog named Sprite was allowed to become honorary college cat. Despite the fact that a statute of 1595 bans dogs from the University, the Jack Russell belonging to bursar's secretary Cheryl Fison was so popular that the college awarded it honorary feline status... Just after the war, Trinity Hall deemed babies to be cats so wives of undergraduates could bring their offspring inside. Asked to comment, Sprite purred contentedly. (CAM, Lent 1999.)

"In examinations the foolish ask questions that the wise cannot answer." - Oscar Wilde.

Village Life: Neil Simmons was gratified when his mimicked hoots apparently brought a response from the owls in his garden at Stokeinteignhead, Devon. His neighbour Fred Cornes had the same notion. They found they had unwittingly been exchanging calls for a year. (Observer, 27.7.1997.)

Football Oddities: 30-1-1946 - Britain's Longest Match: cup-tie replay, Stockport County vs Doncaster Rovers, 2-2 after extra time, play-to-finish abandoned (dusk), $3\frac{3}{4}$ hours!

21-12-1957 - Charlton Athletic 7, Huddersfield Town 6. The away team led 5-1 after 52 minutes but with two minutes left Charlton had made it 6-5. Huddersfield equalised then lost!

17-11-1993 - "international" England vs San Marino started sensationally when mighty England found themselves a goal down after some 8 seconds. Recognising their "minnow" status San Marino kicked off eccentrically, not with a pass but with a long kick down the right wing. The England full-back who gained possession tapped the ball back gently to his goalkeeper. He hadn't noticed San Marino's winger Gualtiery's run along the touchline, enabling him to nip in, shoot, and score. Alas the game then reverted to expectations; England won 7-1.

Newspaper Correction: "Angus Dei made one of his rare devotional appearances in the Guardian...Music, yesterday." (20.x.6)

Oddities, continued.

The full inscriptions on the medallions (12.4) of Henry IX our last rightful hereditary Stuart King can be read thereon in the West Highland Museum, Fort William as follows:

Heads: HEN.IX.MAG.BRIT.FR.ET.HIB.REX.FID.DEF.CARD.EP.TUSC. (Henry 9 Great Britain France & Hibernia (=Scotland) King Defender of the Faith Cardinal Bishop of Tuscany.)

Tails: NON DESIDERIIS HOMINVM SED VOLVNTATE DEI (Not by men's wishes but by God's will.)

Revivals: The Biber tercentenary has popularised the fine music of Bach's forerunner (1644-1704). The "Rob Roy" overture of Berlioz, which fell flat at first performance, is most happy in harmony and melody, and deserves a place in concert programmes. Some tautening by a skilled composer who can work in Berlioz' style will yield a popular "favourite".

A "Brave Utterance": The dark commencement of the 21st century AD and the third Christian millennium, with warclouds and more than one nation deploying WMDs (weapons of mass destruction) prompted the presiding bishop Frank Griswold of the Anglican church in USA to say of the opulent West in December 2002: "The world has every right to loathe us, because they see us as greedy, self-interested and almost totally unconcerned about poverty, disease and suffering."

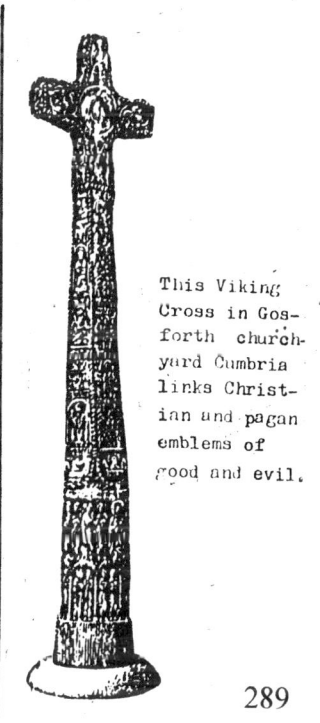

The banner of the Risca Lodge, South Wales Area, National Union of Mineworkers. (John Gorman Collection.) see 9.5.

This Viking Cross in Gosforth churchyard Cumbria links Christian and pagan emblems of good and evil.

7th October. "Bush Telegraph on Coincidences." (D.Tel,5.2.98)

* American presidents Abraham Lincoln and John Kennedy were both shot in the head on a Friday, in the presence of their wives. Both were shot by men who hid in warehouses. Lincoln's secretary, whose name was Kennedy, advised him not to go to the theatre. Kennedy's secretary, whose name was Lincoln, advised him not to go to Dallas. The assassins, John Wilkes Booth and Lee Harvey Oswald, were both in their twenties. Both were shot dead before they could be tried. Lincoln and Kennedy were both succeeded by men called Johnson.

* Albert and Betty Cheetham and Albert and Betty Rivers met recently in a Tunis hotel. The couples discovered that they not only shared Christian names, but that they had married on the same day in the same year. Both husbands had been in the coach building industry and both wives had worked for the post office. There are many examples of the phenomenon Carl Jung called "synchronicity".

* Among the books on the shelves of the <u>Titanic</u> was a novel entitled <u>The Wreck of the Titan</u> by Morgan Robinson. Written in 1898, the story involved a luxury Atlantic liner called the "Titan", which struck an iceberg and sank on her maiden voyage.

- - - - - - - -

8th October. The Passionate Faith of John Neale (see also 11.3).

For the consecration of St Augustine's, Canterbury, 29.6.1848:
"O Mother Church! arise and shine, for lo! thy light is come!
Awake, and give the blind their sight, teach praises to the dumb
Till all the faithful through the world, God's one elected host
Shall welcome the outpouring of a brighter Pentecost;   ball
And there shall be and thou shalt see, throughout this earthly /
One Church, one Faith, one Baptism, one God and Lord of all!"

And during the sad days of the 1866 Cattle Plague, when the poet was found one day on his knees in a Cheshire cowshed:
"All creation groans and travails; Thou O God shall hear its
For of man and all creation Thou alike art God alone.   groan;
Pity then Thy guileless creatures Who, not less, man's suffer-
For our sins it is they perish, let them profit by our prayer,
That our oxen, strong to labour, may not know nor fear decay;
That there be no more complaining and the plague have passed
                                                        away..."

(Then, "with deeper, tenderer pity", Neale prayed
"For the widow, for the orphan, for the helpless hopeless poor;
Helpless, hopeless, if Thou spare not of their basket and their
                                                         store.")

9th October.   F O R E B O D I N G S.   291

"The dark places of the earth are full of the habitations of cruelty" (Psalm 74.20, A.V.). This we know all too well; yet "forewarned is forearmed" - remember the old Irish faith of 18 March! - and Thomas Hardy wrote wisely when he declared: "If way to the Better there be, it exacts a full look at the Worst" (In Tenebris II). The American poet James Russell Lowell had written earlier (1844) about the USA's coming slavery crisis: "So the Evil's triumph sendeth, with a terror and a chill, / Under continent to continent, the sense of coming ill." He went on however to look to "the dim unknown" where "standeth God within the shadow, keeping watch above His own". That's a tough hope not shared by all. Can it be justified?

Lincoln dreamed of his assassination before it happened, and Morgan Robinson foretold the sinking of the Titanic. (7.10). Tennyson and Hardy sensed the coming of World War 1; the 1930s saw widespread anticipations of World War 2, among which the Japanese reduction of Nanking was a precursor that should not be forgotten; and the lamentable and avoidable "cold war" decades sapped countless minds with fear of nuclear annihilation.

A mountaineer avoids chasms; can the human race avoid abysms?! We can at least try! - Hear T.S.Eliot, Choruses from 'The Rock', X:

"The great snake lies ever half awake, at the bottom of the pit of the world, curled
In folds of himself until he awakens in hunger and moving his head to right and to left prepares for his hour to devour.
But the Mystery of Iniquity is a pit too deep for mortal eyes to plumb. Come
Ye out from among those who prize the serpent's golden eyes,
The worshippers, self-given sacrifice of the snake. Take
Your way and be separate.
Be not too curious of Good and Evil;
Seek not to count the future waves of Time;
But be satisfied that you have light
Enough to take your step and find your
                                    foothold."
-Likewise St Peter in Chapter 5 of his first
Epistle (verses 8-9a):- "Be sober, be vigilant;
because your adversary the devil, as a roaring lion, walketh
about, seeking whom he may devour: Whom resist, stedfast in
                                            the faith..."

This passage is read daily during the late evening "Compline".

10th October.   **R E C O V E R Y.**

T.S. Eliot indulged himself in obscurity at times, and I prefer poets who make their meaning clear. Eliot, in <u>The Rock</u> (written for an interwar London pageant) wrote simply, as in yesterday's passage (9.10), and also in canto II:

"Of all that was done in the past, you eat the fruit, rotten or ripe...
For every ill deed in the past we suffer the consequence:
For sloth, for avarice, gluttony, neglect of the Word of GOD,
For pride, for lechery, treachery, for every act of sin.
And of all that was done that was good, you have the inheritance.
For good and ill deeds belong to a man alone, when he stands alone on the other side of death,
But here on earth you have the reward of the good and ill that was done by those that have gone before you.
And all that is ill you may repair if you walk together in humble repentance, expiating the sins of your fathers;
And all that was good you must fight to keep with hearts as devoted as those of your fathers who fought to gain it.
The Church must be forever building, for it is forever decaying within and attacked from without;.
For this is the law of life; and you must remember that while there is time of prosperity
The people will neglect the Temple, and in time of adversity they will decry it.

What life have you if you have not life together?
There is no life that is not in community,
And no community not lived in praise of GOD.
Even the anchorite who meditates alone,
For whom the days and nights repeat the praise of GOD,
Prays for the Church, the Body of Christ incarnate.
And now you live dispersed on ribbon roads,
And no man knows or cares who is his neighbour
Unless his neighbour makes too much disturbance,
But all dash to and fro in motor cars,

Familiar with the roads and settled nowhere.
Nor does the family even move about together,
But every son would have his motor cycle,
And daughters ride away on casual pillions.

Much to cast down, much to build, much to restore;
Let the work not delay, time and the arm not waste;
Let the clay be dug from the pit, let the saw cut the stone,
Let the fire not be quenched in the forge.

John Ruskin

Among Britain's greatest Victorians was Ruskin who in later life established craft-industries in the English Lake District. In his pot-pourri of letters <u>Fors Clavigera</u> (The Angel of Destiny) he writes about the Advent prayer for "grace... to put upon us the armour of light". He remarks that the <u>industry</u> of light alone is not enough for there are evil forces around - "the powers of ill" mentioned near the end of Tennyson's 2nd Locksley Hall poem. (see 1 Peter 5.8+, 12 Oct.)

11th October. "The (Georgian) Magistrate's Pocket-Book"; or, an epitome of the duties and practice of a Justice of the Peace, by Wm Robinson, Esq., Ll.D. (Charles Hunter, 1825).

- - - - - - -

This fascinating work, the pre-industrial forerunner of our "Stone's Justices' Manual", provides a late lok at feudal England before democracy and the vote were won. The J.P. was a figure to be respected and even feared for his autocratic power in his community. By Robinson's time the enclosure of common land had spawned a poverty-stricken urban proletariat, held down not by chattel-slavery but by Master-and-Servant law:

Disputes between Masters and Servants, in Husbandry etc. On complaint on oath, by any master, mistress, or employer, against any such servant, artificer, &c., for any misdemeanour, miscarriage, or ill-behaviour in his service, 1 Justice may hear, examine, and determine the same, and issue his warrant to apprehene such servant, &c. and punish the offender by commitment to the House of Correction there to be corrected (that is, whipped, by 1 Geo. 4 c.57), and kept to hard labour for (not exceeding) one calendar month; or otherwise by abating part of his wages, or by discharging him from his service (20 Geo. 2 c. 19 ss 2,5).

Swearing. ...forfeit as follows, viz. as day labourer, common soldier, sailor or seaman, 1 shilling; every other person below the degree of a gentleman, 2s; every person of or above..5s; ... to the poor (19 Geo. 2 c.21 ss1,10). A Justice of the Peace, omitting his duty, Pen. 5£, Half to the poor, H. to him that will sue in any court of record. (Ibid. s6).

Apples and Pears. Selling or buying apples or pears by any other measure than a round measure, $18\frac{1}{2}$ inches diameter within the hoop, and 8 inches deep (called the water measure), Pen. 10s. H. to the informer, H. to the poor (1 Anne st.1 c15 s 1).

Cattle. Wantonly and cruelly beating, abusing, or ill-treating cattle, Pen. not exceeding 5£ nor less than 10s to the king ...(3 Geo.4 c.71 ss 1,2).

Women. The indecent and immoral practice of selling a wife is a misdemeanour. Whipping women convicted of offences is prohibited...imprisonment and hard labour in the Common Gaol or House of Correction not exceeding six nor less than one month, or solitary confinement, not exceeding seven days at any one time, shall be adjudged in lieu thereof...(1 Geo. 4 c.57 ss.2,3).

- - - - - - -

(Note the great local discretion of J.Ps, and the easing of harshness when George 4 acceded. Schoolgirls were legally beaten to nearly the end of 20th century, as were some female naval cadets at least until the 1950s - a little-known fact.)

<u>12th October.</u>   "<u>The Loving Eye And Patient Hand</u>
            <u>Shall Work With Joy And Bless The Land.</u>"

So reads the inscription over Keswick's Primavera Restaurant, in the building by the River Greta which housed from 1894 to 1984 the "Keswick School of Industrial Arts" which owed much for its inspiration to Canon and Mrs Rawnsley. The Canon was a long-serving vicar of Crosthwaite, nicknamed "The most active volcano in Europe"; and the founder of the National Trust.

John Ruskin (studied on 23, 24 & 28.1) lived at Brantwood, Coniston in later life, and established in Lakeland a Ruskin Lace & Linen Industry, some products of which are on show in that village's museum. Having argued against capitalism to the point of damaging his health in clashes with industrialists, he devoted himself to direct labour (e.g. roadwork at Oxford) and to romantic ventures like his Guild of St George. The village museum displays the text - perhaps his - "Hundreds of people can talk for one who can think, but thousands can think for one who can see."

The glory of Keswick and Lakeland is in Variety - always something new to see! In Summer 1951 I led parties of 20 or so from the CHA (Co-operative Holidays Association) hostel in Borrowdale for days in the high fells. At 6pm we would find ourselves at Buttermere Head too tired to want to walk the Honister Pass home; and would ring for three taxis at 17s 6d each (2/6 per head). But we had to get out and walk the steep 1-in-4 bit which the cars could not manage! Transport has changed since then, when buses were far more primitive, though more decorous, than today's. They had succeeded the opentopped chars-à-bancs, with folding covers, of the 1920s. For pictures see Irvine Hunt's "Lakeland Transport" (Rusland, Penrith 1978)

(Charsabancs? - the public would never accept this as the correct plural of the ineptest importation in the history of our tongue, or that charabancs was a singular noun (French: car with benches). I recall my primary teacher agreeing with her class that "sharrer" wasn't so silly!)

CAMP COFFEE

You care to hear so much of my views —

You will think how miserable I felt when I woke up at half-past 3 this morning and thinking — discovered I had made a mistake in the date — I'm so awfully sorry I can't think how it happened ——— that I have been going about this week in a way unusual to me and so lost a day — I'm so dreadfully sorry but nothing can alter

with my dearest love
Kate

Kate Greenaway, *Letter to Ruskin*

13th October.   Lake Poets for the 21st Century.

In autumn 1994 I received a postcard from a friend who was in a café at Pooley Bridge on lake Ullswater. He wrote:

Absolutely Soaked.

Tent awash, mud reigns,
Rain; stair-rodding.
Grass yellow, sky grey.
Walking limited, lakes full.
Otherwise - superb. A.H.G.

Then at the Wordsworth Winter-School in February 2002 we had the pleasure of welcoming two Argentinian ladies who brought down our average age very considerably. These 30-year-olds worked as teachers of English in their Spanish-speaking homeland; were in love with our national culture as vested in Shakespeare, Wordsworth and the Celtic "fringe"; and enjoyed singing our traditional songs (6.7 &c.) which they knew far better than most of us offshore-islanders. I wrote for them:

Two teacheress-girls from Rosario,
In Grasmere for winter safario,
  Sang tunefully-vocal
  Airs Celtic and local;
Do you think we could coax them to tarry? - No!

Hope ("Angie" Cifré.)

The sun is shining up in the sky Around me,
Green, red and golden images And crystal clear sounds.
A dove gently across the sky, Sweet giggles from the kids
In the playground, And the murmur of a stream.
Walking along a winding path, What's my guiding light?
My friend's helping hands, My beloved's smile.
Hope...I step forth into your paradise;
Soon peace will fill our hearts, Bliss will touch our souls.
I once wondered..."Where's Hope?"
"She" seemed to be out for a while then,
And now I believe "She" is back in my life.

(Above - Coledale Inn 017687.78272;
Top - Keswick Theatre 017687.74411)

The Shrine (Silvia Duarte.)

Mist-enshrouded lies a shrine of unruffled mossy stone whipped by the wind, lashed by the rain. It endures still, the ghostly shape of an aching soul in search of comfort will approach to worship in the midst of its own darkness till the impending eventide sheds its silence.

295

14th October. Grand Old Man of British Politics.

The St Deiniol's Library in Hawarden, North Wales, houses a quarter of a million books, and was founded by his children in memory of William Ewart Gladstone (1809-98), who was an M.P. for nearly all the time from 1833 to 1896, and four times Prime Minister. Roy Jenkins' fine biography (Macmillan 1995) portrays Gladstone's excessive energy, tree-felling, 'rescue' work among prostitutes, verbose oratory, workoholism and passion for books. St Deiniol's expands his own large library, and welcomes visitors 10 - 4 except Sundays to its free exhibition. Ring 01244.532350 for terms for residential or other use of the library itself; no one is barred for lack of funds.

Gladstone's attempts to solve the problems of Ireland were unmatched till Mo Mowlam and the 1998 Good Friday Agreement. He veered between conciliation and coercion of nationalists, and an episode of 1881 led a balladeer to declare that
"It was the tyrant Gladstone and he said unto himself,
I never will be easy till Parnell is on the shelf,
So make the warrant out in haste / And take it by the mail,
And we'll clap the pride of Erin's isle / Into cold Kilmainham jail."
(For the meteoric career of the spellbinding Irish patriot see "Parnell & the Englishwoman" (H. Leonard, Penguin 1991).

---

296 Karen Maloney tells of meeting a charming Irish missionary nun in Goa in 2003, who had been a schoolgirl in a strict convent school when the church authorities failed to prevent malpractices by those in power. The Victorian Sr Mary Benedict would insist, contrary to the balladeer and general use, that the first syllable of Parnell's name be accented; whereupon a poetess wrote naughtily that "Our pronounc'd Irish Nationalist yarn'll / Treat matters less ghostly than carnal. / Said he, 'Mrs O'Shea / And I had it away - / Or my name isn't Charles Stewart Parnell!" The ditty was found circulating in school; and when the authoress with wise modesty omitted to claim it was hers, the Sister caned all the girls in the class, thus ensuring that the limerick was remembered, to appear now!

15th October. Clash of Eminent Victorians, (among whom Gladstone and Tennyson were chief.)

There was a bond of close friendship between politician and poet all their lives, which was triggered by their warm affection for Arthur Hallam whom Gladstone knew at Eton College and Tennyson at Cambridge University prior to Hallam's early death which prompted the famous In Memoriam sequence of poems. The growing divergence of views on the Irish question and other issues in later life did not destroy their friendship, even when the Poet Laureate aimed at the Prime Minister some lines urging negotiation with the Opposition over the Redistribution and Franchise Bills: "Steersman, be not precipitate in thine act..." One wonders how Attlee would have dealt with unsolicited political advice from say T.S. Eliot.

In September 1883 Tennyson joined Gladstone and a large party for the cruise on the "Pembroke Castle" up the west coast to Kirkwall and thence across the North Sea to Denmark. The poet's grandson and biographer writes that to the two girls in the party, Mary Gladstone and Laura Tennant (20 or so) "the whole experience was like a play, and the old poet threw himself heart and soul into the romance and fun of it." When Laura said to Gladstone's son as they looked at snowcapped Scafell "Isn't it lovely", a deep voice behind them said "Yes, and cold like some women I know"; and Tennyson stalked silently around them on deck "in his black sombrero and long cloak".

But the explosive "Locksley Hall Sixty Years After" drew a pained response from Gladstone, who _did_ accept the need to be reminded that his government hadn't purged the slums (Have we yet?). He was however proud of the social progress gained, and (with a "middle-classy" perspective) didn't want the Queen's jubilee marring by "tragic tones". In fact Tennyson, with a poet's vision exceeding the politicians', feared a "mighty wave of evil" ahead. (World War 1 alas). He didn't believe in the inevitability of human progress; and he held correctly that "The truth is the wave advances and recedes".

Writing in "The Bookman" magazine soon after Tennyson's death in 1892, his fellow-poet W.B. Yeats offered his fine general verdict, to the effect that Victoria's laureate had maintained his poetic standard and had become a greater and deeper man as the years had passed. No longer basing his hopes on political skills or technical advance, he had grasped that it _is the health of hearts_ that is paramount.

16th October. "Return To The Centre".

Professor Stephen Hawking asks (15.9) whether the universe needs a Creator..."and who created him?" Well, every river needs a Source; and the poet Christopher Smart's "Song to David" exults resplendently with the verse:

> "He sang of God - the mighty source
> Of all things - the stupendous force
> On which all strength depends;
> From whose right arm, beneath whose eyes,
> All period, power, and enterprise
> Commences, reigns and ends."

The five arguments for the existence, or rather the reality of God which Aquinas proposed (see 2.4) fail to command universal acceptance and are best seen as indications; indeed a mystic writer claimed that "by love He can be gotten and holden, but by thought never" ("The Cloud of Unknowing.")

I remember the Observer headline which I read in bed on St Patrick's Day 1963 (not being at mass that Sunday morning in that heady year, being no more than an 83% regular!) It read "Our Image of God must go", which was the paper's addition to an article in which the then bishop of Woolwich, John Robinson, introduced his forthcoming controversial book "Honest to God". Of course it must, for we see as through a glass darkly; but this fact didn't avert furious controversy. For myself I prefer the Pelican paperback "The Shaking of the Foundations" by Paul Tillich, establishing the old understanding that God isn't a giant-size irascible paterfamilias but is the "Ground of all being" within and beyond us and all things (Isaiah 57.15).

Dom Bede Griffiths was the Roman Catholic Prior of Farnborough Abbey until he went to India in 1955 to live in ashrams which were Christian communities adapted to Hindu ways. His fine book "Return to the Centre" (Collins 1976) has this to say concerning the Sacred Mystery: "What is the true Self ...the true Centre of man's being? Is it the ego, making itself independent, seeking to be master of the world, or is there an 'I' beyond this, a deeper Centre of personal being, which is grounded in the Truth, which is one with the universal Self, the Law of the universe? This is the great discovery of Indian thought, the discovery of the Self, the Atman, the Ground of personal being, which is one with the Brahman, the Ground of universal being. It is not reached by thought; on the contrary, it is only reached by transcending thought. Reason, like the self   (continues opposite.

16.10 conclusion.

of which it is the faculty, has to transcend itself. As long as it remains turned towards the senses, to the material world, it will always remain defective, unable to discover the Truth. But the moment it turns inwards to its Source and knows itself in its Ground by a pure intuition, then it knows the truth of its own being and the being of the world, and then it becomes really free. 'You will know the truth, and the truth will make you free.' This is redemption, to be set free from the senses and the material world and to discover their Ground and Source in the Self, which is the Word of God within. The Fall of Man is the fall from this Ground, this Centre of freedom and immortality, into subjection to the senses and this material world, and Reason is the serpent. Reason can either be subject to the eternal Law, the universal Reason, and then it becomes Wisdom, it knows the Self, or it can seek to be the master of the world, and then it becomes demonic. It is the demon of the modern world. In every generation the Fall of Man is repeated, but never, perhaps, on a wider scale than today.

How then to recover from the Fall, how to return to the Centre? This is the problem of the modern world, but it has been the problem of the world from the beginning. Every ancient culture, as Mircea Eliade has shown, built its life round such a Centre. It might be a building, a temple, a city, or simply the home; it might be a place - a mountain, a grove, a burial ground; or it might be a person - a priest or king or seer. But always it was a point where contact could be made with the Source of being. It was a point where heaven and earth converge, where human life is open to the infinite Transcendence. This was the essential thing, to keep contact with the Transcendent, so that human life did not become closed on itself. But the modern world has removed every such point of contact. Everything has become profane, that is, outside the sphere of the holy. Temple and palace, priest and king, sacred grove and mountain, all must be abolished, so that the world of nature and the world of man alike may be emptied of a transcendent significance, of any ultimate meaning. No wonder that there is a rebellion among the young against this drab, one-dimensional world. Young people now come to India from the West, seeking to recover the sense of the sacred, the inner meaning of life, which has been lost in the West. But India too is losing it rapidly. Wherever modern civilization spreads, all holiness, all sense of the sacred, all awareness of a transcendent Reality disappears. This is just another Fall of Man.

But, thank God, there are still sacred places in India - sacred mountains and caves, sacred rivers and trees and plants and animals, sacred places where people go...

temples where the old sacred rites continue." So have we in Britain even though "Modern science and technology are the fruit of the tree of the knowledge of good and evil..Not evil in themselves..they become evil when..separated from wisdom. Science is the lowest form of knowledge, (that) of the material world through the discursive reason. Philosophy is above science, because it goes beyond the material world..but it is still confined to discursive reason. Theology is above philosophy..open to transcendent reality, but its methods are still those of science and philosophy. Only Wisdom can transcend Reason and know the Truth..intuitively..in its Ground... science when separated from wisdom is always a knowledge of good and evil (and) brings a corresponding evil in its train.. Medicine..brings with it the disaster of overpopulation" and physical science the Bomb and environmental pollution. This is because they have developed without relation to heaven - to the trancendent Reality, Law, Tao (pron. 'dow') which keeps heaven and earth in harmony. Humanity to survive needs a _metanoia_, a total change of heart, dethroning that science which imprisons us in the narrow world of the conscious mind.

Griffiths' diction is so exact that summary is difficult; but his is the Psalmist's prayer (85.6): "Wilt Thou not turn again and quicken us that Thy people may rejoice in Thee?" He died in 1993 following his major contribution to harmony of religion, whereby Christians can say "There are many Divine Revealers; Jesus came as Holy Redeemer."

299

17th October. <u>MUSIC BUSINESS.</u>

I recently took a package containing Schubert's "Death and the Maiden" string quartet, orchestrated by Mahler and recorded on CD (compact disc), to post as a gift. The lady behind the counter weighed it, sold me the stamps, and asked "Is it valuable?" My reply left her smiling though speechless: "Commercially no, it's a second-hand CD fetching £1, or £2 at the most; spiritually it's priceless, for it's a recording of one of the world's finest pieces of chamber music, by Schubert."

In these days of a vast industry in commercial "pop-music" it is salutary to recall that Schubert's string quintet which he completed during the last few months of his short life, and which is honoured as a supreme masterpiece of chamber music for a handful of performers, perhaps unsurpassed, perhaps only equalled by the mature Beethoven's last quartets, lay gathering dust for two decades on his publisher's shelf until the minor composer Diabelli found it there and pushed the firm to print it. Schubert himself died in poverty.

Footnote on Brahms (21-23.8): A BBC Radio 3 "Discovering Music" programme featuring his Academic Festival Overture mused on why he chose this pot-pourri of student songs for the "Full Monty" scoring with the largest orchestra he ever required. I think that the generally-formidable composer was happily enjoying a light-hearted field-day and worked things up to a fine climax just for fun; and what better reason? On another occasion a friend, visiting the composer for lunch, was asked by the home-help to wait since the master was working. A few minutes later came the noise of a dog barking in the study. Then a genial Brahms came out to greet his friend, who managed to peep into the work-room. There was no dog.

— — — — — — —

<u>18th October.</u> Hoping there's a St Luke's Summer to enjoy on and around this feast-day before the greys of Halloween set in, here's <u>AN APPEAL TO CATS IN THE BUSINESS OF LOVE</u>, by Thos. Flatman, 1637-88; line 4 altered, 5 to 8 omitted.

— — — — — — —

Ye cats that at midnight spit love at each other,
Who best feel the pangs of a passionate lover,
I appeal to your scratches and your tattered fur
To prove that love's business is more than to purr.
  Men ride many miles, Cats tread many tiles,
  Both hazard their necks in the fray;
  Only cats when they fall From a house or a wall
  Keep their feet, mount their tails, and away!

19th October. Mists and Mellow Fruitfulness.

John Keats' celebratory "Ode to Autumn" employs the above phrase in its first line. His bright "Ode on the Poets" alas is less well known, for it proclaims their "priestly" role in lighthearted phrases of a fantasy-Heaven "Where the daisies are rose-scented, And the rose herself has got Perfume which on earth is not..." I like its final quatrain:

> Bards of Passion and of Mirth
> Ye have left your souls on earth!
> Ye have souls in heaven too,
> Double-lived in regions new!

Arthur O'Shaughnessy's ode "The Music-makers" concurs and adds a proclamation of how the saving word spreads "soul by soul and silently":

> They had no vision amazing
> Of the goodly house they are raising;
> They had no divine foreshowing
> Of the land to which they are going:
>
> But on one man's soul it hath broken,
> A light that doth not depart;
> And his look, or a word he hath spoken,
> Wrought flame in another man's heart.

Percy Shelley could be very polemic; the Masque which he wrote after the massacre of workers at Peterloo, Manchester in 1819 urges the oppressed "proles" to unite non-violently:

"Rise like Lions after slumber / In unvanquishable number" - but see Paul Foot's "Red Shelley" (1980, ch .6) for Reform vs Revolt.

Two pregnant verses from Edward Fitzgerald's version of "The Rubáiyát of Omar Khayyám of Naishápúr":

> Oh, Thou, who Man of baser Earth didst make,
> And who with Eden didst devise the Snake;
> For all the Sin wherewith the Face of Man
> Is blacken'd, Man's Forgiveness give - and take!
>
> The Ball no Question makes of Ayes and Noes,
> But Right or Left as strikes the Player goes;
> And He that toss'd Thee down into the Field,
> He knows about it all - HE knows - HE knows!

A verse from a 15th or 16th century popular song, which was used by several composers in their Masses, was poignant too:

> Western wind, when wilt thou blow,
> The small rain down can rain?
> Christ, if my love were in my arms,
> And I in my bed again!

- - - - - - - -

So (Keats again): "Souls of poets dead and gone, What Elysium have ye known? - Happy field or mossy cavern - choicer than the Mermaid Tavern?"

20th October. "McManus's Law." 302

Alas great extremes of riches and poverty exist in today's England, all attempts to lessen which have foundered on the rocks of what seems a permanent range of human personalities.

My Law notes that a powerful moneyed Establishment culls the people's wealth every 200 years or so:

```
1066   -  Norman Conquest.
1381   -  Poll-tax (triggered by cost of war with France.)
1536+  -  Dissolution of the Monasteries.
1760+  -  Enclosure Acts, depopulating rural common-land.)
1980+  -  Thatcherite trawls and privatisations.
```

Incidentally the name McManus is widespread in the Irish counties of Fermanagh and Roscommon, as branches of the Maguire and O'Connor ascendancies there. It should be Mac-Maghnuis or MacMagnus, where Magnus (Latin: great) comes from the Nordic saint of that name, who is the dedicatee of Kirkwall, Orkney's lovely cathedral. Magnus is in turn thought to be a diminutive of Charlemagne (French emperor).

(I came, I saw, I conquered-Caesar)

(from 3.10 - conclusion of millenary hymn.)

And now the torch of mission
Has passed into our hands,
With confident compassion
Help us fulfil thy plans;
As clothed in God's whole armour
We bear the Spirit's sword,
Women and men all witness:-
One Church, one Faith, one Lord.

We look ahead in gladness,
Strengthened in ministry,
United in the blessing
Of Holy Trinity;
So with the saints in glory
We hymn thy love outpoured,
In word and deed proclaiming
One Church, one Faith, one Lord.

21st October. "Nisi Dominus Custodierit Civitate."

Latin was the universal Western language of the Middle Ages, and it is a pity that its elegance is largely lost from today's schools – though its difficulty made it a mixed blessing and indeed a source of boredom and misery to many pupils. Many Victorian towns and cities used it for their mottos; the text above from Psalm 127 (R.C. 126) vs.1 is the Halifax choice (28.4) and appears in translation on the arches in Leeds Town Hall:

"Except the Lord build the house they labour in vain that build it; Except the Lord keep the city the watchman waketh but in vain."

This Leeds hall (28.4 also) is one of the most ornate masterpieces of Northern confidence. The stage is backed by a huge organ with pipes finish- in white but decorated in blue and orange, and sur- mounted by a Yorkshire Rose "Window", albeit not transparent, in similar colours. Around the walls is a miscellany of unconnected slogans:

Leeds Town Hall.

```
LEEDS INTERNATIONAL CONCERT SEASON
            1996/97
        BBC PHILHARMONIC
SAT 12TH OCT/96  7.30PM
£12.00  AREA    LEEDS TOWN HALL
ROW 7        SEAT  30

LEEDS INTERNATIONAL CONCERT SEASON
            1996/97

        BBC PHILHARMONIC
SAT 12TH OCT/96
      7.30PM
     LEEDS TOWN HALL
£12.00 inc. VAT    AREA
ROW  7      SEAT   30
   NO REFUNDS OR RETURNS
```

Honesty is the best policy.	Trial by jury.
Weave truth with trust.	Goodwill towards men.
Industry overcomes all things.	Deo regi patriae.
In union is strength.	Magna Charta.
Auspicium melioris aevi.	Forward.
God in the highest.	Labor omnia vincit.

303

The reader may care to devise six texts for the 21st century. to replace those thought weak. For my suggestions, and for translations of the Latin ones above, please see **25** October.

Fort William's old railway-station beside Loch Linnhe (pron. 'Lin') – alas demolished after the steam era to make way for a necessary ring-road.

22nd October. Thornley's Sorrow and Pride. (A saga of coal.)

Thornley village lies 5 miles east of Durham city and a little further north of Sedgefield. Its pit was sunk in 1834 and closed in 1970 although still workable, the steel industry opting then for Australian coal. Seemingly desolate through the loss of shops and pubs too, there remains a vibrant spirit worthy of the place where the Durham Miners' Association began.

John Gully who founded the mine was a "self-made" venturer and M.P. for Pontefract. He used Cornish sinkers, German overseers, and a local builder who ran up limestone hovels for the "green labour" - farmworkers driven from the land by enclosures, etc. The dirt-floored houses had but a small pantry and a single room 15ft. by 12, with ash-heap sanitation and water sold from a cart at 1d a bucket.

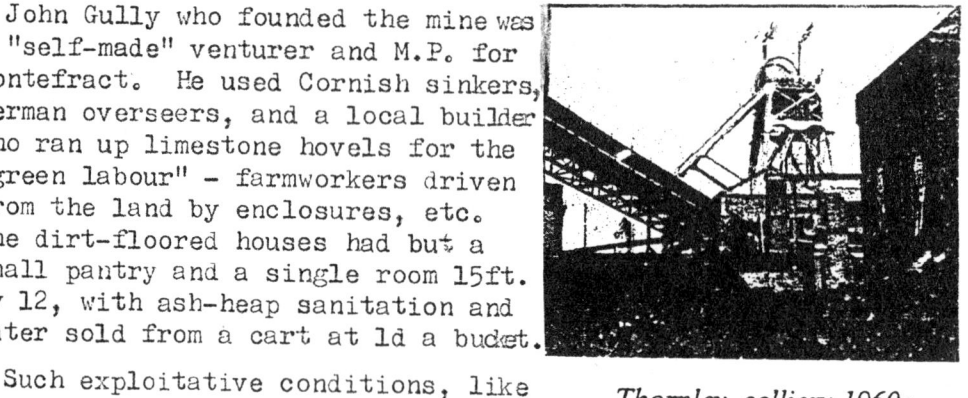

Thornley colliery 1960s

Such exploitative conditions, like those in the pit, need remembering since uncomfortably similar ones still exist in the Third World, with ourselves the remote exploiters via the money-system and its impersonal workings. As Studdert Kennedy warned (Lies, H&S 1919); "If the man of superior abilities is not a public servant he is a parasite, and more unworthy of his manhood than an ignorant and drunken pauper. If he uses his ability to serve himself at the expense of his fellow-men, to get on and get over them, his success is the measure of his failure. He is like those enormous bloated flies that buzz round the dead on a battlefield." Strong words, and it may be kinder to wonder what defect of psychology leads people to seek more wealth than they can use whilst Lazarus starves at the gate. Go to Nantyglo in the younger South Wales coalfield and see the towers erected by the coalowner to keep the pitfolk who made him rich out of his grounds!

In 1842 a new law stopped women and young children working below ground in the mines.

23rd October. ## *Shades of the Prison House!*

With Irish immigrants and old Durham families joining the Thornley workforce, an explosive situation developed and was detonated in 1837 when Gully appointed Richard Heckles, a noted mining engineer and opponent of organised labour, as pit manager. The Chartist cause, parliamentary democracy, became linked with that of working conditions, leading to a Thornley riot in 1839 which was pacified by the appearance of the military. But the "Bond System" (29.6) tied miners to their pit for a year under a contract with strict legal provisions, so that they were little more than wage-slaves. Heckles enforced it dictatorially at Thornley, at the same time stubbornly breaking the law himself by refusing to have the pit's weighing-machine tested and stamped by the Government.

In 1842 the Thornley miners' union helped set up a N.E. Miners' Association, which engaged William Prowting Roberts as lawyer. Then on 24 November 1843 the Thornley men struck against unfair management. Heckles fined each miner 2s. 6d., then invoked the Master and Servant Act when the strike continued. Warrants for 68 arrests were issued, and Durham magistrates heard the case. First in the dock was John Cookson: "A man cannot get a living if the bond is carried out in its strictness; if a man is fined for a quart of splint" (dark stone in his coaltub). The Bench applied the letter of the law and jailed the men for six weeks; but they had scorned Roberts' case that the unstamped machine subverted the bond, and the lawyer obtained a habeas corpus writ from higher authority in London, and had the men released.

THORNLEY COLLIERY.

£10. REWARD.

WHEREAS, on the Night of Monday, the 12th Instant, a serious Riot took place in the Village of Thornley; when the Doors and Windows of the Houses of several of the Men who have resumed their work at the Thornley Colliery were broken with large Stones, and two Guns were fired at the Door of Stephen Bones, and one at the Door of William Craddock, both Men had been working Coals on that Day.

Notice is hereby Given,

That the above Reward will be paid, by the Thornley Coal Company, to any Person who will give such Information as will lead to the Conviction of any one or more of the Parties concerned in the breaking of the Doors and Windows, or firing the Guns.

NIXON AND BRIGNAL, PRINTERS, DURHAM.

Clashes occurred elsewhere in the coalfield, e.g. at Silksworth in 1891 when Lord Londonderry had 106 families of striking miners evicted. But the UK needed coal, so force could not be overplayed! And happily the old Thornley banner, which led the first Gala in 1872, has been replicated in the Miners' Hall in the village that helped create the NUM. The new banner was paraded at the 119th Durham Miners' Gala on 12.7.2003, blessed in the cathedral before Tony Benn's talk, & borne out to Blaydon Races.

24th October.   Horrific Perils and Hairsbreadth Escapes.

What is it in the human psyche that prompts the production and enjoyment of desperate situations? How tantalising for Tantalus in Greek mythology, for example, to be in the situation described in Book XI of Homer's "Odyssey" (tr. Pope):

> "There Tantalus along the Stygian bounds
> Pours out deep groans; (with groans all hell resounds)
> Ev'n in the circling floods refreshment craves,
> And pines with thirst amidst a sea of waves;
> When to the water he his lip applies,
> Back from his lip the treach'rous water flies.
> Above, beneath, around his hapless head,
> Trees of all kinds delicious fruitage spread...
> The fruit he strives to seize; but blasts arise,
> Toss it on high, and whirl it to the skies!"

Some consolation was offered to this king, banished to Hades for lèse-majesté against the gods, when Orpheus passed through with his golden lyre, seeking his lost wife Eurydice. Others in the mythology suffered comparably dire fates - Danaus' daughters who had stabbed their husbands to death on their wedding-nights were doomed to fill a sieve with water; and Sisyphus had to roll a heavy stone uphill that was always slipping down again.

Prometheus, chained to an icy rock for thirty years till he was rescued by Hercules, had his liver torn out daily by an eagle. With no transplants available, he drew Shelley's eulogy:

> "To suffer woes which Hope thinks infinite;
> To forgive wrongs darker than death or night;
> To defy Power, which seems omnipotent;
> To love and bear; to hope till Hope creates
> From its own wreck the thing it contemplates.
> Neither to change, nor flatter, nor repent;
> This, like thy glory, Titan, is to be
> Good, great and joyous, beautiful and free;
> This is alone Life, Joy, Empire, and Victory."

Seven young Athenians had to be sent to Crete every nine years to be delivered to the Minotaur to placate King Minos. And poor Andromeda was chained to a rock as sacrifice to stay a sea-monster from ravaging her father's kingdom; whereupon Perseus flew in on his winged horse Pegasus to slay it by showing it the Gorgon's head - Burne-Jones' swordwork in his famous painting, seen in gouache in Southampton art-gallery and in oils at Strasbourg, enhances the drama. Perseus married the girl, and now they look down from the starry heavens to guide our mariners!

25th October.   **Taciturn Tales.**

No British Prime Minister has been further away from the agenda of tonguesters or spin-doctors than Clement Attlee (1945-51; see 18.7), who was stated never to use one word when none would do. At the fiftieth birthday party of the celibate bachelor Bishop Mervyn Stockwood, unfairly nicknamed "Merv the perv", there was a lively discussion on John Robinson's controversial book "Honest to God" (16.10). The retired Attlee sitting in a corner said tersely "Never read the book." On another occasion a young canvasser for Labour at a council election failed to recognise the former Prime Minister and asked if he was a supporter. Getting the answer "Yes", he followed instructions and said would he like to join the Party. "Already a member" was the reply. Attlee had his faults, over Ireland and nuclear weapons, but was benign and sincere, and not above writing his own comic "epitaph" (see 29.12):

Some said he was never a starter,
There were many who thought themselves smarter;
But he ended PM,
CH and OM,
An Earl, and a Knight of the Garter.

Answers 21.10 then suggestions: Portent of better times, Ruled by God for our land, Labour conquers all; Bach Beethoven Brahms, Words end - music begins, Peace and Plenty, Love.

Letters to the departed can raise smiles among us who linger. There was one to Mr J.S. Bach, BBC, London complimenting him on his music; and in 1970 a letter reached Canterbury some 8 centuries late, addressed to one T.A. Becket, Esq. Then in 1996 the German publishers Bertlesmann wrote to Thomas Hardy at Dorchester Library asking his opinion on computers in libraries. The librarian said Geography's OK, History's haywire.

More dubious is the tale of René Descartes' New Year Party in Paris, to which Isaac Newton and his mother were invited. The evening flew merrily with good wine, gay dances, and cheery music; but alas young Isaac cast hungry eyes on the refreshments on the side-table, and moved towards them when midnight had struck. His mother, wishing to avoid a scene in the hush that had descended, caught his arm and scribbled him a note which read "I think they're for 1 am." Finding this next morning, Descartes misread it as "I think there-fore I am", pondered its message, and based his philosophical work on it.

Finally it is said that an O-level European History examination had the question "Write briefly on 5 of the following: Napoleon, Haynau, Garibaldi, Pio Nono, Bismarck..." A candidate responded "Pio Nono was Pope Pius IX, who gained that nickname because when a railway station in Vatican City was projected, he threw up his hands in horror and cried "NO, NO!" (Actually a previous pope had vetoed the trains.)

26th October.   "Cry, The Beloved Country."

Racism, a major issue of social justice, came to crisis in South Africa during four decades of Apartheid ("separate development" - in theory- of black, white and 'coloured' peoples) till it ended in President de Klerk's release from prison of his great successor Nelson Mandela. Here is Alan Paton at the start of that era, in his above-named 1948 "story of comfort in desolation", telling of an elderly black father, the Reverend Stephen Kumalo, who has come to Johannesburg to seek his son who has got into bad company. His young friend the Revd. Theophilus Msimangu helps him in his fear, all too justified by the end of the novel, that the vagabond life would draw his son into violent crime. "Yes, Msimangu was right. It was the suspense, the not knowing, that made him fear this one thing... He would return with a deeper understanding to Ndotshemi...And might not he himself be grandfather to a child that would have no name? This he thought without bitterness tho' with pain..Back!

back knowing better the things that one fought against, knowing better the kind of thing that one must build. He would go back with a new and quickened interest in the school, not as a place where children learned to read and write and count only, but as a place where they must be prepared for life in any place to which they might go. Oh for education for his people, for schools up and down the land, where something might be built that would serve them when they went away to the towns, something that would take the place of the tribal law and custom. For a moment he was caught up in a vision, as man so often is when he sits in a place of ashes and destruction.

"Yes — it was true...the tribe that had nurtured him, & his father and his father's father, was broken. For the men were away, and the young men and the girls were away, and the maize hardly reached to the height of a man.
— There is food for us, my brother.
— Already?
— You have been here a long time.
— I did not know it.
— And what have you found?
— Nothing.
— Nothing?
— No, nothing. Only more fear and more pain. There is nothing in the world but fear and pain....
— Then I say it is time to turn. This is madness, that is bad enough. But it is also sin, which is worse. I speak to you as a priest.
Kumalo bowed his head. You are right, father, he said. I must sit here no longer."

We too in 21st century Britain also find our traditional ways of life at risk. We too have no continuing city.

Community-values are constantly attacked by TV consumerist pressures and by the glitter of supermarkets & sports.

Our schools need to fortify the young against the idolatry of money & "success". We need wise & able teachers; not O & A-level grades, SATs & League Tables. Values are paramount!

308   - - - - - continues.

27th October.   School for the Blind.   (cont'd from 26/10).

It was a wonderful place, this Ezenzeleni. For there the blind, that dragged out their days in a world they could not see, here they had eyes given to them. Here they made things that he for all his sight could never make. Baskets stout and strong, in osiers of different colours, and these osiers ran through one another by some magic that he did not understand, coming together in patterns, the red with the red, the blue with the blue, under the seeing and sightless hands. He talked with the people, and the blind eyes glowed with something that could only have been fire in the soul. It was white men who did this work of mercy, and some of them spoke English and some spoke Afrikaans. Yes, those who spoke English and those who spoke Afrikaans came together to open the eyes of black men that were blind.

His friend Msimangu would preach this afternoon, in the chapel that he had seen.

*

"Msimangu opened the book, and read to them first from the book. And Kumalo had not known that his friend had such a voice. For the voice was of gold, and the voice had love for the words it was reading. The voice shook and beat and trembled, not as the voice of an old man shakes and beats and trembles, nor as a leaf shakes and beats and trembles, but as a deep bell when it is struck. For it was not only a voice of gold, but it was the voice of a man whose heart was golden, reading from a book of golden words. And the people were silent, and Kumalo was silent, for when are three such things found in one place together?

    I the lord have called thee in righteousness
    and will hold thine hand and will keep thee
    and give thee for a covenant of the people
    for a light of the Gentiles
    To open the blind eyes
    to bring out the prisoners from the prison
    And them that sit in darkness
    out of the prison house.

"And the voice rose, and the Zulu tongue was lifted and transfigured, and the man too was lifted, as is one who comes to something that is greater than any of us. And the people were silent, for were they not the people of the blind eyes? And Kumalo was silent, knowing the blind man for whom Msimangu was reading these words:

    And I will bring the blind by a way that they knew not
    I will lead them in paths that they have not known
    I will make darkness light before them
    and crooked things straight
    These things I will do unto them
    and not forsake them.

"Yes, he speaks to me, there is no doubt of it. He says we are not forsaken. For while I wonder for what we live and struggle and die, for while I wonder what keeps us living and struggling, men are sent to minister to the blind, white men are sent to minister to the black blind. Who gives, at this one hour, a friend to make darkness light before me? Who gives, at this one hour, wisdom to one so young, for the comfort of one so old? Who gives to me compassion for a girl my son has left?

"Yes, he speaks to me, in such quiet and such simple words. We are grateful for the saints, he says, who lift up the heart in the days of our distress. Would we do less? For do we less, there are no saints to lift up any heart. If Christ be Christ he says, true Lord of Heaven, true Lord of Men, what is there that we would not do no matter what our suffering may be?

"I hear you, my brother. There is no word I do not hear..."

Paton's story adds that Msimangu is known as a preacher, yet is despised by some for the folly of "making the hungry patient, the suffering content, the dying at peace" when his golden voice could "raise a nation." Certainly the Guid Book includes a "social gospel" ("Hate the evil, and love the good, and establish justice in the marketplace" - Amos 5.15) - yet this prophetic ministry needs holding in balance with the pastoral, e.g. Isaiah 42 above.

"You need theology before you can have social justice" - Donald Soper

OPENING
of the
LANCASTER & CARLISLE RAILWAY,
On Tuesday, the 15th December, 1846.
Admit the Bearer to the 1st CLASS CARRIAGES.

The Opening Train will leave { Lancaster at..........11
Kendal Junction at....13
Penrith at............2 }
and return from Carlisle the following morning at half past 8.

A Train will leave Carlisle at Twelve, remaining at Penrith in time to return with the "Opening Train."

"I do not believe in the big way of doing things" - Mother Teresa of Calcutta.

309

An early Inter-City railway ticket; Liverpool to Manchester was earlier but lacked the terror of crossing Shap Fell!

28th October. THE CITY OF YORK. (Minster, south view.)

I find it hard to say which is the more thrilling: the view of the three-towered cathedral in bright sun, or that of the blue streamlined steam locomotive "Mallard" at the entrance to the Great Hall of the National Railway Museum (happily free admission from spring 2003 there, if alas no longer at the Minster.) The locomotive still holds the world record speed for steam traction - 126mph in 1938.

My first visit to the Minster, in 1984 before the fire caused by thunderbolt, was unusual in that a large Alsatian dog was merrily running around the nave, successfully dodging all the staff as they tried to catch it or coax it away.

The 1990s repairs to the west front and doorway show that the local stonemasons can produce work in no way inferior to that of their great medieval predecessors. The Dean's Court Hotel faces that front across the piazza, and used to display a notice saying that the view of the Minster from the hotel was the finest in York - unless the view of the Dean's Court Hotel from the Minster was preferred!

310

THE WORKS OF MERCY
FEED THE HUNGRY.
CLOTHE THE NAKED.
GIVE DRINK TO THE THIRSTY. VISIT THE IMPRISONED.

Where High Church Ceremonies are in use, things can go wrong in many ways. My 1960s friend Will O'Connor, a Morecambe vicar who chaired the local CND Group, had been curate of such a church in Crewe. Two of the choirmen were Low Church and always protested against the incense by coughing and spluttering when censed. One day the young man with the thurible, the metal can on chains with burning incense, whispered to Will "It's gone out! What shall I do?". Told to go through the motions, he rattled the cold can - and the choirmen coughed as usual.

29th October. When is a Girl not a Girl?

When Norman Moss revised his British-American dictionary, he commented that his feminist editor railed against traditional language that unintentionally slights women. He granted that a US 'fox' is an attractive woman, not girl, and also that female undergraduates are women (to list them as 'freshmen' won't do; even 'freshfolk' is preferable); yet he baulked against accepting that every post-pubertal female must be called a woman, and added that if his son takes an undergraduette out, he'll say he goes out with a girl. I wholeheartedly agree.

Thus 'girl' is in order for a young adult in a sexual context (such as 'glamour girl') where 'woman' hints at irregularity ('scarlet woman'); also in a romantic one (the girl from Ipanema) where 'young woman' sounds detached and businesslike, and 'lady' may imply social aspirations ('I want a Lady in my arms tonight!') Yet in less intimate contexts 'girl' can belittle - the 23-year-old who answers the telephone is a girl, whilst the one who practises law is a woman. Moss says we lack terms for women that are the equivalent of 'fellow', 'bloke' and 'guy', for 'chick', 'bird' and other colloquial words coined by men are diminishing. Here he overlooks 'lass', 'damsel', 'maid' and the Scots 'hizzie' that are still there to be used. Clearly however the girl/woman distinction will always depend partly on context like that between boy and man. We need sensitivity in choosing.

The English tongue isn't static - in the 1930s it was contemptuous to call a woman a 'female', but females now abound in 'heartsearch' columns. Nor is it symmetrical; a man is seldom said to be 'widowered', and I have never heard of 'biandry'. I go further than Moss in saying that 'girl' and 'boy' are used of older people in the context of warm friendship; I recently heard one of a group of five or six ladies in their sixties say to the other bus-travellers "This is our stop, girls".

Whilst it is discourteous to use 'girl' or 'boy' to someone who is known to dislike it, or who is seen as low in status, it is unacceptable for a small minority of people to try and force the entire usage of words into a new mould. (Does 'gay' still mean 'mirthful'? Wordsworth's "daffodils" poem affirms that meaning.) My patience is sorely tried by those who challenge my usages whilst being themselves prone to use bad language and/or composite nouns such as 'girlfriend'! "Ah, that's different", they say; whereupon I liken them to the Red Queen in "Alice", who said that when she uses a word it means what she chooses. Language is social and not to be privatised. As Melancthon urged, 'In All Things Charity'. (Latin: In omnibus caritas - NOT "Love on the bus"...)

30th October. COPYRIGHTS & WRONGS – (A Bridge Too Far!)

When Julia Ward Howe sent her verses "Mine Eyes Have Seen The Glory" to the "Atlantic Monthly" magazine for publication in February 1862, the paper sent her a cheque for four dollars in payment. She probably thought little of this, for, married to a senior medical officer in Lincoln's northern army, she was not financially dependent on her poetic output. Sibelius, however, had to rely on his musical royalties, at least until the proud Finnish nation granted him a pension. Like Beethoven before him he wrote and sold trifles of lighter music for what they could earn. In 1904 he parted with his rights over <u>Valse Triste</u> on derisory terms, and regretted his mistake for a full half-century when the wistful piece proved to be an unrepeatable popular "hit". Was this the worst bargain since Esau sold his birthright for a bowl of lentil soup with bread roll? – (Genesis 25.34; – but see below!)

The labourer is worthy of his or her hire, in the arts as elsewhere, and it is sad to recall that Schubert's String Quintet, one of the greatest of all chamber works, lay gathering dust for two decades on a publisher's shelf before Diabelli located it long after the death of the impoverished composer. The contrast with the "muzac industry" of the too-opulent West of today, with ephemeral "hits" winning vast fortunes, is discreditable – and if this seems to be a value-judgement, it's meant to be one. Copyright to prevent literary "piracy" and to secure some sort of income for the artist, and for dependants in the wake of death, has the general approval of society. But the mid-1990s extension by the European Union (EU) of copyright from 50 to 70 years from death is another matter! Half a century is plenty for two generations of family to make good any shortfall from the artistic life. The extension enables a third generation to prey on public culture!

Unfortunately in our "Western World" (the USA also has embraced extended copyright to 70 years as against the norm of 50 elsewhere) there is a climate of opinion which fails to rein in financial business which needs moral control. The recipients of undue royalties fall foul of Ruskin's dictum (28.1 – and here I make an exception to my efforts to avoid repetitions): "The principle of righteous dealing is, that if the good costs you nothing, you must not be paid for doing it."

It appears therefore that the acceptance by European nations of the right of the EU to issue commercial directives is an Esau-type blunder on vaster scale than that of Sibelius!

31st October. # Christian Halloween - is it trick or treat?

THE coming of autumn darkness, writes Shirley Toulson in "The Celtic Year", is "the season at which the veil between time and eternity can easily become transparent".

The Celts, in the era when they embraced Christianity, had to slaughter the cattle that couldn't be fed through winter. The bones were burnt in bon(e)fires.

The sorrow of the season reminded them of human mortality and was not banished by the feasting on plentiful meat, for the winter would bring death to humans as well as to beasts, through hunger, cold, and illness. Halloween marked the death of the year, for their New Year began on November 1 with the winter season of Samhain.

It was a time when evil spirits could appear to triumph over the good.

Now in our very different society, with well-warmed houses and Calderdale Council to clear the roads, we hesitate to personify the dark forces operating in our world and through our spirits.

Yet St Paul was right when he warned the Ephesians (ch 6, vs 12) that life entails spiritual conflict; and Tennyson wrote in "Locksley Hall Sixty Years After" that

". . . there may be those about us whom we neither see nor name,

Felt within us as ourselves, the Powers of Good, the Powers of Ill,

Strowing balm, or shedding poison in the fountains of the Will."

The new language of psychiatry supplements but does not displace this traditional religious understanding, and the stage is set for the spooks, skeletons, and broomsticks of this season — alas trivialised in our over-comfortable consumerist society by "trick-or-treat" and other frivolities which forget the spiritual side of life!

When Donald Coggan was Archbishop of Canterbury he released a report, commissioned by a previous archbishop, which affirmed the genuineness of paranormal events, but warned that "psychic and spiritual studies" are vulnerable to risks and to fraud.

Real ghosts appear to be benign, and Harry Griffin, who at 85 is still the Lakeland correspondent of "The Guardian" newspaper, relates a fine story in his 1960s book "In Mountain Lakeland", about the very bold climber C. F. Holland's "strange experience in the fells during the First World War". (continues on 1 Nov.)

313

"Viewpoint" article in Todmorden News. By Frank McManus publ. 25.10.1996.
Griffin continues in post at 92, 2003.

1st November.   Genuine Ghosts and Spurious Spooks.

Continuing my Halloween article (31.10) on this "All Saints' Day": Holland reported that when he descended Hollow Stones one summer afternoon after climbing on Scafell Crag, he was most unexpectedly joined by his friend the great mountaineer Siegfried Herford, whom he hadn't heard to be on leave from France. They talked about the days they could have together when the war was over; and then Herford had to cross over into another valley, promising he would see Holland again as soon as possible. But days later Holland received a letter saying that Herford had died on active service on the day of their last chat!

This is a fine example of a type of story which, though rare, is by no means unique — a departing spirit being granted a last look at a favourite spot on earth. Ghosts, it seems, are generally benign, though troubled spirits are reported, quite apart from fraudulent productions. Perhaps only one person in tens of thousands sees a ghost, but enough do to establish the concept in the public mind.

Thomas Hardy the novelist and poet had a lifelong wish to see a ghost, and eventually saw one, his grandfather's, in Stinsford churchyard on Christmas Eve 1919, when he was 79. "A green Christmas" it said, and Hardy replied courteously "I like a green Christmas". When it entered the church Hardy followed - but it was nowhere to be seen.

My late friend Guendoline Haddock, widow of our family doctor, told me in the 1980s when she was about 80, that after a patient of her husband had died of a distressing condition, his widow despaired and rejected the Church. Guen persuaded her to return for midnight communion of Christmas; and they were sitting together half way up the left side of the nave, waiting for the service to begin, when Guen saw the deceased man, restored to health, pass up the aisle and sit on the right near the front. His widow did not see him. It is meaningless to ask whether Guen saw a vision or a hallucination; she simply saw it, and many could testify to her stable sanity and integrity.

So the veil is thin; "supernature" is part of nature: and All Saints-tide is no trick but a joyful treat. On 31.7 I mentioned Bp How's fine hymn "For All The Saints"; and I have a happy memory of the Centenary Evensong (1987) at All Saints' Church in the Durham pit-village of Eppleton (18.2), with music by Hetton Silver Band & talk by Bp David Jenkins.

2nd November.   The Tragedy of Nadezhda.

Alas for Tchaikovsky, two years after he reached the relative peace of mind of his 5th symphony (23.9) his "best incomparable friend" Mme von Meck stunned him by writing that she was near ruin and had to stop his annuity, yet still had infinite love for him. He replied that money had no effect on his friendship, but this went unanswered. In October 1893, the month before Pyotr died, his niece who was also Nadezhda's daughter-in-law mediated at his request and reported that she, ill with tuberculosis, had whispered "I knew I was no longer necessary to him...our correspondence was still a joy to me but I didn't feel I had any right to please myself alone if it had become a burden to him...why didn't he write again?" It appears that her son-in-law Pahulsky had withheld Tchaikovsky's letters from her; and the unanswerable question arises: In whose interests, hers or her family's? Her sorest trial, hinted Anna the mediator, "was the agonising last illness of her beloved eldest son"; and she felt guilty of letting her friendship with Tchaikovsky (pictured) lead her to neglect her family. "I must atone for my sin", she repeated; and, ending the correspondence which she misjudged as no longer vital, she returned to the Church and the Faith.

Six days after receiving her last letter, Tchaikovsky was working on his chilling symphonic ballad "The Voyevoda"; later he wrote "The Sleeping Beauty" and "Nutcracker" ballets and the opera "The Queen of Spades", along with shorter works. But he was set on writing "a grand symphony forming the keystone of all my works", and in late 1892 he wrote a programme: "The ultimate essence of the plan of the symphony is LIFE. First part - all impulsive passion, confidence, thirst for activity. Must be short. (Finale, DEATH - result of collapse.) Second part, love; third, disappointments; fourth ends dying away (also short)." This might have applied to the work he was completing only to recast some of its material into his brief and seldom-performed Third Piano Concerto. By mid-February 1893 he had begun his 6th symphony, which he described to his nephew Davidov as having a "programme which shall remain a mystery to everyone - let them guess away...The programme itself is subjective to the core." Later he preferred his brother Modest's title "Pathétique", only to discard this as well as "Programme Symphony" and leave just the number. It was first performed in St Petersburg on 16th October 1893, and nine days later Tchaikovsky was dead. (see over)

3rd November. TCHAIKOVSKY'S FAREWELL.

This Sixth Symphony is a popular favourite which moves from the darkness of mystery to that of despair. Its first movement is an emotional and brilliant portrayal of the passion and tragedy of life, rightly described by Professor Tovey, in his "Essays in Musical Analysis", as "the climax of Tchaikovsky's artistic career" - "perhaps the finest thing (he) ever wrote" - its ending for solemn trumpets and trombones over a descending scale for plucked strings being "a crowning beauty that greatly strengthens the pathos". The finale is a lament. In between are a graceful waltz in 5:4 time and a most breathtaking march that also ends with the motto of Beethoven's 5th. The detailed programme has been guessed at as expected for over a century. The critic Rostislav Hofmann compared the 6th and 4th symphonies - both are most emotional in their 1st and 4th movements; each looks back on love in its 2nd movement and has a military march in the 3rd. "The 6th looks to us like a response to the 4th, and its cancellation, unless it is simply 'The Reproach'..!" I think this is very plausible and at least an ingredient in its inspiration. Also is Pyotr saying "Before I leave this world, let me show you how I really can compose!"?

Mystery followed. Tchaikovsky spoke of his symphony with pride and without death-wish; yet having finished his work and lost his love, did he dice with death in drinking unboiled water and thus contracting cholera? Guessing away, we must surely be thankful for the gentle composer and his loving female friend.

THE CHURCH OF ST. ANTHONY. CARTMEL FELL

4th November, "DEAR DIRTY DUBLIN" (G.W. Target, 1974.)

Grandmother cooks for the large family.

...would you need a thick iron pot about two feet across...
"Will you be bringing me the bastable now?"
...with a flat lid to it, and a couple of lugs for hanging over the open fire if you've a need, and three stumps of legs for standing to the side of the hearth or in the oven.

And, for a table of plates to be filled the like of ours, you need a couple or three pounds of good fat neck of lamb, being the cheapest cut, a dozen or so fresh potatoes, three or four good big onions, and a sprig of young thyme. You leave the meat on the bone, just chopping it small as you've a mind to. Then you slice two or three of the potatoes, and line the bottom of the pot with them to cook away and thicken the juices you'll be getting. Then a layer of sliced onions, then the meat. A fist of rough salt, a scatter of pepper, then the thyme, and the rest of the onions, and then in with the whole potatoes. A good pint of water, cover the pot with the lid, and cook in the oven for a couple of hours till the smell of it has everybody waiting hungry...

— — — — — —

Though you'll be blessed by Saint Anthony himself to be finding a stew the like of _that_ in the Restaurants of Dublin today! True, if you've the money there's no end of Fine Fayre for your table: Dublin Bay Prawns, Clarenbridge Oysters, Boyne Salmon...but my grandmother cooked for more than money.

Sunday evening in the frontroom
after coming back from Benediction, tea finished, and the fire lit, and the gramophone in its polished walnut cabinet, the sort you'd have to keep winding...and these scratchy old records...never heard since with the same joy and innocence...Count John McCormack himself?... I can hear (my choice) to this day...

>Kathleen Mavourneen, the grey dawn is breaking,
>The horn of the hunter is heard on the hill,
>The lark from her light wing The bright dew is shaking:
>Kathleen Mavourneen, what, slumb'ring still?
>O hast thou forgotten how soon we must sever?
>O hast thou forgotten this day we must part?
>It may be for years, it may be for ever;
>O why art thou silent, the voice of my heart?
>It may be for years, and it may be for ever:
>Then why art thou silent, Kathleen Mavourneen?

5th November.   SHOULD LISZT BE LISTED?

Classifying and making lists of things is a popular human activity — longest rivers, highest mountains and so forth. It is a bold and foolish person who ventures an opinion on greatest footballers or musicians — so here goes with my Premier League of all-time great orchestral composers. (I demur to judge their predecessors from the great days of vocal church-music — Palestrina, Victoria, Lassus, Byrd, Tallis...)

Handel	1685-1759.	Berlioz	1803-1869.
Bach	1685-1750.	Wagner	1813-1883.
Haydn	1732-1809.	Brahms	1833-1897.
Mozart	1756-1791.	Tchaikovsky	1840-1893.
Beethoven	1770-1827.	Sibelius	1865-1957.
Schubert	1797-1828.	Vaughan Williams	1872-1958.

Many favourite composers, including my own Mendelssohn and Dvorak; the northerners Delius and Grieg; and many loved mainly for a single work or style, e.g. Chopin, Faure (Requiem), Elgar (Enigma), and Britten (Young Person's Guide) have perforce been omitted, perhaps to sneak in as and when my mood changes. All whom I have named are male; as in literature with the Brontë sisters, so in music until fairly recently, female composers felt it necessary to publish their work as that of men. Even Clara Schumann passed off some of hers as her husband Robert's. Happily times have changed. My list is personal; yet surely the three B's (say) occupy a higher level of creative art than do lighter musicians.

Malcolm Muggeridge, 20th-century journalist, broadcaster and raconteur, gained the nickname St Mugg because of his disillusionment with social endeavour and his too "other-worldly" hopes. Rightly recognising much decadence in postwar Western "culture", his "Chronicles of Wasted Time" (Collins, 1972, book 1, p.15) declare: "As for literature and the arts...listen to the Missa Solemnis after the Beatles..." "I was born into a dying, if not already dead, civilisation, whose literature was part of the general decomposition...At the beginning of a civilisation, the role of the artist is priestly but at the end, harlequinade...From Plainsong to the Rolling Stones, from El Greco to Picasso, from Chartres to the Empire State Building...from Pascal's Pensées to Robinson's Honest to God. A Gadarene descent down which we all must slide..!" True, but too heavy-handed, for renewal needs joy or 'twill fail.

6th November.

The Blaydon Races.

Many parts of Britain have their own "quasi-national anthem"; "London Pride" to "I belong to Glasgow"; Yorkshire's "Ilkley Moor baht 'at" to Cumbria's "John Peel" - the traditional one who lies in Caldbeck churchyard; and Cornwall's fine "Floral Dance" (in and out of Helston's houses on 8th May to "the band of peculiar tone Of the cornet, clarinet and big trombone..."); and of course the Lincolnshire Poacher. For zest, however, I doubt that the North-East's "Blaydon Races" can be surpassed, for all its doggerel words. The races are long since defunct, as alas is Geordie Ridley's show for which the song was written as an early "commercial" - perhaps the most successful of such! Here's the chorus, which won and wins the hearts of the local community, and some verses; with acknowledgement and thanks to http://geordiepride.demon.co.uk/blaydon_races.htm (visit for more.)

"Ah went to Blaydon races, 'Twas on the 9th of June Eighteen hundred and sixty-two On a summer's afternoon, I took the bus from Balmbra's And she was heavy laden, Away we went along Collingwood Street That's on the road to Blaydon." (Chorus as below.)

"We flew across the Chain Bridge Reet into Blaydon Toon, The bellman he was calling then, They called him Jackie Broon. I saw him talking to some chaps An' them he was persuadin' To gan an' see Geordie Ridley's show At Mechanics' Hall in Blaydon." (Chorus as below.)

"Now when we got to Paradise There were bonny games begun - There were four and 20 on the bus And how we danced an' sung; They called on me to sing a song So I sang 'em Paddy Fagan - I danced a jig an' I swung me twig The day I went to Blaydon."

Chorus: "Oh me lads, you should've seen us gannin' Passin' the folks along the road An' all of them were stann- /in'; All the lads an' lasses there They all had smilin' faces Gannin' along the Scotswood Road To see the Blaydon races."

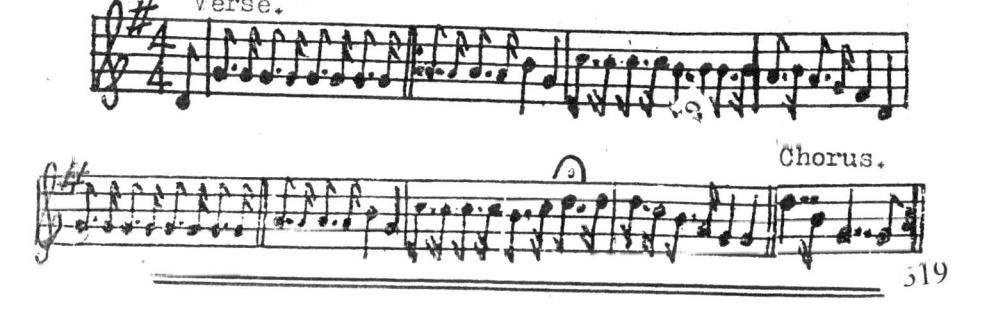

319

Summary of Contents.

September:

6 - Juror of the Year, &c.
7 - Chit-chat & Clap-trap.
8 - In Such a Night.
9 - Tickleby Tomcat village.
10 - National Hubris.
11 - Parlour Songs.
12 - Bp Ailbe & the Wolf.
13 - Old England around 1900.
14 - Browning's Lost Leader.
15 - Space and Time.
16 - Iona of my Heart.
17 - Richard Rolle on Women.
18 - Monster Rhondda Demo.
19 - Bouch's Belah Viaduct.
20 - Chess problems.
21 - Tchaikovsky essay, also each day to
24 - History of Courting.
25 - Curses & Verses.
26 - Hildegard of Bingen.
27 - South Polar Sunrise.
28 - Postal Challenge.
29 - A Wink Too Soon.
30 - Elegies in Country Church-yards.

October:

1 - Creationism v Evolution.
2 - Harvest celebrations.
3 - The Millennial Hymn.
4 - Animal Ethics.
5 - Green Witches & Dead Cats.
6 - Sweetie the Rat.
7 - Coincidences.
8 - John Neale verses.
9 - Forebodings.
10 - Recovery.
11 - Georgian Magistrates.
12 - Keswick & Lakeland.
13 - Lake Poets for 21st Century
14 - Gladstone & Hawarden.
15 - Eminent Victorian Spat.
16 - Bede Griffiths' teaching.
17 - Music Business.
18 - Cats In Love.
19 - Mists & Mellow Fruitfulness
20 - McManus's Law.
21 - Leeds Town Hall.
22 - Thornley's Sorrow & Pride.
23 - Jailing of Miners.
24 - Escapes and Perils.
25 - Taciturn Tales.
26 - Paton's African novel.
27 - The Blind School.
28 - Tales of York and Crewe.
29 - Girls, Babes & Dames.
30 - Copyrights and Wrongs.
31 - Trick or Treat?

November:

1 - Spooks.
2 - Tchaikovsky's best friend.
3 - Tchaikovsky's farewell.
4 - Dublin around 1950.
5 - Should Liszt be Listed?
6 - On the Road to Blaydon.

320

"Raise the Song of Harvest-Home" - see 2nd October.

THE GOMER PRESS LIMITED, in 2003 published at £8.99 retail THE COLLECTED POEMS OF IDRIS DAVIES. Order via local bookshop!

'THE MORN ON OUR MOUNTAINS'

Mardale before Flooding for Haweswater Reservoir
(late 1930s)

A Book for the Dark Days
(7th November to 7th January)

"The March and the Muster" Part 6

Frank McManus

Looking South to Mardale Green at the Head of the Dale, showing (from left to right) The Dun Bull Inn, Harter Fell, Nan Bield Pass, Rough Crag, Chapel Farm, The Church and Riggindale Farm. Grove Brae and Goosemire are below in the trees.

"A Light That Doth Not Depart." − (foreword, "The Morn on our Mountains.")

after
"LA VÉRITÉ"
by
Jules Lefebvre.
(1884 − 1912)
Musée d'Orsay
322 Paris.

Near the beginning of the "Elders" chapter of Dostoevsky' novel "The Brothers Karamazov" (i.e Pt 1, Bk 1, ch.5), the 19-year-old Alyosha, on his way to join the local monastery as a novice is presented as a precocious and modern young man in pursuit of truth and yearning for an immediate heroic act to perform and "prove himself". Unlike other such youths he was convinced of immortality and God; and the novelist notes that had he decided otherwise, he would without delay have embraced atheism and Socialism, "for Socialism is more than the question of labour; above all it proposes a modern structural expression of atheism,,,the deliberate forming of society as a Tower of Babel built without God." All this from an author who at 27 lay under sentence of death for "socialist" activity before having a last-minute commutation to Siberia!

Yet in chapter 5 of the next book, Mr Miusov during a discussion in the monastery quotes a "security-agent" as saying the Establishment hardly fears revolutionaries except "a few odd men...terrible people, Christians and Socialists at the same time. A Christian Socialist is far more dreadful than one who is an atheist." He adds that he can't help recalling these words in the present company; whereupon he is directly challenged by Father Paissy: "You apply the to us and call us socialists, don't you?"

In Britain of course socialist tradition includes Christianity as a source among others — Trade Unions, Co-ops, Marxism, Chartism etc. "When Adam delved and Eve span, Who was then the gentleman?" asked the wild hedge-priest John Ball. Rainbro' the Leveller challenged Oliver Cromwell on equality. F.D. Maurice and Bishop Westcott (1.5) led for socialism in the 19th century; William Temple in the 20th − whilst Geoffrey Studdert Kennedy's "Democracy and the Dog-collar" (Hodder 1921) studied the aloofness between Organised Religion and Organised Labour finding the former not sincere enough, and the latter too unspiritual! Verb. sap., I fear!

7th November.   "Thorns into Roses, and Winter to May."   323

Now that the dark evenings are here again, we turn to our firesides if we are lucky enough to have them, and to families and friends whether we are or not. I turn merrily to the bottle too, yet I heed the Health Warning that UK hedonism necessitates:- Too much alcohol harms your health. We need to avoid being dependent for social pleasure on any substance bar food, fuel, clothing, air, water and so forth, and to be able to be convivial without strong drink. This being said, why not

'Put Round The Bright Wine'?

[musical score]

Put round the bright wine, for my bosom is gay,
The night may have sunshine as well as the day.
Oh welcome the hours! when dear visions arise
To melt my kind spirit, and charm my fond eyes.
When wine to my head can its wisdom impart,
And love has its promise to make to my heart;
When dim in far shade sink the spectres of care,
And I tread a bright world with a footstep of air.

Yes, mirth is my goddess, come round me, ye few,
Who have wit for her worship, I doat upon you:
Delighted with life, like a swallow on wing,

I catch ev'ry pleasure the current may bring:
The feast and the frolic, the masque and the ball,
Dear scenes of enchantment! I come at your call;
Let me meet the gay beings of beauty and song,
And let Erin's good humour be found in the throng.

If life be a dream, 'tis a pleasant one sure,
And the dream of tonight we at least may secure.
If life be a bubble, tho' better I deem,
Let us light up its colours by gaiety's beam.
**Away with cold vapours, I pity the mind
That nothing but dulness and darkness can find:**
Give me the kind spirit that laughs on its way,
And turns thorns into roses, and winter to May.

This was one of the Irish folksongs which Beethoven set, for money and relaxation, whilst working on the serious masterpieces of his final decades. Unlike the Scottish one that Estelle is made to perform in the Berlioz sketch (9th Aug) it is 100% forward-looking. Also set was England's "Miller of Dee".

A coin or two I've in my purse, to help a needy friend;   A little I can give the poor, and still have some to spend.

8th November. MRS DOSTOEVSKY - A 50-Rouble Fee.

Among the world's great novelists Russia's Fyodor Dostoevsky (1821-1881) stands in high esteem as possibly the finest of all. After six years at Petersburg Military Engineering Institute and one in the army, he turned to literature and was attracted by radical socialism, only to be jailed then sentenced to death as an activist for forcible seizure of power. Reprieved at the last moment and exiled to Siberia for a decade, he married Maria Isayeva in 1857 only to lose her to tuberculosis in 1864, by which time Fyodor was back in Petersburg and his vocation of letters. After an affair and an unsuccessful courtship, Dostoevsky found himself in a parlous plight through having assumed responsibility for the 33000-rouble debts of his late brother's magazine Epoch. A shyster publisher took them over subject to his giving them a complete new novel (The Gambler) by 1 November 1866. With the work going badly and a penalty-clause threatening, his friends persuaded his to engage a stenographer-copyist.

The night-school secretarial teacher Olkhin was approached for help, and he sent the 20-year-old Anna Grigoryevna Slitkina to visit the novelist, which she did in a state of happy excitement mingled with some apprehension, plus satisfaction at having an independent job with a 50-rouble fee in prospect. After a grumpy start Fyodor rallied as he found that his shorthand-scribe speeded up his composing so that the time-problem was overcome. He shared his history with "Anya" and asked to meet her after the project was finished, then paid a second call on her unannounced, to ask her to visit his house next day to plan their work on Crime & Punishment.

Then on 8 November 1866 he was cheerful and excited when she arrived, and he told her he had dreamt of finding a diamond among the letters and papers in his rosewood box, but couldn't remember what became of it. They spoke as usual about what they had done since they last met, and he said he had devised a plot for another novel, involving a young woman's psychology. A failed artist, older than his years, had met a girl of 22 or so - 'Anya' to give her a name - and thought he might find happiness with her. But with so big a difference in age and personality, would it ring false to have them fall in love? Anna recognised Fyodor's own life-story but not herself as the girl, since she whom he had previously courted was called Anya too. Driven on by careful responses, he asked if the artist were he and the girl she, would she marry him; to which she replied yes she'd always love him. And she, his diamond, did, and stabilised him for his great vocation.

9th November.   The Power of the Dog.

In the mid-1980s I "dog-sat" for a week in London for a friend visiting Iona. For two days the dog was distant, though friendly. He then "melted" and "fell in love with me", showing great affection. After three more days, however, he started to pine, especially when I went out leaving him; and this alas escalated to misery when I was due to return home. Then I shared this story in 1996 with a Todmorden friend, who told me of a local dog, being cared for when her "master" was away for some weeks, that disappeared as he was returning, and made her own way to his house a mile away.

A notable instance of "Canine ESP (Extra-sensory perception)" relates to "the famous" (or furious) "dog Wessex" which Thomas Hardy's second wife Florence obtained in 1913. This wire-haired fox-terrier snapped at servants and postmen and tore Galsworthy's trousers when he visited. But when William Watkins of the London Dorset Society visited the Hardys' home Max Gate near Dorchester in Spring 1925, Wessex, who liked him, greeted him in the hallway with joyful barks but suddenly these gave way to a pitiful whine. Florence has told that she could find nothing amiss; but even when the company had settled, the dog sometimes pawed Mr Watkins then gave a quiet howl. The guest left cheerfully after the social evening; yet Wessex was unexpectedly silent when the telephone rang early next morning, and lay with head down as word came that Watkins had died suddenly at his hotel. Wessex had known!

— — — — — —

GREETINGS - - - from
Mr. and Mrs. THOMAS HARDY
Max Gate (and the dreaded
Dorchester   dog Wessex!)   Xmas 1923

Hardy's last poems include:
DEAD "WESSEX" THE DOG TO THE HOUSEHOLD

Do you think of me at all,
   Wistful ones?
Do you think of me at all
   As if nigh?
Do you think of me at all
At the creep of evenfall,
Or when the sky-birds call
   As they fly? . . . .

Should you call as when I knew you,
   Wistful ones,
Should you call as when I knew you,
   Shared your home;
Should you call as when I knew you,
I shall not turn to view you,
I shall not listen to you,
   Shall not come.

10th November. "Many Long Years Ago."

The Cambridge Union (university debating-society) at a mid-20th-century meeting considered the following motion: "In 1612AD the Pilgrim Fathers landed on the Plymouth Rock. In the opinion of this House it would have been a far better thing if the Plymouth Rock had been landed on the Pilgrim Fathers".

The native Americans who suffered ethnic cleansing and the expropriation of their lands by Europeans would agree. The world is ever so. The settlers' "Thanksgiving" for survival, and harvest, is observed yearly in the USA on the last Thursday in November; and in 2002 I was privileged to be invited to the traditional dinner, pumpkin pie and all, in the Illinois prairie homestead of my brother's friends. American hospitality and kindness is often great. If only the US voters can evolve into the "alert and intelligent citizenry" who alone (said Eisenhower) can secure the proper meshing of the industrial/military complex with our peaceful aims and goals! The US Music Supervisors' Conference in 1931 criticised the choice of "The Star-Spangled Banner" (3.3), and other songs ("Marseillaise" &c.) which arose from particular wartime episodes, to serve as national anthems. For all their merit, shared by other such songs (27.11), their repeated use in schools, as with flag-ceremonies, instils that narrow patriotism which can become "the last refuge of the scoundrel" (Dr Samuel Johnson), and does not serve the good of the world.

Julia Howe's hymn (24.11) falls into a different category yet can be misused by those who miss its theological nature. The wife of Abraham Lincoln's chief medical officer in the Slavery Rebellion or Civil War, she saw the northern army on manoeuvre, heard the soldiers singing "John Brown's Body", and was urged as poetess to write some good words to the tune. Waking in her hotel at grey dawn next day, she found to her astonishment that "the wished-for lines were arranging themselves in my brain. I lay quite still until the last verse had completed itself...searched for an old piece of paper... and began to scrawl the lines" in the darkened room. She went back to sleep, and later sent the verses to the "Atlantic Monthly — which sent her a cheque for $4 in payment!

Lincoln's hat and umbrella; Chicago History Museum.

Drawn by Otto J. Schneider.

11th November. MARTINMAS-DAY, which like Candlemas 2.2 was used in some places for hiring-fairs of farmworkers in the agricultural era. Martin served in the Roman army until he, giving half his cloak to a beggar, had a vision of Christ and gave up soldiering. Brief imprisonment made him the "patron saint of conscientious objectors"; then he became Bishop of Tours in c.372 and a founder-builder of the Church in France.

"Remembrance-day", in the wake of WW1 which ceased on 11.11.1918 with strange appropriateness on the feast of a pacifist saint, is Europe's contribution to the commemorative season which begins at Halloween with All-Saints'-tide. It is now clear that the Great War was young Europe's holocaust, and a greater evil than any for which it was undertaken. In fairness we note that no-one foresaw the four-year stalemate of trench warfare. Gerard Hughes S.J. has written that all who gave their lives deserve our respect, but it cannot be God's will that we should kill each other. Siegfried Sassoon the poet (16.6) wrote:

"Sneak home, and pray you'll never know
The hell where youth and laughter go." - also

"Look up, and swear by the green of the spring that you'll never forget" - which gave John Masters the title for his last novel of his WW1 trilogy Loss Of Eden. By 1935 Sassoon was a pacifist and member of the Peace Pledge Union; by 1939 he nevertheless felt there was nothing for it but fight WW2, though theological pacifists like Gilbert Shaw (4.3) stood firm in the perplexities of those dreadful years.

The plain old church of St Martin, Martindale (off Ullswater in the English Lake District; well worth visiting from the steamer-pier at Howtown, as is St Peter's nearby. (fine new windows cf. Shap).

<u>12th November.</u>   "New Occasions Teach New Duties" (Lowell).

   The use of the poppy emblem must not be allowed to blind us to the entirely new situation of the 21st century. Whereas the war-remembrances of those we loved and lost used to relate mainly to servicefolk, war's casualties are now over 80% civilian — so we need to build for peace, with Pope Paul VI's watchword reminding us that "Peace is the fruit of anxious daily care to ensure that each person lives in justice as God intends". As for remembrance, I find it hard to say what needs remembering and what is best forgotten. Though Hardy was wise to say that "If way to the Better there be, it exacts a full look at the Worst", we mustn't dwell on horrors to the point of ourselves being dragged down. Isaiah had a word too — "Cease to dwell on things gone by..."! (43^{18})

<u>Note on the origins of World War 1:</u>
   The industrial era, initiated by Britain, had gained momentum in Western Europe and the USA by the final decades of the 19th Century. Germany, formed from the Prussian states, and France vied commercially and for territory, and established large conscript armies. Britain was fearful of the build-up of German naval strength, and a popular demand for more capital warships arose under the jingoistic slogan "We want 8, and we won't wait". Germany feared an inevitable French attempt to regain Alsace and Lorraine which she had annexed in 1870. All this was complicated by Balkan problems to the S.E. of the weakening Austro-Hungarian empire, and by relationships with Turkey and radicalism in pre-revolutionary Russia.

   Hardy's ominous "Channel Firing" poem of April 1914 mused on "gunnery practice out at sea":
        "All nations striving still to make
        Red war yet redder, mad as hatters..."
Britain was threatened by the risk of German control of the channel coast and ports of France, and had long since guaranteed the integrity of Belgium. The assassination in Sarajevo of the Austrian heir-apparent lit the powder-keg of an overfine "balance of power and interests" that toppled into an unforeseen abyss of disaster. Austria deemed Serbia's apology inadequate, and her mobilisation triggered similar processes elsewhere. As A.J.P. Taylor has urged, it is hard to reverse a mobilisation which has fuelled soldiers' pugnacity, and the inflexibility of railway-scheduling made it impossible, alas. Soon Germany struck pre-emptively into France and outflanked her defences by a frightful violation of Belgian neutrality which was the <u>proximate</u> cause of Western war.

<u>13th November.</u> <u>The Dear Old Church of England.</u>

Much loved, much mocked, by a few hated, with history glorious at times, inglorious at others (see 3.10), our 'C. of E' still aims at trying to help and serve everyone in our land who wishes it. Not the same in any two places – compare Martindale (11.11) with Grimethorpe of colliery-band fame, now gutted of industry – she has suffered shrinkage, now checked in some places, as values and faith have weakened following horrific world wars and a growth of materialism in the morally decadent Western world.

In order to hold and extend our ground, modern liturgies i.e. forms of service have been compiled in today's style and language. Beautiful new traditions have emerged from places such as Iona and Taizé. The Roman church has given up on Latin, and the C. of E. has produced books and pamphlets to supplement its noble Book of Common Prayer (but the graphs of falling numbers over recent decades show not the slightest change of gradient as a result!). This flawed treasure, used zestfully, is rich in diction as in doctrine; and its Litany, brief Communion, Lenten Commination, and Psalms remain priceless. Unlike the bulky Worship Anthology produced for the 21st Century under the inaccurate title 'Common Worship' it fits the pocket, is giveable to brides and at baptisms, and finds a niche in cottage, city 'bedsit' and stately home. I'm not opposed to the modern productions, especially when they use worthy language, but the traditional Western rite is far too good to be abandoned. It's commitment and passion that succeed, whether Scouse or Tudor-style.

"Really, Frank, your daybook isn't going to sell if you go on and on about the Moral Theory of the Atonement!" (*)

(*) That Christ by His teaching and example moved men and women to love and repentance and so effected their salvation, healing their alienations from self, community and God. (Put forward by Peter Abelard (C12) & Hastings Rashdall (C20). (cf. 14.2, 6.4)

329

14th November. Chrissie Answers.

Some tricky queries have come my way recently. I feel fortunate that I have been able to call on the services of the North-East's favourite counsellor for replies to the more awkward ones:

<u>From Miss Rosie-Jane Catcher (Pevensey)</u>
Some radical papers and magazines have stopped using "feminine designations" e.g. actress, authoress, priestess. Ought they?

Dear Madam,
No. If sex is irrelevant to vocation, mentioning it in passing doesn't matter. We needn't amend Yeats' memorial to read, "Equestrian, pass by!" — and it's plain silly to say a horseman's inferior to a woman, or an authoress to a male author. If we conceal sex, we concede the prejudice that women (sometimes men) are inferior. Furthermore the ban is selective, for "waitress" and "dinner-lady" pass unchallenged, and nobody spoke of "King Elizabeth the King Parent". It might, however, be better to call female vicars "presbytresses", because of their tresses.

(16.6)

<u>From the Lord Bishop, The Palace, Barchester.</u>
Thank you for your nice letter, but unfortunately the Dean hasn't spoken to me since I followed your advice. What can I do?

My dear Tommy,
Meet me at noon this Thursday in the Saracen's Head; tell Mrs Proudie that you're being interviewed <u>re</u> the Hogglestock Pyx.

<u>From the Editor:</u> How honest is that, please; I'll believe the <u>best</u>!
Dear Sir, 100%; Would you besmirch me?

<u>From the Head Girl, Barchester Comprehensive School.</u>
I love carol-singing but I don't really fancy "Lo He abhors not the Virgin's womb" in "O come, all ye faithful". A bit anatomical, I say, and wrong to imply that anything about Jesus' mother might possibly have repelled Him. What say you?

Dear Sue, It just means He condescended to share all our life. But it isn't in the Latin, and we could sing "Rests He in Mary's arms by Joseph's side!" (contd opposite.

15th November. Deservedly Lonely Hearts?

Let room be found for Heartsearch pleas rejected by other publications:

<u>Vengeful</u> female, 29, seeks man to destroy. Box 491.

<u>Professional</u> female, 32, getting over broken engagement with idiot, WLTM male. Will not be responsible for own actions. Box 492.

<u>Girl</u>, 28, heart broken, lonely, disillusioned, WLTM anybody. Box 493.

<u>Spinster</u>, 25, seeks male to exorcise certain feelings. Box 494.

<u>Dumpee</u>, 36, very vexed, seeks fun for retaliation purposes. Box 495.

<u>Athletic</u> male, 26, jilted, bitter, angry and confused, seeks female company, n/s, gsoh. Box 496.

<u>Male</u>, 27, seeks companion for constant reassurance. Box 497.

<u>Caring</u> sincere male, 24, recently chucked, WLTM anyone just to annoy her. Box 498.

<u>Gentleman</u>, 44, recently returned from Monte Carlo, WLTM young blonde woman, cat-walk model type. Exchange photos. Box 499.   (acknowledgements to Metro newspaper.)

14.11 (Chrissie Answers) continued:

From <u>Major H.A. Greenhorn, MFH</u> (Slack-on-Hebden).
Vaughan Williams wrote two popular Fantasias, one on the old song <u>Greensleeves</u>, and one "on a theme by Thomas Tallis" the Tudor composer. In what work by Tallis did it appear?
Dear Major Greenhorn,
   Queen Elizabeth I's archbishop Matthew Parker published in 1567 "The Whole Psalter", with metrical versions of the 150 Old Testament Psalms and supplementary material including Tallis' eight settings of which VW used No. 3, an acrostic poem on the name MATTHEVS PARKERUS in praise of Psalm 119 (S.A.E. for copy) and a poem extolling "The Vertue of the Psalmes". Psalm 2 runs:

Why fum'th in fight the Gentiles' spite, in fury raging stout?
Why tak'th in hand the people fond, vain things to bring about? (set to the
The Kings arise, the Lords devise, in counsels met thereto,   VW tune.)
Against the Lord with false accord, against his Christ they go.

16th November. Musical Bumps.
(That's the name of a party-game in 1930s, now forgotten.)

We don't want things to go wrong at a concert yet we can smile if occasionally they do. I'm told that a famous northern orchestra performing the third "Leonora" overture by Beethoven was taken aback when the offstage trumpeter missed his cue to sound a fanfare. He had been put in the corridor behind the stage of the milltown's only hall, and seen by the local bobby through the glass doors. His explanation of lurking there with trumpet won the response "That's a likely story, come with me!"

"Punch" cartoon, 1844, 'Der Freischütz at the Haymarket'.

- - -

(suggesting the Shakespearian idea of simplicity, placards replacing stage scenery.)

- - -

I myself saw a percussionist dislodge a tubular bell in the final bars of "Pictures at an Exhibition", only to catch it before it hit the ground and disrupted the final clangour.

Hugh Vickers' "Even Greater Operatic Disasters" (Papermac, 1983) has some good yarns. During a Manchester performance of Wagner's "Ring" cycle in 1976 Siegfried lifted the breastplate from the sleeping Brunnhilde. Starting back as needed at the words "Das ist kein Mann" he heroically ignored the note which she had put on her breast: "Do not disturb, Early Morning Tea 7.30am."

Richard Strauss's "Salome" causes disquiet in operatic circles by reason of its questionable taste. When a company took it to Australia the theatre-manager objected to the very gory head that the producer had brought; then the large soprano fell out with the stagehands who got their own back by replacing it with ham sandwiches which were unveiled to the dialogue: <u>Herod</u>: "Daughter of Herodias you blaspheme". <u>Salome</u>: "I care not, I will kiss his mouth".

At the New York Metropolitan Opera in 1937, in "Lohengrin", Melchior, tricked in his bridal chamber by Telramund, failed to find the desired sword under his bed, and with great presence of mind substituted a short left to the jaw of his astonished cuckolder. Then in Dublin a paralytically-drunk tenor in "La Boheme" couldn't find Mimi's "chelida manina" to grasp

17th November. "Yanks", or Summer-time in Gorsley. (book review.)

I am concerned about the relative lack of attention to and availability of the writings of George W. Target. Of his fine novels from around the 1960s it seems that "The Teachers" is best-known, probably because its tale of a London primary school staffed by intriguing characters latches on to the early experiencs of many of us, as it evokes an era before the mechanisation by Ofsted, standard assessment tests and so forth. 'Penguin' published it after it had appeared as a Duckworth hardback. Other Target novels are no less fine; I recently discovered The Patriots (1974), about a pair of IRA bombers in London, the man a thug, the girl a true patriot - not a topic to endear its author to the then British establishment or public! The man escapes; the girl gets caught after she has sickened of the use of violence.

George Target's novel "The Americans" (Duckworth 1964) reaches a very sensational climax during a CND march to the H-bomb missile base on Gorsley Common. His tale however is also a cameo of workaday life that glorious summer in a Kentish town based on Bromley where he lived. (Gorse replaces Broom.) The young courting couples still went steady then, even when laced with a fair shot of delinquency:-

* the impeccable Tom Wallington and his Carol;
* the up-market Peter Devas and Pam Wheeler-Bennet, shotgun-wed children of Mayor and Alderman;
* Greg and Sandra;
* Tony Fuller and tiresome little Moira;
* the undesirable Danny Hills and compliant Doris;
* David and Susan;
* the heroic Barty and Becky from oppressed groups;
* and hapless Chuck whose Joyce "wouldn't even let him make first base, yet came to grief all the same,-'in the smoke'". (Psalm 119.83!)

It is a pity that misplaced "patriotism" in our Establishment has blanketed out what is among the very greatest of our 20th-century novels, seeing it as subversive which it is not. The broad canvas of Gorsley life during that hot summer is built, like a Sibelius symphony, into a marvellous mosaic out of innumerable fragments of the "day of small things" - the Catford Hot Cats, the angling club, the milk now having come, "the whistle, the closing gates, the green flag..." - the whole, like much else of the GWT oeuvre,

333   　　— — — — —   (continued at foot overleaf

18th November.   Still On Target!

George Target's other books include "Evangelism Inc." (critique of Billy Graham & Co.), "Watch With Me" (devotional), "Bernadette" (definitive biography of Devlin, Westminster M.P. at 21 the youngest ever) and "Scenes of War" (published by the Fellowship of Reconciliation & hard to obtain):

"To tell of war", he writes, "it is necessary to risk rhetoric — for nothing so wicked, so monstrous, so irreligious, ought to be spoken about in the innocent, comely, loving and lovely words of common speech... Not

GWT, mid-thirties c.1960.

the rhetoric of propaganda, the lies told in what we are assured is the Cause of Truth and Peace...but the rhetoric of pity, compassion, suffering, patience, forgiveness" where Hope rests.

"And then there was Jock, came from the tenements of Glasgow — and Tosher from along the Old Kent Road, always on the scrounge...Dave, Jim, Arthur, Tom, Mike...All dead...Yes, the many men so beautiful, ranked now in the tended rows of Military Cemeteries as they had once stood so easy in other, living, breathing ranks...For how else, except in ranks, battalions, regiments, uniforms, blind and obedient, can so many of us be brought to the killing of our unknown Brothers? the numbing of conscience?..'God be merciful to me a sinner...'"

"The Great Golden Legend is that the Dead Have Died That We Might Live, that They Gave Their Tomorrows For Our Todays. 'Give your life?' Taffy used to say. 'You get it taken, boyo!' Taffy...buried him next to the Italian...pinched half the flowers..."

17.11 (Review of "The Americans") continued.

being (to quote a friend's letter to me) "so cheering to revisit" since "life needs 'spicing up' with dabs of 'it'"! All this in the context of serious faith, with old prayers made to cover present needs, and the sight of a trainload of nuclear missiles eleciting this from Cranmer's litany — "O holy, blessed, and glorious Trinity, three Persons and one God: have mercy upon us miserable sinners". Excellent!   F.McM.

— — — — — —

(Please order from your library this book; The Teachers; The Scientists; The Triumph of Vice; The Patriots; Bernadette etc. I'll welcome any comments on them which you care to send.) 334

19th November. Two of England's Greatest.

This brief letter from me appeared in the _Guardian_ on 29.9.92, in reply to "Centipede's" article on the 20th century's greatest symphonies. My recklessly-terse rejoinder reviewed Vaughan Williams' output. His No. 6 caused a sensation in 1948 when it followed the serene No. 5 which had brought balm during the terrible war years. Wilfrid Mellers (11.1) said that "In the furious turmoil of the first few bars Eden is obliterated". A marvellous paradisal tune crowns the first movement, only to yield to

YOUR omission of England's greatest symphonist, Ralph Vaughan Williams, seems either inexplicable or deliberately provocative. His No. 3 may be too intimate, No. 4 too raucous, No. 6 too destructive, No. 7 a shade too programmatic, and No. 9 too tough; but his Fifth is a near-perfect gem, and No. 2 (his own favourite, the "London") is what I'd take to a desert island if limited to one work, for it covers the entire spectrum of human feeling.

the baleful rhythms and fanfares of the doom-laden second, in which they are followed by a quiet passage of dark beauty and pathos and a cataclysmic climax on drums and brass. This in turn dies away before the jazzy noise of the third, followed only by a hushed and wispy epilogue whose strange beauty needs many hearings before it is fully grasped. One comment I heard after an early performance was "It frightened the knickers off me!" - and yes the general opinion, which RVW's denials failed to eradicate completely, was that it expresses the havoc of and desolation after World War 2. But Mellers points out that "The death of the heart may occur in many contexts, especially in our brutishly mechanised world". I have no disc or tape of this magnificent "6th", for I agree with Beethoven's verdict on "furious turmoil": "O friends, not these sounds! Let us attune our voices more joyfully and more acceptably!"

Dr Joseph Needham (20.8) had many claims to fame, as biochemist, Chardin scholar, and Sinologist whose encyclopaedia of Chinese science and civilisation has filled a void in Western understanding. As Anglican "Reader" and Christian Socialist he linked with Conrad Noel's tradition at Thaxted Church. His article "Laud, The Levellers, and the Virtuosi" (publisher not known to me) amplifies the aftermath of Reformation plunder: "In 17th-century England...even in religion there was a moment of equal-poise...before the medieval tradition, in the form of the C. of E., ceded the power to the Protestant and Puritan bodies...perhaps but an aspect of the passing of power (of which) the civil war and the Commonwealth were the outward and visible signs...The abolition of the laws against usury; the "freeing" of trade from galling restrictions...the complete removal..of economic life from theological control — all signified the triumph of the middle class." (But see Rev. 2 4,5!)

20th November.   "Single Vision and Newton's Sleep."   336

There is a consensus among our very great poets that the universe can't be contained in the conceptual cage of physical science however splendid. Wordsworth wrote that he never wilfully yielded to life's tendency (Prelude, 1850, XIV, 160) to "substitute a universe of death/ For that which moves with light and life informed,/ Actual, divine and true".

Tennyson confirms this in "The Voice and the Peak"; "A deep below the deep,/ And a height beyond the height!/ Our hearing is not hearing,/ And our seeing is not sight." And the visionary William Blake prays God for deliverance from mechanical philosophies which he denotes as Newton's sleep. It is impossible to survey Blake briefly and adequately; let some of his "Auguries of Innocence" speak for themselves:

"A Robin Redbreast in a cage
Puts all Heaven in a rage;

He who shall train the horse to war
Shall never pass the Polar Bar.

The wild deer wandering here and there
Keep the human soul from care.

Kill not the moth nor butterfly,
For the last judgment draweth nigh.

Nought can deform the human race
Like to the armourer's iron brace.

When gold and gems adorn the plough,
To peaceful arts shall Envy bow.

The whore and gambler, by the state
Licensed, build that nation's fate.

The emmet's inch and eagle's mile
Make lame philosophy to smile.

A truth that's told with bad intent
Beats all the lies you can invent.

Joy and woe are woven fine,
A clothing for the soul divine."

Ruskin memorial cross, Coniston churchyard.

Follow a light that leaps and spins,
  Follow the fire unfurled!
For riseth up against realm and rod,
A thing forgotten, a thing downtrod,
The last lost giant, even God,
  Is risen against the world.
	For our God hath blessed creation,
	  Calling it good. I know
	What spirit with whom you blindly band
	Hath blessed destruction with his hand;
	Yet by God's death the stars shall stand
	  And the small apples grow.

(from "The Ballad of the White Horse" - G.K. Chesterton.)

21st November.   A Family Treasure.   337

Gift of P. Howson

George Formby Jr., ukulele man and popular pre-war entertainer with his Window-cleaner's and Chinese Laundry songs among many others, and holder of an early "golden disc" for a million sales, with his fiancée Patricia Hewson in her Preston home. Theirs would have been the second marriage of widower George, but he died before it could take place. The photograph is inscribed to my parents, in Pat's writing that can be seen over the coffee-pot: "To Frank & Louie, with love, xPatx." Pat's mother and mine were long-standing friends long before Pat knew George; and I can just remember visiting their Penwortham home (where I think the photograph was taken) when I was a young boy.

---

from "The Patriots" by George W. Target (17-18.11):
(*) "What they'd really like...is the chance to be charging us for the very air we breathe!" (I warm to that; When I chaired Grange-over-Sands Council's water authority my pay was nil; now the chairmen get fat-cat salaries!)
(*) "Those who choose to walk through fire must count the cost."
(*) "Desperation is the driving force of extremism."

Translate: "FORFO OISTO PONDERO VER"   (solution - 29.11)

22nd November. "A Quickness that my God hath Kiss'd." 338

A quick look (pun!) at Prayer, defined thus quaintly by Henry Vaughan...First from the Book of Common Prayer (BCP):

"O God, merciful Father, that despisest not the sighing of a contrite heart, nor the desire of such as be sorrowful; Mercifully assist our prayers that we make before thee in all our troubles and adversities, whensoever they oppress us; and graciously hear us, that those evils, which the craft and subtilty of the devil or man worketh against us, be brought to nought; and by the providence of thy goodness they may be dispersed; that we thy servants, being hurt by no persecutions, may evermore give thanks unto thee in thy holy Church; through Jesus Christ our Lord.

"O Lord, arise, help us, and deliver us for thy Name's sake."
- - - - - -   (from The Litany).

"O merciful and mighty God, who hatest nothing that thou hast made; who through thine only-begotten Son Jesus Christ hast overcome death, and opened unto us the gate of everlasting life: We humbly beseech thee graciously to behold this thy family in this demi-paradise and vale of tears; and to receive our supplications and prayers for all men and women in thy holy church, for all who do not know the Lord Jesus, and for all who by word or deed reject his universal faith. Take away all ignorance, blindness and hardness of heart, and contempt of thy word, that we may truly serve thee and be brought home as one flock by our Lord Jesus, that great Shepherd of the sheep, who is alive and reigns with thee and the Holy Ghost, ever one God, world without end. Amen." (from the Good Friday and Easter collects and G.W. Target, "The Americans", adapted.)

1. THEY who trod the path of labour follow where My feet have trod;
They who work without complaining do the holy will of God;
Nevermore thou needest seek Me; I am with thee everywhere;
Raise the stone and thou shalt find Me; cleave the wood and I am there.

2. Where the many toil together there am I among My own;
Where the tired workman sleepeth there am I with him alone.
I, the Peace that passeth knowledge, dwell amid the daily strife;
I, the Bread of heaven, am broken in the sacrament of life.

3. Every task, however simple, sets the soul that does it free;
Every deed of love and mercy done to man, is done to Me.
Nevermore --
—*Henry Van Dyke*, 1852-1933.

No. 601, Old Methodist Hymnal, Victorian industrial era. The "Nevermore" chorus is from the Gospel of Thomas, found lately.

23rd November.   Making The Pathways Neat.

Thomas Hardy's poem "During Wind and Rain" draws for detail on his first wife Emma's "Recollections" of her Plymouth childhood and her family departure from friends in pouring rain, by train to live in Cornwall. It offers, with magical illustrations, the flow and ebb of human life, its intimate joys and ultimate doom. "We pass; the path that each man trod / Is dim, or will be dim, with weeds: / What fame is left for human deeds / In endless age? It rests with God." (Tennyson, In Memoriam, Canto 73). Here now is Hardy:

They sing their dearest songs—
He, she, all of them—yea,
Treble and tenor and bass,
 And one to play;
With the candles mooning each face. . . .
 Ah, no; the years O!
How the sick leaves reel down in throngs!

They clear the creeping moss—
Elders and juniors—aye,
Making the pathways neat
 And the garden gay;
And they build a shady seat. . . . .
 Ah, no; the years, the years; across
See, the webbed white storm-birds wing.

They are blithely breakfasting all—
Men and maidens—yea,
Under the summer tree,
 With a glimpse of the bay,
While pet fowl come to the knee. . . .
 Ah, no; the years O!
And the rotten rose is ript from the wall.

They change to a high new house,
He, she, all of them—aye,
Clocks and carpets and chairs
 On the lawn all day,
And brightest things that are theirs. . .
 Ah, no; the years, the years; ploughs.
Down their chiselled names the rain-drop

I am reminded of Wordsworth's "Journey down the Duddon" in 30 or so dullish sonnets which offer a "God's-eye view" of all the lovely Lakeland river, "Child of the clouds", down to where "Majestic Duddon" passes the Broughton water-meadows which are my earliest memory at 3 or 4, to expand "o'er smooth flat sands" at Foxfield and Millom. There follows the great and famous "Afterthought" which is a final flash of genius:

> I THOUGHT of Thee, my partner and my guide,
> As being pass'd away.—Vain sympathies!
> For, backward, Duddon! as I cast my eyes,
> I see what was, and is, and will abide;
> Still glides the Stream, and shall for ever glide;
> The Form remains, the Function never dies;
> While we, the brave, the mighty, and the wise,
> We Men, who in our morn of youth defied
> The elements, must vanish;—be it so!
> Enough, if something from our hands have power
> To live, and act, and serve the future hour;
> And if, as toward the silent tomb we go,   [dower,
> Through love, through hope, and faith's transcendent
> We feel that we are greater than we know.

Self, 18 mths, feeding tortoise (1929).

24th November. **WHAT BANGED?** (Some Nibbles and Quibbles.)

The Nobel physics prize was awarded in October 2006 to two scientists for helping to prove that the universe began with the Big Bang. Can anyone please say what banged? An explosion is an event in time, and is inconceivable that there could have been one "when time was yet unknown" (15.9). Nor can anything be known if there be no Mind or Minds to do thee knowing!

— — — — — —

"His Day is marching on": Services of Remembrance can risk accidental harm if they are too selective. After the so-called "Battle Hymn of the Republic" (10.11, 16.12) had ended the event in St Paul's Cathedral on 14th September 2001 in consolation of the Victims of the New York outrages five days previously, a "broadsheet" press-correspondent wrote that is was "primarily a battle hymn for an elect nation". He failed to recognise it as a theophany portraying God's action in history. "Behold, he cometh with clouds...and all kindreds of the earth shall wail because of him." (Revelation 1.7). Our own heroic Sheila Cassidy, in "Good Friday People" (DLT, 1971), devotes chapter 18 to the "Day of Yahweh" theme of the Old Testament Prophets, e.g. Habakkuk 3 and Zephaniah 1.14-16: "The great day of the Lord is near...a day of wrath...trumpet and alarm against the fenced cities and the high towers"! So also Julia Howe: "He is sifting out the souls of men before his judgement seat" — all men and women on all sides of any conflict, not validating "an alliance that should use its military power to crush the terror" (Daily Mail!)

The U.S. slavery-rebellion of 1861-5 pierced many true hearts as a "terrible swift sword". The pacifist Senator Sumner set aside his views, thinking temporary war was less evel than entrenched slavery; and as Lincoln's foreign minister was eventually to "weep like a woman" at the bedside of the stricken President. Today's pacifists are spared such "testing by the imperatives of love"; war is now too total to afford room for the reckonings of just-war theory! It is only on All Souls Day that the even larger death-toll of world hunger and curable illness is acknowledged by us "Christians"

— — — — — — —

Scotland's greatest 20th-century divine, George MacLeod (17.5), concurred with Michael Ramsey (14.4) in refuting the "Hurd school of churchmanship" which would "keep politics out of religion", seeking ease in a "Castle of Orthodoxy" assured of Jesus as High Priest within whilst following the Jehovah's Witnesses in not applying His Kingship to the world outside. "Only One Way Left" — Cunningham Lectures 1954, publ. Iona.

Stir-Up Sunday 25th November 1996 — so called because the "collect" or day's prayer in the C. of E. Book of Common Prayer for the Sunday next before Advent runs: "Stir up, we beseech thee, O Lord, the wills of thy faithful people; that they, plenteously bringing forth the fruit of good works may of thee be plenteously rewarded; thro' JC our Lord".

Inevitably this led to the old custom of stirring the ingredients of the year's Christmas pudding so that it had time to improve on standing. Nowadays the Co-op and other large groceries sell such excellent puddings that the skills of home production are at severe risk.

The collect at Holy Communion is followed by Jeremiah's prophecy of the righteous King, and of future deliverances such as eclipse the exodus from slavery in Egypt.

This passage, and the four preceding verses which begin the 23rd chapter of "Jeremiah" by warning Israelite pastors not to prey upon or scatter the Lord's people — leaders of churches and religious bodies please note! — have been versified by me as follows:

"Woe to the shepherds who scatter the sheep On the mountains and every high hill,/ Who rule and devour them and carelessly sleep, Never binding the broken or ill;/ For the days are a-coming and now they begin When the Scion of David shall reign,/ And His people shall know He effaces their sin And shall dwell in their lands once again."

To this may be added such verses as these, each with chorus:
*) "Out with the bomb-blessing prelates and lords, The killjoys that smother our life./ Out with the statesmen who strive for rewards, Dividing our lands by their strife,/For the days.."
"Come stir up our wills that they waver no more,/And order our steps in thy peace,/ That wisdom may triumph o'er weapons of war, And the fruits of the Spirit increase,/ For the days.."
*) (Bp Gerald Ellison of Chester refused to bless Polaris c.1960)

26th November. **Byron's True Friend!**

In the grounds of Newstead Abbey where the poet George Gordon Lord Byron lived before "fleeing" England, there stands an impressive memorial to his beloved dog Boatswain (Bo'sun), which delights visitors more than it did his acquaintances!—

>   Near this Spot
>   are deposited the Remains of one
>   who possessed Beauty without Vanity,
>   Strength without Insolence,
>   Courage without Ferocity,
> and all the virtues of Man without his Vices.
>   This praise, which would be unmeaning Flattery
>   if inscribed over human Ashes,
>   is but a just tribute to the Memory of
>
>   B O A T S W A I N, a D O G,
>
>   who was born in Newfoundland May 1803
>   and died at Newstead Nov`r`. 18th 1808.

When some proud Son of Man returns to earth,
Unknown to Glory but upheld by Birth,
The sculptor's art exhausts the pomp of woe,
And storied urns record who rests below:
When all is done, upon the Tomb is seen
Not what he was, but what he should have been.
But the poor Dog, in life the firmest friend,
The first to welcome, foremost to defend,
Whose honest heart is still his Masters own,
Who labours, fights, lives, breathes for him alone,
Unhonour'd falls, unnotic'd all his worth,
Deny'd in heaven the Soul he held on earth:
While man, vain insect! hopes to be forgiven,
And claims himself a sole exclusive heaven,
Oh man! thou feeble tenant of an hour,
Debased by slavery, or corrupt by power,
Who knows thee well, must quit thee with disgust,
Degraded mass of animated dust!
Thy love is lust, thy friendship all a cheat,
Thy tongue hypocrisy, thy heart deceit,
By nature vile, ennobled but by name,
Each kindred brute might bid thee blush for shame,
Ye! who behold perchance this simple urn,
Pass on, it honours none you wish to mourn,
To mark a friend's remains these stones arise
I never knew but one — and here he lies.

342

"Terrorism is the poor man's war; war is the rich man's terrorism." — Peter Ustinov. We need to be rid of both.

27th November. "Old Abe Lincoln Came Out of the Wilderness, 343
              Many long years ago." - and that, with repet-
itions and two weak verses, "Old Jeff Davis tore down the
government" & "But old Abe Lincoln built up a better one", is
all there is to the Yankee Civil War song except for its tune
(which resurfaced in the Great War as "We are the King's Navee").

These are rousing songs of comfort for soldiers away from
home, and I enjoy them even though war needs taking off human-
ity's agenda for the new millennium. They and their tunes
used to be very familiar, but may have been marginalised by
commercial sound, in which case they can be sought on I.T.
and from libraries. "Marching through Georgia" sanitises the
scorched-earth policy of Sherman which desolated the South,
so that Lincoln's name is abhorred to this day in Charlestown!

"Bring the good old bugle, boys, we'll sing another song;
Sing it with a spirit that will start the world along,
Sing it as we used to sing it, fifty thousand strong,
While we were marching through Georgia. (Chorus) Hurrah! Hur-
  rah! We bring the jubilee! Hurrah! Hurrah! The flag that
  makes you free! So we sang the chorus from Atlanta to the sea.
                                                        While etc.
"Yes, and there were Union men who wept with joyful tears,
When they saw the honoured flag they had not seen for years;
Hardly could they be restrained from breaking forth in cheers,
                                                        While etc.
"So we made a thoroughfare for Freedom and her train,
Sixty miles in latitude, three hundred to the main;
Treason fled before us, for resistance was in vain, While etc!"

Then, merrily parodied to run "Mary had a little lamb, its
fleece was white as snow, Shouting out the battle cry of free-
the call to rally round the anti-slavery cause went: dom..."

"Oh we'll Rally Round the Flag, boys, we'll rally once again,
Shouting out the battle cry of freedom;
We will rally from the hillside, we'll gather from the plain,
Shouting out the battle cry of freedom.
 (Chorus) The Union for ever, Hurrah, boys, hurrah!
Down with the traitor, Up with the star, While we rally etc.

"We will welcome to our numbers the loyal, true, and brave...
And although they may be poor not a man shall be a slave, etc.

"So we're springing to the call from the East & to the West...
And we'll hurl the rebel crew from the land we love the best,
                                                        etc!"
Fine words (over the top? - but no! - ours is the bloodless
fight in the wake of those, Him, who gave innocent blood for all!)

28th November.   **"Awareness, Awareness, Awareness!"**   344

Anthony de Mello, S.J, who died in 1987, was widely known for his retreats, seminars and spiritual teaching of a distinctive character over 18 years. He directed the Sadhana Institute in Poona, India, and his writings include the 'Fount' paperback (1990) entitled "Awareness" (which was his main theme).

He offers a view of human motivation which warns that kind human deeds are not simply altruistic but generally stem from a degree of enlightened self-interest since they please the doer! Awareness of this checks our pride, and tells us not to expect too much from our fellows or to judge them too harshly; for all save the awakened few pursue self-interest, whether in coarse or refined ways. We therefore should not feel let down or rejected when they disappoint or oppose us, but should swap our illusions for reality, and dreams for facts, so that our lives gain meaning and beauty. Confidence takes over from being too dependent on others' words & whims. We can observe things, then our thoughts, then ourselves as thinkers of thoughts. de Mello recalls a fable of a lion that approached some sheep and was amazed to find another lion among them which bleated like a sheep and showed by its behaviour that it thought it was one. He took it to a pond and showed it their reflections, whereupon it grasped its nature and started roaring! I think, and my objects of thought include "me myself". "I" am more permanent than my "me" which is known by name, clothes, diction, behaviour etc., all of which change in ways that my awareness outlasts. The "me" in which suffering exists is no longer identified with when one observes it after "stepping out"!...and so forth with Tony de Mello's insights which can but be hinted at in this sketch.

This detachment which he commends does not stop our acting against perceived injustice. Indeed we do so more effectively when not blinded by negative feelings against offenders. Also our interdependence is not poisoned by demanding too much from others; it is contact with reality that banishes loneliness, not just human company as such!

Something similar applies to religious practice; God, says Tony, "would be much happier if you were transformed than if you worshipped". Cardinal Martini told of an Italian couple who arranged for their wedding-reception to be in the church courtyard; but it rained and the priest was coaxed to let it take place in the church. Upset by the hilarity he spoke to his assistant who pointed out that Jesus enjoyed the Cana wedding. "Ah but they had no Reserved Sacrament there!" he rued, his ritual sense blown up to exceed reality and love!

<u>29th November.</u>   "F O U R S Q U A R E."   St Paul's Cathedral.

a reproach to much of contemporary London building!

See 25 May for its pre-decessor, lost, 1666, by fire.

<u>Puzzle solution</u> from 21.11: "FOR/FOOLS/TO/PONDER/OVER".
(Not Latin, of which my generation of school-pupils said:
"Latin is a dead language, Dead as dead can be; First it
killed the Romans, Now it's killing me." - But it's a beautiful language if dreary to learn, and campaigners for a universal language might have done better defending it than by opting for "Esperanto". "Caesar sed passus sum iam" means "But, Caesar, I have suffered already", and not as it sounds when spoken. Another "howler" relates to a French report of the emotive response to an orator by his audience: "Le peuple ému répondit", rendered by pupil "The purple emu laid another egg.")

"Plunge into the heat of battle and keep your heart at the lotus feet of the Lord." (Lord Krishna, Hindu Bhagavad-Gita.)

       Moll Flanders, a girl of the street
       Was skilled in the art of deceit;
         Transported for crime,
         Moll repented in time -
       She's the felon who fell on her feet. (V.E.Cox).

"The story is repeated, The world is ever so; All virtue 345
seems defeated And hope sinks very low; But those once persecuted Their triumphs yet attain, And evil executed Is turned
           to Easter's gain." (Will O'Connor.)

30th November.   "WANNABE CELEBRITY?"   346

Andy Capp, famous around 1960s for lazing whilst his wife did all the domestic work. Necessary in the era of exhausting manual work, this was perpetuated by some husbands in better days.

"A small-time businessman, 55 years old", writes Tony de Mello (see 28.11), "is sipping beer at a bar and he's saying, "Well, look at my classmates, they've really made it." They've got their names in the newspaper; do you call that making it? One is president of the corporation; the other has become the Chief Justice. "Do you call that making it?

"Who determines what it means to be a success? This stupid society!...Being president of a corporation, having a lot of money has nothing to do with being a success in life. You're a success in life when you wake up!...You have no worries; you're happy. That's what I call being a success. Having a good job or being famous or having a great reputation has absolutely nothing to do with happiness or success. Nothing! All he's really worried about is what his children will think about him, what the neighbours will think about him...He should have become famous. Our society and culture drill that into our heads night and day. People who made it! Made what?! Made asses of themselves, because they drained all their energy getting something that was worthless...And do you know why that happens? Only one reason: They identified the "I" with some label — with their money or their job or their profession. That was their error."

I think we damage people by treating them as celebrities, though a few of them are wise enough to value their work as an end in itself. Tony de Mello's warnings do not deny a person the quiet contentment of finding his or her true role in life and fulfilling it as well as is humanly possible!

"God give me life till my work is done and work till my life is o'er" — Winifred Holtby, friend of Vera Brittain and author of the great 1930s novel "South Riding."

1st December. "Chill December brings the sleet..."

With the dark teatimes upon us, we look forward to Christmas brightness, all too often "jumping the gun" and turning a consumerist Winterval into Autumnval (which is even worse!) Some old customs from the following list still **survive, however.**

5th – St Nicholas' Eve; gifts exchanged in continental Europe & "Boy Bishops installed till 28.12 when they preach swansong sermons. This in medieval England happened only at Bury St Edmund's, but is now more widespread; I imagine we will have a Girl Bishop or two presently!

6th – St Nicholas' Day; he was the Bishop of Myra whose secret munificence included tossing bags of gold into the homes of the poor. Hence the Santa Claus outfit, evolved from bishops' robes, and his gifts via chimneys. He has merged with and all but superseded the northern Father Christmas.

9th – Celebration of the red red Robin who comes bob bob bobin' along. "The Robin Redbreast and the Wren
Are God Almighty's cock and hen." (Trite!)

12th – Tin Can Bands perform at Broughton, Northants at midnight to exclude gypsies seen as malign influences. (Illegal!)

13th – St Lucy's Day, carefully celebrated in the alarming old custom of girls in white dresses with evergreen crowns, and some at least with lit candles in their crowns as in Sweden. "Lucy light, Lucy light, Shortest day and longest night" – (or so it was, roughly speaking, till we lost the Julian calendar in 1752). Latin for "light" is "lux, lucis". In England the custom has largely been replaced by Christingle events in which children and others hold oranges and candles.

16th – St Tibba's Day, celebrated at her well at Ryhall, Rutland by the gathered fowlers and falconers. Also "O Sapientia" -16.12.

21st – St Thomas' Day (also observable on 3.7), mentioned by Thomas Hardy near the start of "Far from the Madding Crowd" with shepherd Oak watching his flock by the twinklings of the stars as they slowly wheeled their way around the sky. "St Thomas Gray, St Thomas Gray, Longest night and shortest day" – (compare 13th above; did the calendar-change yield this jingle?) Some girls slept with onions under pillows hoping to have visions of their future husbands, or sang: "Good St Thomas, do me right,/ Let my true love come tonight,/ That I may see face to face / And in my arms his form embrace." Labourers went "Thomasing" to collect gifts from farmers; or "Corning" or "Gooding", exchanging hollysprigs for flour.
(to 23.12)

2nd December. Down the Rabbit Hole, & other Curiosities. 348

The governing bodies of sports find it necessary to lay down interpretations of unusual situations that occasionaly crop up. The "Decisions on Golf Rules" by the Royal and Ancient Club of St Andrew's (2002-3) hold that if the ball enters Burrowing Animal Hole out of Bounds and comes to rest in Bounds, then under rule 25.1 the player may drop the ball, without penalty, within one club-length of the point on the ground directly above its position in the burrow.

— — — — — — —

"Lips in pistol, Mist in times; Cats in crystal, Mice in chimes." - James Thurber. (Spellings.)

— — — — — — —

Around the turn of the century it was reported that during the hockey match between the diocesan clergy and Mothers' Union the Bishop of Truro, Bill Ind, was sent off the field by the referee. His offence was to have told the official who had given an anti-clergy decision that he'd be happy to exercise his guide dog for him if it would help. Collusion to give a laugh was suspected. (For more on bishops see 7 January).

Decision: no lead for England
(Picture:- Lisbon 24.6.04!)

— — — — — — —

"The Magistrate" magazine for June 2004 thanked Victoria Wyer JP of Wiltshire for the following sentence from a defence solicitor's letter: "My client did not fragrantly flout the law."

— — — — — — —

"Bishopesses" - Ray Simpson's "Exploring Celtic Spirituality" contains a paragraph about an Irish tradition which can not now be either proved or disproved. I have come across the episode elsewhere, in connection with St Brigid's installation as abbess of Kildare, a double foundation with female and male houses. The paragraph, Reproduced by permission of Hodder and Stoughton Limited, reads:

"When Brigid became a nun in the 6th century one old bishop, Ibor, was so struck by the aura of holy fire over her that he unintentionally read the words for the consecration of a bishop over her. He told a remonstrating colleague: 'I have no power in this matter: this dignity has been given by God to Brigid'."

— — — — — — —

In early 2004 a church organist from Maghull wrote (alas I do not have the source) that he had "been an organist in the Anglican Church or over 50 years, and the music has deteriorated at the same rate as the language. 300 years of sublime words and music have given way to lachrymose ditties, Noddy tunes and worship songs." I share this concern - see opposite.

3rd December. Bright The Vision That Delighted. 349

[musical notation]

I like to visit England's "Northern Lakes", not least Derwentwater and the Borrowdale Valley south of Keswick. I take the liberty of entering the fine oak pulpit in Stonethwaite Church if nobody else is there, to sing a verse or two of Richard Mant's hymn on the vision of Isaiah in ch.6 of his book:

BRIGHT the vision that delighted
  Once the sight of Judah's seer;
Sweet the countless tongues united
  To entrance the prophet's ear.

2 Round the Lord in glory seated,
  Cherubim and seraphim
 Men Filled his temple, and repeated
  Each to each the alternate hymn:

3 'Lord, thy glory fills the heaven;
  Earth is with its fullness stored;
Unto thee be glory given,
  Holy, holy, holy, Lord.'

4 Heaven is still with glory ringing,
  Earth takes up the angels' cry,
'Holy, holy, holy,' singing,
  'Lord of hosts, the Lord most high.'

5 With his seraph train before him,
  With his holy Church below,
 Women Thus conspire we to adore him,
  Bid we thus our anthem flow:

6 'Lord, thy glory fills the heaven;
  Earth is with its fullness stored:
Unto thee be glory given, (see also
  Holy, holy, holy, Lord.'   5.1.)

The poignancy is that the pulpit was taken from Holy Trinity Church, Mardale before Haweswater was flooded to make a vast reservoir in the late 1930s; and the hymn was sung at the final church-service (see 18.12). Its words were specially apt for the valley-head, first (or 2nd to Wasdale?) for grandeur in all Lakeland. "No one who walked up the valley and saw the fields carpeted with wild flowers and the hedges in a glory of bloom, and the great rhododendron bushes clustering round the Dun Bull Inn, could fail to regret that it was their last flowering before the water began to flood during the following winter." - M.Fraser, 'Companion into Lakeland' (1937 — see also 11.10).

I find hymns of around the 19th century far superior to many of the worship-songs that are promoted nowadays; these tend to be deliberately repetitive, and more expressive of the singers' feelings than of the splendours of the Faith. The exclusion (or abbreviation) of St Patrick's Breastplate is scandalous, and I say that publishers have a nerve to update the 1906 "English Hymnal" and the 1925 "Songs of Praise" for younger gatherings, both of which had Percy Dearmer and Ralph Vaughan Williams among their literary and musical editors though of course there are fine 20th-century hymns and tunes to add, & simpler harmonies for St Patrick's hymn & others.

For a lighthearted survey of "Hymns Bad & Worse" please see 15 December before the survey of seasonal hymns next day. A point worth stressing now is that ancient Christian art and hymnody excels modern, in focusing on the "Triumph of the Cross" no less than on its blood and anguish. (continues 4.12)

4th December. "Tell Me the Old Old Story!"

(cont?. from 3.12.) Today's churches which display "stations to the cross" on their interior walls, to portray scenes en route to Calvary, should surely add "stations beyond the cross" showing Mary Magdalene mistaking the risen Jesus for the gardener, etc. Kenneth Leech has written (loc. cit. 5.4): "The more ancient the crucifixes the more likely they are to show Christ as victor...", and has commended Fortunatus' fine hymns, of which "Sing my tongue" is ideal for Good Friday Veneration. "Songs of Praise" boldly sets it to "Grafton" aka "Tantum Ergo" in the major mode. (Why not "Regent Sq." or "Westminster Abbey"?)

(Venantius Fortunatus, 530-609, was a Latin poet from near Venice. Said to be lazy and a gourmet, which were as nought alongside his work as biographer of St Martin and of his platonic female friend the deserted Queen Radegunde, he settled near her at Poitiers where he became bishop in his late 60s. To Radegunde he wrote: "Even though the clouds are gone and the sky is serene, the day is sunless when you are absent." He sent her roses and lilies. The "fragment of the True Cross" which she obtained in 569 inspired his great Passiontide hymns.)

Another day which calls for a cheerful song is Trinity Thursday, the traditional "Corpus Christi" festival of thanksgiving for Holy Communion and the formation of Christ's people as His Body on earth. In the 14th & 15th centuries there were great processions of craft-guilds and town councils, and the long processional hymn by Thomas Aquinas, "Praise O Sion, praise thy Master" has been set by S.H. Nicholson (in A&M Rev. as No. 622) to a tune from which, as with the last verse below, I have evolved:

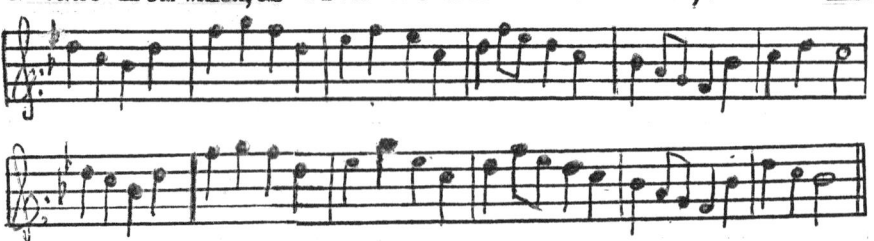

2* Sing to-day, the mystery showing
Of the living, life-bestowing
  Bread from heaven before thee set;
E'en the same of old provided,
Where the Twelve, divinely guided,
  At the holy Table met.

5 What he did at Supper seated,
Christ ordained to be repeated,
  His memorial ne'er to cease :
And, his word for guidance taking,
Bread and wine we hallow, making
  Thus our Sacrifice of peace.

11

Lo the angels' food is given;
See the pilgrims' bread from heaven
Which on dogs can ne'er be spent;

Thou Who this on earth bestowest,
Bring us where Thy face Thou showest,
Guests to share Thy nourishment.

th December. Tressall's "Ragged Trousered Philanthropists" (28.1) contains its hero's Oration on how the "boss-class" corners an unfair share of the fruits of its capital and of employees' labour. The justification put forward was that since owners bore all the risks of business-failure, the workers were entitled to a basic wage but not to a share in the prosperity of good times. This ignored the fact that the workforce could lose its entire livelihood on being sacked or "stood off". Now however Tressall's clarity has been lost through the emergence of impersonal multinational firms within a "global market" that divides the world into nations of the rich and of the desperately poor.

The trick is very simple! Only some 3% of UK money-supply is issued by Government (9.3); the other 97% is made out of nothing by finance-houses (banks etc.) that have the nerve to charge interest for making it available. This predation is mirrored in the widespread drawing of dividends by passive shareholders "who neither toil nor spin" (Gaitskell), so "the rich get all the pleasure" (26.4)! "Ain't it all a blooming shame?"!

Studdert Kennedy wrote ("Democracy & the Dog Collar", 1921 p.60) that "...the system is not a system, it's a growth...out of human nature"-Urged by the unholy spirit, lord & doomster of decay,that proceedeth from the financial predation industry, that with the playboys and girls of the western world together is worshipped and glorified, that spake by the spindoctors. Come Holy Ghost!

6th December. "ORIANA".

This little-known yet beautiful drawing by the pre-Raphaelite artist Wm. Holman Hunt appeared in a volume of early Tennyson poems published in 1857. The artist's model is believed to be his first wife Fanny Waugh.

The poem tells a sad non-classical tale of the heroine who bids farewell "in the yew-wood black as night" to the archer who had just plighted his troth to her by light of moon and star. Alas 'twas her heart that his "damned arrow" pierced when it went aside as she watched the battle.

7th December. The Cheviot, The Stag, and The Black, Black Oil.

It was my great good fortune to find in my Selkirk B&B (p.8) a copy of this 1973 "Ceilidh Play with Scenes, Songs and Music of Highland History from the Clearances to the oil strike". This presentation was compiled co-operatively by the 7.84 Theatre Company, thus named to emphasise that 7% of Britons then "owned" 84% of British property. It was performed in 27 Scottish halls large and small around May 1973; then 27 listed (including 2 in Belgium) that autumn, and 6 in Eire in late June 1974, after which it was televised and published by West Highland Press and then by Methuen, with explanatory notes and illustrations under the copyright of actor John McGrath. The tale begins with the Highland Clearances after Culloden when absentee landlords evicted their villagers to make way for hardy Cheviot sheep that were judged more profitable than tenants' rent. Strathnaver under the 3rd Duke of Sutherland was among the worst, and Patrick Sellar the bailiff was tried and acquitted of murder following the death of a woman in her late 90s when her home was burnt. He appears with James Loch the "Improver" to sing "High Industry" on stage to the tune "Bonnie Dundee":

As the rain on the hillside comes in from the sea
All the blessings of life fall in showers from me
So if you'd abandon your old misery -
I will teach you the secrets of high industry:

Your barbarous customs, though they may be old,
To civilised people hold horrors untold -
What value a culture that cannot be sold?
The price of a culture is counted in gold. (Chorus: As the rain..)

(Loch) There's many a fine shoal of fish in the sea
All waiting for catching and frying for tea -
And I'll buy the surplus, then sell them you see
At double the price that you sold them to me. (Chorus)

(Sellar) I've money to double the rent that you pay,
The factor is willing to give me my way
So off you go quietly - like sheep as they say -
I'll arrange for the boats to collect you today. (Chorus)

Don't think we are greedy for personal gain,
What profit we capture we plough back again,
We don't want big houses or anything grand,
We just want more money to buy up more land. (Chorus).

8th December. <u>Wearing The White Waistcoat.</u> (pictured 16.7)

In the Ceilidh Play a Reader then declares that the Isle of Rhum was cleared of 400 souls "to make way for one sheepfarmer and 5000 sheep". Historical characters then appear including Queen Victoria herself who sings: "These are our mountains/ And this is our glen/ The braes of your childhood/ Are English again", and the 3rd Duke, recruiting for the Crimea War, only to be told by an old man: "You robbed us of our country and gave it to the sheep. Therefore...let sheep now defend you." Depopulation of the seven crofting counties continued through the years when sheep gave way in turn to the stalking of deer and grouse – in 1755 they held 20% of Scotland's population; in 1851, 13%; in 1951, 5%; in 1972, 3%. "In those days" says McGrath "the capital belonged to southern industrialists. Now it belongs to multi-national corporations with even less feeling for the people than Patrick Sellar." He refers to the exploiters of the late 20th century oil strikes, typified by Texas Jim who updates the "High Industry" song, varying the chorus to end: "Then you'll open your doors to the oil industry", and continuing, supported by a worried Whitehall civil servant:

> There's many a barrel of oil in the sea
> All waiting for drilling and piping to me
> I'll refine it in Texas, you'll get it, you see
> At four times the price that you sold it to me.

There are fun-items in the script to lighten its seriousness, and it is followed by the traditional ceilidh – but not before a master of ceremonies – Liz Maclennon spoke the part during the Oban performance to the 1974 conference of the Scottish Nationalist Party – has warned that "Nationalism is not enough. The enemy of the Scottish people is Scottish capital, as much as the foreign exploiter".

Sadly there are few such radical presentations in early 21st century Britain. The great Scots divine George MacLeod, who famously founded the Iona Community, said in his 1954 Cunningham Lectures that "the whole West" may well, as suggested (21.6) under "Standards in Commerce and Politics", be fulfilling, albeit unconsciously, the role of the cartoon capitalist with his watchchain and top hat. "You and I are sporting a sort of collective white waistcoat. There is no proletariat to rise in Britain or the US. But...what if Africa and S.E. Asia now, make rich the Western world? Are we so certain that they will never rise?...The real problem of our time is not domestic but global." We must plan quickly and fairly; for leaving things to the money market and local rulers has beggared the 3rd World!

9th December. __KISS AND TELL!__ or
ELECTION FIREWORKS 5.11.58.

The author (30) with 40-something Barbara Castle and youngish Harold Wilson, preparing for Frank's eve-of-poll meeting at the Morecambe & Lonsdale byelection in the then safe Tory seat.

(Shadows whited out to Harold's detriment!)

The CND issue loomed large and had our support. My personable opponent Basil Ferranti claimed descent from a Doge of Venice. Asked if I could match this I said "Judging from my name I'm descended from the High Kings of Ireland". Published in the Lancs. Evening Post this delighted my father's workmates, and him too. Then Basil was asked his hopes and said his wife would be 23 on polling day and 'twould be a nice gift for her to come first; an easy pleasantry from a well-placed candidate, yet to this day I am amazed that every digit in the result is either 1 or in 23 (or multiple) both left to right and bottom to top. Our Lab. vote was up on 12005 in 1955.

Tory	23923
Lab.	12692
Maj.	11231

Harold and Barbara went on to high State office, which eventually cost Harold his health. Both wished to reverse Heath's entry into the European Community as having been ill-founded. In 1975, encouraged by concessions claimed by Foreign Secretary Jim Callaghan, Wilson and Cabinet called for "Yes" votes in the referendum, whilst Castle remained opposed. The Prime Minister allowed public disagreement but, according to his close friend Barbara's diary, was "almost beside himself" with rage when she helped organise the anti-Government campaign. "No one had done more than he had to keep the party together... and he had had enough of it. 'So this is all the loyalty I get. No one would have brought you back into Government but me.' At that, something snapped in me and (to foot opposite.

10th December.   Poetic Premier and a Bumpy Road.   355

Visit Cwmcoed in Gwent's Ebbw Fach vale, and if you drive or go by bus along Attlee Road you'll be kept wide awake by its posse of "sleeping policemen". This is one of the few places named for Britain's post-war Prime Minister in a century that became more critical of its politicians than Gladstone's. Yet Clement Attlee's admirers honour him as main architect of the UK's most caring social system at least since the Reformation. His biographer Francis Beckett (see also 29.12) shows that his subject belies his "sheep in sheep's clothing" reputation. He dared say of Churchill: "Trouble with Winston. Nails his trousers to the mast. Can't get down." He admonished Truman (US president) over Hiroshima and threatening to "nuke" North Korea, but proved helpless to avert Cold War and the British nuclear arsenal. He failed to recognise that Ireland was on the road to civil conflict. Yet he derided unprincipled politics, and the Daily Herald's anonymous verse was probably his:
(parodying The Red Flag, late 1950s - 2.5)
"With heads uncovered swear we all To have no principles at all; If everyone will turn his coat We'll get the British people's vote."
(Beware of those who act on this!)

9.12 (concl.)   I retorted, 'I have never been so insulted in my life. I thought you had chosen me on merit. I am the best Minister you've got (*) and you can have my resignation in ten minutes flat.' He began to climb down.
(*) she was!   'You can have mine. Of course I chose you on merit. But this campaign you are organising is intolerable.'"

Invited to a meeting of senior ministers, Barbara was met by "a gloomy scene...Harold..obviously in a shattered state...Jim ..head in hands. 'Have a drink,' said Harold morosely..'I was very insulting to Barbara just now and I apologise...' I went over and kissed him affectionately on the forehead. 'And I'm sorry if I upset you, but I'm afraid I can't withdraw,' I replied. 'Don't I get a kiss?' said Jim gloomily. 'God knows I need it.' So I kissed him too...Harold had obviously calmed down a bit, but he was still in a pretty neurotic state. He wasn't going to accept Barbara's resignation or anybody else's ..He must represent the whole movement or nothing at all..." Michael Foot mediated a modus vivendi as the Yes and No campaigns began. This episode highlighted the complementarity and mutual need of Castle & Wilson, both genuine & passionate.

11th December.   Chinese Proverb and English Patchwork.   356

"If there is righteousness in the heart there will be beauty in the character.

"If there is beauty in the character there will be harmony in the home.

"If there is harmony in the home there will be order in the nation.

"When there is order in the nation there will be peace in the world."

— — — — — —

Compare T.S. Eliot, Chorus V, *The Rock*.

"If humility and purity be not in the heart, they are not in the home; and if they are not in the home, they are not in the City." And Chorus VIII:
"Our age is an age of moderate virtue
And of moderate vice
When men will not lay down the Cross
Because they will never assume it.
Yet nothing is impossible, nothing,
To men of faith and conviction.
Let us therefore make perfect our will.
O God, help us."

```
ADTRN£003.20
FROM:031 Ilkley
TO  :013 Grassington YDN
UC5528    S  1      SU 74
    J  8       B6573
15-Apr-04 13:34 Tkt:0153
```
VALID FOR 24 HOURS
FROM TIME SHOWN

Thank you for travelling
Horseless Carriage
01756 753123
www.prideofthedales.com

(The excellent small bus-company in lovely Wharfedale, "Pride of the Dales", retains on its tickets the term from the earliest days of motoring, "Horseless Carriage".)

— — — — — —

Seen at a London Church! ↓

In the early 1990s, before I took press-cuttings, *The Times* printed a letter from Noël Jones, then Bishop of Sodor & Man and an opponent of women's priesting, criticising Bishop Jim Thompson of Bath & Wells who had spoken in support. Noël railed against his writing from the idyllic moated palace in comfortable Wells in a way that upset many churchpeople in the more humdrum everyday world. He in turn was attacked by a correspondent who asked, after Matthew 7.3, "Why beholdest thou the moat that is round thy brother's palace. but considereth not the sea that is around thine own?"

12th December. "THE PATRIOTS" (1974) - another Target novel.
(I attempted to review this book but can only offer notes!)

- - - - - - -

George Target followed this novel with one called "The Triumph of Vice"! - but the fact that the Peace Process in Ireland "holds" through public support after a decade is a Triumph of Virtue after two more or less violent centuries from 1798. "The Patriots" encapsulates the atmosphere of the Troubles at their peak, when to be Irish in England was sufficient for being an object of suspicion. The novel is so splendid as to be unreviewable, by me at least. - One of GWT's greatest; yet little known at the time, for our Establishment blanketed it with silent suppression, and it is suspected that copies were bought up and destroyed! Target's style is unusual in that, whilst many authors set out parallel stories in chapters before they converge, he does so in paragraphs of a page or less, keeping things on the boil, with felicity of diction that reminds me of Hardy. "The pale moon was setting behind the grey rooftops" of London, far from rosy Tralee. "'Ready, Dark Rosaleen?' 'Yes...' 'Select own objective in area. Morning rush. You're doing bloody great, so you bloody are! Clicks off...silence...'" "The main speaker, Lord Brockway, had been introduced to much applause, and then the Chairman handed the mike to Bernadette Devlin." "God save Ireland." (& England, & all. Amen.)
F.R.M.

THE WORKS OF WAR DESTROY HOMES AND LAND·SEIZE FOOD SUPPLIES · CONTAMINATE WATER·IMPRISON DISSENTERS·INFLICT WOUNDS· BURNS· KILL THE LIVING

☆
God In Everything

(A Panentheistic Parody of 'Brahma' by Ralph Waldo Emerson.) ------

I am the batsman
   and the bat,
I am the bowler
   and the ball,
The umpire, the
   pavilion cat,
The groundsman,
   roller, stumps
   and all.

"SAGA" Oct. 2005
Prom premiere
I don't decry Mark Ellen's "10 best CDs of the millennium so far", but I'm convinced that the greatest music of the 2000s was written in 1913 but only released in 2001 – namely *A London Symphony* by Vaughan Williams in its original version, performed at this year's Proms.

To hear music anew from the days before classical composers abandoned consonance has been my great joy, especially the first half of the 1913 Finale with the heavenly lost Andantino just before the tremendous climax.
FRANK MCMANUS, *Todmorden*

LET US LIVE BY OUR LABOUR.

13th December. Sufficient is whose arm alone? Can our defence be sure?

It is almost a commonplace truth that war is a fruit of human aggression (see 17.12 foot) so that conversely "It is a greater joy to destroy wars with words than men with weapons & a true glory to win peace by peaceful means". (*) Sadly the wages of human sin cannot be frozen, and violence breeds violence so that wars tend to cause further wars. Hitler's lieutenant Hermann Goëring claimed that a Government can always persuade its nation to support a war by claiming that it is in imminent danger of invasion or destruction. Thus the UK Parliament concurred in the US attack on Iraq because a security dossier was distorted to imply that the West could be made victim to attack by weapons of mass destruction at 45 minutes' notice. Clearly armed force is powerless to dry up the wellsprings of evil - a World War costing 55 million lives cannot be described as "stopping Hitler". Rich nations which truly seek peace need to develop the United Nations into a world-authority with minimum human and democratic standards for all nations, and an international law and policing service to uphold them. "Law Not War", as Gaitskell said over Suez 1956. "They who take the sword shall perish by the sword" declared Another (Matthew 26.52), and His apostle Paul taught that the crucial fight is spiritual with spiritual weapons (Ephesians 6.10-18; 2 Cor. 10.3-4). "Steel kills the sinner but cannot excise the sin" (Studdert Kennedy, *Pictorial Weekly* 13.7.1929).

The pacifist (Latin *pacificio*, I make peace) if quietist is a coward, but if obedient to Paul VI's maxim (12.11) is anything but! S/he cannot expect, any more than anyone else, freedom from trials and tribulations; yet there are many traditional promises of divine defence (18.3; see also Psalm 121, RC 120). Onward Christian Soldiers, but your battle is on a distinctive plane. President Dwight D. Eisenhower of the US knew this well! In a 1953 speech he said that no people on earth can as such be termed an enemy; national security is only achievable in co-operation with fellow-nations; nations are entitled to choose their own economic and governmental systems; a nation's hope of lasting peace needs basing not on any arms-race but on just relations and honest understanding with others. "Every gun that is made...every rocket fired signifies...a theft from those who hunger and are not fed...We pay for a single destroyer with new homes that could have housed more than 8000 people...This is not a way of life at all, in any true sense. Under the cloud of threatening war, it is humanity hanging from a cross of iron." (see also 3.3) (*) St Augustine

14th December.   Madame Souris a une Maison!   359

Jan Boyes' delightful letter of 26.6.2004 in the <u>Guardian Review</u> reminds me of my own enjoyment, at age 6 or 7, of G. Gladstone Solomon's 1926 book "Le Français Pour Les Jeunes". Beginning with the above fact that Mrs Mouse has a House, it progresses to the sad story of its 3rd Lesson:

> Ces petites souris n'ont pas de père.
> Il est mort.
> Le chat l'a tué.
> Le chat est méchant; il n'est pas bon.
> Le père était bon.
> Il avait une longue queue.
> Mais il est mort; — tué par un chat!
> Pauvre Papa Souris!
> Pauvre père!
> Méchant Monsieur le Chat!

Angelo Roncalli, later Pope John 23.

Its author was highly successful in thus winning the attention of this primary-school pupil of St Philip's CE School, Southport (monogram SPS, local rendering Southport Potted Shrimps), in the early 1930s ere the darkness thickened. Boyes of Alfriston adds that later "we read that the favourite toys of (Papa's) son Louis and Louis' friend Pierre Lapin are guns, so perhaps we are expected to hope that the younger generation of mice and rabbits will be able to hold their own." Today's happier remedy is to feed cats so well that they forget to hunt! For further mouse-studies see 25.1, 16.3, and 5.1 (follows).

I thought being pregnant was bad enough, but now I'm homeless too.

If you are on means tested benefits, or other low income, & you have an OL14 or HX7 postcode, your cat (male or female) can be neutered free of charge. But funds are limited so don't delay. Hurry & telephone *01422 845501* for details.
Calder Valley & District Cats Protection

HOUSE MOUSE (MUS MUSCULUS)

Ask at local library for nearest C.P. branch.

15th December.   **Hymns Bad and Worse.**
                                  (plus the odd gem)

   Isaac Watts (1674-1748) liberated English hymnody from the straitjacket which limited it to metrical versions of the Old Testament Psalms. The glories of his best work such as "When I survey the wondrous cross" are not diminished by the fact that he penned some disasters (see also 10-11.3). "There's not a sin that we commit Nor wicked word we say, But in the dreadful book 'tis writ Against the judgement day" for example. More grizzly, though perhaps comforting to harassed teachers, was: "When children in their wanton play Served old Elisha so; And bid the prophet go his way, 'Go up, thou baldhead, go!': God quickly stopt their wicked breath And sent two raging bears, That tore them limb from limb to death, With blood, and groans, and tears"! (Charming! - how could they catch all 42?) Happily John M. Neale campaigned successfully against such horrors, which had grieved him as a child (11.3).

   Metrical psalms were often arid; Tate & Brady rendered Ps.1.1 "How blest is he who ne'er consents By ill advice to walk, Nor stands in sinners' ways, nor sits Where men profanely talk." Yet their Psalter has the quaint Ps.42.1: "As pants the hart for cooling streams When heated in the chase, So longs my soul, O God, for thee, And thy refreshing grace" - which makes me wonder if there can be composition by luck, and if monkeys may tap out Shakespeare after all. At any rate it is surely worthier than the 1980s offering: "As the deer pants for the water, So my soul longs after you..." which proceeds to make silver rhyme with giver, and king with anything. (Yet firms have copyrighted it, though I wouldn't sing it if they paid me. I think it borders on simony to copyright words of faith, even though Beethoven had to exact payment in order to keep alive.

My own verses are marked © solely to guard against piracy; non-commercial reproduction welcome if my © is appended.) Now what of Ps.137.9: "How blest that jolly trooper goes, Who, riding on his naggie, Shall take thy wee bairns by the toes And ding them on the craggie?"!! Was it written to take 1st prize for awfulness as send-up of Scots dourness? (see 25.1)

see 3.12

Borrowdale Church (Stonethwaite)

16th December. "Now The Darkness Gathers".

The more northerly the latitude, the tighter the grip of the midwinter dark, until at the Arctic Circle the sun fails to rise at the solstice. Yearning for daylight can become intense by later December, though this can be mitigated by the the Christmastide activity and "bright lights" of the "developed West", so that our spiritual longing for uplift in days of sadness is not so well symbolised as in earlier times. Even so our need for solace and deliverance may need avid expression:

> "Jolly old Kursimass it's time tha didst coom
> An' drive all our grief-clouds away;
> Coom gladden our hearts and let everey home
> Have cause to be merry this day." (Yorkshire verse).

Or, in the churchy language of the Great Advent Antiphons:

"O come, O come Emmanuel! And ransom captive Israel
That mourns in lonely exile here Until the Son of God appear...

"O come, thou Lord of David's Key! The royal door fling wide
   (from the Latin *Veni veni Emmanuel.*)   and free..."

This is one of several powerful hymns that to our loss have been crowded out of our popular culture by commercial bludgeon which has turned the virtue of sensible "Christmas shopping" into the vice of inordinate spending which affronts the poor. These Advent hymns include "Come Thou long-expected Jesus"; translations of Nicolai's "Wachet Auf", much loved by Bach; "Lo He comes" (see also 20.12); and Julia Howe's "Mine eyes have seen the glory". They relate to Jesus' return as well as to Christmas.

In 1998 my ex-mayoress Julia asked me to write verses for a "Witness against Excessive Shopping", to end with the standard final verse of Brooks' "O little town of Bethlehem". They are:

O mighty city, Manchester, (*)
How shrill thy musac's cry!
Amidst its skirl the shoppers whirl -
"Come buy, come buy, come buy!"
Yet in thy bright lights' flicker
Old wisdom whispers strong, and pence,
"Good Christmas sense ain't pounds,
It's knowing right from wrong."

So when you give or entertain
Don't just give price or pelf,
Give heart and love, e'en God above,
And make some gifts yourself;
Salute the Sally Army,
Defy the gods of greed,
And keep some back for darker days,
And care for those in need.

Now here we sing, glad news we bring
To bad folk and to good,
To shopgirls, lads and laden dads
And profiteers in food:-
Just pause and think when buying drink
Or selling plastic ware,
It's not the price that makes things nice
Or measures mothers' care.

O holy Child of Bethlehem,
Descend to us, we pray;
Cast out our sin, and enter in,
Be born in us today.
We hear the Christmas Angels
The great glad tidings tell:
O come to us, abide with us,
Our Lord Emmanuel.

(*) or, for example, "O famous town of Todmorden".

361

17th December. "The mourning of the nations."

Anthologies of sermons don't sell like hot cakes, and are hardly my most favourite reading! Yet maybe an exception deserves to be made for Paul Tillich's short collection "The Shaking of the Foundations" (SCM 1949) which he compiled in New York City in 1947. Tillich (1886-1965) was a German army chaplain in WW1 then a theology teacher in universities till forced to flee in 1933 for criticising Nazism. He became a US citizen in 1940 and wrote his Systematic Theology volumes.

"The Shaking" argues that old prophecies such as Isaiah's "Earth shall reel like a drunkard" (24.20) had become fact and not metaphor in the wake of WW2 and the fate of Warsaw, Berlin and Hiroshima. Nuclear physicists had loosed the destructive energies which had been bound in our material world since the original fiery chaos ("big bang"? - but how can such an event in time happen "when time was yet unknown"? - I digress) had gained the cohesive structures of this fertile planet. Then man appeared, discovered the key to unlock the bound forces of the ground, and used them destructively. Yet the prophetic spirit has not disappeared from the earth. Just as the doom of Europe was prophesied before the world wars (15 Oct), so US soldiers who walked through Europe's ruins included some who saw with "visionary clarity" the doom of their own land's towns and cities, "decades before the final catastrophe"!!

Such prophets arouse hatred like Jeremiah did of old, and are called traitorous defeatists; but the prophets stood their ground because beyond the sphere of destruction they saw the sphere of salvation. Like the Psalmist they said of God the Source: "...the foundations vanish but Thou shalt endure" (Ps.102.26). The old must die in order that the Eternal may create the new! (see John 12.24 which is the motto-text of Dostoevsky's "The Brothers Karamazov".)

— — — — — — —

My title "The mourning of the nations" does not however come from Tillich, but from the 1940 journal of Angelo Roncalli who later became Pope as John XXIII the great and good. Perhaps thinking of his native Italy whose dictator Mussolini had made common cause with Hitler, he noted that if the Gospel law of life, which limits the use of wealth and power and declares the principles of justice and harmony, is violated, the terrible sanction of war is willed by men and nations through their representatives. "He who instigates war and foments it is always the Prince of this world, who has nothing to do with Christ."

18th December.   "Nature, also, mourns for a lost good."   363

Paul Tillich used this sentence by Schilling as a title for a sermon and a chapter-heading in his collection of discourses. Human life is marked by experiences - "Paradise Lost" and "Paradise Regained" - and even when earth recovers from tragedy, and the green grass conceals the bloody battlefields, some of its lost glory seems irretrievable. "There hath past away a glory" wrote Wordsworth after celebrating the present joy of Maytime in his great "Intimations of Immortality" ode. Nowhere is this more poignant than in the Mardale valley of the eastern Lake District, which was depopulated and drowned over some years from 1935, to make a huge reservoir for thirsty Manchester to use drinkable water for hosing, flushing and industrial coolant purposes when rainwater would have served.

The final service in the excellent little Holy Trinity Church on 18.8.1935 brought the community together in desolation, even whilst "O God our Help" and "Bright the Vision" were attempted bravely by the 81 souls crowded into the 75-seat building, and by several hundreds outside to whom the service was relayed by loudspeaker, including a lecturer with whom I worked at Lancaster F.E. college in the 1950s, and Mardale's last vicar who had returned from retirement but was too devastated to go in.

Technology helps out - Frederick Barham, Mardale's vicar 1910-1934, winds gramophone to get tunes in the absence of the organist. (Jn. Graham, Shap History Society.) For Black Hole of Swindale see 27.12 (foot)

The flooding was sacrilegious. Regaining Paradise needs unlimited time (the slow movement of Schubert's String Quintet portrays this). Meantime we find "Strength in what remains behind" and, communing with nature, draw divine sorrow & hope. (Rom.8.19-22; Rev.21.1; Isa.65.17):

19th December.   MID-CENTURY STEEL-TOWN CHRISTMAS.

(reproduced with kind permission from "The Coal was Dark & Deep", by John Stephenson, Vicar of Eppleton 1979-1995.)

"CONSETT, in North-West Durham, came to prominence in the 1830s, when lead and iron ore were discovered in the nearby moorland, leading to the formation of Consett Iron Company..."

(John Stephenson goes on to tell of the dark times of the 1930s, with unemployment and desolating poverty, then adds:)

"That was Consett, and to the lad who spent 25 years of his life there, the magic memories remain primarily in connection with Christmas: walking by the river Derwent through the snow from Shotley Bridge to Castleside, always with the huge blast furnaces & cooling towers & chimneys dominating the skyline...the snow untrodden by human foot, the wild red & scarlet berries on the holly trees peeping through the heavy white blanket of snow, giving the impression of Christ's own blood, almost as if God were saying through nature that in the springtime, at Easter, when the crocuses & the daffodils are holding their heads high after winter's slumber, there is a death - Good Friday - followed by resurrection, "The Lord is risen!"...O yes, there was a war on during the first five years of the 1940s, but it was remote from us, except for the menacing searchlights criss-crossing in the night sky, and the barrage balloons suspended in mid-air, just in case a German aeroplane, bearing bombs, came our way...the wail of the air-raid siren made us fearful, and the drone of an aeroplane at night as we lay in bed kept us anxiously on edge, awake, afraid to sleep in case we didn't wake to a new day...but it was in December 1943, in Consett Parish Church, that this writer first heard the beautiful music of Bach's "Sheep May Safely Graze", and it was always in December when we woke up on Christmas morning to find a stocking draped over the bottom of the bed, and inside the stocking a bar of chocolate, an apple, an orange, some nuts, a silver sixpence or threepenny-bit...the light went on shining in the darkness and Consett was preserved...the familiar houses & shops and the parish church & the cinemas, untargeted by bombers, went on standing as before, and the red pillar box on the street corner where we posted our Christmas cards still stood silently & proudly, its two-inch covering of snow making it appear to have a hat. Life's familiar things must never be despised, for it was with a handful of dust that God made the earth, even if it was man who covered Consett with muck."

Consett's town-motto, E FERRO FERRUM TEMPERATUM (Out of irom comes steel or tempered iron) recalls the theologian's text for creation, E NIHILO NIHIL (Out of nothing can come nothing).

Christmas "Bah! Humbug!"

As Britain has become richer for all outside the poverty-trap, [we] have come close to a two-week hibernation, which some enjoy [bu]t others don't. Mr Scrooge's famous riposte (above) has its [ap]peal to those who see the sad irony of "gluttony before the TV", [an]d drunkenness in some town-centres: — All this for a festival [na]med in honour of the Christ-child born in poverty and soon to [be] a refugee. (Berlioz' "L'enfance" follows the famous 'Shep[he]rds' Farewell' with a cold reception to the Holy Family at [Po]rt Said, until a scorned Ishmaelite household welcomes them. [He]ine called the work a nosegay of exquisite blooms of melody.)

Mr Scrooge deserves a hearing, whilst we hear the churc[h] [co]unterclaim that this "Christmas" cornucopia is part of the [wo]rld's darkness that Christmas enlightens. I have a friend who [if] alone on 25.12 would happily take a sandwich lunch to the Top [A]thens ruins which symbolise Emily Brontë's Wuthering Heights.

Poultry is all too often reared in crates and killed by callous mechanical/electrical methods (contrast 1835 below).

Loneliness besets those without families, and homeless folk find the doors of libraries and public amenities closed.

(continued overleaf.)

Eastern Daily Press 17.3.2002

Picture: EDP LIBRARY

The Norwich-London coach – with fowl passengers.
(around 1835).

It is a Christmas coach, I vow,
And whirls along in pride,
For all its outside passengers
Are food for the inside.

With bottles broach, "The Norfolk coach"
As good a toast as heard is;
And long live they who feast today
Upon its Christmas turkeys.

365

<u>21st December,</u>   <u>Saint Thomas's Wake.</u>

On this "shortest day", dedicated to the apostle who was not rebuked for doubting, I continue yesterday's list of Yuletide hesitations.

* Some are ensconced too long with "difficult" relatives.

* The world's sorrows encroach and may engulf. My title is that of Sir Peter Maxwell Davies' commemorative music for those who suffered in the two-night air-attack on Manchester just before Christmas 1942 which killed thousands.

* The irony or shame of modern war is highlighted in the "Sonnet composed after seeing Mr Blair on TV upholding the Iraq airstrikes against a background of the Downing Street Christmas Tree" by Karen Maloney 16.12.1998 (not reproduced here because of its ephemeral context; yet did not Jesus forbid His followers to call down fire on "enemy" heads? - Luke 9$^{51-56}$).

— — — — —

So I continue with John Stephenson's "The Coal is Dark", in which he contradicts the popular claim that Christmas is essentially for children. It is for them among others! -

"Sometimes our journey through life seems anything but a winter wonderland: a loved one suddenly dies, or, after a long illness, cancer claims a relative or friend...sometimes ambition is frustrated, sometimes a friend lets us down badly, and our lives seem to be in the grip of a hard, cruel frost...nothing seems to grow in the world of nature because of the severe cold, yet even in a long hard winter, red berries appear.

"December is a dark month, but the Christian Church's celebration of the birth of Jesus (God-become-Man) brings light where there is darkness, hope where there is despair, and we all know that without hope life is cruel and hard.

"The mid-winter Festival of Christmas, although it is about the birth of a child, is for grown-ups, not (as most people think) for children. Why? Because grown-ups, unlike children, have experienced despair in their lives, and therefore it's grown-ups, not the children, who need to have their hopes rekindled, and their bitterest memories defrosted...God, Saviour, not Superman, looks out of the eyes of a weak, helpless baby, a baby dependent on the care and concern of a human mother, surrounded by cattle and clay in a smelly stable because the world was too frosty to give Him (Jesus) a proper welcome, except by common shepherds, and by three kings from Persian lands afar, the Magi, with their precious gifts." So:

"O come, thou Branch <u>of Jesse!</u> <u>draw</u> The quarry from <u>the lion's claw!</u>"

22nd December.   **HARDY PERENNIALS.**   367

Thomas Hardy (1840 – 1928) is England's much loved if over-pessimistic "Laureate of Loss".

Christmas Eve, and twelve of the clock,
　"Now they are all on their knees,"
An elder said as we sat in a flock
　By the embers in hearthside ease.

We pictured the meek mild creatures where
　They dwelt in their strawy pen,
Nor did it occur to one of us there
　To doubt they were kneeling then.

So fair a fancy few would weave
　In these years! Yet, I feel,
If some one said on Christmas Eve,
　"Come; see the oxen kneel

"In the lonely barton by yonder coomb[1]
　Our childhood used to know,"
I should go with him in the gloom,
　Hoping it might be so.

Illustration caption: We Christmas-carolled down the Vale, and up the Vale, and round the Vale, We played and sang that night as we were yearly wont to do — A carol in a minor key, a carol in the major. Then at each house: "Good wishes. Many Christmas joys to you!" © F. McManus 1981. — THOMAS HARDY

"THE OXEN" (Above) recalls an old belief or fantasy of Dorset farming-folk before their traditional ways, portrayed in poems and in novels including "Far from the Madding Crowd", succumbed steadily to the mechanisation of thought and life.

[1] Farmyard in the hollow.

The comic masterpiece "The Rash Bride" (illustrated) eclipses its own tragic story of the Mellstock Quire on its rounds, so spirited is its diction. Too long to set out in full, it deserves hunting out of Hardy collections or selections. The custom of carolling deserves to be kept up, as it is at this season for charity and/or evangelism in many places, by singers and instrumentalist with qualified leaders rather than by ad hoc groups of children. I've taken part during Iona Abbey Christmas-party weeks as well as here in Todmorden.

Other seasonal poets include Tennyson, Davies, Rossetti and Kipling, whose "Eddi's Service" with an ox and a donkey for congregation, commemorates St Wilfrid's landing at Selsey, where the Saxon chapel still stands:

But the Saxons were keeping Christmas,
　And the night was stormy as well,
Nobody came to the service,
　Though Eddi rang the bell ....

'Wicked weather for walking',
　Said Eddi of Manhood End.
'But I must go on with the service
　For such as care to attend.' ...

23rd December.   "Blazing Fire and Christmas Treat".   368

Concluding the list of midwinter festivals begun on 1.12:

23rd - Tom Bawcock's Eve at Mousehole near Penzance (pronounced Mouzle). This brave fisherman put his boat out in storm and brought in a catch that saved the villagers from near-starvation. He is commemorated in the Star-Gazey Pie that is cooked there from fish on this day every year.

24th - Christmas Eve, after noon on which my mother would put up the decorations in the 1930s. Dewsbury Minster rings the Devil's Knell, a unique passing-bell custom from the Middle Ages. In the agricultural era, when a villager died it was made known by ringing Nine Tailors (tollers? tellers?) on the church bells; in some places two twos for a child, three threes for a woman, four fours for a man, followed in each case by a stroke on the tenor bell per year of age of the deceased. In Dewsbury this was extended to celebrate Christ's defeat of the devil by five fives plus one toll per year _anno domini_, with scorers to avert error and careful timing to end just as the midnight mass began. The custom arose when a son of the squire was sentenced to die for murdering a servant, but was reprieved on condition that he financed this custom, "to keep him mindful of his sins and the village folk of their salvation".

25/6/7/8th - Christmas/Boxing/St John's/Holy Innocents' Days. the 26th is not named for the "sport" of boxing but from the custom of young servants receiving boxes of seasonal gifts from the gentry as they left to rejoin their families for their holiday till the Twelve Days of "Xmas" were over. The 26th of course is the "feast of Stephen", though I find it odd that this first Christian martyr is commemorated so soon after Jesus' official birthday, instead of allowing a few shadowless days until we recall Herod's infant victims.

CHRISTMAS EVE 1946

The shepherds watch tonight again
  The star above the byre
Where Mary's child is born again
  Unto the heart's desire.

The angels sing tonight again
  Of God who gives to earth
His gift of love and joy again
  To all who seek his mirth.

The wise men walk tonight again
  To Bethlehem afar
To worship and to praise again
  The babe beneath the star.

And we shall sing tonight again
  The songs of other years,
Until our hearts are young again
  Behind our hidden tears.

24th December, 1946   Idris Davies (see also 9,11,12.5; 24.12).

24th December.   "Brighter Visions Beam Afar."

> "The time draws near the birth of Christ:
>   The moon is hid; the night is still;
>   The Christmas bells from hill to hill
> Answer each other in the mist.
>
> "Four voices of four hamlets round.....
>   That now dilate, and now decrease,
>   Peace and goodwill, goodwill and peace,
> Peace and goodwill, to all mankind."
>
> (Tennyson, *In Memoriam*, canto 28.)

Phil Mathison has an effective Christmas Eve ghost-story in *Railway Magazine* for January 2004 which was on sale in advance of that month. Set in the days of steam, the night freight-train to Normanton is half-an-hour down at Carlisle, as fireman Geoff Holmes joins driver Jack Whiteley for the run south, via Settle. Anxious to reach home in Leeds by midnight, they flog the engine to such fury over the bleak moor and viaduct at Ribblehead that Holmes pleads with the driver to ease off, but in vain. A distant signal near Settle is approached at top speed but turns green in the nick of time. On reaching Holbeck shed where a local crew take over at 11.50, the fireman tells the foreman that he'll never fire for Whiteley again — only to be told that Jack had died last night in lodgings.

(from Latin Bible printed in Venice 1588 & now in library of Gonville & Caius College, Cambridge.)

A STAR IN THE EAST

When Christmastide to Rhymney came
 And I was six or seven
I thought the stars in the eastern sky
 Were the brightest stars of heaven.

I chose the star that glittered most
 To the east of Rhymney town
To be the star above the byre
 Where Mary's babe lay down.

And nineteen hundred years would meet
 Beneath a magic light,
And Rhymney share with Bethlehem
 A star on Christmas night.

"Console thyself, thou wouldst not seek Me if thou hadst not found Me."
(Pascal, Pensée 552)

<u>25th December.</u> "The Nativity of Our Lord, or the Birth-day of Christ, commonly called Christmas-Day." (so-called in The Book of Common Prayer).

Bruce Kent, in an obituary note for Lord Hugh Jenkins, a former Labour M.P. for Putney who was active in the Campaign for Nuclear Disarmamebt (CND), wrote in the <u>Guardian</u> 28th January 2004, that: "On Christmas Day 1945 he (Jenkins) left the studio (of Rangoon Radio) in charge of a Burmese independence activist, who played 'Colonel Bogey' before the King's speech, and 'Mad Dogs and Englishmen' immediately afterwards".

The fine carol "While Shepherds Watched" is not quite ubiquitous for the Scots have a version which begins: "While humble shepherds watched their flocks". Choirs have vied for the most flamboyant tune for the familiar words when an alternative to the usual "Winchester Old" is desired. I recall carolling in Todmorden streets where children were astonished when we sang it to the melody stolen for "Ilkley Moor baht 'at". I think our local tune "Shaw Lane" is the best of all —

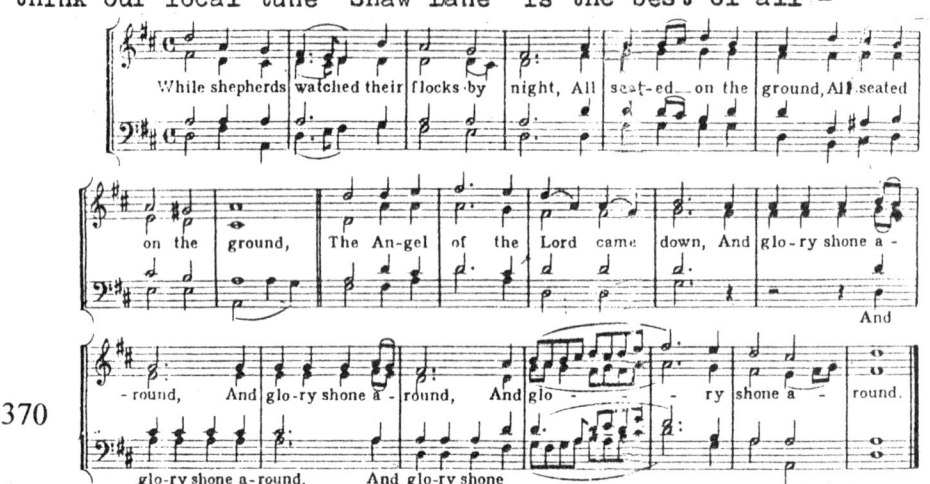

[Musical score: "While shepherds watched their flocks by night, All seated on the ground, The Angel of the Lord came down, And glory shone around, And glory shone around, And glory shone around."]

Among the many modern poems for Christmas Day John Betjeman's "Christmas" is deservedly popular, with its bells that call "Even to shining ones who dwell / Safe in the Dorchester Hotel". For earnest seriousness we may turn to Hopkins:

Moonless darkness stands between
Past, O Past, no more be seen!
But the Bethlehem star may lead me
To the sight of Him who freed me
From the self that I have been.

Make me pure, Lord: Thou art holy;
Make me meek, Lord: Thou wert lowly;
Now beginning, and alway;
Now begin, on Christmas day.
      Gerard Manley Hopkins.

26th December.   Good King Wenceslas cried out:
"It is not surprising;
All these parsons round about,
Demythologising:
'Hebrew sheep were kept at home
When the frost was cruel.
Shepherds never let them roam —
Who'd be such a fo-o-ol!'"

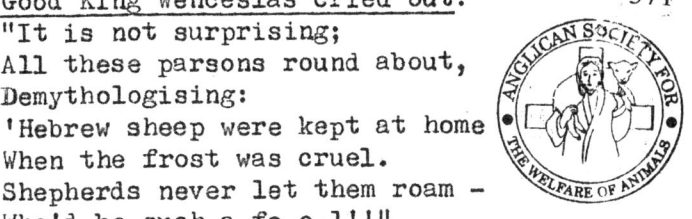

This 1960s verse isn't subversive, for Jesus' birthday is unknown, and 25 December is simply an "official birthday" like the Queen's. The bleak midwinter doesn't feature in the Bible, but was seized upon by early Christians so that the returning sunlight might symbolize the True Light (John 1.9) Who brings healing to human souls (16.12). Possibly the Babe of Bethlehem was born in March or early spring?

The Oxford Book of Carols (1928), like the English Hymnal (1906), had Percy Dearmer as an editor and Ralph Vaughan Williams as Musical Editor. It is a fine resource-book. Carol 137, "Masters in this hall", was written to an old French air arranged by Gustav Holst: "Masters in this Hall,/ Hear ye news today, / Brought from over sea,/And ever I you pray:" — followed by a Nowelling chorus celebrating the holy birth.

In 1979 I was a part-time Open University tutor-counsellor; and when Head Office failed to record an assignment-grading I blamed it on bureaucracy and sent a determined letter which began "My dear Computer". It replied thus with the compliments of the Assignment Records Office:

"Dear Frank, Had we but world enough, and time,
The system's mystery I should explain in rhyme,
Thou by my transistor's side
Wouldst problem-solving logic find demystified.
But, as it is, my little metal universe
Cannot murder Marvell's verse
For hours on end. Otherwise
Enquiries from people less charming than yourself would never get replies.."

This reached me on Christmas Eve so I replied, with Nowell chorus, and quoting my tutor-number to help the dear computer:

"Lord of Walton Hall,
Hear ye news today?
Does your quasi-mind
Ever watch and pray?

Can you write a hymn?
(Marvellous your verse;

Writes each modern poet
Doggerel far worse.)

Carol liked her grade!
I like Carol too —
Yet 25645,...
9 is fond of you.

'Shepherds as of right
Leap and dance and sing'
But can you be saved
By the newborn King?"

(We can but hope!) So:

"May your circuits scintillate, As your keyboards oscillate!"

27th December. — *From a Youthful Diary, Grange-o-Sands 1956.*
(when as Chemistry lecturer at Lancaster & Morecambe F.E.
college I lived there with my wife Benita & our Alsatian Si.)

23.3 - "School" very tense with a flock of inspectors in. This system is useless to rectify national faults, and local faults are covered by "window-dressing"!

16.4 - Naked man reported to have walked at church-time yesterday along Bare promenade, Morecambe, of all places!

24.5 - Ben took one cat into the bedroom in the small hours and found three under the eiderdown when she woke. Empire Day!

27.6 - My "Good Homes Needed for Kittens" notice at college defaced by (a) cat-poison advert. (b) remarks on Davy Crockett hats, & (c) note by F.T.- "Nephews of above also available".

20.7 - The Libraries Committee, on which I serve, considered three girls for two posts, and eliminated the most attractive one on the advice of the maiden lady officials.

13.8 - Delightful devilry by Simon who was seen four times eating dry dogmeal as a cover for scone-stealing.

14.8 - Mrs R's granny died last week aged 100 yrs & 1 day, having just extracted a message from the Queen and a tray from the Mayor of Barrow-in-Furness.

25.8 - *Tribune* quotes Bernard Shaw: "Titles distinguish the mediocre, embarrass the superior, and are disgraced by the inferior."

(continued from 18.12) - SWINDALE, Lakeland's Secret Valley.
   Immediately south of Mardale the small valley of Swindale nestles among its hills. I only discovered its small-scale yet characteristic scenery when I was 75. A map drawn by the Lake District's celebrated cartographer Alfred Wainwright is reproduced as an appendix in this book, to scale $2\frac{1}{2}$ inches per mile.

   Swindale is but 2 miles long and is a substantial walk from public transport *via* the links shown by Wainwright. Best use a van or car that carries a bicycle. Drive from Bampton to Swindale Head, drop friends, return $1\frac{1}{4}$ miles to Swindale Foot (near "N" of "Bampton" on map) to park without blocking the narrow road. Cycle to friends, park bike at Swindale Head, walk upstream crossing Hobgrumble Gill by bridge, then bear right up faint zigzag path to 1300 feet, then left to topmost spectacular Black Hole, "Sarah's Pool"! If with an able pal (for safety) scramble down carefully & swim. Go home, read Sarah Hall's "Haweswater", and weep.

28th December.   "On the Third Day of Christmas".   373

Some people may feel that "Christmas" is over by teatime on 25.12, to be followed by family trips made necessary by our nomadic careers. Well and good; but I regret that community-celebrations are minimal during the "12 Days", with even the "25th" anticipated by gun-jumping early festivities. It's a pity that <u>Messiah</u> is performed so early in December, and the Bach <u>Christmas Oratorio</u> sung in a 3-hour marathon when it was written to be performed in six parts spaced through the Dozen Days as in the composer's settled township. Yet retirees must not begrudge the UK lifestyle, and need to rejoice when "oafish louts remember Mum" (Betjeman) with garish gifts!

We can and should enjoy the carols throughout the season, with the ever-popular "We Three Kings" in a fresh set for 6.1. To conclude this topic I mention Bede's hymn for the Holy Innocents' Day, with the only possible consolation for grief over child victims of Herod or anyone else, "Whom in their woe earth cast away,/ But heaven with joy received today" (Engl.Hymnl.35). Nor need we push our minds too hard, for as James Montgomery the radical politician and jailbird wrote in "Angels from the realms of glory", we may enjoy our "times of arrival":-

"Sages, leave your contemplations; Brighter visions beam afar;
Seek the great Desire of Nations; Ye have seen his natal star."
                                                           (Ref. Haggai 2.7)

Finally, the much-loved "Lo! He comes with clouds descending", Charles Wesley's fine hymn of the Second Coming which is based on an earlier and rougher original by John Cennick, was turned by Martin Madan (1726-90) into a nice composite of both, in which the judgment is social as well as individual. It runs:

a great work of reference.

1. Lo! He comes with clouds descending,
   Once for favour'd sinners slain;
Thousand thousand Saints attending
   Swell the triumph of His train:
     Alleluia!
God appears on earth to reign.

2. Every eye shall now behold Him,
   Robed in dreadful majesty;
Those who set at nought and sold Him,
   Pierced and nail'd Him to the Tree,
     Deeply wailing,
Shall the true Messiah see.

3. Every island, sea, and mountain,
   Heav'n and earth, shall flee away,
All who hate Him must, confounded,
   Hear the trump proclaim the Day:
     Come to judgment!
Come to judgment! come away!

4. Now redemption, long expected,
   See in solemn pomp appear!
All His saints, by man rejected,
   Now shall meet Him in the air:
     Alleluia!
See the Day of God appear!

5.* Answer thine own Bride and Spirit,
   Hasten, Lord, the gen'ral Doom!
The New Heav'n and Earth t'inherit,
   Take thy pining exiles home:
     All creation
Travails! groans! and bids Thee come!

6. Yea, Amen, let all adore Thee,
   High on Thine eternal throne;
Saviour, take the power and glory:
   Claim the Kingdom for Thine own:
     O come quickly!
Alleluia! Come, Lord, come!

from Penguin Book of Hymns (1990)

*Today's books weaken this alas by preferring Wesley's "Glorious scars" verse (which though fine isn't "popular") and by varying the ending from that of the Bible itself!

29th December. Still More Schoolgirl Audacity.

Francis Beckett's biography "Clem Attlee" (Richard Cohen Books, 1997, £20) provides a deal of new and little-known information on "a massively underestimated Labour prime minister, as its jacket-cover rightly describes its subject who was in No. 10 from 1945 to 1951. It deserves hunting out and reading, for no brief review can do justice to a Prime Minister who was wrongly called a sheep in sheep's clothing by Churchill – the accolade "a modest little man with plenty to be modest about" almost certainly did not come from that source. Incidentally the limerick "Few thought he was even a starter" (mellowed by much telling into my version of 25.10) appeared only in a note to his brother.

I can but pass over the heady politics of the building of NHS and Welfare State in the face of postwar austerity, and will touch on his humour and poetic prowess instead. Among the verses cited by Beckett are his exchange in June 1951 with Ann Glossop (15) of Penrhos College, Colwyn Bay, who dared to address Britain's Head of Government thus:

> Would you please explain, dear Clement
> Just why it has to be
> That Certificates of Education
> Are barred to such as me? . . .
>
> I've worked through thirteen papers
> But my swot is all in vain
> Because at this time next year
> I must do them all again . . .
>
> Please have pity, Clement,
> And tell the others too.
> Remove the silly age-limit
> It wasn't there for you.

Clearly delighted by this missive amidst cares of office, Attlee responded in like doggerel, marked "SECRET", no doubt to the surprised delight of the schoolgirl:

> I received with real pleasure
> Your verses my dear Ann
> Although I've not much leisure
> I'll reply as best I can.
>
> I've not the least idea why
> They have this curious rule
> Condemning you to sit and sigh
> Another year at school.
>
> You'll understand that my excuse
> For lack of detailed knowledge
> Is that school certs were not in use
> When I attended college.
>
> George Tomlinson is ill, but I
> Have asked him to explain
> And when I get the reason why
> I'll write to you again.

(G.T. was Minister of Educn.)

Two Attlee tales, one most likely spurious and later adapted to Kinnock's era, the second true:- The P.M., with guests in the Central Lobby as the Speaker's procession approached, saw an M.P. friend and called "Neil!" They knelt. Then Lord Pakenham, later Longford, demurred on being made First Lord of the Admiralty, 1951; whereupon Attlee replied "The Navy survived Winston Churchill & Brendan Bracken) - it'll probably survive you."

30th December. "The Queen's Matrimonial Ladder". 375

No, not our Elizabeth II! The title is that of William Hone's book published in London in 1820. It has a cartoon by George Cruikshank which shows King George IV being revived by a bottle of "Essence Bergam" being put under his nose after he had fainted on hearing that his estranged Queen Caroline had returned to England. Hone added verse:

"Ah! what was that groan? - 'twas the Head of the Church,
When he found she was come - for he dreaded a search
Into what he'd been doing; and sorely afraid for   /for'.
What she might find out, cried 'I'll not have her prayed
And the Bishops, obeying their pious Head, care took
That the name of his wife should be out of the Prayer Book!"

(Of course the satirist's word 'Head' is poetic (?) licence. Henry VIII arrogated it but Elizabeth I modified the royal appellation to 'Governor', which remains as a mere formality.)

A previous cartoon portrays George, as "Prince of Whales", attempting to use his bulk to sink Caroline's ship. The dissolute royal couple brought a greater palace-scandal to Britain than any of the late 20th century.

The goldfish-bowl lives that are forced on the Windsors by the media and prurient public would destroy many a family in one way or another. Elizabeth and Philip have been in post since TV was in its cradle, & have developed methods of coping which younger royals can hardly emulate. For decades I was a royalist because of risk of assassination run by "political Heads of State"; I now have changed my mind because of cruel intrusiveness on the part of photographers and journalists. We should have a low-key ceremonial Head of State, elected say for 8 years with eligibility for one further term; this when the reign of Queen Elizabeth II is ended.

MCLEAN'S CROSS, IONA
WOOD-ENGRAVING BY JULIA WROUGHTON

31st December. "Seven Swans...and a Partridge."

With Christmastide still with us, I share the suggestion by "WHLF" in the Crosthwaite parish magazine that "The Twelve Days of Christmas" may be more than just a nonsense-song. S/he suggests that it may be, or have begun as, a 'teaching' song for the Christian faith from the years when few children could read or write. (Compare the 'Dilly Song' (10.6).)

Certainly "my true love" could be God, and the partridge Jesus, for the mother-bird traditionally feigned injury to decoy its predators away from its nestlings for which she is ready to sacrifice herself. The tree is that of the cross, as per 1 Peter 2.^{24}. The the two turtle-doves (Luke 2.^{24}) may denote the Old & New Testaments <u>via</u> the prophetic Baptist and Jesus. Thereafter things become somewhat conjectural and far-fetched; and WLHF's suggestions deviate from "Dilly" for Nos. 3 (French Hens / Faith, Hope, & Love, main gifts of the Spirit); 6 (Geese A-Laying / Days of Creation); 7 (Swans - sacraments); 9 (Ladies Dancing / Fruits of the Spirit); 12 (Drummers / Items of Faith in the Apostles' Creed). Folklore-cum-low-culture!

<u>New Year's Eve</u> spells Tennyson seriously and Burns convivially! -

"Ring out, wild bells, to the wild sky,
The flying cloud, the frosty light.
The year is dying in the night;
Ring out, wild bells, and let him die...

Ring out the thousand wars of old,
Ring in the thousand years of peace..."

"...And we'll tak a cup o' kindness yet,
For auld lang syne."

(Both these poems need locating in a good anthology & reading in full.)

Picture for careful colouring - or photocopying for home-made cards!

Christmas 200 .

"Crown Him the Lord of Peace."

<u>1st January 1996.</u> - <u>New Year's Day</u> - and a more likely New Millennium Day than 1.1.2000 or even 1.1.2001. Our calendar is a few years "slow", for Herod who met the wise men ceased to be king by 4BC. The <u>Waits' Carol</u> (1642) includes these verses, as No. 28 in the Oxford Book of Carols, for singing to the tune "Greensleeves":

THE old year now away is fled,
The new year it is entered;
Then let us now our sins down-tread,
And joyfully all appear:
  Let's merry be this day,
  And let us now both sport and play:
  Hang grief, cast care away!
  God send you a happy New Year!

2 The name-day now of Christ we keep,
Who for our sins did often weep;
His hands and feet were wounded deep,
And his blessed side with a spear;
His head they crowned with thorn,
And at him they did laugh and scorn,
Who for our good was born:
  God send us a happy New Year!

3. And now with New Year's gifts each friend
Unto each other they do send:
God grant we may all our lives amend,
And that the truth may appear.
  Now, like the snake, your skin
  Cast off, of evil thoughts and sin,
  And so the year begin:
  God send us a happy New Year!

Easier said than done maybe, but at least the snake gets a more honourable mention than in other contexts.   377

The trouble with 1st January is that it tends to become a faint echo of Christmas Day, and an anticlimax. Perhaps only the very churchy know it as the feast of Jesus' Naming (verse 2 line 1), or as Day 7 of the 12 Days of Christmas. Modern Britain hibernates for half the day then watches routine television, for the broadcasting media set their store on New Year's Eve except for traditional morning concerts from Vienna. Even the local Scottish flavour of Hogmanay has largely been lost - it arose because dour Presbyterians in the Kirk discouraged Christmas celebrations for reasons which pass my understanding - though the sentimental singing of "Auld Lang Syne" survives amid too much "pop".

In my childhood the adults were still careful over "letting the old year out" at midnight and over being "first-footed" by the desired tall, dark and handsome male - human, though seeing a black cat was also benign. Anyway, "God send us a <u>Happy New Year</u>".

<u>Felicitous Firms</u> exist alongside the Happy Families of 10.9! Musicians may recall "Thomas Tallis & Co., Cheese Factors" (Manchester 1950s) and "Delius Taxis" (Bradford 1990s). My favourite remains "W. Katz Ltd., Manufacturing Furriers" (London '70s).

<u>2nd January.</u> APHORISMS ON SOCIETY. ("No such thing." - Thatcher)

* "The desire for more than we need dehumanises us and leads to the disintegration of civil society." - Thomas Aquinas. (1227-1274) Summa Theologica 2a 2ae Q118 arts 5&8.

* "The spoil of the poor is in your houses." - Isaiah 3:14.

* "The rich man's wealth is his strong city, and as an high wall in his own conceit." - Proverbs 18:11.

(That can be literally true, with high walls around stately homes, and the "Nantyglo Towers" near Brynmawr, Gwent, that a coalowner had built to safeguard his privilege from encroachment by destitute colliers. On the grand scale, the poet Dr Elisabeth Adler wrote from Berlin in 1991:

* "I live now in the part of the world
where the rich man's wealth
protects him like a high wall
and the unemployed, the old and the handicapped
are outside the wall and excluded.
Europe will be a fortress,
will be protected by a high wall of wealth,
will shut its gates to the poor and to the foreigner.
God, who made me leap over the wall, where are you?")

* "Cash-payment is not the sole nexus of man with man." - Thomas Carlyle, Past and Present, bk.iii, ch.9.

* "The love of money is the root of all evil." - Paul, 1 Tim 6:10.

* "You cannot inject the principles of ethical socialism into an economy based on private greed; You cannot do it!" - Aneurin Bevan 1959.

(Michael Foot quotes Bevan as saying of the British people in 1959:

* "History gave them their chance and they didn't take it.")

(David Lloyd George, Chancellor of the Exchequer 1908-1915, was the last politician to confront the moneyed Establishment when in office. Damaged by WW1, he had by then saved countless senior citizens from the workhouse. He said:

* "A fully-equipped duke costs as much to keep as two dreadnoughts."
* "Aristocracy is like cheese; the older it gets, the higher it becomes."
* "The British aristocracy is the ultimate issue of Norman plunder, Reformation pillage, and Royal indiscretion." - (this in reply to Edward VII's accusation of class warfare.)

Alas a new strain of fat cats has evolved! For a final assessment please see 7 Jan. (inside the back cover).

3rd January. **Uncle** Henry entertains the Family in the warm
Parlour, though outside the frost was cruel, in the days
before "wireless" and TV, and the mild winters after 1947.
His recitation was very popular in the early 20th century.

THE GREEN EYE OF THE LITTLE YELLOW GOD.
(by Brangby Williams (1911) - music-hall star)

There's a one-eyed yellow idol to the north of Khatmandu,
There's a little marble cross below the town;
There's a broken-hearted woman tends the grave of Mad Carew,
And the Yellow God forever gazes down.

He was known as "Mad Carew" by the subs at Khatmandu,
He was hotter than they felt inclined to tell;
But for all his foolish pranks, he was worshipped in the ranks,
And the Colonel's daughter smiled on him as well.

He had loved her all along, with a passion of the strong,
The fact that she loved him was plain to all.
She was nearly twenty-one and arrangements had begun
To celebrate her birthday with a ball.

He wrote to ask what present she would like from Mad Carew;
They met next day as he dismissed a squad;
And jestingly she told him then that nothing else would do
But the green eye of the little Yellow God.

On the night before the dance, Mad Carew seemed in a trance,
And they chaffed him as they puffed at their cigars;
But for once he failed to smile, and he sat alone awhile,
Then went out into the night beneath the stars.

He returned before the dawn, with his shirt and tunic torn,
And a gash across his temple dripping red;
He was patched up right away, and he slept through all the day,
And the Colonel's daughter watched beside his bed.

He woke at last and asked if they could send his tunic through;
She brought it, and he thanked her with a nod;
He bade her search the pocket saying, "That's from Mad Carew,"
And she found the little green eye of the god.

She upbraided poor Carew in the way that women do,
Though both her eyes were strangely hot and wet;
But she wouldn't take the stone and Mad Carew was left alone
With the jewel that he'd chanced his life to get.

When the ball was at its height, on that still and tropic night,
She thought of him and hastened to his room;
As she crossed the barrack square she could hear the dreamy air
Of a waltz tune softly stealing thro' the gloom.

His door was open wide, with silver moonlight shining through;
The place was wet and slippery where she trod;
An ugly knife lay buried in the heart of Mad Carew,
'Twas the "Vengeance of the Little Yellow God."

There's a one-eyed yellow idol to the north of Khatmandu,
There's a little marble cross below the town;
There's a broken-hearted woman tends the grave of Mad Carew,
And the Yellow God forever gazes down.

Mt Everest - detail of picture from
my student who moved to Khatmandu!

379

4th January.   "LOCKSLEY HALL 200 YEARS ON."   380

"All the world's a stage" wrote Shakespeare, and places
which were the scenes of impassioned happenings at one period
of time often serve entirely different purposes later on. In
honour of Tennyson's "Locksley Hall Sixty Years After" (22-3.6;
24-5.8), a remarkable integrative poem to which little if any-
thing need be added, and at a friend's suggestion, I offer:-

When the Lindsay County Council couldn't balance its accounts,
And its Cabinet Committee quailed before the dread amounts
It was forced to pay as interest whilst neglecting all its schools
With the dreaded threat of OFSTED deeming teachers useless tools.
There arose Sir Godfrey Holtby saying "We'll be surcharged all,
If not jailed by Blair and Blunkett - so we'll have to sell the Hall
"But it's our touristic showpiece - Tennysonian is its fame!"
Pleaded Lady Susan Brittain (and there's nothing like a Dame
To uphold our threatened values and our culture that was rich
Ere it crumbled into dust before the moneypeople's itch):
"'Tis the place, and all around it, as of old, the curlews call"
Quoth the lady, with her tales of olden love in Locksley Hall,
Stories too of early death, of lonely service, "sad retreat -
Till squire Leonard won in Forty-five his Labour council-seat!
But the upkeep grew beyond him, so he gave the Hall that we
Might bring all our city children out for days by moor and sea.
There are pictures in the hallway midst displays of Lincoln life:
N-ewton, Tennyson and Thatcher - scenes 'of business, love and strife'.
Then the picnic-garden yields delight in days of summer sun,
And the evening's splendid concert fills the paradise of fun.
Will you sell this to a pop-star or a fat tycoon from Leeds?
Will you set a football-wizard's feet above the people's needs?
Is there not one Council left that durst sustain the people's power?-
Hoping that the hour may pass, will shape its heart to front the hour?"
But the fire-alarm's loud clangour drove the Chairman from the chair,
And the meeting stands adjourned a week - and who will then be there?
Will they follow Light and Right to help Love conquer at the last
When each stormy moment's flown away to mingle with the Past?

From the North-East.
　"I'd never go to war for Mr. Blair,   (Revd John
　　He treads a path that angels wouldn't dare." Stephenson.)
...and in lighter vein:
　　Did you hear of the pitman who tried to cross a homing
pigeon with a woodpecker? The idea was so it would knock on
on the door when it arrived with its message.

"THE PRICE OF LIBERTY IS ETERNAL VIGILANCE" - J.P. Curran, 1790.

5th January ("Twelfth Night"). "TO ANOTHER MOUSE" (after 25.1)

With acknowledgement to CHD Associates, 4D Church Road, Tweedmouth, the source of the Marshall Hattersley limerick "The people still flock to the poll" (see 15th July), I am happy to share John Hargrave's report (1992) that "a workman demolishing a wall in Honiton, Devon had found a mouse's nest made of shredded Treasury notes." He adds, with due acknowledgements to the shade of Rabbie Burns:

Ah, Mousie, thou'rt a canny snicket /To tak an' use the Bankers' ticket!
Thy housin' problem made thee sneak it /Without a qualm!
I wish I had thy sense to nick it /To keep me warm!

Tha's beggar'd up the Bankers' **Promise** /To **Pay**, an' paper'd thy sma' palace,
To keep thee snug from winter's malice/Wi' paper blanket;
Nor kenn'd it was the Bankers' fallace/That should be thankit!

Instead o' savin bits o' paper /Thou chaw'd 'em up — a cantie caper!
Each needle-point a wee-bit traitor /To gnaw an' shred it!
Tha'll surely hear o' something later /Caa'd Social Credit.(x)

What ithers sav'd wi' stint an' trouble /For thy sharp tuttie-pegs to nibble,
Gies common sense to Bankers' drivel/ Of dearth an' debt;
While thy scant wit ignores the Riddle,/We'll solve it yet!

(x) — Social Credit: the doctrine that "The creation of the original issue of money should be maintained as the exclusive monopoly of national Government" (Abraham Lincoln); and not that of finance-houses who create then lend it on interest (see 9.3)

(Cont'd from 3.12) More Mardale Verses.
(Addition, written 10.6.2006 Trinity Eve.)

The Mardale clearance was commemorated on 18.8.1985, the 50th anniversary of the farewell-service in Mardale Church. The same order of service was followed, in the open air near the dam, on that wet day. Another repetition seems likely to take place on the 100th anniversary, and I venture to propose these additional verses for the final hymn:

7 Here we have no lasting city,　　　　　(Starred line based
　Now the Dun Bull sells no ale;　　　　　on the toast on page
Men Yet we laud in pride and pity　　　　196 of Sarah Hall's
　Noble exiles from this dale. (*)　　　splendid novel
　　　　　　　　　　　　　　　　　　　　　　　　"Haweswater".)

8 Still the Mardale hills are glorious,
　Still the Mardale hills are grand.　　　(verse 8 sets
Women Climb these hills and be victorious;　　an old song
　Here we see our Promised Land.　　　　of Mardale.)

9 Lord, thy glory.....

381

6th January. **TWELFTH DAY; EPIPHANY** (Christ made known to the wider world through the arrival of the Magi from afar).

- - - - - - -

Well, so that is that. Now we must dismantle the tree,
Putting the decorations back into their cardboard boxes –
Some have got broken – and carrying them up to the attic.
The holly and the mistletoe must be taken down and burnt,
And the children got ready for school. There are enough
Left-overs to do, warmed up, for the rest of the week –
Not that we have much appetite, having drunk such a lot,
Stayed up so late, attempted – quite unsuccessfully –
To love all our relatives, and in general
Grossly overestimated our powers. Once again
As in previous years we have seen the actual Vision and failed
To do more than entertain it as an agreeable
Possibility, once again we have sent Him away,
Begging though to remain His disobedient servant,
The promising child who cannot keep His word for long...

(Sufferings) will come, all right, don't worry; probably in the form
That we do not expect, and certainly with a force
More dreadful than we can imagine. In the meantime
There are bills to be paid, machines to be kept in repair,
Irregular verbs to learn, the Time Being to redeem
From insignificance. The happy morning is over,
The night of agony still to come; the time is noon:
When the Spirit must practise his scales of rejoicing.
God will cheat no one, not even the world, of its triumph.

[W. H. AUDEN, from *For the Time Being*]

- - - - - - -

This poem is less well known than T.S. Eliot's "A cold coming we had of it, Just the worst time of the year..." I am reminded of Schubert's 'Winterreise' songs on the same theme. Auden is easy to understand, for our emergence from Christmas retreats or cocoons can be painful as we take the load of everyday life and work. In 1996 the UK had also an "Epiphany of the Golden Calf", the Lotto jackpot of £42m tempting 90% of adults to buy tickets, for motives ranging from fun, through wistful longing, to brazen avarice in a world where millions go hungry. Eliot's "Rock" (see 9,10.10) makes bold to say:

All men are ready to invest their money
But most expect dividends.
I say to you: *Make perfect your will.*
I say: take no thought of the harvest,
But only of proper sowing.

7th January. "Some of my Best Friends are Bishops!"

Clerihew from RAF servicefolk in WW2, told by Bp Richard Hare, retired near Bassenthwaite Lake: "The nicest name in German / Is Hermann", / Said Goëring, / Purring.

The sweetest "rebuke", nay correction, that I can recall was penned in Ely Contact by Peter Walker who was bishop there in the 1980s, and who incidentally publicised the Adler poem (2 Jan) in a Church Times article. Of Don Cupitt, the Dean of Emmanuel College, Cambridge, he wrote that he was passionately concerned for the humanising of religion. But who will keep this fragile flame burning but the great Lover of humanity who lit it in the first place...in this sad world..?"

I don't know any bishopesses, so Emily Brontë's Last Lines must stand in:

No coward soul is mine,
No trembler in the world's storm-troubled sphere:
　I see Heaven's glories shine,
And faith shines equal, arming me from fear.

　O God within my breast,
Almighty, ever-present Deity!
　Life – that in me has rest,
As I – undying Life – have power in Thee!

　Vain are the thousand creeds
That move men's hearts; unutterably vain;
　Worthless as withered weeds,
Or idlest froth amid the boundless main.

　To waken doubt in one
Holding so fast by Thine Infinity;

So surely anchored on
The steadfast rock of immortality.

　With wide-embracing love
Thy Spirit animates eternal years,
　Pervades and broods above,
Changes, sustains, dissolves, creates, and rears.

　Though earth and man were gone,
And suns and universes ceased to be,
　And Thou were left alone,
Every existence would exist in Thee.

　There is not room for Death,
Nor atom that his might could render void;
　Thou – Thou art Being and Breath,
And what Thou art may never be destroyed.

☆
By hook
Or by crook

School-pupil's essay: "The bishop came for confirmation...now I know what a crook looks like!"

(*) To conclude the Aphorisms (2.1) and indeed the Daybook, I quote the message for 1997 from Bp Nigel McCulloch (then Wakefield, now Manchester.) "Important though politics and economics are, they cannot on their own provide the answers to life's problems. Our society will not be made better simply by new laws or a new government. What is needed is a change of heart." (see Wm. Temple 15.7 & G.S. Kennedy 5.12)

I'll be last
In this book.

"Thus saith the Lord God:..A new heart also will I give you, & a new spirit will I put within you." (see Ezekiel 36²⁶; also Lam.5²¹, Jude²⁴/⁵, Heb.13²⁰¹).

Summary of Contents.

November:

7 - Thorns into Roses.
8 - A 50-Rouble Fee.
9 - Power of the Dog.
10 - Many Long Years Ago.
11 - Martinmas remembrance.
12 - Forward be our Watchword.
13 - Dear old "C. of E."
14 - Chrissie Answers.
15 - Deservedly Lonely Hearts.
16 - Musical Bumps.
17 - Summertime in Gorsley.
18 - Still On Target.
19 - Needham and RVW.
20 - Follow the Fire Unfurled.
21 - Patriots.
22 - Godkissed Quickness.
23 - Making The Pathways Neat.
24 - Nibbles and Quibbles.
25 - Woe to the Shepherds...
26 - Byron's friend Bo'sun.
27 - Out Of The Wilderness.
28 - de Mello on "Awareness".
29 - Foursquare.
30 - Successful Failures.

December:

1 - Chill December.
2 - Down the Rabbit-Hole.
3 - Bright The Vision.
4 - Old old stories.
5 - Financial predation.
6 - Oriana.
7 - Cheviot, Stag, & Black Oil.
8 - White Waistcoat.
9 - Cabinet Kiss 'n Tell.
10 - The Attlee Road.
11 - Proverb & Patchwork.
12 - Patriots and Pussycat.
13 - Destroy Wars with Words.
14 - Méchant M. le Chat.
15 - Hymns Bad & Worse.
16 - The Darkness Gathers.
17 - Mourning of Nations.
18 - Mardale marred.
19 - Consett in N.W.Durham.
20 - Bah! Humbug!
21 - St Thomas's Wake.
22 - Hardy Perennials.
23 - Midwinter Festivals.
24 - The Desire of Nations.
25 - Mad Dogs & Englishmen.
26 - Doggerel Far Worse.
27 - From a Youthful Diary.
28 - Don't Jump the Gun!
29 - Ann's Audacity.
30 - Prince of Whales.
31 - Ring Out the Darkness.

January:

1 - The Waits' Carol.
2 - Aphorisms on Society.
3 - Uncle Henry & Mad Carew
4 - "3rd Locksley Hall".
5 - A Capital Gain.
6 - Bills to be paid.
7 - By hook or by crook.

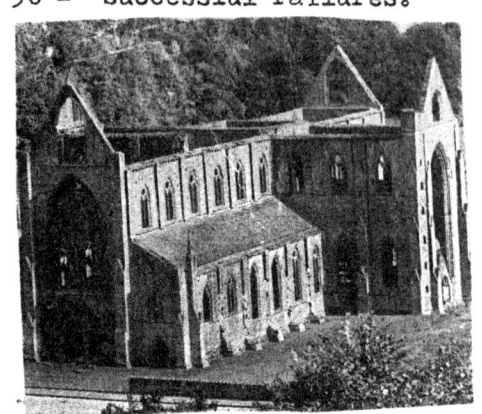

Tintern Abbey, visited by Wm. Wordsworth as a young tourist - on an occasion which led him to write a magnificent poem a few miles up the Wye valley.

DURHAM COUNTY COUNCIL

v

APPENDIX: SWINDALE, LAKELAND'S SECRET VALLEY (from 18 & 27.12)

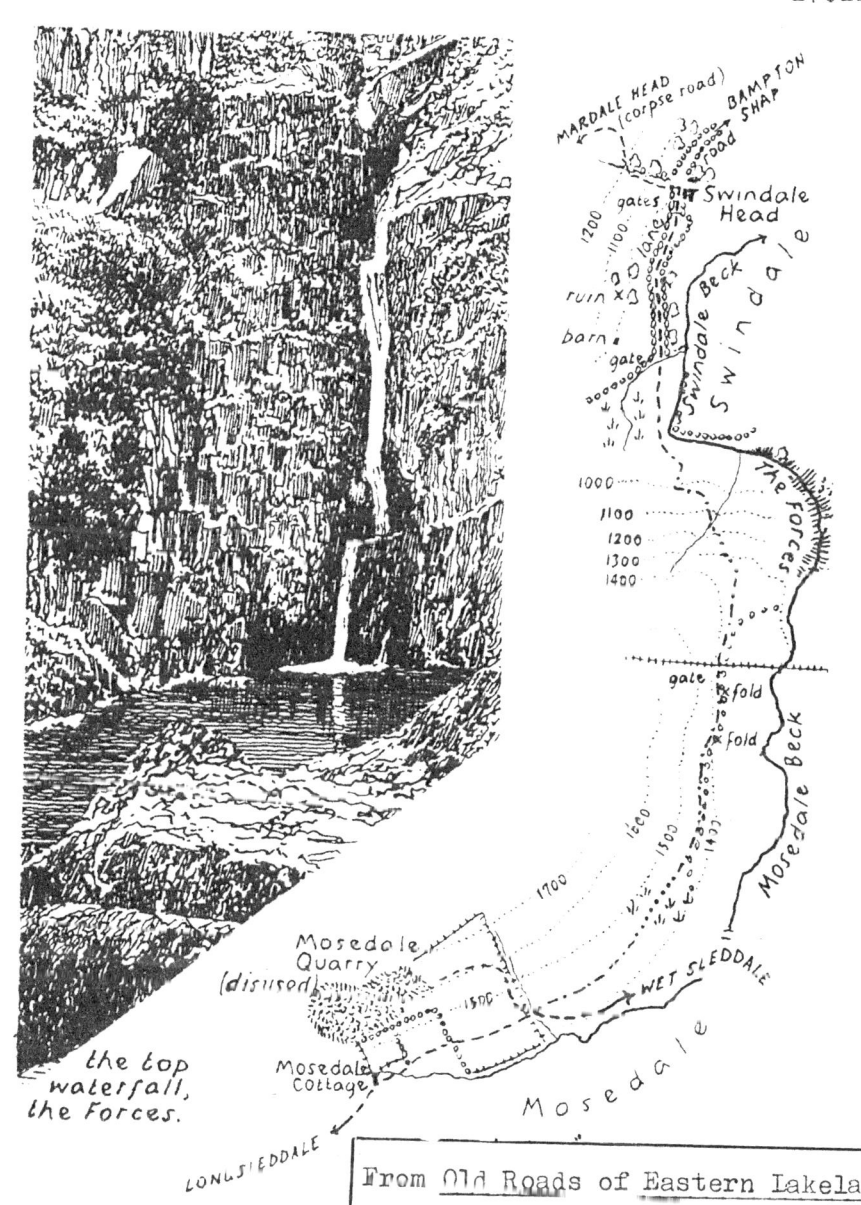

the top waterfall, the Forces.

PS to 27.12: Wainwright says go down ravine's west side, others demur! Pic: Sarah's Pool.

From *Old Roads of Eastern Lakeland* by A. Wainwright, copyright © The Estate of A. Wainwright, 1985. Reproduced by permission of Frances Lincoln Ltd.

"The Splendour of the Morning." - (postlude and valediction.)

    I have been urged to express the overall purpose of my Daybook, but must confess to a mixed and muddled motivation! Trying to give fun and pleasure is an ingredient of course, whilst the serious aim is to give pause for thought via a free-range sort of National Syllabus of topics to explore.(I grant that my Modern Language section is of the scantiest (14.12)!) I fear that young minds are being regimented, and both culture and creativity blocked out, by governmental directives to schools (e.g. standard assessment tests) and by the hated "league tables" which set school against school, and teacher against child. Dickens denounced an earlier Age of Control in "Hard Times" (27.7); & A.N. Wilson, in "The Victorians" pp.283-4 tells of their depriving the poor of their traditional education, in favour of compulsion "in places strictly assigned to them according to income & social status." A lonely dissenter from the Forster Act of 1870 establishing this was Archdeacon Denison of Taunton, who was appalled that power over children would fall to an uncaring State. Of course much good was and is done in schools, but credit for this is due to teachers, pupils and administrators in spite of the flawed framework and unfair resourcing between 'top' and 'sink' schools and universities - our national disgrace!

    "<u>Our Earthly Leaders Falter</u>", wrote Chesterton; so if "official" systems of training and entertainment yield a dumbed-down generation able to understand IT and mobile telephones in a false "global village" yet in isolation from their local neighbours and communities, it is time for those of us who can read the signs of the times to "Rise like lions after slumber In unvanquishable number" (Shelley) and <u>get ourselves wise</u>. Don't leave things to the professionals in sport, faith, entertainment, politics - whatever - the Devil's big British win is the unspoken widespread attitude that "you don't do things with serious responsibility unless you get paid, or get good marks or some clear personal benefit".

(continues.

Engineering Work will mean that the Virgin West Coast Main Line will operate an amended train service, a summary of which is shown below:
  Additional train services will replace the replacement bus service between Carlisle and Glasgow Central.
newstatesman ● 6 June 2005   Virgin Train leaflet (Frank McManus)   **THIS ENGLAND**

Postlude (conclusion).   vii
"Getting and Spending, We Lay Waste Our Powers." (8.2)

The "global village" is not a village! I don't mind a very occasional telephone-call from a local trader, but I resent getting up to five in a day from people whose dialect puts them in the Indian subcontinent, offering me low-cost telephoning or other goodies. They do so as part of a paid job and can have no real concern for my affairs. By contrast a village is a smallish locality with residents who generally know one another.

Money is being worshipped as an idol! When the popular Mayor of London set out to reduce city-congestion, he had no better idea than to use the power of the purse, charging motorists £5 per day to drive in central London, so as to force some to use public transport. This was followed by railway-company proposals for higher peak fares to force some on to the roads!

"Break the System!" - is this our task for survival? It all depends how you set about it. The Soviet experience had its successes and was deliberately damaged and undermined from the West, but all too often it was oppressive and grey. Studdert Kennedy wrote (Lies, H.& S.1919) that nobody wants to see Capitalism destroyed more than he did; but he did not "have the slightest faith in its being destroyed, except to land us in something far worse, unless its destruction is carried out by new men." "The system...is a growth...out of human nature. The world...has jolly well got to grow out of it." Kautsky stressed "the absolute necessity of a change of heart and mind in the people before we can...run things on a co-operative basis."

Quo Vadis? (where do we go from all this?)

Paul said it (2 Timothy 4.2): "Preach, teach, reprove, in season, out of season."

Educate, agitate, organise; advertise!

Draw strength from friends, faith, arts; Nature, Old wisdom, New wisdom, Hope, Love.

Ending with Finland's epic Kalevala:

"I have shown the way for singers,
Showed the way, and broke the tree tops,
Cut the branches, shown the pathways.
This way therefore leads the pathway,...
Widely open for the singers,
For the young, who now are growing,
For the rising generation.   (1-cf. 20.4)

ountain, Tonypandy Square

ACKNOWLEDGEMENTS.

My gratitude for permission to publish goes to Dr Elisabeth Adler for her poem; Bishops David Lunn and Peter Walker for writings in their diocesan magazines; the Literary Executors of Vera Brittain for her writings; Julie Burchill for an extract from the Guardian; Faber and Faber Ltd for lines of 'Annus Mirabilis' from Collected Poems by Philip Larkin; & of 'Choruses from the Rock' from ditto by T.S. Eliot, and of 'For the Time Being' & 'You are silly..' from do. by W.H. Auden: Pat Forrest for Martin Forrest's verses; Gomer Press Ltd for poems by Idris Davies; Simon Hart for his Times article; Denis Healey for extracts from My Secret Planet; David Higham Associates for extracts from Frances Lloyd George's The years That Are Past, Malcolm Muggeridge's Chronicles of a Wasted Time, and Jeremy Seabrook's Working Class Childhood, published respectively by Random House Ltd, Collins, & Victor Gollancz); Norman Iles for his poem; John Julius Norwich for items in Still More Christmas Crackers, 1990-9, publ. Viking; Bernard Massey for information about the hymn-tune Blaenwern; extract from Cry The Beloved Country by Alan Paton, published by Jonathan Cape, reprinted by permission of The Random House Group Ltd; The Society of Authors as Literary Representative of the Estate of John Masefield for A Consecration and Seekers; SPCK for extracts from The Cry of the Deer by David Adam; John Stephenson for his writings; Templegate Publications for the extract from Bede Griffiths' Return to the Centre; The Estate of Robert Service for lines from his poems; the Watchtower Bible and Tract Society for the extract from Awake magazine; and a number of others for small items and some of untraceable origin. In connection with Vyvian Holland's An Explosion of Limericks, Cassell PLC, a division of the Orion Publishing Group (London), ask me to state that all my attempts at tracing the copyright holder were unsuccessful. Some further acknowledgements appear in the text by request. Every effort has been made to seek permissions, and if any copyright-holder has been overlooked I apologise and will rectify this in any future edition. I must also record my deep gratitude to all authors of the splendid out-of-copyright older items which I have used!

INDEX.

Brief indications of contents are listed at the end of each of the six parts of this Daybook, i.e. immediately following the items for 29th February, 3rd May, 5th July, 5th September, 6th November and 7th January. A short classified index follows:-

An INDEX of Limericks and some main themes' main entries.   ix

16.1 duck; **29.1** laughs anatomical, Bp of Glasgow, cricketing Lord, Euro, Brunnhilde's distress, Bianca, lady of Kent; **27.3** Jael, homme de Dijon, Carr, Sultan of Oman, Girl of golden West, Curate of Kew, Pussy; **5.5** Debra, lady of Sydenham, Eminem, Precede us O Lord; **12.6** virtue of genes (by the late Lord Limerick), Becquerel, Pascal; **15.7** people flock to poll; **3.8** Siddal; **14.8** lion, man of St Bees, man of Calcutta, Oak, Daedalus, Kilkenny cats; **26.8** blonde alone; **6.9** lady from Dingle; **25.9** Dex; 13.10 girls from Rosario; **14.10** Parnell; **25.10** Attlee; **29.11** Flanders.

Clerihews: **25.2** Davy, Needham, Grieg, Royal Phil., Buss/Beale, Charles II; **6.9** Narcissus; **7.1** Goëring.

Tennyson: **28.2** Young man's fancy, old man's sorrow; **5.3** The harbour bar (Kingsley); **21.3** Vision & rubbish; **22.3** Hallam, In Memoriam; **26.3** Height beyond height; 24.4 Victoriana; **1.5** Hope; **4.5** Owl; **22.5** Maud (frolic); **21.6** philosophy/rail-slip; 22-3.6 Locksley Hall Sixty Years After, second part; **20.8** envoi; **24-5.8** start of 2nd L.H.; **15.10** Gladstone spat, Yeats' verdict; 24,31.12 seasonal; 4.1 "3rd Locksley Hall"!!

Wordsworth: 4.2 railway philippics; **7.2** Natural piety; **8.2** sonnets; **10.2** parodies; **27.4** cities; **18.6** role of poet's mind; **23.11** Duddon farewell; **12.12** poetic vocation.

Major Poets; (alphabetical): Auden 30.9 6.1; Barnes 26.5; Belloc 2.3 ; Blake 20.11; Brontë E, 7.1; Browning 14.9; Burns 25-6.1; Byron 11-12.2 29.4; Causley 19.9; Chesterton 30.9 & 20.11; Davies 9,11,12.5 23-4.12; Eliot 9,10.10 11.12 6.1; Hardy 29.2 9,12,23.11 22.12; Herrick 9.1; Hood 29.9; Hopkins 25.12; Housman 24.6; Keats 20.1 19.10; Kingsley 5.3; Kipling 23.4 27.5 4.7 22.12; Macauley 14.6; Masefield 2,15.2; Milton 11.7; Morris 3.5; Newbolt 25.4; Owen 24.5; Sassoon 16.6; Scott 16.4; Service 4.8; Shakespeare 8.9; Shelley 19,24.10; Von Eichendorff 27.1; Yeats 23.3 19.10.

Original verse: 19.1 8.5(+Iles) 3,20.6 5.7 16.9 3.10 25.11
                                      16.12 (4,21.1 ??!!)

Hymns: Aquinas 4.12; Cotter 28.3; Coxe 6.4; Dalmon 14.1; Donaldson 30.8; Fortunatus 5.4 4.12; Heber 1.0; How 31.7; Mant 3.12; Neale 15.3 17.6 8.10; O'Connor 16.5 3.6 29.11; Patrick 2.6; Smart 16.10; Squires 2.10; Tate 25.12; Wesley/Cennick/Madan 28.12; van Dyke 22.11.

Monetary Justice: 11,24,27,28.1; 8,9.3; 15.7; 5.12 (best revisited in that order.)

Divinity: 21.2 18.3 2,5,6,7.4 30.4+
 15-16.5 26.5 2.6 17.6 22.7 23.8 15.9 1.10 16.10 16.12 6,7.1.